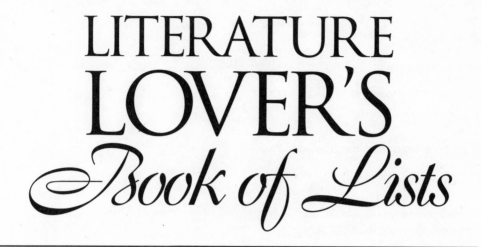

LITERATURE
LOVER'S
Book of Lists

SERIOUS TRIVIA FOR THE BIBLIOPHILE

JUDIE L.H. STROUF

PRENTICE HALL PRESS

Library of Congress Cataloging-in-Publication Data

Strouf, Judie L. H.,
    Literature lover's book of lists : serious trivia for the bibliophile / Judie L.H. Strouf.
      p.   cm.
    Includes bibliographical references and index.
    ISBN 0-7352-0017-3
    1. Literature--Miscellanea. 2. Books and reading--Miscellanea. 3. Literary recreations. I. Title.
    PN43.S77 1998   98-25544
        802--dc21   CIP

Prepared for trade publication by the Stonesong Press, Inc.

Printed in the United States of America

10 9 8 7 6 5 4 3 2

ISBN 0-7352-0017-3

ATTENTION: CORPORATIONS AND SCHOOLS

Prentice Hall books are available at quantity discounts with bulk purchase for educational, business, or sales promotional use. For information, please write to: Prentice Hall Special Sales, 240 Frisch Court, Paramus, NJ 07652. Please supply: title of book, ISBN, quantity, how the book will be used, date needed.

PRENTICE HALL PRESS
Paramus, NJ 07652

A Simon & Schuster Company

On the World Wide Web at http://www.phdirect.com

Prentice Hall International (UK) Limited, *London*
Prentice Hall of Australia Pty. Limited, *Sydney*
Prentice Hall Canada, Inc., *Toronto*
Prentice Hall Hispanoamericana, S.A., *Mexico*
Prentice Hall of India Private Limited, *New Delhi*
Prentice Hall of Japan, Inc., *Tokyo*
Simon & Schuster Asia Pte. Ltd., *Singapore*
Editora Prentice Hall do Brasil, Ltda., *Rio de Janeiro*

ABOUT THIS RESOURCE

The Literature Lover's Book of Lists is a compendium of useful, whimsical, and necessary information for people of all ages who love to read, at whatever level. It is not necessary to read this book from beginning to end. It is a book to browse and thumb through, surveying the scope of its contents and making mental notes. Later, when you need particular information for your own curiosity or in relation to something you are reading (or planning to read), you can turn to *The Literature Lover's Book of Lists* and use the table of contents to locate the exact list quickly. Placement of various lists within specified categories is arbitrary. Many lists could have been included in other sections, so it will be most helpful to embark on a thorough overview when you first acquire the book.

The book is organized in three ways: alphabetically, chronologically, and logically. When possible, a general, though not exact, alphabetical arrangement is used to assist in finding items in the table of contents (example: themes); when chronology seems more important, the organization shifts to accommodate this (example: literary periods); logic prevails when it is more sensible to present certain information together or ahead of adjacent information (example: drama section).

The first section consists of broad lists about literature: main types of literature, Nobel Prize winners, an extensive literary glossary with pronunciation aids, literary and Biblical allusions, famous characters, gods and goddesses, famous places from literature, and literary criticism. The chapters that follow present hundreds of books and author lists, arranged in various ways: age group, genre, theme, literary period, and others. Section II will be especially valuable for parents who are eager to encourage their children to read or are concerned about school reading curricula. Drama and poetry have their own separate sections. SECTION 4: POETRY... REFLECTION OF THE SOUL, for example, details seventeen different types of poetry from ballad through sonnet, contains a poetry glossary, and explains stanza types, versification, poetic devices and more.

Other lists highlight African American, Native American, Spanish, and other world literatures. The special contributions of female authors are emphasized. One of the longest of the forty-eight lists is SECTION 6: THEMES... UNDER ONE UMBRELLA, which pertains to literature about young adult concerns such as child abuse/rape, divorce, eating disorders, family relationships, teen sex and pregnancy, searching for self, and runaways. SECTION 7: LITERARY PERIODS...INTO ONE ERA AND OUT THE OTHER provides background information for historical and literary perspective. It records literary, dramatic, and other events from the Renaissance through 1900. The section also defines classicism, romanticism, and neoclassicism, and chronicles fiction from around the world by decade.

In a somewhat lighter vein, there is SECTION 8: POTPOURRI... WEIRD, WHIMSICAL, AND WORTHWHILE. Here are off-beat, unusual lists such as rare book values, last words of authors, epitaphs, literary lapses, weird tidbits about authors, as well as useful, practical lists on the Dewey Decimal and Library of Congress classification systems.

In addition to personal experience, thousands of books and other materials were studied to compile the 198 lists herein. Of course, no work of this magnitude can escape error or controversy: Language changes, authors' names are spelled differently in various countries and times, and sources can be mistaken on particular items. Because we want this to be the most accurate and useful resource book available to the general reader, we invite you to send comments and suggestions for future editions to Lit Lists, 633 Pine Street, Harbor Springs, Michigan 49740.

Judie L. H. Strouf

About the Author

Judie L. H. Strouf graduated from Central Michigan University with a B.S. degree in English and Middle School/Secondary Teaching Certificate. She then earned an M.A. degree in Guidance and Counseling K–12 from Western Michigan University and pursued further course work at both Western Michigan and the University of Michigan. For more than three decades, she has taught literature, English, drama, advanced composition, creative writing, remedial reading, journalism, and social studies in the Michigan public schools. A Fulbright Scholarship, awarded by the U.S. Office of Education, enabled Stouf to spend a year in Chipping Norton, England, as English Department Head, Chipping Norton Grammar School. This experience gave her a special perspective on British literature and culture. Her books for teachers, *Hooked on Language Arts! Ready-to-Use Activities* and *Worksheets for Grades 4–8* (1990), *America's Discovery Activities Kit: Ready-to-Use Worksheets for the Age of Exploration* (1991), and *The Literature Teacher's Book of Lists* (1993), all published by The Center for Applied Research in Education, have become best-sellers. A fourth book, *Hooked on the USA: Activities for Studying the States*, was published by J. Weston Walch in 1993.

In addition to writing, Stouf spends time teaching piano, reading, and travelling. Along with her husband of forty years, she has visited most of the continental United States, Alaska, Hawaii, Europe, Scandinavia, Great Britain, and Africa.

CONTENTS

SECTION 5: DRAMA... THEREBY HANGS A TALE 215

SECTION 6: THEMES... UNDER ONE UMBRELLA 239

SECTION

1

Literature . . . An Introduction

LITERATURE IS...

1. a pleasure which arises not only from the things said, but from the way in which they are said; and that pleasure is only given when the words are carefully or beautifully put together into sentences — *Stopford Brooke*

2. the thought of thinking Souls — Thomas Carlyle

3. a transmission of power...literature is a power line, and the motor...is the reader —*Charles P. Curtis*

4. a kind of intellectual light which, like the light of the sun, may sometimes enable us to see what we do not like—*Samuel Johnson*

5. only what people would say to each other if they had the chance — *Christopher Morley*

6. language charged with meaning to the utmost possible degree — *Ezra Pound*

7. in many of its branches no other than the shadow of good talk — *Robert Louis Stevenson*

8. the notation of the heart — *Thornton Wilder*

9. an analysis of experience and a synthesis of the findings into a unity — *Rebecca West*

10. the product of inquiring minds in revolt against the immovable certainties of the nation— H. L. Mencken

11. news that stays news — *Ezra Pound*

12. the orchestration of platitudes — *Thornton Wilder*

So what is literature? For the purposes of this book, the word *literature* is used in its broadest sense to encompass the many types of writing shown in the list below.

autobiographies	films	philosophical treatises
biographies	folktales	plays
comic books	journals	poetry
diaries	legends	political documents
epics	letters	religious writings
epitaphs	literary criticism	short stories
essays	magazine articles	sketches
fairy tales	novels	speeches

2. Main Types of Literature

POETRY

Lyric Poetry
- elegy
- ode
- simple lyric
- song
- sonnet

Narrative Poetry
- ballad
- epic
- metrical romance or tale

Dramatic Poetry
- masque (mask)
- monologue
- poetic plays
    - comedy or farce
    - history
    - melodrama
    - tragedy

Other Poetry
- descriptive
- didactic or moralistic
- pastoral
- satiric

PROSE

Autobiography

Biography

Essay

Letters/Diaries/Journals

Prose Drama

Prose Fiction
- adventure or experience tale
- novel
- novelette
- allegory
- romance
- short story

Other Prose
- journalism
- historical
- literary criticism and review
- scientific
- travel

3. Literary Pyramid

Readers should move upward on the literary pyramid. Those who feel less confident might begin at a comfortable level near the bottom and take small steps toward "better" literature. Of course there is worthy literature on every step, and each genre has its own classics. In general, however, the more difficult—and ultimately the most rewarding—literature will be nearer the top of the pyramid. Enjoy the climb!

CLASSICS					
LITERARY CRITICISM					
NOVEL	ALLEGORY	SATIRE			
EPIC POETRY	POETIC DRAMA				
ODE	SONNET	ELEGY	EASY LYRIC POETRY		
NOVELETTE	AUTOBIOGRAPHY	BIOGRAPHY	ESSAY		
SHORT STORY	WESTERN	MYSTERY	ADVENTURE	ROMANCE	
MELODRAMA	POP MAGAZINE	LETTER	DIARY	JOURNAL	FARCE
FABLE	COMICS	COMIC-FORMAT BOOK	LIMERICK	SONG OR BALLAD	

4. Nobel Prizewinners for Literature

The Nobel Prize for Literature has been awarded nearly every year since 1901 to an individual who has benefited humanity by producing distinguished literary works. The prize is named after Alfred B. Nobel, the Swedish chemist who invented dynamite and bequeathed the interest from $9,000,000 to be used for the Nobel Prizes. This list includes only prizewinners from North and South America, Great Britain, Australia, South Africa, and Ireland, mainly because they are readily available in English.

1907 —Rudyard Kipling *(Great Britain)*

1923 —William Butler Yeats *(Ireland)*

1925 —George Bernard Shaw *(Great Britain)*

1930 —Sinclair Lewis *(United States)*

1932 —John Galsworthy *(Great Britain)*

1936 —Eugene O'Neill *(United States)*

1938 —Pearl S. Buck *(United States)*

1945 —Gabriela Mistral *(Chile)*

1948 —T. S. Eliot *(Great Britain)*

1949 —William Faulkner *(United States)*

1950 —Bertrand Russell *(Great Britain)*

1953 —Winston Churchill *(Great Britain)*

1954 —Ernest Hemingway *(United States)*

1962 —John Steinbeck *(United States)*

1967 —Miguel Angel Asturias *(Guatemala)*

1969 —Samuel Beckett *(Ireland)*

1971 —Pablo Neruda *(Chile)*

1973 —Patrick White *(Australia)*

1976 —Saul Bellow *(United States)*

1978 —Isaac Bashevis Singer *(United States)*

1980 —Czeslaw Milosz *(United States)*

1981 —Elias Canetti *(Great Britain)*

1982 —Gabriel Garcia Marquez *(Colombia)*

1983 —William Golding *(Great Britain)*

1987 —Joseph Brodsky *(United States)*

1990 —Octavio Paz *(Mexico)*

1991 —Nadine Gordimer *(South Africa)*

1992 —Derek Walcott *(Trinidad and Tobago)*

1993 —Toni Morrison *(United States)*

1995— Seamus Heaney *(Ireland)*

5. Literary Terminology

In order to better understand literature, it is helpful to know and to be able to pronounce the following words. Examples are given for many terms. Those preceded by an asterisk (*) indicate that additional information or examples are included in the lists specified in parentheses. See also List 81, Poetry Glossary; List 95, Figures of Speech; and List 115, Drama Glossary.

abstract (ab-STRAKT)— Word or idea referring to a generality, state of being, or quality that is not represented by an object or immediately accessible to the five senses.

*allegory (AL-uh-gore-ee)— Writing that has a deeper meaning hidden beneath the obvious one. (See List 126, Allegories; and List 146, Symbolism in Literature.)

*alliteration (uh-lit-uh-RAY-shin)— Repetition of sounds at the beginning of words. Ex: Slug in the slime. (See List 96, Alliteration from A to Z.)

*allusion (uh-LOO-shun)— Reference, without explanation, to a work of literature, a character, a principle, and so on, assuming that the reader is familiar with its implications. (See List 6, Allusions: Literary; List 7, Allusions: Biblical; and List 120, Allusions: Shakespearian.)

anadiplosis (an-uh-di-PLOH-suhs)— Repetition of an important word in a phrase or clause (often the final word) in the next phrase or clause. Ex: Truth brings freedom; freedom brings responsibility.

analogy (an-AL-uh-gee)— Comparison of two dissimilar things that are alike in some way, often using simile or metaphor. Ex: He reminded me of a pig eating his swill.

antagonist (an-TAG-uh-nist)— Person who opposes or competes with the main character, hero, or heroine; often the villain.

antihero (AN-tuh-HERE-oh)— Character, usually the protagonist, who faces a series of problems and events in a story, but often is going against traditional societal standards.

antithesis (an-TITH-uh-sis)— Opposing view; view contrasted with thesis (main idea). Ex: (Thesis) All men are created equal; (Antithesis) Some men are more equal than others.

aphorism (AF-or-iz-uhm)— Wise saying, usually brief, reflecting a general truth. Ex: Haste makes waste.

bibliography (bib-lee-OG-ruh-fee)— List of written works or sources on a particular subject.

bildungsroman (BIL-duhnks-roh-MAHN)— Fiction depicting the moral and intellectual growth of a protagonist, often intended for the education and guidance of others. Ex: *David Copperfield.*

blurb— Short publicity quote on book jacket or brochure to promote book.

bowdlerize (BOHD-luh-reyez)— To excise material deemed objectionable from a piece of writing. (Named after Thomas Bowdler, who censored and deleted passages and words from Shakespeare's plays in 1818.)

burlesque (ber-LESK)— Literary form which ridicules or mocks.

catharsis (kuh-THAHR-suhs)— Therapeutic release of emotion upon identifying with and being moved by a piece of literature.

catastrophe (cuh-TAS-truh-fee)— Final event of a dramatic work, usually ruin or death.

characterization (kar-ik-ter-uh-ZAY-shin)— The process of developing a character in a narrative or drama, often through the conflict of the plot.

circumlocution (ser-kum-loh-KEU-shin)— Writing or speaking that goes around the subject instead of getting directly to the point. Ex: This was not unlike…

*classicism (KLAS-i-siz-uhm)— Literary (and other artistic) movements of ancient Greece and Rome, using strict forms, accenting reason, and characterized by restraint. Opposite is romanticism. (See List 154, Classicism.)

cliche (klee-SHAY)— Trite, overused idea or statement. Ex: Have a nice day.

climax (KLEYE-max)— High point in the plot where the reader is most intrigued and does not yet know the outcome.

coherence (koh-HEER-uhns)— Clarity in connecting ideas.

*comedy (KOM-uh-dee)— Fictional writing that has a happy ending for its major characters and contains humor. (See List 117, Shakespeare: Complete Plays and Poems; and List 134, Humor.)

conciseness (kuhn-SEYES-nis)— "Tight" writing; use of only the necessary words to express thoughts.

concision (kuhn-SI-shin)— See conciseness above.

concrete (kon-KREET)— Opposite of abstract; refers to specific people and things that can be perceived with the five senses.

conflict (KON-flikt)— Opposing elements or characters in a plot.

connotation (kon-uh-TAY-shin)— Feelings and associations added to specific word meaning. Ex: *mother*— kindly, self-sacrificing, nurturing woman. See also *denotation* below.

consonance (CON-suh-nuhns)— Repetition of similar consonant sounds, with changes in intervening vowel sounds.

convention (cuhn-VEN-shin)— Accepted literary form of the past.

copyright (KAH-pee-reyet)— Legal rights to published works which stop anyone else from using the work without permission.

critic (KRID-ik)— Person who evaluates literature or other art.

*criticism (KRID-uh-siz-uhm)— Essays and critiques evaluating a writer or his work, based on set standards, according to the philosophy of the critic. (See List 14, Literary Criticism; List 15, Schools of Criticism; and List 16, U.S./British/Irish Critics.)

denotation (dee-noh-TAY-shin)— Dictionary meaning of word. Ex: mother— female who bears or adopts a child. See also *connotation* above.

denouement (day-new-MAHN)— Outcome, resolution, solution of a plot.

dialogue/dialog (DEYE-uh-log)— Speaking and conversation between characters in stories, plays, and in person.

*didactic (deye-DAK-tik)— Describes literary works meant to teach a moral or lesson. (See List 49, Fables: Aesop.)

doppelgänger (DOHP-uhl-GENG-er)— Personification of a character's darker side; ghost.

double entendre (dew-blahn-TAHN-druh)— Double meaning of word, phrase, or sentence, often raucous or sexual in implication. Ex: All eyes to the rear.

editorial (ed-uh-TORE-ee-uhl)— Newspaper or magazine article expressing opinion of an editor or publisher.

ellipsis (ee-LIP-suhs)— Three dots (…) to show words have been left out of a quotation or to indicate the passage of time.

*envoy/envoi (EN-voy or AHN-voy)— Brief postscript to book, essay, or poem; often the concluding stanza to a ballade, summarizing the poem. (See List 85, French Verse Forms; and List 93, Sestina.)

epigram (EP-uh-gram)— Witty, often paradoxical, saying or brief poem. Ex: Absence makes the heart grow fonder— of somebody else.

*epitaph (EP-i-taf)— Inscription on tombstone or marker for the dead. (See List 178, Epitaphs of Authors.)

*eponym (EP-ah-nim)— Person whose name is the source of a new word. Ex: Peter Magnol (magnolia). (See List 179, Eponyms.)

*essay (ES-say)— Short prose work expressing author's views on a subject. (See List 46, Essays: Collections; List 47, Essays: Informal; and List 48, Essay Masters.)

*euphemism (YEW-fuh-miz-uhm)— More palatable word for less pleasant subject. Ex: "lady of the evening" is a euphemism for "prostitute." (See List 181, Euphemisms and Oxymora.)

*fable (FAY-buhl)— Story with moral or lesson about life, often with animal characters possessing human characteristics. (See List 49, Fables: Aesop.)

fabliau (FAB-blee-oh)— Short, metrical tale told by minstrels in twelfth and thirteenth centuries, often spicy and satiric.

fiction— Any literature about imaginary events or people.

fiction, interactive— Stories that give the reader choices in the way the plot develops by making certain decisions along the way.

fiction, popular— Fiction aimed at the mainstream population. Ex: romances; detective stories.

*fiction, science— Fiction concerning advanced technology, usually imagined, not actual scientific advancements. (See List 69, Science Fiction Masters.)

first-person narration— Story told from first person point of view, usually using "I."

flashback— Jumping backward in the chronology of a narrative, often through a dream or musing sequence.

foil— Character opposite or different from the protagonist, used to highlight the protagonist's traits; incidents or settings may also be used as foils.

*folklore/folktales— Stories and legends transmitted by word of mouth, rather than in writing. (See List 12, Mythological and Legendary Characters; List 51, Fairy Tales/Folktales/Myths/Legends; List 56, Folklore (American): Imaginary Characters; and List 57, Folklore (American): Real Characters.)

foreshadow (FORE-sha-doh)— Hints during the narrative about what will happen later; can be literal hints or symbolic hints.

genre, literary (ZHAHN-run, LID-uh-rer-ee)— Kind or type of literature; literary classification. Ex: novel; science fiction.

hero— Character, usually the protagonist, who rises above and conquers a series of problems and events in the story.

homonyms (HOM-uh-nimz)— Words that sound alike, are spelled alike, but have different meanings. Ex: trunk (of tree and a suitcase).

homophones (HOM-uh-fohnz)— Words that sound alike (includes homonyms and also words that have different spellings). Ex: sea and see.

*hyperbole (high-PER-buh-lee)— Use of extreme exaggeration for effect. Ex: His breath could wilt a flower. (See List 95, Figures of Speech.)

i.e. (EYE-EE)— That is (followed usually by explanatory matter).

ibid. (IB-id)— Used in footnotes and bibliographies to refer to the source mentioned directly above.

idiom (ID-ee-uhm)— Phrase in common use that does not literally mean what it says. Ex: Hold on to your hat and pocketbook.

*imagery (IM-ijree)— Creation of mental pictures by pertinent word choice and heightened description. Ex: His leathery, sun-abused face was ridged like corrugated cardboard. (See List 95, Figures of Speech.)

in medias res (in-MAYD-ee-uhs-RAYS)— Beginning in the middle of events. Ex: *Odyssey* by Homer (opens in the middle of a journey).

irony (EYE-ruh-nee)— Phrases or words with meanings quite different from what is actually stated. Ex: "Brutus is an honorable man."

*jargon (JAHR-guhn)— Words peculiar to any particular occupation. Ex: Flyboy = pilot.

*juvenilia, literary (jew-ven-NIL-ee-uh, LID-uh-rer-ee)— Literature produced during youth; or literature suited to young readers. (See List 18, Best-Selling Children's Books; List 19, Juvenilia Enjoyed by All; List 20, Middle School Reading List; and List 193, Weird and Wonderful Tidbits.)

kenning (KEN-ing)— Short metaphorical expression referring to something without naming it, primarily used in Old English and Norse poetry. Ex: He was plunged into the sea of fire (hell).

*legend— Story handed down, generation to generation, often thought to be at least partially true historically. (See List 12, Mythological and Legendary Characters; List 51, Fairy Tales/Folktales/Myths/Legends: Collections; List 56, Folklore (American): Imaginary Characters; and List 57, Folklore (American): Real Characters.)

litotes (LEYE-tuh-teez)— Understatement, where a positive is expressed as a negative. Ex: He is not a bad dancer.

malapropism (MAL-uh-prop-iz-uhm)— Confusion of similar-sounding words which often ends up sounding humorous. Ex: The Calvary had well-groomed horses. (cavalry; Calvary)

*metaphor (MET-uh-for)— Comparison of unlike things without using the words like or as. Ex: Her lips were rose petals. (See List 95, Figures of Speech.)

*moral— A lesson the literature is teaching; fables usually teach a lesson about life. (See List 49, Fables: Aesop.)

motif, literary (moh-TEEF, LID-uh-rer-ee)— Recurrent words or phrases.

*mythology (mith-OL-uh-gee)— Traditional tales about goddesses, gods, heroes, and other characters, often telling about the creation of the universe, talking about death, or otherwise philosophically explaining human existence. (See List 11, Gods and Goddesses; List 12, Mythological and Legendary Characters; and List 51, Fairy Tales/Folktales/Myths/Legends: Collections.)

narration (nar-RAY-shin)— Telling a story.

narrator (NAR-ay-ter)— Person telling the story.

n. b. (EN-BEE)— Note well (followed by important point to remember).

*nom de plume (nahm-duh-PLOOM)— Pen name or pseudonym used by author. (See List 189, Pseudonyms of Famous Writers of the World.)

*novel (NOV-uhl)— Long, fictional prose story. [See List 64, The Novel Masters: (American); List 65, The Novel Masters: (Other Than American); and List 66, Novelists and Storytellers: Women.]

novella (noh-VEL-uh)— Short novel with fewer characters than novel.

*novel, gothic— Novel with medieval setting suggesting mystery and/or horror. (See List 58, Gothic and Regency Romance.)

novel, historical— Full-length fiction book, using historical facts as its basis for plot or setting, but including imaginary characters and dialogue.

*novel, picaresque (pik-uh-RESK)— Novel characterized by young hero of lower-class, unrespectable background, who leaves home and is faced with a harsh, cruel world, and eventually conforms to its realities. (See List 67, Novel: Picaresque.)

nuance (NYU-ahns)— Slight shade of meaning or detail.

op. cit. (OP-SIT)—- Used in footnotes/bibliographies to refer to work previously cited or quoted.

*oxymoron (ahks-uh-MORE-on)— Use of paradoxical or opposite words for effect. Ex: poor little rich girl. (See List 181, Euphemisms and Oxymora.)

paradox (PAR-uh-doks)— Contradictory statement that makes sense. Ex: She loved and hated him at the same time.

paraphrase (PAR-uh-frayz)— Restatement of writing, keeping the basic meaning, but telling it in one's own words.

parody, literary (PAR-uh-dee, LID-uh-rer-ee)— Satire imitating an author or work with the aim of mockery.

passage, purple— Writing that contains flowery, ornate language, often in the midst of otherwise dull passages.

*personification (per-son-uh-fuh-KAY-shin)— Literary device where writer attributes human qualities to objects or ideas. Ex: Fear raised its ugly head. (See List 95, Figures of Speech.)

plagiarism (PLAY-jer-iz-uhm)— Using other people's work as one's own without crediting the true author. (This is illegal and punishable in a court of law.)

*play— Story written to be acted out by actors on a stage; contains dialogue and stage directions; drama. (See List 109, Drama Masters; List 110, Twentieth-Century Master American Dramatists; List 117, Shakespeare: Complete Plays and Poems; List 121, Popular High School Productions; and List 122, Long-Running Broadway Plays.)

play, miracle— Early drama based on religious stories; saint play.

*play, morality— Early drama involving teaching and preaching of moral principles, usually by allegorical characters. (See List 109, Drama Masters.)

play, mystery— Early dramatizations of the Old and New Testaments.

plot— Structure of the literature; the way it is put together; the unfolding or sequence of the events.

*poetry— Poem collection; genre characterized by rhythm, rhyme (sometimes), and stanzas, as opposed to prose. (See lists in Section 4, Poetry... Reflection of the Soul, for examples of most types of poetry.)

point-of-view— Perspective from which the story is written; can be omniscient (all-knowing), first-person ("I"), shifting between characters, or other.

*prose—- Literature written in sentences and paragraphs, as opposed to poetry or verse. (See List 2, Main Types of Literature.)

protagonist (pro-TAG-uh-nist)— Main character, hero, or heroine in a written work.

proverb— Saying, adage, or maxim, usually short and generally believed to be true. Ex: A stitch in time saves nine.

*pseudonym (SOO-duh-nim)— Name author uses instead of his/her real name; nom de plume. (See List 189, Pseudonyms of Famous Writers of the World.)

*pun— Play on words; words put together in such a way as to be humorous.

question, rhetorical (ruh-TOR-uh-kuhl)— Question asked without expecting an answer; used for effect. Ex: Oh, what does it matter, anyway?

realism, literary— Literature reflecting real life, rather than imaginary or idealistic life.

redundancy (ree-DUHN-din-see)— Repetition that is unnecessary and awkward, as contrasted with intentional repetition for a particular effect. Ex: rich, wealthy individual.

resolution (rez-uh-LOO-shin)— Clarification, solution, or outcome of the conflict in a story.

rhetoric (RET-er-ik)— Persuasive writing.

roman à clef (roh-mahn-ah-KLAY)— Novel based on actual people and places, but written as fiction instead of fact.

*romance (roh-MANS)— Story about heroic deeds, mysterious settings, or love. (See List 58, Gothic and Regency Romance.)

*romanticism (roh-MAN-tuh-siz-uhm)— Literary moment characterized by emotion, imagination, and goodness of people; little emphasis on reason. Opposite of classicism. (See List 166, The Romantic Period.)

sarcasm (SAHR-kaz-uhm)— Form of irony which seems to praise, but really criticizes. Ex: Mother *always* knows best!

*satire (SA-teyer)— Literature that makes fun of social conditions or conventions, often for the purpose of creating change. Ex: *A Connecticut Yankee in King Arthur's Court* by Mark Twain. (See List 126, Allegories.)

sequel (SEE-kwuhl)— A subsequent work similar to an original, often with the same characters. Ex: Star Trek I, Star Trek II…

setting— Time and place of a story. Ex: Nineteenth-century England.

*simile (SIM-uh-lee)— Comparison of one thing to another using the words *like* or *as*. Ex: Her lips were like rose petals. (See List 95, Figures of Speech.)

*spoonerism (SPOON-er-iz-uhm)— Sound reversal in words to produce a humorous effect. Named after William Spooner, English preacher. Ex: heard in the band; bird in the hand.

*story, short— Fiction story shorter than a novel, often having a surprise ending. (See List 70, The Short Story: Characteristics; List 71, Short Story Collections; List 72, The Short Story Masters; and List 73, Short Works.)

style— The way an author characteristically expresses him or herself (short sentences, flowery language, etc.)

*symbol (SIM-buhl)— A word or object that stands for something else. Ex: dove = peace. (See List 146, Symbolism in Literature; and List 147, Symbols.)

synonym (SIN-un-nim)— Words meaning the same. Ex: mix, blend.

synopsis (sin-OP-sis)— Summary or condensed statement of a literary work.

*tale, fairy— Fanciful, imaginary story about a hero or heroine overcoming a problem, often involving mystical creatures, supernatural power, or magic; often a type of folktale. (See List 50, Fairy Tales and list 51, Fairy Tales/Folktales/Myths/Legends: Collections.)

*theme/thesis (THEEM/THEE-sis)— Main idea in a piece of literature; topic or subject. (See lists in Section VI, Themes : Under One Umbrella.)

*thriller— Story or movie filled with suspense. (See List 42, Detective and Spy Stories/Thrillers/Mysteries; List 43, Detective Stories: Sherlock Holmes; List 52, Fantasy/Horror/Ghosts: Stories; List 53, Fantasy/Horror/Ghosts: Collections; and List 125, Adventure Stories: True.)

tone— Mood brought forth by story or poem. Ex: sadness.

*tragedy (TRA-juh-dee)— Literature, often drama, ending in catastrophe for the protagonists after dealing with a series of problems. (See List 117, Shakespeare: Complete Plays and Poems.)

understatement (UHN-der-STAYT-muhnt)——Form of irony where the author intentionally understates the facts. Ex: We have a little problem here (referring to an impending catastrophe).

*verse— Writing with rhyme and meter, as opposed to prose; often verse refers to poetry of a less serious nature. (See List 82, Ballad; List 86, Grue; List 88, Limerick; and List 103, Humorous Poetry: Short.)

villain (VIL-in)— Character in a story or play who opposes the protagonist; the "bad guy."

6. ALLUSIONS: LITERARY*

Good literature is often peppered with allusions, and the authors assume a modicum of understanding on the reader's part. An allusion (not to be confused with an illusion) is a reference to a well-known character, story, setting, author, or myth in a subsequent speech or writing. Sometimes the present meaning has changed from its original source.

---

* Note: The source for some of this material is *Grand Allusions* by Elizabeth Webber and Mike Feinsilber, Farragut Publishing Company, Washington, D.C., 1990.

You will find literature difficult to understand and appreciate if you do not have the literary background to recognize mythological characters, Shakespearian and Biblical references, previous important writings, and other literary allusions. (See List 7, Allusions: Biblical; List 12, Mythological and Legendary Characters; and List 120, Allusions: Shakespearian.)

Artful Dodger (from Dickens's novel, *Oliver Twist*)— The Artful Dodger, nickname of Charles Dickens's character Jack Dawkins, was the head pickpocket in Fagin's gang. Now any skillful crook is called an artful dodger.

Augean Stables (from Greek mythology)— Hercules had to clean out the Augean Stables, which was a monumental task because it hadn't been done in 30 years. Now Augean Stables refer to any very difficult cleanup, actual or figurative.

Babbitt (from Sinclair Lewis's *Babbitt*)— Babbitt was a character who rebelled slightly against society's standards, but generally returned to conformity because of social pressures. Now a Babbitt refers to any average, conforming American with no imagination.

beau geste (from Wren's *Beau Geste*)— P. C. Wren's character, Beau Geste, dies heroically. Now any grand gesture, statement, or act of sacrifice for another is called a beau geste.

belling the cat (from an old fable and *Piers Plowman*)— The fable tells of a mouse's suggestion to put a bell around the neck of the cat so they could tell when the cat was in the vicinity. However, the question of who was to have the courage to bell the cat was a difficult one because of the inherent danger. Now a person who bells the cat is the person who has courage to stick his neck out for his friends despite putting himself at risk.

Big Brother is watching you (from George Orwell's *1984*)— The novel warns that government could invade our privacy. Big Brother now refers to any government or ruler that tries to dictate, eavesdrop, or gather personal information on its citizens.

Bligh (from *Mutiny on the Bounty* by Nordhoff and Hall and an actual British Naval officer involved in mutinies)— The novel's Captain Bligh was a tyrant. Now any person who is cruel, unreasonable, and tyrannical is a Captain Bligh.

Boswell (from James Boswell)— Boswell wrote a renowned, detailed, admiring biography of Samuel Johnson. Now an author who writes about a friend in glowing, admiring terms is referred to as that person's Boswell.

Brahmin— The author Oliver Wendell Holmes and his friends in nineteenth-century Boston formed a close literary, social, and political group and were prolific in their writings and criticisms. The members of this group were often referred to as the Boston Brahmins (from the Hindi *Brahman*, meaning of highest class). Now the term refers generally to any socially prominent and intellectually refined individual.

brave new world (from Huxley's *Brave New World*)— Aldous Huxley used this term satirically to portray a regimented, technological world without a heart or soul. The term is often used sarcastically or ironically to depict "advances" in our society which may in fact lead humanity to ruin.

brobdingnagian (from Swift's *Gulliver's Travels*)— Brobdingnag was the place where the giants lived in this satire by Jonathan Swift. Now anything extremely large is called brobdingnagian. (Note: Stresses in *brobdingnagian* are on the first and third syllables.)

Byronic (after Lord Byron)— George Gordon, Lord Byron, was an English Romantic poet who was considered a bit of a rake in his day. Now the term refers to any person who is like Byron himself or whose writing includes handsome, sad, brooding, and appealing characters like Byron's.

catch-22 (from Heller's *Catch-22*)— Joseph Heller's protagonist, Yossarian, tried to get out of dangerous jobs in the Air Corps by claiming insanity. However, the doctors told him anyone who wanted to avoid combat was sane, and if he really was crazy, he wouldn't be sane enough to apply for a discharge. This is the circular "catch-22." Now any situation where you lose no matter which decision you make is called a catch-22.

Cheshire cat (from Carroll's *Alice in Wonderland*)— The Cheshire cat in Lewis Carroll's story grinned all the time and could disappear and reappear at will, leaving only its grin. Now people who grin from ear to ear or wear a puzzling smile are said to be grinning like a Cheshire cat.

Damon and Pythias (from Greek legends)— Pythias was sentenced to death, but let out for a specified time for a parental visit if Damon took his place while Pythias was gone. Pythias got back just before they were to execute his friend, and they were both let go. Now any close friends are sometimes called Damon and Pythias.

Dantesque (after Dante)— Dante wrote with epic scope, vivid detail, and allegory. Now any writing resembling this is considered Dantesque.

Dickensian (after Dickens)— Charles Dickens wrote novels showing the poverty, injustices, and misery of Victorian England. Now situations or writings about similar topics are sometimes called Dickensian.

dog in the manger (from an old fable)— In the fable a dog prevented an ox from eating the hay though he had no use for it himself. Anyone who tries to spoil something for someone else, even though it is of no use for himself, is now called a dog in the manger.

Don Juan (from Tellez's *El Burlador de Seville* and Byron's epic poem *Don Juan*)— Gabriel Tellez (Tirso de Molina) told about the life and loves of Don Juan, the chief character in his play. Today we refer to a man who is a playboy or philander as a Don Juan.

Dorian Gray (from Wilde's *The Picture of Dorian Gray*)—-Oscar Wilde's character, Dorian Gray, a handsome but corrupt man, wanted to stay young and handsome forever, but of course, could not. A Dorian Gray, today, is anyone who clings to youth and is afraid of aging.

East Lynne (from Wood's *East Lynne*)— Mrs. Henry Wood's novel was a tear jerker about a woman who abandons her husband, only to return in disguise so she can rear her children. The phrase now refers to any play that is an overly sentimental tear jerker.

Elmer Gantry (from Lewis's *Elmer Gantry*)— The protagonist in Sinclair Lewis's novel was a corrupt, but successful, evangelist. Now any self-serving fundamentalist minister is called an Elmer Gantry.

Everyman (from an old play *Everyman,* of unknown authorship)— In the play, Everyman represented every man or all men. The term is still used in this sense.

Faulknerian (after Faulkner)— In his novels and short stories, William Faulkner's characters seemed to be driven by hidden forces beyond their control, and the plots included tragic violence set in the South. Any later work similar to his writings, characters, or settings is said to be Faulknerian.

Faustian (from a body of literature by Marlowe, Goethe, and others)— Faust sold his soul to the Devil to gain power, youth, and wealth. In modern usage, a Faustian bargain is one in which a person sacrifices everything to obtain immediate gratification, but pays the price later on.

for whom the bell tolls (from Donne's *Devotions*)— John Donne said "no man is an island" and that all people shared a common fate. He used the phrase: "Never send to know for whom the bell tolls: it tolls for thee." The expression continues to have a similar meaning in later works.

Gatsby (from Fitzgerald's *The Great Gatsby*)— F. Scott Fitzgerald's character, Jay Gatsby, was a crooked, but appealing, millionaire who deceived others about his past. A Gatsby is someone who gives in to his own fantasies and obsessions and represents ostentatious and lavish living.

gilded age (from Twain/Warner novel)— Mark Twain's novel, *The Gilded Age* (co-authored) deals with greed in post-Civil War America. The phrase has come to denote the post-Civil War era.

heart of darkness (from Conrad's *The Heart of Darkness*)— The phrase derives from Joseph Conrad's story of the character Marlow's searching through a dense jungle for another man. Heart of darkness now refers to the dark side of the human soul.

Holy Grail (from legends of King Arthur and Christian legends)— The Holy Grail, object of knightly quests, was the lost cup that Jesus supposedly drank from at the Last Supper. In current usage, a search for the Holy Grail signifies any difficult or possibly unattainable goal.

Homeric (after Homer, the Greek writer)— Homer's epics, the *Iliad* and the *Odyssey,* were mythological, heroic, and immense in scale. Today anything that is larger than life is referred to as Homeric.

Horatio Alger (from Horatio Alger's stories)— Alger's stories deal with poor boys who became rich. Now anyone who makes good after being born into a life of poverty is referred to as Horatio Alger.

Kafkaesque— Franz Kafka's writings, often surreal and bizarre, often presented characters thwarted by red tape and authoritarian bureaucracy. Now any literature or situation similar to this is called Kafkaesque.

last hurrah (from O'Connor's novel)— *The Last Hurrah,* written by Edwin O'Connor, was based on the life of James Curley, a former Boston mayor. The last hurrah refers to the last speech or function of a prominent person, particularly a politician, before retiring or leaving office. It has come to stand for the final action of a person before the end of a career.

leviathan (from Book of Job in the *Bible* and Hobbes's *Leviathan*)—-The Biblical Leviathan was a giant sea monster. Today anything that is huge and monstrous is said to be a Leviathan.

Lilliputian (from Swift's *Gulliver's Travels*)— In Jonathan Swift's story the Lilliputians were tiny people who were able to work together to subdue the giants. Now anything very tiny that can control something larger than itself is called Lilliputian.

Lochinvar (from Scott's *Marmion*)— Sir Walter Scott's long story-poem told of Lochinvar, a handsome hero, in love with Ellen. Today a Lochinvar is any handsome young, heroic-type man in pursuit of a lovely lady.

Machiavellian (From Machiavelli's *The Prince*)— Niccolo Machiavelli thought people were basically evil and that it was sometimes necessary to use evil means in order to rule. The term in present use refers to anyone who is merciless, clever, and unethical to obtain goals, particularly politically.

man for all seasons (after Thomas More)— Thomas More, author of *Utopia*, was sent to prison and executed because he refused to accept King Henry VIII as head of the Church in England. He was called a man for all time or a man for all seasons for sticking to his beliefs so strongly. Now a man for all seasons is any respected person who stands up for his ideals under pressure.

Moby Dick (from Melville's *Moby Dick*)— In Herman Melville's story, Captain Ahab relentlessly pursued Moby Dick, the whale, which had many symbolic meanings. Now Moby Dick has come to represent any monstrous obsession.

munchkin (from Baum's *The Wonderful Wizard of Oz*)— Frank L. Baum's Munchkins were diminutive, lively people. Now people use the term to describe a physically small person, often affectionately.

noble savage (from Jean Jacques Rousseau's writings)—This expression refers to an uncultivated person who is really more worthy and sensible than some of his or her "civilized" counterparts.

Oedipus complex (from Greek mythology and Sophocles's *Oedipus Rex*)—The mythological Oedipus unwittingly killed his father and married his mother. The Oedipus complex, delineated by Sigmund Freud, is a child's powerful erotic attachment to the parent of the opposite sex, creating rivalry with the parent of the same sex.

Orwellian (after George Orwell)— George Orwell's novel *1984* expressed his disillusionment with communism, totalitarianism, and bureaucracy. Today, the term *Orwellian* is used to describe anything bleak and oppressive, especially a political situation.

Peck's bad boy (from George Peck's writings and sketches)— Peck's character was a mischievous boy whose tricks and annoying behavior caused problems and embarrassment to others. In modern usage, anyone who causes embarrassment by gauche behavior is a Peck's bad boy.

Peter principle (from *The Peter Principle: Why Things Always Go Wrong*)— Laurence J. Peter's book theorized that people tend to rise to their level of incompetence. The same meaning applies today: You do well, you are promoted; but eventually you are promoted to a job you cannot do. This is the Peter principle.

Peyton Place (from Metalious's *Peyton Place*)— Grace Metalious's novel was about the evil lurking beneath the respectable facade of a community. Now the term is used to describe any situation where the veneer of respectability is suspect.

pilgrim's progress (from Bunyan's *Pilgrim's Progress*)— John Bunyan's character, Christian, overcame all obstacles through faith. Today anyone who overcomes worldly problems is said to have made a pilgrim's progress.

Platonic love (from Plato's *Symposium*)— The love Plato speaks of is based purely on mental and spiritual closeness. Thus any strong but nonsexual affinity for another person is called platonic.

Promethean (from Greek mythology, Aeschylus, and others)— Prometheus was a Greek god who defied authority and was punished. Prometheus has been alluded to in various ways in literature (sometimes for his defiant attitude, sometimes for the punishment he received, and sometimes as a hero for his independence). Today a Promethean person is anyone who is independent, defiant of authority, and willing to make sacrifices for his beliefs.

Pygmalion (from Greek mythology)— The mythological Pygmalion sculpted a statue of the ideal woman and fell in love with it. Any story or situation where a mentor takes on a pupil, remakes the person, then falls in love with the resulting creation is compared with the Pygmalion myth.

Queeg (from Wouk's *The Caine Mutiny*)— Herman Wouk's character, Captain Queeg, was an erratic, unstable commander who persecuted his subordinates. The name has come to denote any petty, incompetent person in a leadership position.

quixotic (from Cervantes's *Don Quixote*)— Miguel de Cervantes's character, Don Quixote, steadfastly sought knightly glory, colliding with everyday reality. Today anyone who pursues idealized, impractical goals is called quixotic.

Rabelaisian— François Rabelais wrote with bawdy or grotesque humor. Now anyone who writes in the same vein or behaves like Rabelais' characters is called Rabelaisian.

Rube Goldberg— Cartoonist Rube Goldberg drew fanciful, complex machines that did simple things. Thus any procedure that makes a simple task seem complicated is compared to a Rube Goldberg contraption.

Runyonesque— Damon Runyon wrote about the seamier side of New York, and his likeable characters were gamblers and scoundrels. We now refer to any underworld person or even a personable or likeable rogue as Runyonesque.

Shangri-la (from Hilton's *Lost Horizons*)— James Hilton portrayed a land of eternal youth and peace in his novel. Now Shangri-la has come to mean any idyllic place.

shot heard round the world (from Emerson's "Concord Hymn")—-Ralph Waldo Emerson's poem told of the first shot fired against the British in the Revolutionary War. Now a shot heard round the world refers to any dramatic statement or action that begins something important or greatly influences later events.

silent spring (from Carson's *Silent Spring*)— Rachel Carson wrote about the destruction of our environment by the use of herbicides and pesticides, referring to a silent spring without birds and other creatures. Now the words refer to any ecological calamity.

Socratic method (from Socrates/Plato interactions)— Plato's teacher, Socrates, used a question-and-answer method of teaching instead of lecturing. This method is now referred to as the Socratic method.

Svengali (from DuMaurier's *Trilby*)— Trilby, George DuMaurier's beautiful character, fell under the hypnotic spell of Svengali, a musician who was turning her into a singer. Today anyone who has (or tries to obtain) power over someone else through strength of personality is called a Svengali.

tabula rasa (from Latin, "blank state")— The British philosopher John Locke talked about a student's mind as being a "tabula rasa." He meant by this that the student's mind was fresh and unsullied, ready to be inscribed with knowledge. This expression has the same meaning today.

Trojan horse (from Virgil's *Aeneid*)— In Virgil's epic, the Greeks conquered Troy by filling a large, wooden horse with their soldiers and tricking the Trojans into letting it through the city gates. Today, any seemingly innocent maneuver that is designed to harm an adversary is called a Trojan horse.

Tweedledum and Tweedledee (from Carroll's *Through the Looking Glass* and Byrom's poem)— John Byrom used the terms Tweedledum and Tweedledee to satirize two competing schools of musicians, and Lewis Carroll used the names for his quarrelsome identical twins. Tweedledum and Tweedledee have come to denote any two things that are hard to tell apart.

ugly American (from *The Ugly American* by Lederer and Burdick)— In this novel, the protagonist, an American operative abroad, got his nickname because he was physically ugly. The phrase, however, has come to describe overbearing American policies or behavior in foreign countries.

utopia (from Thomas More's *Utopia*)— Thomas More depicted an ideal society in this work. A utopia—the term literally means "nowhere" in Greek—is any perfect place, state of being, or government.

Walter Mitty (from Thurber's "The Secret Life of Walter Mitty")— James Thurber's character, Walter Mitty, was a quiet, unassuming man who had daydreams of grandeur and heroic episodes. A person today who fantasizes about unrealistic, brave deeds is Mittylike, Mittyish, or a Walter Mitty.

Willy Loman (from Miller's "Death of a Salesman")— Arthur Miller's play had as its protagonist Willy Loman, a salesman whose life was crumbling about him and who eventually committed suicide. In present use, a Willy Loman is any person who is working hard trying to earn a living, but is not being very successful and is therefore a pathetic figure.

7. ALLUSIONS: BIBLICAL

This list contains Christian stories and Biblical characters often alluded to in literary works. The remarks, taken from a multitude of sources including encyclopedias, the Bible itself, scholarly works concerning the Bible, and books on allusions frequently found in literature, represent a consensus of Protestant, Catholic, and Jewish traditions. See also List 140, Religion: Biblical Quotations.

Abraham and Isaac— Abraham, reportedly 100 years old, and his wife, Sarah, had an only son named Isaac. God asked Abraham to sacrifice the son as a burnt offering and Abraham promised he would. Then at the last possible moment, God provided an animal for sacrifice instead. The story showed that if you have faith and are willing to give up anything God asks, he will bless you later.

Adam and Eve— The first two humans on earth were Adam and Eve. Eve persuaded Adam to eat of the forbidden tree of knowledge of good and evil, and thereby began the sins of man. God banished them from the Garden of Eden and relegated them to work and grow their own food forever.

Apostles, the Twelve— An apostle is a person who is sent by God with a message for the people. The apostles of Jesus were Matthew, Peter, James (the Greater), John, Judas Iscariot, Matthias, Philip, Bartholomew, Thomas, James (the Lesser), Simon, and Thaddeus.

Armageddon (from the Book of Revelation in the New Testament)— Armageddon is the scene of a battle between the forces of good and evil, ending the world. Armageddon is now used to describe any fierce confrontation resulting in mutual destruction.

Cain and Abel (from the Book of Genesis in the Old Testament)— Cain and Abel were twin brothers, sons of Adam and Eve. Cain murdered his brother, Abel, and God put a mark on Cain so everyone would know he was a murderer, but also so people would know he was under God's protection. In the present day, the mark of Cain refers to the stigma of anyone who has committed a crime or is an outcast by societal standards.

city on a hill (from the Book of Matthew in the New Testament)— The city on the hill appears in the Sermon on the Mount. Jesus described a "City that is set on a hill that cannot be hid," a place that was the "light of the world." This referred to a place that would be a shining example and a model to others, and the phrase is still used in that sense.

Daniel in the lion's den— Daniel was an Old Testament prophet who went through many trials and tribulations in Babylon. He had four visions of the end of the world, and these visions were the basis for the Book of Revelation. Now a person confronted with difficulties is compared to Daniel in the lion's den and is encouraged to hold up in the face of adversity or persecution, as he did.

David and Goliath— When Goliath, the great Philistine warrior, challenged the Israelites to combat, young David accepted the challenge and felled Goliath with a single stone from his sling. Now anyone who confronts great odds is considered a David going against a Goliath.

Elijah and Jezebel— A wicked Phoenician princess who became the wife of Ahab, king of Israel, Queen Jezebel was opposed to Elijah's monotheistic views and forced him to leave Phoenicia. She was thrown out a palace window, killed, and eaten by dogs, as Elijah had predicted. A Jezebel now is any wicked or shameless woman.

Esther and the king of Persia— Esther and her foster father, Mordecai, helped deliver the Jews from persecution by the king of Persia.

feet of clay (from the Book of Daniel in the Old Testament)— Nebuchadnezzar dreamed of someone having a gold head, silver arms, brass belly, iron legs, and feet of clay. Daniel predicted the feet of clay were the weakness and foretold the fall of Nebuchadnezzar's empire. The expression "feet of clay" now refers to the flaw of an otherwise strong and admirable person.

four horsemen of the apocalypse (from the Book of Revelation in the New Testament)— In his view of the end of the world, St. John saw four horses (white, red, black, and pale) representing the horrors of war: conquest, slaughter, famine, and death. Today the "four horsemen" phrase is used to represent any four men of ill repute or those who will bring catastrophe or destruction.

good Samaritan— Samaritans lived in Samaria at the time of Jesus. They honored Moses as the only prophet, but were at odds with other Jews. Jesus told a parable of a Samaritan who did what he thought was right even under pressure from others. Now a good Samaritan is anyone who does the right and courageous thing.

Jacob and Esau— These twin boys were born to childless Isaac and Rebekah in answer to prayer. Esau, a hunter, and Jacob, a shepherd, fought over the promise of spiritual privileges and birthright. Sometimes people refer to any arguing or greedy family members as being like Jacob and Esau.

Jesus— Jesus of Nazareth, son of Mary and God, became a religious teacher and leader. His followers founded Christianity.

Job— The Old Testament tells of Job, whose family was killed, stricken with illness, and deprived of his worldly goods. He kept his faith during his suffering, though he complained loud and long as the result of a wager between God and Satan. The story showed that God did not punish people because they sin, and that no one was immune from suffering, even the pious and guiltless. Today people talk of the "patience of Job," alluding to this story.

Jonah and the whale— Jonah was an Old Testament prophet. He tried to escape God's command to go to Assyria and preach, but God brought a storm upon his ship. The crew threw him overboard, and he was swallowed by a whale. Later the whale vomited Jonah out and then Jonah went to Assyria and preached repentance as he had been commanded earlier. The story showed God's love for both Jews and Gentiles.

Joseph— Husband of Mary, the mother of Jesus; a carpenter by trade, Joseph was a kind husband and father.

Joshua and the battle of Jericho— Joshua succeeded Moses and led Israel in conquering Canaan. The fall of the city of Jericho was a major battle ending in victory for the Israelites.

Judas Iscariot— One of the twelve Apostles, Judas betrayed Jesus to the authorities for a handful of silver coins. He later repented and returned the money he had been given, but apparently either hanged himself or fell to his death. Today a Judas is a traitor.

Lazarus (from the Book of John in the New Testament)— Lazarus was brought back to life by Jesus. Now someone who survives a disaster or rises again from apparent defeat is often called a Lazarus.

Lot and his wife— Lot was Abraham's nephew and lived in Sodom until God destroyed the city because of its wickedness. Lot escaped, but his wife was turned into a pillar of salt because she looked back at the burning city.

Mary— Mary, wife of Joseph, was the mother of Jesus, who was conceived without intercourse. She was at the crucifixion and the burial tomb, and saw Jesus after his resurrection.

Moses— At God's request, Moses led the Hebrews out of Egypt and guided them through the desert to the edge of Canaan. This flight from bondage is referred to in the Bible as the Exodus. When the Egyptians pursued the Hebrews, God drowned the Egyptians in the sea. Moses also led his people to a sacred mountain where God appeared amid lightning and thunder. God gave Moses the Ten Commandments and Moses established Israel's laws.

Noah and the flood (Noah and the ark)— Noah was a good man who lived in an age of sin. God wanted to save him and his family from a great flood that wiped out nearly everything and so commanded Noah to build an ark and to take two of every creature with him into the ark. Noah did so, and after the deluge, received a blessing of fertility. He later was guilty of drunkenness, but his sons, Ham, Shem, and Japheth became the legendary ancestors of the tribes of the ancient Middle East.

Peter (Simon or Simon Peter)— Simon, son of Jonah, was an important disciple of Jesus and was called "the rock" on which the church would be built. He was a fisherman from Galilee, and become a spokesperson for the other disciples. He witnessed the transfiguration and crucifixion of Jesus. Three times he denied he knew Jesus after Jesus was arrested and condemned. He is a saint of the Roman Catholic Church.

prodigal son— The parable of the prodigal son relates the story of a spendthrift son, who upon repentance and returning home, was warmly welcomed by his father. Any young man who is wayward and then forgiven by his family after he changes his ways and returns home is now called a prodigal son.

Rachel— Rachel is one of the four Jewish matriarchal figures of the Bible. She was the second wife of Jacob and the mother of Joseph.

Ruth— The story of Ruth, a widow who remarried and became an ancestor of King David, showed how God worked behind the scenes in everyday events.

Samson and Delilah— Samson, an Israelite judge renowned for his strength, was betrayed to the Philistines by his mistress, Delilah. Now any hard-hearted, disloyal woman is called a Delilah, and a well-built, physically strong man is called a Samson.

Sodom and Gomorrah (from the Book of Genesis in the Old Testament)— Sodom and Gomorrah were cities that God destroyed because their people were so sinful. Today, any place deemed unwholesome is referred to as a Sodom and Gomorrah.

Solomon, King— Solomon, the third King of Israel, was the son of King David. He reigned for about 50 years, became rich, wrote books, and was considered a wise man. People refer to the wisdom of Solomon when referring to someone who is fair and astute.

Thomas (doubting Thomas)— Thomas was one of the twelve Apostles. He would not believe that Jesus was resurrected from the dead until he actually saw the wounds on Jesus after he reappeared. Now anyone who doubts or questions things which others believe is called a doubting Thomas.

wise men, three— The three wise men were considered the first Gentiles to acknowledge Jesus' divinity. They were magi (astrologers, magicians, dream interpreters, or philosophers) who came from the East, guided by a star, to pay homage to the baby Jesus in Bethlehem and give him gifts of frankincense, gold, and myrrh. Although not named in the Bible, later tradition calls them Gaspar, Melchior, and Balthazar.

8. QUOTATIONS FROM LITERATURE

Students of literature and avid readers should be familiar with these famous quotations. They are in alphabetical order. (See also List 120, Allusions: Shakespearian; and List 140, Religion: Biblical Quotations.)

"A book of verses underneath the bough, a jug of wine, a loaf of bread— and thou beside me singing in the wilderness— oh, wilderness were paradise enow!"
   – **Omar Khayyam,** *Rubaiyat*

"A foolish consistency is the hobgoblin of little minds…
   – **Ralph Waldo Emerson, "Self Reliance"**

"A little learning is a dangerous thing."
   – **Alexander Pope, "An Essay on Criticism"**

"All animals are equal, but some animals are more equal than others."
   – **George Orwell,** *Animal Farm*

"All for one and one for all."
   – **Alexandre Dumas,** *The Three Musketeers*

"All is for the best in this best of all possible worlds."
   – **Voltaire,** *Candide*

"A man's a man for a' that."

– Robert Burns, "Is There for Honest Poverty"

"A man's reach should exceed his grasp."

– Robert Browning, "Luria"

"And so, my fellow Americans, ask not what your country can do for you; ask what you can do for your country."

– John F. Kennedy's inaugural address

"And therefore never send to know for whom the bell tolls; it tolls for thee."

– John Donne, *Devotions upon Emergent Occasions*, Meditation XVII

"An iron curtain has descended across the continent."

– Winston Churchill, speech on March 4, 1946

"A penny saved is a penny earned."

– Ben Franklin, *Poor Richard's Almanack*

"A small leak will sink a great ship."

– Ben Franklin, *Poor Richard's Almanack*

"A thing of beauty is a joy forever."

– John Keats, "Endymion"

"Beauty is truth, truth beauty— that is all ye know on earth, all ye need to know."

– John Keats, "Ode on a Grecian Urn"

"Because I could not stop for death he kindly stopped for me..."

– Emily Dickinson, "The Chariot"

"But I have promises to keep, and miles to go before I sleep..."

– Robert Frost, "Stopping by Woods on a Snowy Evening"

"Call me Ishmael."

Herman Melville, *Moby Dick*

"Cogito, ergo sum." (I think; therefore I am.)

Renè Descartes, "Pensées," *Discours de la methode* (Part IV)

"Come live with me and be my love."

> – Christopher Marlowe, "The Passionate Shepherd to His Love"

"Death, be not proud, though some have called thee mighty and dreadful for thou art not so …"

> – John Donne, "Death"

"Do not go gentle into that good night. Rage, rage against the dying of the light."

> – Dylan Thomas, "Do Not Go Gentle into That Good Night"

"Drink to me only with thine eyes."

> – Ben Jonson, "To Celia"

"East is east, and west is west, and never the twain shall meet."

> - Rudyard Kipling, "Ballad of East and West"

"Elementary."

> – Sir Arthur Conan Doyle, "The Crooked Man" and other Sherlock Holmes stories

"Far from the madding crowd's ignoble strife their sober wishes never learned to stray."

> – Thomas Gray, "Elegy Written in a Country Churchyard"

"Four score and seven years ago our fathers brought forth upon this continent a new nation…"

> – Abraham Lincoln, "Gettysburg Address"

"Full many a flower is born to blush unseen and waste its sweetness on the desert air."

> – Thomas Grey, "Elegy Written in a Country Churchyard"

"Gather ye rosebuds while ye may."

> – Robert Herrick, "To the Virgins, to Make Much of Time"

"Give me your tired, your poor, your huddled masses yearning to breathe free, the wretched refuse of your teeming shore."

> – Emma Lazarus, "The New Colossus" (on the base of Statue of Liberty)

"God bless us, every one!"

> – Charles Dickens, *A Christmas Carol*

"God's in his heaven— all's right with the world."

> – Robert Browning, "Pippa Passes"

"Good fences make good neighbors."

— **Robert Frost, "Mending Walls"**

"Had we but world enough, and time, this coyness, lady, were no crime."

— **Andrew Marvell, "To His Coy Mistress"**

"Happy families are all alike; every unhappy family is unhappy in its own way."

— **Leo Tolstoy, *Anna Karenina***

"Home is the sailor, home from the sea, and the hunter home from the hill."

— **Robert Lewis Stevenson, "Requiem"**

"How do I love thee? Let me count the ways."

— **Elizabeth Barrett Browning, "Sonnets from the Portuguese"**

"I am the master of my fate; I am the captain of my soul."

— **William Ernest Henley, "Invictus"**

"I celebrate myself, and sing myself."

— **Walt Whitman, *Leaves of Grass***

"I have a dream…"

— **Martin Luther King, Jr., Lincoln Memorial speech**

"I have nothing to offer, but blood, toil, tears, and sweat…"

— **Winston Churchill speech, May 13, 1940, House of Commons**

"I'm nobody! Who are you? Are you a nobody, too?"

— **Emily Dickinson, untitled poem**

"In Flanders fields the poppies blow between the crosses row on row…"

— **John McCrae, "In Flanders Field"**

"I think that I shall never see a poem lovely as a tree."

— **Joyce Kilmer, "Trees"**

"It is a far, far better thing I do, than I have ever done."

— **Charles Dickens, *A Tale of Two Cities***

"It was the best of times, it was the worst of times."

— **Charles Dickens, *A Tale of Two Cities***

"I wandered lonely as a cloud."

     – **William Wordsworth, "Daffodils"**

"Let him now speak, or else hereafter forever hold his peace."

     – **Book of Common Prayer of the Anglican Church**

"Listen my children, and you shall hear of the midnight ride of Paul Revere."

     – **Henry Wadsworth Longfellow, "Paul Revere's Ride"**

"Nobody dast blame this man. A salesman is got to dream, boy. It comes with the territory."

     – **Arthur Miller, *Death of Salesman***

"No man is an island."

     – **John Donne, *Devotions upon Emergent Occasions*, Meditation XVII**

"Off with her head! Off with his head!"

     – **Lewis Carroll, *Alice's Adventures in Wonderland***

"Oh, wad some pow'r the giftie gie us to see oursels as others see us!"

     – **Robert Burns, "To a Louse"**

"One if by land, two if by sea."

     – **Henry Wadsworth Longfellow, "Paul Revere's Ride"**

"Open, sesame."

     – **"Ali Baba and the Forty Thieves" from *Arabian Nights***

"Poems are made by fools like me, but only God can make a tree."

     – **Joyce Kilmer, "Trees"**

"He who, mixing grave and gay, can teach and yet give pleasure, gains a vote from each."

     – **Horace, *De Arte Poetica***

"Rose is a rose is a rose."

     – **Gertrude Stein, "Sacred Emily"**

"Ships that pass in the night, and speak each other in passing…"

     – **Henry Wadsworth Longfellow, "Elizabeth"**

"Shoot, if you must, this old gray head, but spare your country's flag."

> – **John Greenleaf Whittier, "Barbara Frietchie"**

"The best laid schemes o' mice an' men gang aft a-gley…"(go oft awry)

> – **Robert Burns, "To a Mouse"**

"The female of the species is more deadly than the male."

> – **Rudyard Kipling, "The Female of the Species"**

"Theirs is not to reason why, theirs but to do and die."

> – **Alfred, Lord Tennyson, "Charge of the Light Brigade"**

"The land was ours before we were the land's."

> – **Robert Frost, "The Gift Outright"**

"The mass of men lead lives of quiet desperation."

> – **Henry David Thoreau,** *Walden*

"The only thing we have to fear is fear itself."

> – **Franklin Delano Roosevelt's inaugural address, March 3, 1933**

"The paths of glory lead but to the grave."

> – **Thomas Grey, "Elegy Written in a Country Churchyard"**

"The reports of my death are greatly exaggerated."

> – **Mark Twain (Samuel Langhorn Clemens) in a message to newspapers in the United States after they published stories claiming he had died abroad.**

"The world is too much with us."

> – **William Wordsworth, "The World Is Too Much With Us"**

"There is no frigate like a book to take us lands away…"

> – **Emily Dickinson, "There Is No Frigate Like a Book"**

"There is no joy in Mudville—mighty Casey has struck out."

> – **Ernest Lawrence Thayer, "Casey at the Bat"**

"They also serve who only stand and wait."

> – **John Milton, "On His Blindness"**

"Things fall apart; the center cannot hold…,"
    – **William Butler Yeats, "The Second Coming"**

"Those who cannot remember the past are condemned to repeat it."
    – **George Santayana, *The Life of Reason: Reason in Common Sense***

"'Tis better to have loved and lost than never to have loved at all."
    – **Alfred, Lord Tennyson, "In Memoriam"**

"To be great is to be misunderstood."
    – **Ralph Waldo Emerson, "Self Reliance"**

"Trust thyself."
    – **Ralph Waldo Emerson, "Self Reliance"**

"…two roads diverged in a wood, and I— I took the one less travelled by, and that has made all the difference."
    – **Robert Frost, "The Road Not Taken"**

"Was this the face that launched a thousand ships?"
    – **Christopher Marlowe, *Doctor Faustus***

"Water, water, everywhere nor any drop to drink."
    – **Samuel Taylor Coleridge, "The Rime of the Ancient Mariner"**

"We hold these truths to be self evident, that all men are created equal…"
    – **Declaration of Independence of the United States**

"We, the people of the United States, in order to form a more perfect union,…"
    – **Preamble to the Constitution of the United States**

"What happens to a dream deferred? Does it dry up like a raisin in the sun?"
    – **Langston Hughes, "Harlem"**

"Whoso would be a man must be a nonconformist."
    Ralph Waldo Emerson, "Self Reliance"

"Yesterday, December 7, 1941,— a date which will live in infamy…"
    – **Franklin Delano Roosevelt, speaking about the Japanese attack on Pearl Harbor**

"You're a better man than I am, Gunga Din!"
    – **Rudyard Kipling, "Gunga Din"**

9. Influential Writers from Around the World

All the following writers and their works profoundly influenced the thinking of the western world and helped shape our culture. Any serious student of literature should be acquainted with all of them. The following influential male writers are listed in alphabetical order, along with selected major works. For lists of influential women, see List 151, Women: Important Writers; and List 152, Women Writers: Women's Issues. For a historical perspective, see lists of literary, dramatic, and other events for various time periods in Section VII, Literary Periods… Into One Era and Out the Other.

Aeschylus — Greek tragedian. *Prometheus Unbound*

Aesop — Greek fabulist. *Fables*

Anderson, Hans Christian — Danish author. *"The Emperor's New Clothes"; "The Princess and the Pea"; "The Ugly Duckling"*

Aquinas, Thomas — Italian philosopher/priest. *Summa Theologica*

Aristophanes — Greek comedic playwright. *The Clouds; Lysistrata*

Aristotle — Greek philosopher. *Rhetoric; Poetics; Metaphysics; Politics*

Augustine, St. — Roman Catholic saint and writer. *The City of God; Confessions* (autobiography)

Balzac, Honore de — French novelist. *The Human Comedy; Père Goriot*

Baudelaire, Charles — French poet. *The Flowers of Evil*

Beckett, Samuel — Irish playwright. *Waiting for Godot*

Casanova, Giovanni Jacopo — Italian author. *Memoirs*

Cervantes, Miguel de — Spanish author. *Don Quixote*

Chekhov, Anton — Russian short story writer and playwright. *The Cherry Orchard; The Three Sisters; Uncle Vanya*

Copernicus, Nicolaus — Polish astronomer. *On the Revolution of Heavenly Bodies*

Dante — Italian author. *Divine Comedy*

Darwin, Charles — British scientist. *Origin of Species and the Descent of Man; The Voyage of the Beagle*

Dostoyevsky, Fyodor — Russian author. *The Brothers Karamazov; Crime and Punishment*

Dumas, Alexandre — French novelist. *The Three Musketeers*

Einstein, Albert — German-Swiss physicist. *Relativity: The Special and General Theories*

Emerson, Ralph Waldo — American essayist. *Self-Reliance; The American Scholar*

Euripides — Greek tragedian. *Bacchae; Medea; The Trojan Women*

Flaubert, Gustave — French novelist. *Madame Bovary*

Fontaine, Jean de la — French fabulist. *Fables*

Franklin, Benjamin — American essayist, politician, and inventory. *Autobiography, Poor Richard's Almanack*

Freud, Sigmund — Austrian psychiatrist. *The Interpretation of Dreams; Civilization and Its Discontents*

Goethe, Johann Wolfgang — German novelist and dramatist. *The Sorrows of Young Werther; Faust*

Grimm, Jacob and Wilhelm (The Brothers Grimm) — German linguists and folklorists, Collection of folk tales, including: "Hansel and Gretel"; "Little Red Riding Hood"; "Rumpelstiltskin"; "Snow White and the Seven Dwarfs"

Hobbes, Thomas — British philosopher. *Leviathan*

Homer — Greek poet. *Iliad; Odyssey*

Hugo, Victor — French novelist. *Les Miserables; The Hunchback of Notre Dame*

Ibsen, Henrik — Norwegian playwright. *A Doll's House; Ghosts; An Enemy of the People; Hedda Gabler*

Joyce, James — Irish poet and novelist. *Ulysses; Finnegan's Wake; Portrait of the Artist as a Young Man*

Kafka, Franz — Austrian writer. *The Metamorphosis; The Trial; The Castle*

Khayyam, Omar — Persian poet. *Rubaiyat*

Machiavelli, Niccolo — Italian philosopher. *The Prince*

Mann, Thomas — German novelist. *The Magic Mountain; Death in Venice; Buddenbrooks; Doctor Faustus*

Marx, Karl — German political philosopher. *Communist Manifesto; Das Kapital*

Mill, John Stuart — English philosopher and essayist. *On Liberty*

Moliere (Jean Baptiste Poquelin) — French playwright. *The Misanthrope; Tartuffe*

Montaigne, Michel de — French essayist. *Essays*

More, Sir Thomas — British writer, philosopher. *Utopia*

Newton, Sir Isaac — British scientist/mathematician. *Philosophiae naturalis principia mathematica* (Principia)

Ovid — Roman poet. *Metamorphoses; The Art of Love*

Paine, Thomas — Colonial American pamphleteer. *Common Sense*

Pasternak, Boris — Russian novelist. *Dr. Zhivago*

Plato — Greek philosopher. *Republic; Symposium*

Plutarch — Greek biographer. *Lives*

Proust, Marcel — French novelist. *Remembrance of Things Past*

Rabelais, Francois — French writer. *Gargantua and Pantagruel*

Remarque, Erich Maria — German novelist. *All Quiet on the Western Front*

Rousseau, Jean-Jacques — French philosopher and writer. *Confessions; Emile; The Social Contract*

Sartre, Jean-Paul — French philosopher. *Being and Nothing; No Exit*

Solzhenitsyn, Alexander — Russian writer. *One Day in the Life of Ivan Denisovich; The Gulag Archipelago*

Sophocles — Ancient Greek tragedian. *Antigone; Oedipus Rex; Oedipus at Colonnus*

Thoreau, Henry David — American writer, *Civil Disobedience; Walden*

Tolstoy, Leo — Russian novelist. *Anna Karenina; War and Peace*

Verne, Jules — French author, "father" of science fiction. *Around the World in Eighty Days; Twenty Thousand Leagues under the Sea; From the Earth to the Moon; Journey to the Center of the Earth*

Virgil — Roman writer. *Aeneid*

Voltaire (Francois Arouet) — French novelist/philosopher. *Candide*

Zola, Emile — French essayist and novelist. *J'accuse; Germinale*

10. FAMOUS CHARACTERS FROM LITERATURE

See also List 6, Allusions: Literary; List 7, Allusions: Biblical; List 11, Gods and Goddesses; List 12, Mythological and Legendary Characters; and List 120, Allusions: Shakespearian.

Ahab, Captain — Main character in Melville's *Moby Dick*, who is determined to exact revenge on the white whale.

Aladdin — Character in *Arabian Nights*. Whenever Aladdin rubbed his lamp, a genie would appear and give him anything he wished.

Alice — Main character in *Alice in Wonderland* and *Through the Looking Glass* by Lewis Carroll.

Antonio — Character in Shakespeare's *The Merchant of Venice*, who is asked to give a pound of flesh to repay his debt to Shylock, the money-lender.

Antony, Mark — Character in Shakespeare's *Antony and Cleopatra* and Julius Caesar. A general and friend of Caesar; later became a triumvir, one of three Roman government administrators.

Baba, Ali — Protagonist, who opens the cave of gold, saying, "Open, Sesame," in *The Arabian Nights* tale, "Ali Baba and the Forty Thieves."

Babar — Elephant character in several books by Jean and Laurent de Brunhoff.

Babbitt — Main character (real estate agent) in book of same title by Sinclair Lewis. He put money before all else and was a boor.

Beast — Character in *Beauty and the Beast*, who is kind and loving despite his hideous appearance. Finally turns into a prince and marries Beauty.

Beauty — Beautiful female character in *Beauty and the Beast*, who falls in love with Beast.

Beauty, Black — Horse in Anna Sewell's famous story by that name.

Beauty, Sleeping — Princess in fairy tale by same name. She is put under a spell to sleep for 100 years, but when a handsome prince kisses her, the spell is broken.

Beowulf — Main character in eighth-century epic of the same name; slayed Grendel, the monster, but was killed by a dragon.

Bones, Bram — Ichabod Crane's rival for the love of a young lady in Irving's *The Legend of Sleepy Hollow*; scares Ichabod.

Brothers Karamazov — Brothers in Dostoyevsky's novel by the same name are Ivan, Alyosha, Smerdyakov, and Dmitri. Dmitri is accused of killing his father.

Brutus — Character in Shakespeare's *Julius Caesar*; led conspiracy against Caesar and murdered him.

Bumpo, Natty — Main character in Cooper's *The Leatherstocking Tales*; adopted the Indian way of life.

Butler, Rhett — Male character in Margaret Mitchell's *Gone With the Wind*; Scarlet's third husband.

Casey — Baseball player in Thayer's "Casey at the Bat," who strikes out in the ninth inning.

Cat, Cheshire — Cat from *Alice in Wonderland* that can disappear, leaving only his grin behind.

Catherine — Female character in Emily Bronte's *Wuthering Heights*, who is the object of Heathcliff's obsessive love.

Christian — Main character in John Bunyan's allegory, *The Pilgrim's Progress*.

Cid, El — Hero of twelfth-century Spanish epic *Poem of the Cid*.

Cinderella — The fairy-tale heroine who has two mean step-sisters and an uncaring step-mother.

Cleopatra — Character in Shakespeare's *Antony and Cleopatra*; Queen of Egypt.

Copperfield, David — Main character in Dickens' novel by same name; story exposes cruel treatment of children in 19th-century Great Britain.

Cordelia — Character in Shakespeare's *King Lear;* the only one of Lear's daughters who is sincere about her love for him.

Crane, Ichabod — Main character in *The Legend of Sleepy Hollow.* He is a lanky schoolteacher frightened by the Headless Horseman (put in his path by a rival for his girlfriend).

Cratchit, Bob — Character in Dickens's *Christmas Carol,* who worked for Scrooge and was Tiny Tim's father.

Crusoe, Robinson — Main character from Defoe's book of same name; he was shipwrecked on an island and survived for years.

d'Artagnan — Main character in Dumas's *The Three Musketeers;* a friend of the musketeers, Porthos, Athos, and Aramis.

Desdemona — Wife of Othello in Shakespeare's play by same name. Killed by Othello in a fit of jealous rage.

Dorothy — Main character in L. Frank Baum's *The Wonderful Wizard of Oz* who, with three friends, finds herself in an enchanted kingdom. Her last name was Gale.

Dracula, Count — Vampire in Bram Stoker's novel.

Dumpty, Humpty — Character of a nursery rhyme; also met by Alice in her adventures in *Through the Looking Glass.* Humpty is an egg.

Dwarfs, Seven — Happy, Bashful, Dopey, Sneezy, Grumpy, Doc, and Sleepy are the seven dwarfs in the Disney film *Snow White.*

Emile — Title character in Jean-Jacques Rousseau's *Emile,* which offers an innovative theory of education.

Fagin — Character in Dickens's *Oliver Twist,* who teaches Oliver and others how to be pickpockets.

Falstaff — Shakespeare character in *King Henry the Fourth* and other plays; a lovable rogue.

Faust — Legendary magician and alchemist in plays by Christopher Marlowe and Goethe.

Figaro — Spanish barber created by Beaumarchais and who later appears in operas: Mozart's *The Marriage of Figaro* and Rossini's *The Barber of Seville.*

Finn, Huckleberry — Main character, an orphan in Twain's novel, *The Adventures of Huckleberry Finn,* who shares a series of adventures with Jim, a runaway slave.

Fogg, Phineas — Character in Jules Verne's *Around the World in Eighty Days.*

Fox, Brer — Recurring animal character in *Uncle Remus* stories. Usually loses out to Brer Rabbit.

Frankenstein, Dr. Victor — Doctor/scientist in Mary Shelley's *Frankenstein,* who creates a monster.

Friday — Sidekick to Robinson Crusoe in book by same name.

Gatsby, Jay — Male lead character in F. Scott Fitzgerald's *The Great Gatsby*; tries to get back his former sweetheart after he becomes wealthy.

Goldilocks — Main female character of *The Three Bears*. Goes to bears' house, tries out their things, and is discovered sleeping in baby bear's bed.

Goose, Mother — The reputed source of the children's nursery rhymes collected by Charles Perrault during the seventeenth century.

Gradgrind — Utilitarian and practical character in Charles Dickens's *Hard Times* who comes to see the error of his ways.

Gretel — Female character in fairy tale who, with brother Hansel, wandered in woods, found gingerbread house owned by a witch, but got out of her clutches by outwitting her.

Grinch, The — Dr. Seuss's miserly character in *How the Grinch Stole Christmas*. Now anyone who spoils fun for others is a grinch.

Gulliver — Main character in Jonathan Swift's *Gulliver's Travels*; travels to four fictitious places as Swift mocks human frailties.

Hamlet — Main character in Shakespeare's play by same name; son of Gertrude, former Queen of Denmark and nephew of Claudius, King of Denmark; avenges murder of his father by killing the murderer, his uncle, Claudius.

Hansel — Male character in fairy tale who, with sister Gretel, wandered in woods, found a gingerbread house owned by a witch, but escaped by using his wits.

Hare, March — Character in Lewis Carroll's *Alice's Adventures in Wonderland*.

Hawkins, Jim — Boy in Stevenson's *Treasure Island*, who foils the plans of the pirates.

Heathcliff — Male character in Emily Bronte's *Wuthering Heights*, obsessed with love for Catherine.

Heep, Uriah — Hypocrite and blackmailer in Dickens's *David Copperfield*.

Holmes, Sherlock — Archetypal detective in a series of stories by Sir Arthur Conan Doyle; Holmes always picks up on remote clues and solves the most difficult mysteries.

Hood, Red Riding — Fairy tale heroine, who, dressed in red cape and hood, went to grandmother's house and was tricked by a wolf pretending to be her grandmother.

Hook, Captain — Evil pirate leader in *Peter Pan*, who had a hook for a hand because of a crocodile encounter.

Hyde, Mr. — Evil character in Stevenson's *The Strange Case of Dr. Jekyll and Mr. Hyde*. Hyde is really Dr. Jekyll under the influence of potions and represents the evil side of Jekyll's personality.

Iago — Envious officer in *Othello* who deceives Othello and begins a tragic chain of events.

Jane — Tarzan's mate in the popular comic strip and films.

Jeeves — Wise and resourceful manservant in P. G. Wodehouse's writings.

Jekyll, Dr. — Good character in Stevenson's *The Strange Case of Dr. Jekyll and Mr. Hyde*, who turns into evil Mr. Hyde after he experiments on himself.

Jim — Escaped slave who accompanies Huckleberry Finn in his adventures in Twain's novel, *The Adventures of Huckleberry Finn*.

John, Little — One of Robin Hood's faithful men.

Juan, Don — Character in Lord Byron poem and also Shaw's play, *Man and Superman*; notorious woman-chaser; also known by his Italian name, Don Giovanni.

Juliet — Female title character in Shakespeare's *Romeo and Juliet*; she was in love with Romeo, but their warring families tried to keep them apart.

Knight, White — Character in Carroll's *Through the Looking Glass*.

Legree, Simon — Brutal slave driver in Stowe's *Uncle Tom's Cabin*.

Lennox, Mary — Main character in Frances Hodgson Burnett's *The Secret Garden*. Spends unpleasant childhood in India until she arrives in England and finds a garden to care for.

Lion, Cowardly — Character from Baum's *The Wonderful Wizard of Oz*; seeks courage from the wizard.

Little, Chicken — Chicken character in a story who tells everyone the sky is falling because she got hit on the head with an acorn. The animals believe her, set out to tell the king, but are ambushed on the way and eaten by a fox.

Loman, Willie — Main character in Arthur Miller's *Death of a Salesman*; eventually commits suicide.

Macbeth — Character in Shakespeare's play by same name; general in army of Duncan, King of Scotland; goaded by wife, Lady Macbeth, to murder the king and claim the throne for himself.

Malaprop, Mrs. — Character in Richard Sheridan's *The Rivals*, who keeps mixing up similar words.

Meg, Jo, Beth, Amy — Four sisters, main characters in Louisa May Alcott's *Little Women*.

Micawber — Eternally optimistic character in *David Copperfield*, the quasi-autobiographical tale by Charles Dickens.

Mitty, Walter — Character in Thurber's *The Secret Life of Walter Mitty*, who lives a fantasy life because his own life is so boring.

Mowgli — The Indian boy who wanders away from his family and is raised by a pack of wolves in Rudyard Kipling's *The Jungle Book*.

O'Hara, Scarlet — Manipulative female character in Margaret Mitchell's *Gone With the Wind*.

Othello — Main character in Shakespeare's play by same name. He kills his wife, thinking she had been unfaithful; then kills himself with remorse when he realizes he has been tricked by Iago.

Pan, Peter — Main character in James Barrie's play by the same name; goes to a country where children never have to grow up.

Panza, Sancho — Sidekick of Don Quixote in Cervantes's great novel; Quixote's foil.

Pickwick, Samuel — Title character in Dickens's *The Pickwick Papers*, a naive, good-hearted man who founds the Pickwick Club and has a series of misadventures before retiring from the world.

Pied Piper of Hamlin — Main character in Robert Browning's poem by the same name (and also hero of folktale), who plays his flute and lures all the rats from town. When the people fail to pay him his due, he enchants all the children from the town the same way.

Pinocchio — Wooden puppet in Collodi's story, whose nose grows longer every time he lies. He wants to be a real person.

Pip — Nickname of boy in Dickens's *Great Expectations*; he leaves his real friends because he is consumed with ambition. Full name is Philip Pirrip.

Pollyanna — Main female character in Eleanor Porter's book by the same name. Pollyanna has many rough times, but manages to remain happy and cheerful.

Portia — Female character in Shakespeare's *The Merchant of Venice*, who saves Antonio from having to pay the utmost price for his debt.

Prospero — Main character in Shakespeare's *The Tempest*; he is banished to an island and rules with magic.

Prynne, Hester — Female character in Hawthorne's *Scarlet Letter*, who has to wear a red letter *A* on her dress as a punishment for committing adultery.

Puck — Mischievous fairy in Shakespeare's *Midsummer Night's Dream*.

Puss in Boots — Fairy tale cat, who wore red boots and through a series of clever tricks gained the favor of the king and secured the princess's hand for his master.

Quasimodo — Hunchback bell-ringer in *The Hunchback of Notre Dame* by Victor Hugo.

Quixote, Don — Would-be knight-errant in the novel of the same name by Miguel de Cervantes.

Rabbit, Brer — Animal character in *Uncle Remus* stories. Usually manages to outwit Brer Fox.

Rabbit, White — Character in Lewis Carroll's *Alice's Adventures in Wonderland*.

Rapunzel — Female fairy tale character given to a witch when she was 12 years old; her hair was so long the witch (and the prince) climbed up into the castle tower on it; after several misfortunes, the prince and Rapunzel lived happily ever after.

Remus, Uncle — African-American story-teller in *Uncle Remus* stories; he tells stories about life using animal characters.

Robin, Christopher — Male character in series of A. A. Milne's *Winnie-the-Pooh* books, modeled after the author's son.

Romeo — Title character in *Romeo and Juliet* by Shakespeare, caught in the war between the Capulets and Montagues.

Rowland, Childe — King Arthur's youngest son; with the help of Merlin, the magician, he found his sister, Burd Ellen, and released her from a spell.

Rumpelstiltskin — Dwarf from story by same name who helps the princess spin straw into gold.

Sailor, Sinbad the — Main character in the *Arabian Nights* story "The History of Sinbad the Sailor."

Samsa, Gregor — Character in Kafka's "The Metamorphosis," who is changed into a giant insect.

Sawyer, Tom — Main character in Twain's *The Adventures of Tom Sawyer*, who gets into one scrape after another.

Scarecrow — Character in Baum's *The Wonderful Wizard of Oz*, seeks brains from the wizard.

Scheherazade — Queen in *Arabian Nights*, who told 1001 stories to her husband, the sultan.

Scrooge, Ebenezer — Miser from Dickens's *A Christmas Carol* who always said, "Bah, Humbug" when people wished him a happy Christmas. Has a change of heart about Christmas after three terrifying visits from spirits who show him his past, present, and future.

Sharp, Becky — Main female character in Thackeray's *Vanity Fair* who pursues wealth and power by any means she can.

Shylock — Character in Shakespeare's *The Merchant of Venice* who is a hard-hearted money lender.

Silver, Long John — Villainous, one-legged pirate in Stevenson's *Treasure Island*.

Superman — Comic book hero who can "run faster than a speeding bullet," and "leap tall buildings in a single bound," among other feats. He fights crime and injustice wherever he can.

Tarzan — Male comic book and movie hero who was raised with apes in an African jungle. He is kind and strong.

Thatcher, Becky — Tom Sawyer's sweetheart in Mark Twain's *Tom Sawyer*.

Thumb, Tom — Tiny boy no bigger than a thumb, who never gets any larger. Male character in fairy tale.

Tim, Tiny — Crippled boy from *A Christmas Carol* who is finally helped by the repentant Ebenezer Scrooge.

Tinkerbell, Tinker — Fairy character in *Peter Pan*, who teaches Peter to fly.

Toad, Mole, Rat, Badger — Four characters from *Wind in the Willows* by Kenneth Grahame.

Tom, Uncle — Passive slave in Harriet Beecher Stowe's *Uncle Tom's Cabin*.

Tuck, Friar — One of Robin Hood's faithful men.

Tweedledum and Tweedledee — Overweight twins from *Through the Looking Glass* by Lewis Carroll.

Twist, Oliver — Title character in the novel by Charles Dickens. Grows up without his parents, goes to a workhouse, is abused, runs away, joins a gang, and eventually finds a benefactor.

Two-Shoes, Goody — Character in a nursery tale by Oliver Goldsmith; a poor girl who became very happy after being given a pair of shoes.

Van Winkle, Rip — Character in story by Washington Irving; he goes hunting, falls asleep for 20 years, and returns home to find no one recognizes him.

Watson — Sherlock Holmes's sidekick in Sir Arthur Conan Doyle's series of mysteries.

White, Snow — Character in *Snow White and the Seven Dwarfs*; she tries to escape a wicked step-mother who poisons her.

Winnie-the-Pooh — Toy bear in series of A. A. Milne's books.

Wizard of Oz — Character in Baum's *The Wonderful Wizard of Oz*, who pretends to be brave and powerful to give Dorothy and her friends what they are seeking.

Woodman, Tin — Character in *The Wonderful Wizard of Oz*; he seeks a heart from the wizard.

11. GODS AND GODDESSES*

GOD/GODDESS OF	GREEK	ROMAN	OTHER
Agriculture/harvest	Demeter (f)	Ceres (f) Saturn (m)	Soma (m) <Hindu> Frey/Freyr (m) <Norse>
Dawn	Eos (f)	Aurora (f)	
Dreams/sleep	Morpheus (m) Hypnos (m)	Somnus (m)	
Earth	Gaea (f)	Tellus (f) Terra (f)	
Entrances/exits		Janus (m)	Vayu (m) <Hindu>
Fertility/motherhood	Semele (f)		Isis (f) <Egyptian>
Fire	Hephaestus (m)	Vulcan (m)	Agni (m) <Hindu>
Forests/fields		Sylvanus (m)	
Healing	Asclepius (m)	Aesculapius (m)	Serapis (m) <Egyptian>
Hearth/home/household	Hestia (f)	Vesta (f) Lares and Penates (m)	
Hunt/moon	Artemis (f)	Diana (f)	
King of gods	Zeus (m)	Jupiter/Jove (m)	Odin (m) <Norse> Amon-Ra (m) <Egyptian> Shiva (m) <Hindu> Quetzalcoatl (m) <Mexican>
Love	Eros (m)	Cupid (m) Amor (m)	
Love and beauty	Aphrodite (f)	Venus (f)	Hathor/Athor (f) <Egyptian> Lakshmi (f) <Hindu> Freyja/Freya (f) <Norse>
Marriage	Hera (f) Hymen (m)	Juno (f)	Frigg/Frigga (f) <Norse>
Messenger/science/ invention	Hermes (m)	Mercury (m)	
Moon	Selene (f)	Luna (f)	
Music/poetry/ prophecy/medicine	Apollo (m)	Apollo (m)	Brage/Bragi (m) <Norse>
Queen of gods	Hera (f)	Juno(f)	Shakti (f) <Hindu> Isis (f) <Egyptian>
Rainbow	Iris (f)		Idun/Iduna (f) <Norse>
Sea	Poseidon (m)	Neptune (m)	
Shepherds	Pan (m)	Faunus (m)	
Silence	Harpocrates (m)	Harpocrates (m)	
Spring	Persephone(f)	Proserpina (f)	Idun/Iduna (f) <Norse>

GOD/GODDESS OF	GREEK	ROMAN	OTHER
Sun	Helios (m)	Apollo (m) Sol (m)	Ra (m) <Egyptian> Mitra/Surya (m) <Hindu> Horus (m) <Egyptian>
Thunder	Zeus (m)	Jupiter (m)	Thor/Atli (m) <Norse> Indra (m) <Hindu>
Underworld/death	Hades (m) Persephone (f)	Pluto (m) Dis (m)	Osiris (m) <Egyptian> Hel (f) <Norse>
Vengeance	Nemesis (f)	Nemesis (f)	
War	Ares (m)	Mars (m) Quirinus (m)	Skanda (m) <Hindu> Tyr (m) <Norse>
Wine	Dionysus (m)	Bacchus (m)	
Wisdom/handicrafts	Athena (f)	Minerva (f)	Balder/Baldr (m) <Norse> Ganesh (m) <Hindu>
Witchcraft	Hecate (f)		
Youth	Hebe (f)	Juventas (f)	

*(f) denotes goddess (female); (m) denotes god (male). Note: A good reference is *A Comprehensive Dictionary of the Gods* by Anne S. Baumgartner.

12. MYTHOLOGICAL AND LEGENDARY CHARACTERS

Myths are stories about gods, goddesses, and humans with supernatural powers. They usually attempt to explain the origin of the universe, the operation of natural forces, and the good and evil qualities of humans. The characters below (people, animals, and some combinations) are non-divine beings who appear in myths and legends. See also List 11, Gods and Goddesses.

Achilles — Greek warrior who could only be killed by a wound to the heel. Now we refer to someone's weakness by calling it an Achilles's heel.

Aeneas — Warrior on the Trojan side in the Trojan War and the legendary founder of Rome. A symbol of devotion because he carried his father out of Troy on his back.

Adonis — Extraordinarily handsome Greek boy. Now we refer to any good-looking young man as an Adonis.

Agememnon — Greek king who led his men in the Trojan War. Led tragic life and was finally murdered by his wife.

Amazon — Female warriors in Greek mythology, who were powerfully built and ferocious fighters. Now we refer to any extraordinarily strong, large, or assertive woman as an Amazon.

Androcles — Slave from *Androcles and the Lion* legend. Androcles took a thorn out of a lion's foot; later, when he was "thrown to the lions" as a punishment, he confronted the very same lion, who repaid his kindness.

Antigone — Daughter of Oedipus. Disobeyed the king's order not to bury her brother because he was considered a traitor; she was put to death.

Arachne — Had weaving contest with Athena, Goddess of Wisdom, and belittled the gods. Athena turned her into a spider so she'd have to weave the rest of her life.

Argonauts — Jason's comrades in his search for the golden fleece.

Argus — A creature with 100 eyes who was supposed to watch over Io. He finally closed all his eyes when music lulled him to sleep and his eyes were put in the tail of the peacock.

Arthur, King — Hero of legends about ancient England. Head of the Knights of the Round Table.

Atalanta — Swift-footed maiden who outran all her suitors until Hippomemes (helped by Venus, the goddess of Love) tricked her with the distraction of three golden apples.

Atlas — A giant who had to hold the earth and sky on his shoulders forever because he rebelled against the gods. Now we refer to any very strong person as an Atlas.

Brunnhilde (Brynhild) — In Germanic myths, the Valkyrie who fell in love with Siegfried, but had him killed when she found out he deceived her. Committed suicide.

Cassandra — Prophet in Troy during the Trojan War whom nobody believed. Now we refer to a Cassandra as anybody who predicts bad news.

Cerberus — A ferocious dog with three heads who stood at the gates of the underworld, allowing the souls of the dead to enter but not to leave.

Charon — Boatman who took the souls of the dead across the river Styx into the underworld.

Chimera — A monster who had a lion's head, goat's body, and dragon's tail. Now we refer to any illusion or figment of the imagination as chimerical.

Circe — Sorceress who turned men into swine if they looked at her.

Cyclops — Any of the giants who had a single eye in the middle of their foreheads.

Daedalus — Greek who invented a maze called the Labyrinth. No one could ever escape from it. Made wax wings for his son (Icarus) to escape from Crete.

Damon — Greek legendary figure extraordinarily devoted to his friend, Pythias. Agreed to die in his place.

Dido — Queen of Carthage, Africa, who loved Aeneas and committed suicide when he abandoned her.

Electra — Agememnon's daughter; helped kill her mother and her mother's lover to avenge the death of her father. Now we refer to the Electra complex as the unconscious erotic attraction of a young girl toward her father.

Eurydice — Wife of Orpheus. See Orpheus.

The Fates — Three women who had the power to decide how long people would live and what happened to them. Life was represented by a thread: One Fate spun the thread, another measured it, and the third cut it when a person died.

Galahad, Sir — One of King Arthur's Knights of the Round Table, illegitimate son of Sir Lancelot and Princess Elaine. Purest knight of the Round Table. Galahad now refers to any noble person.

Gawain, Sir — One of the most courteous of King Arthur's Knights of the Round Table.

Godiva, Lady — Legendary English lady who rode nude on horseback through Coventry, covered only by her long, flowing hair. Her husband agreed to annul the taxes he had imposed on the city if she did this.

Gorgons — Female monsters having tusks, claws, and hair of snakes. Perseus was successful in cutting off a Gorgon's head and used it to turn his enemies into stone.

Graces (Chorites) — Three Greek goddesses of fertility: Aglaia, Euphrosyne, and Thalia.

Guinevere, Queen — King Arthur's wife.

Harpies — Ferocious winged creatures with women's faces. Now we refer to a nagging woman as a harpy.

Hector — Trojan warrior and Prince of Troy.

Helen of Troy — A beautiful Greek woman, daughter of Zeus and Leda, who was kidnapped by Paris of Troy. The Trojan War began when the Greeks tried to get her back.

Hercules (Herakles)— Son of Zeus and Alcmene; showed his strength doing impossible deeds called the Twelve Labors of Hercules. Now we refer to any huge task as herculean.

Icarus — Son of Daedalus. Used the wax wings his father made him to escape from Crete. Despite his father's warning, flew too close to the sun, melted his wings, and drowned in the sea.

Io — One of Zeus's lovers.

Iseult (Isolde) — In English and Irish legend, the lover of Tristan. See Tristan.

Jason — Greek mythological hero who sailed in his ship, the Argo, with the Argonauts, and found the golden fleece of a magical ram.

Knights of the Round Table — In Arthurian legend, the 150 knights who convened at a round table designed by Merlin so that no one had the most prestigious place.

Lady of the Lake — Supernatural figure from Malory's *Morte d'Arthur* raises Lancelot and gives King Arthur his sword, Excalibur. (Also name of poem by Sir Walter Scott.)

Laocoön — Priest in Troy during the Trojan War who warned of Greek treachery (the Trojan Horse).

Leprechaun — Legendary Irish elves who can disclose a treasure's location, if someone is smart enough to catch them.

Lancelot, Sir — One of the bravest of King Arthur's Knights of the Round Table.

Little John — One of Robin Hood's merry men, ironically named Little John because of his brawny physique.

Medea — Sorceress who fell in love with Jason. Murdered his bride and others when Jason left her.

Medusa — A female monster with snakes for hair (a Gorgon). When people looked at her, they turned to stone. Perseus killed her by using the reflection in his shield to aim his sword, so he didn't have to look at her directly.

Merlin — Magician and advisor to King Arthur.

Midas — A king who was so greedy he wanted everything he touched to turn to gold. When he got his wish he was aghast because he couldn't eat gold, so he asked the gods to let him live normally again.

Minotaur — A monster (man with bull's head) who killed anyone who entered the Labyrinth. Killed by Theseus.

Modred (Mordred) — King Arthur's antagonist (in some versions his illegitimate son); causes Arthur's downfall.

Muses — Nine daughters of Zeus and Mnemosyne, each representing a different art, such as music, dance, astronomy, and so forth.

Narcissus — Handsome young man who fell in love with his own reflection while staring at himself in a pool. The gods turned him into a narcissus (flower). Now we refer to anyone who is conceited as narcissistic.

Nereids — Sea nymphs who came to the assistance of sailors in Greek mythological tales.

Nottingham, Sheriff of — Antagonist in Robin Hood legends.

Nymph — Mythological female spirits who are minor divinities of nature, dwelling in mountains, woods, and so on.

Odysseus (Ulysses) — Greek who fought in the Trojan War. His ten years of adventure after the war are related in the *Odyssey,* an epic poem by Homer.

Oedipus — King who killed his father and married his mother by mistake. Ended up blinding himself for punishment.

Orpheus — Musician who charmed the ruler of the underworld into releasing his wife, Eurydice; because Orpheus broke his promise not to look at her until he got back to earth, Eurydice disappeared forever.

Orestes — Son of Clytemnestra and Agamemnon.

Pandora — Curious, gifted woman who opened a box she was supposed to leave shut, and let out all the evils of mankind except Hope.

Paris — Prince of Troy who kidnapped Helen (who became Helen of Troy) and began the Trojan War. He killed Achilles with an arrow to the heel.

Pegasus — Winged horse that flew above the earth.

Penelope — Wife of Odysseus; symbol of wifely fidelity.

Perseus — Killed Medusa and turned Phineus, his rival, to stone.

Phoenix — Mythological bird that could set itself on fire, and then rise from its own ashes. Now anyone who rises above severe problems is compared with the phoenix.

Pixies — sprites in English folklore that play pranks on people and lead them astray.

Priam — King of Troy. Killed at end of Trojan War.

Procrustes — Evil giant who either stretched people or cut off their legs to make them fit into a bed. Any effort to enforce conformity to a prescribed pattern is called procrustean.

Prometheus — Giant who stole fire from the gods and gave it to humans.

Psyche — The beloved of Cupid, who loses him temporarily by disobeying his request never to seek his identity.

Punch and Judy — English puppet characters. Punch, who continually beats his wife and baby with a stick, is hunchbacked and has a crooked nose.

Pygmalion — Mythological sculptor who fell in love with his statue (which later came to life) of an ideal woman.

Pythias — Greek character who showed ideal loyalty to his friend Damon.

Robin Hood — Legendary English hero/rogue who, with his merry band of men, robbed the rich and gave to the poor.

Romulus and Remus — Twin boys who were raised by a female wolf. Romulus founded Rome.

Saturn — Father of Jupiter in Roman mythology.

Satyr — Mythological creature that was part man, part goat.

Scylla — Monster with six heads who devoured sailors caught between her and a whirlpool named Charybdis. Now we refer to a choice between two bad options as being caught between Scylla and Charybdis.

Sirens — Alluring creatures, half woman and half bird, who fatally enchanted sailors with their singing.

Sisyphus — King who had to roll a massive boulder uphill forever as punishment for cheating death. We now refer to any hard, uphill battle as a task of Sisyphus.

Sphinx — Female monster with the body of a lion and woman's head who asked a famous riddle and destroyed anyone who could not answer it correctly. When Oedipus solved the riddle, she killed herself.

Tell, William — Legendary Swiss archer who was forced to shoot an apple off the head of his son.

Teiresias/Tiresias — Greek mythological character who was struck blind (myths vary as to how this came about), but was given the gift of prophecy.

Theseus — Athenian hero who married Hippolyta, Queen of Amazons.

Titan — Any of a group of giants who ruled the universe at one time. Zeus and some other gods finally ousted them.

Tristan (Tristram) — Lover of Iseult in British and Irish legends. Both died tragically.

Troll — Mythical Norse dwarf who lived in caves, under bridges, and other hidden places. Now we call any mean person a troll.

Unicorn — Mythological equine animal with a horn projecting from its forehead.

Vampire — Living corpse who needs human blood to live.

Werewolf — Man changed into wolf who prowls around at night doing dastardly things such as killing babies and digging up dead bodies under the light of the full moon.

13. FAMOUS PLACES FROM LITERATURE

Atlantis — Legendary vanished island in the Atlantic Ocean.

Avalon — Island where King Arthur was taken after suffering a mortal wound.

Blefuscu — Island north of Lilliput where the Lilliputians' enemies lived, in Swift's *Gulliver's Travels*. Symbolically represents France.

Brobdingnag — Land in Gulliver's Travels where the people are seventy feet tall.

Camelot — Legendary site in Britain where King Arthur and Knights of the Round Table met. Now refers to any ideal spot or situation.

Elysian Fields — Where the souls of good people went after their death. Now Elysian Fields refer to any place of great happiness.

Forest of Arden — Setting of *As You Like It*, by Shakespeare.

Forest of Birnam — In Shakespeare's *Macbeth*, the king's enemies cut branches from the trees in Birnam forest to disguise their advance on his castle.

Gomorrah — Biblical city destroyed because its people were evil.

Lilliput — Place of little people six inches tall that Gulliver of *Gulliver's Travels* visited. People now refer to anything very tiny as lilliputian. Lilliput symbolically represents England.

Mount Olympus — An actual Greek mountain; mythological home of the gods.

Mudville — City where "Casey at the Bat" plays his fateful game.

Never-Never Land (Neverland) — Place where Peter Pan has all his adventures and no one grows up.

Oz — The kingdom and home of Oz, in Baum's *The Wonderful Wizard of Oz*.

Parnassus — An actual Greek mountain where the Muses supposedly lived, and the mythological home of music and poetry.

Shangri-La — A place of eternal youth and peace from James Hilton's *Lost Horizon*.

Sherwood Forest — The woodland in Nottinghamshire, England, where Robin Hood and his band of men supposedly lived.

Sleepy Hollow — Village in *The Legend of Sleepy Hollow*. Now refers to any small, rural, unexciting village.

Sodom — Biblical city destroyed because its people were evil.

Valhalla — Norse heaven for souls of warriors who died in battle.

14. LITERARY CRITICISM

Critics sometimes analyze literature according to its place in a historical framework; according to theoretical categories (technique, genre, and function); or by other valuative criteria. This list includes famous works on literary criticism and different bases for judging literature. See also List 15, Schools of Criticism; List 46, Essays: Collections; and List 48, Essay Masters.

Poetics — Aristotle. First basic literary criticism text says aim of literature is imitation.

On the Sublime — Longinus. Author's soul is standard by which literature should be judged.

The Art of Poetry — Horace. Literature should please and instruct.

Biographia Literaria — Samuel Taylor Coleridge. Radical and idealistic views about the unifying power of poetry and the differences between fancy and imagination.

The Plain Speaker — William Hazlitt. Author judges literature by his impressions and reactions.

The Renaissance — Walter Horatio Pater. States that we need art for its own sake and should evaluate literature according to the impressions writing makes on us. We should experience our sensations to the fullest.

Anatomy of Criticism: Four Essays — Northrup Frye. A psychological and anthropological approach to criticism.

Creative Criticism — Joel Spingarn. Denounces narrow-minded adherence to past rules of literary criticism; first to use term "new criticism."

The Well-Wrought Urn — Cleanth Brooks. Literature must be analyzed according to inner structure; proponent of "new criticism."

Tensions in Poetry — Allen Tate. Essay states tenets of the "new criticism."

Understanding Poetry — Robert Penn Warren and Cleanth Brooks. We should analyze literature by close textual study; advocates "new criticism."

The New Criticism — John Crowe Ransom. Literature has to be judged on its own merit, not in relationship to its genre, its author's background, or its historical relationship.

15. Schools of Criticism

Over the years critics have judged literature in different ways, so works of literary criticism represent different conceptions of what is important about literature and how it should be evaluated. Below are some of the major "schools" of criticism, a major proponent of each approach, and a general statement of basic philosophy. See also List 14, Literary Criticism; and List 16, U.S./British/Irish Critics.

Classicism — *Aristotle*
Literature should please and instruct.

Neoclassicism — *Samuel Johnson*
Good literature relies on the authority of ancient literature and good taste, as reflected by an educated elite.

Impressionism — *William Hazlitt*
Literature should be judged by the impressions it makes on us.

Aestheticism — *Walter Pater*
Literature (as art) is needed for its own sake and valued on artistic merits; pursuit of beauty is highest value.

Modernism — *T. S. Eliot*
Literature of value should not be over-emotional, but an escape from emotion; it should have continuity and objectivity.

Structuralism (Semiotics) — *Roland Barthes*
The internal structure should be studied and analyzed formally to determine literature's value.

Deconstructionism — *Jacques Derrida*
Reaction against structuralism, which is condemned as an anti-humanistic over-analysis of literature.

New criticism — *John Crowe Ransom*
Literature should be read closely and considered independently of who its author is or where it is historically placed.

16. U.S./British/Irish Critics

Critics often exert a powerful influence on which works are published and which are appreciated. Though they write with great authority, and often with great wit and elegance, their assessments of literary quality often vary widely. Moreover, the judgment of critics in one generation is sometimes disputed by later critics, and books that are classics in one era may be devalued in time to come. The following were important critics from the English-speaking world. See also List 14, Literary Criticism; and List 15, Schools of Criticism.

James Agee (*Film*)
Joseph Addison (*Literary*)
Matthew Arnold (*Literary*)
Brooks Atkinson (*Drama*)
Robert Benchley (*Drama*)
William Cullen Bryant (*Literary*)
Anthony Burgess (*Literary*)
John Ciardi (*Literary*)
Samuel Taylor Coleridge (*Literary*)
Bosley Crowther (*Film*)
Thomas de Quincey (*Literary*)
John Dryden (*Literary*)
T. S. Eliot (*Literary*)
Clifton Fadiman (*Literary*)
Penelope Gilliatt (*Film*)
Robert Graves (*Literary*)
William Dean Howells (*Literary*)
Randall Jarell (*Literary*)
Samuel Johnson (*Literary*)
Ben Johnson (*Literary*)
Pauline Kael (*Film*)
George S. Kaufman (*Drama*)

Walter Kerr (*Drama*)
C. S. Lewis (*Literary*)
Amy Lowell (*Literary*)
James Russell Lowell (*Literary*)
Hugh MacDiarmid (*Literary*)
Mary McCarthy (*Literary*)
Howard Nemerov (*Literary*)
Joyce Carol Oates (*Literary*)
George Orwell (*Literary*)
Ezra Pound (*Literary*)
John Ruskin (*Art*)
Delmore Schwartz (*Literary*)
Karl Shapiro (*Literary*)
Stephen Spender (*Literary*)
Algernon Charles Swinburne (*Literary*)
Allen Tate (*Literary*)
Robert Penn Warren (*Literary*)
Dame Rebecca West (*Social criticism*)
Edmund Wilson (*Literary*)
Virginia Woolf (*Literary*)
Alexander Woolcott (*Drama*)

S E C T I O N

2

Books...
For All
Ages

17. BEST-SELLING BOOKS

American Red Cross First Aid Book

American Spelling Book (Noah Webster)

The Bible

The Common Sense Book of Baby and Child Care (Benjamin Spock)

Guinness Book of World Records

In His Steps (C. M. Sheldon)

Infant Care (U.S. Department of Health and Human Services)

A Message to Garcia (Elbert Hubbard)

The McGuffey Reader (Henry Vail)

Quotations from the Works of Mao Tsetung (Mao Tsetung)

The Road Less Traveled (M. Scott Peck)

The Truth That Leads to Eternal Life (Jehovah's Witnesses)

Valley of the Dolls (Jacqueline Susann)

The World Almanac (Mark S. Hoffman, ed.)

18. SELECTED BEST-SELLING CHILDREN'S BOOKS

Amy the Dancing Bear

Are You There, God? It's Me, Margaret

Baby Donald's Busy Play Group

Baby's Animal Friends

Bedtime Hugs for Little Ones

Benji

The Big Golden Book of Dinosaurs

Blubber

The Book of the Sandman

Carl Goes Shopping

The Cat in the Hat

The Cat in the Hat Comes Back

Charlotte's Web

The Children's Bible

Disney Babies A to Z

Dr. Seuss's ABC

Egermeier's Bible Story Book

The Eleventh Hour

Farmer Boy

Find Waldo Now

Freckle Juice

Freckles

The Girls of the Limberlost

The Giving Tree

Glow-in-the-Dark Night Sky Book

Go Ask Alice

The Great Waldo Search

Green Eggs and Ham

Hop on Pop

International Children's Bible

Joyful Noise: Poems for Two Voices

The Little Engine That Could

The Little House in the Big Woods

The Little House on the Prairie

The Little Prince

The Littlest Angel

Love and the Facts of Life

Macmillan Dictionary for Children

The Magic Locket

The Market Square Dog

My First Atlas

Nothing to Do

On the Banks of Plum Creek

One Fish, Two Fish, Red Fish, Blue Fish

The Outsiders

Pat the Bunny

The Real Mother Goose

Richard Scarry's Best Word Book Ever

Sesame Street Hide-and-Seek Safari

The Silver Slippers

Song and Dance Man

Stuart Little

Superfudge

Swan Lake

The Tale of Peter Rabbit

Tales of a Fourth Grade Nothing

That Was Then, This Is Now

The Very Busy Spider

The Way Things Work

When Is My Birthday?

Where the Red Fern Grows

Winnie-the-Pooh

Where the Sidewalk Ends

The Wonderful Wizard of Oz

19. JUVENILIA ENJOYED BY ALL

Aesop's Fables — Collection of short fables attributed to Aesop, possibly a Greek writer, often featuring animals as main characters and teaching lessons about life. (See also List 49, Fables: Aesop.)

Alice's Adventures in Wonderland — Lewis Carroll's classic about a young girl who falls into a rabbit hole and has a series of adventures.

The Blind Men and the Elephant — Fable and poem by John G. Saxe about six blind men, each touching a different part of an elephant and describing it, insisting that he alone knows what the elephant is like.

The Cat in the Hat; The Cat in the Hat Comes Back — Two humorous picture books in verse by Theodore Seuss Geisel (Dr. Seuss) about a whimsical cat and his adventures.

Elsie Dinsmore Stories — Books for very young girls written by Martha Finley in the nineteenth century and very popular at that time.

The 500 Hats of Bartholomew Cubbins — Humorous book by Theodore Seuss Geisel about a boy who had just one hat. When Bartholemew meets the king, he is told to take his hat off, but new hats keep appearing until the king rewards the boy with gold.

The Goose that Laid the Golden Eggs — Fable retold by La Fontaine about a goose that lays golden eggs and makes his master rich. The man is so greedy that he cuts open his own goose to get more eggs, thus killing the goose and ending his streak of good fortune.

The Grasshopper and the Ant — Fable retold by La Fontaine about an ant who works hard storing up grain for the winter while the grasshopper sings; when the grasshopper gets hungry, the ant tells him to go dance.

How the Grinch Stole Christmas — Humorous picture book in verse by Theodore Seuss Geisel, about a mean "grinch" who tries to ruin everybody's Christmas by stealing presents, etc. until he finally sees the true meaning of Christmas.

The Jungle Book — A novel by Rudyard Kipling, nineteenth-century British author, about a boy who is adopted by animals and lives and learns in the jungle.

Just So Stories — Collection of children's stories by Rudyard Kipling, mixing nonsense and reality; excellent for reading aloud.

The Little Engine That Could — Story by Watty Piper about a little train engine that succeeds in climbing a steep mountain by repeating, "I think I can," and eventually "I thought I could!"

The Little Red Hen — Folk tale about a hen who keeps asking for help while planting her grain, but gets no takers. When she harvests her wheat and makes her bread, she eats it by herself, too.

Millions of Cats — Book by Wanda Gag about an old man and woman who wanted a cat so they wouldn't be lonely. They couldn't choose which was the prettiest, and so had millions of cats who clawed each other to death, each insisting he was the prettiest. They ended up with one very special kitten.

Pinocchio — Book by Collodi (Carlo Lorenzini), about the adventures of a wooden puppet who wants to become a human boy. Whenever he lies, his nose grows longer and longer.

Pollyanna — Book by Eleanor Porter about a girl who is always positive and optimistic about everything.

Reynard the Fox — Translated into many languages, this old fable tells of the sly fox, Reynard, and a powerful wolf, satirizing social and political power struggles.

Robinson Crusoe — Novel by Daniel Defoe, eighteenth-century English author, about a sailor surviving a shipwreck on an island.

Treasure Island — Book by Robert Louis Stevenson, nineteenth-century Scottish author, about the adventures of a boy who goes aboard ship with some pirates to search for treasure shown on a map he has found.

The Trumpet of the Swan — Written by E. B. White, this is the story of Louis, a trumpeter swan without a voice, who manages to win the love of Serena, a beautiful swan. The courage and love shown by Louis are inspirational.

Uncle Tom's Cabin — Novel by Harriet Beecher Stowe, nineteenth-century American author, about the immorality and evil of slavery.

The Wind in the Willows — Book by Kenneth Grahame, English author, about the adventures of several animal characters (Rat, Mole, Toad, Badger).

Peter Pan — Play by J. M. Barrie, Scottish playwright, about a little boy who lives in Never-Never Land, learns to fly, and doesn't want to ever have to grow up.

The Secret Garden — Book written in the early twentieth century by Frances Burnett about a girl sent to England after the death of her parents. She finds an old garden and restores it and herself to happiness.

The Tale of Peter Rabbit — Story by Beatrix Potter, English author, about a rabbit that gets into trouble by going into Mr. McGregor's garden.

Through the Looking Glass — Lewis Carroll's book about Alice, who climbs through a mirror to see what's on the other side, and in so doing meets many now-famous characters.

The Ugly Duckling — Story by Hans Christian Andersen about a baby bird in a family of ducks who is different and uglier than the rest, only to find upon maturing that he is a beautiful swan.

Uncle Remus: His Songs and His Sayings — Fables recorded by Joel Chandler Harris in which Uncle Remus, a black man, tells a series of stories to a white boy, often about the adventures of Brer Rabbit and Brer Fox. Brer Rabbit usually gets the upper hand.

Winnie-the-Pooh — A. A. Milne's classic story of Edward Bear (Winnie-the-Pooh) and his adventures with Christopher Robin, Piglet, Eeyore, Kanga, and Baby Roo.

The Wonderful Wizard of Oz — Novel by L. Frank Baum, American author, about the adventures of a girl and her dog who are whisked by tornado to the land of Oz, where they meet a scarecrow without a brain, a cowardly lion, and a tin woodsman without a heart.

20. MIDDLE SCHOOL READING LIST

The following books comprise a general fiction list for middle school students. The books are tried and true, popular, often included on reading lists from various societies and associations, and with the exception of a few old favorites, fairly contemporary.

Across Five Aprils

All-of-a-Kind Family

Animal Farm

The Arm of the Starfish

The Best Christmas Pageant Ever

Bridge to Terabithia

Brighty of Grand Canyon

Bunnicula: A Rabbit Tale of Mystery

Call It Courage

The Cat Ate My Gymsuit

Confessions of a Prime Time Kid

Dirt Bike Racer

Discontinued

A Dog on Barkham Street

Frankenstein

From the Mixed-Up Files of Mrs. Basil E. Frankweiler

The Great Gilly Hopkins

Hatchet

The Hero and the Crown

Hitty: Her First Hundred Years

How to Eat Fried Worms

In the Year of the Boar and Jackie Robinson

It's Like This Cat

Johnny Tremain

Julie of the Wolves

Just One Friend

Leif the Unlucky

M. C. Higgins, The Great

The Moves Make the Man

Mr. Popper's Penguins

My Brother Sam Is Dead

National Velvet

Old Yeller

One Fat Summer

Owls in the Family

The Pushcart War

Rabbit Hill

Rasco and the Rats of NIMH

The Red Pony

Roll of Thunder, Hear my Cry

Sarah, Plain and Tall

Sign of the Beaver

The Slave Dancer

Sounder

Stone Fox

Summer of My German Soldier

Summer of the Monkeys

Summer of the Swans

Thimble Summer

Tiger Eyes

To Be a Slave

Trouble with Tuck

Trumpet of the Swan

With You and Without You

Wuthering Heights

The titles below are favorites from a 1990 survey of 300,000 young children in the Reading is Fundamental network, otherwise known as RIF.

Charlotte's Web (E. B. White)

Superfudge (Judy Blume)

Where the Red Fern Grows (Wilson Rawls)

Tales of a Fourth Grade Nothing (Judy Blume)

Honey I Shrunk the Kids (Hiller and Faucher)

Indian in the Cupboard (Lynne Banks)

Charlie and the Chocolate Factory (Roald Dahl)

James and the Giant Peach (Roald Dahl)

There's a Boy in the Girls' Bathroom
   (Louise Sachar)

Where the Sidewalk Ends (Shel Silverstein)

Island of the Blue Dolphins (Scott O'Dell)

The BFG (Roald Dahl)

21. Junior High Reading List: Oldies, but Goodies

These books were selected from a longer list of books called "Summertime Favorites," compiled by the National Endowment for the Humanities. Published before 1960, they often appear on book lists of public and private schools throughout the United States.

The African Queen — C. S. Forester

Alice's Adventures in Wonderland — Lewis Carroll

Amos Fortune: Free Man — Elizabeth Yates

A Bell for Adano — John Hersey

The Big Sky — A. B. Guthrie

The Bridge Over the River Kwai — Pierre Boulle

The Bridges at Toko-Ri — James Michener

Cimarron — Edna Ferber

The Count of Monte Cristo — Alexandre Dumas

Dandelion Wine — Ray Bradbury

Death Be Not Proud — John Gunther

Drums Along the Mohawk — Walter D. Edmonds

Ethan Frome — Edith Wharton

Gone With the Wind — Margaret Mitchell

Gulliver's Travels — Jonathan Swift

A High Wind in Jamaica — Richard Hughes

The Hunchback of Notre Dame — Victor Hugo

The King Must Die — Mary Renault

King Solomon's Mines — H. Rider Haggard

Kon-Tiki — Thor Heyerdahl

The Last of the Mohicans — James Fenimore Cooper

Le Morte D'Arthur — Sir Thomas Malory

Life With Father — Clarence Day

Little Men; Little Women; Jo's Boys — Louisa May Alcott

The Little Prince — Antoine de Saint-Exupery

Member of the Wedding — Carson McCullers

Men of Iron — Howard Pyle

Mutiny on the Bounty — Charles Nordhoff and J. N. Hall

Mysterious Island — Jules Verne

A Night to Remember — Walter Lord

The Ox-Bow Incident — Walter Clark

The Pearl — John Steinbeck

The Pilgrim's Progress — John Bunyan

Profiles in Courage — John F. Kennedy

A Raisin in the Sun — Lorraine Hansberry

Rebecca — Daphne Du Maurier

Ring of Bright Water — Gavin Maxwell

The Scarlet Pimpernel — Emma Orczy

The Sea-Wolf — Jack London

A Separate Peace — John Knowles

Shane — Jack Schaefer

The Thirty-Nine Steps — John Buchan

The Time Machine — H. G. Wells

A Tree Grows in Brooklyn — Betty Smith

Two Years Before the Mast — Richard Dana

Up From Slavery — Booker T. Washington

The Virginian — Owen Wister

22. LITERATURE FOR YOUNG ADULTS

Below are partial contents of *Beacham's Guide to Literature for Young Adults*, Kirk H. Beetz and Suzanne Niemeyer, editors (Walton Beacham, 1989). The book is frequently used by teachers and contains extensive, candid writeups on these and many other books. See also List 20, Middle School Reading List; List 23, Just Good Reading for Teens; and List 28, Reading List for the College Bound.

Abe Lincoln Grows Up — Carl Sandburg

Adam of the Road — Elizabeth Janet Gray

After the Rain — Norma Fox Mazer

Albert Einstein — Elma Ehrlich Levinger

Alexander the Great — Charles Mercer

All-American — John R. Tunis

All the King's Men — Robert Penn Warren

American Painter in Paris: A Life of Mary Cassatt — Ellen Wilson

Amos Fortune: Free Man — Elizabeth Yates

Are You in the House Alone? — Richard Peck

Are You There God? It's Me, Margaret — Judy Blume

The Bells of Bleecker Street — Valenti Angelo

The Birds of Summer — Zilpha Keatley Snyder

Black Beauty — Anna Sewell

Black Jack — Leon Garfield

The Bumblebee Flies Anyway — Robert Cormier

Caddie Woodlawn — Carol Ryrie Brink

Caesar — Darwin Isenberg

Catch-22 — Joseph Heller

Cathedral: The Story of its Construction — David Macaulay

The Cay — Theodore Taylor

Chase Me, Catch Nobody — Erik Christian Haugaard

The Chestry Oak — Kate Seredy

Chief Joseph: War Chief of the Nez Perce — Brent Kenneth Ashabranner and Russell Gerard David

A Child in Prison Camp — Shizuye Takashima

Children of the Fox — Jill Paton Walsh

The Chocolate War — Robert Cormier

A Christmas Carol — Charles Dickens

Cloudy-Bright — John Rowe Townsend

Conqueror and Hero: The Search for Alexander — Stephen Krensky

Crazy Horse: Great Warrior of the Sioux — Doris Shannon Garst

Daniel Boone — James Daugherty

A Day No Pigs Would Die — Robert N. Peck

A Day of Pleasure: Stories of a Boy Growing Up in Warsaw — Isaac Bashevis Singer

Dear Mr. Henshaw — Beverly Cleary

Dinky Hocker Shoots Smack — M. E. Kerr

Dobry — Monica Shannon

The Door in the Wall — Marguerite de Angeli

Durango Street — Frank Bonham

The Eagle of the Ninth — Rosemary Sutcliff

The Egypt Game — Zilpha Keatley Snyder

The Endless Steppe: Growing Up in Siberia — Esther Hautzig

Eskimo Boy — Pipaluk Freuchen

Far Away and Long Ago — William Henry Hudson

The Fighting Ground — Avi

Footsteps — Leon Garfield

Friedrich — Hans Peter Richter

Gandhi — Olivia Coolidge

Ginger Pye — Eleanor Estes

Girl with a Pen: Charlotte Bronte — Elisabeth Kyle

Gone With the Wind — Margaret Mitchell

Good Night, Mr. Tom — Michelle Magorian

Great Ambition: A Story of the Early Years of Dickens — Elisabeth Kyle

Hans Brinker; or, The Silver Skates — Mary Mapes Dodge

Hans Christian Andersen — Rumer Godden

Harriet Tubman: Conductor on the Underground Railroad — Ann Petry

Heidi — Johanna Spyri

Henry Reed, Inc. — Keith Robertson

A Hero Ain't Nothin' but a Sandwich — Alice Childress

Homesick: My Own Story — Jean Fritz

The House of Sixty Fathers — Meindert DeJong

I Am the Cheese — Robert Cormier

I Heard the Owl Call my Name — Margaret Craven

I, Juan de Pareja — Elizabeth B. De Trevino

I Know Why the Caged Bird Sings — Maya Angelou

Incident at Hawk's Hill — Allan W. Eckert

Invincible Louisa — Cornelia Lynde Meigs

Ishi: Last of his Tribe — Theodora Kroeber

Jane Addams: Pioneer for Social Justice — Cornelia Lynde Meigs

Josh — Ivan Southall

Journey to an 800 Number — E. L. Konigsburg

Journey to Topaz — Yoshiko Uchida

Journey Toward Freedom: The Story of Sojourner Truth — Jacqueline Bernard

The Jungle — Upton Sinclair

King of the Wind — Marguerite Henry

Langston Hughes — Milton Meltzer

The Lantern Bearer: A Life of Robert Louis Stevenson — James Wood

Laughing Boy — Oliver La Farge

Lincoln: A Photobiography — Russell Freedman

Little House in the Big Woods — Laura Ingalls Wilder

Little Women — Louisa May Alcott

The Machine Gunners — Robert Westall

Madame Curie — Eve Curie

The Mask of Apollo — Mary Renault

The Master Puppeteer — Katherine Paterson

Master Rosalind — John Louis Beatty and Patricia Beatty

The Matchlock Gun — Walter D. Edmond

Maudie and Me and the Dirty Book — Betty Miles

Meet the Austins — Madeleine L'Engle

Men of Iron — Howard Pyle

Michelangelo — Elizabeth Ripley

Miracles on Maple Hill — Virginia Sorensen

My Darling, My Hamburger — Paul Zindel

Never Cry Wolf — Farley Mowat

Of Mice and Men — John Steinbeck

Our Eddie — Sulamith Ish-Kishor

The Outsiders — S. E. Hinton

Pendragon: Arthur and His Britain — Joseph P. Clancy

Penn — Elizabeth Janet Gray

Penrod — Booth Tarkington

The Pigman — Paul Zindel

Pollyanna: The Glad Book — Eleanor H. Porter

The Power and the Glory — Graham Greene

Prairie-Town Boy — Carl Sandburg

A Proud Taste for Scarlet and Miniver — E. L. Konigsburg

Queenie Peavy — Robert J. Burch

Rascal: A Memoir of a Better Era — Sterling North

Rifles for Watie — Harold Keith

The Road to Agra — Aimee Sommerfelt

Roller Skates — Ruth Sawyer

A Room Made of Windows — Eleanor Cameron

Rumble Fish — S. E. Hinton

Samurai of Gold Hill — Yoshiko Uchida

The Secret Garden — Frances Hodgson Burnett

A Separate Peace — John Knowles

Shadow of a Bull — Maia Wojciechowska

Shane — Jack Schaefer

Shelley's Mary: A Life of Mary Godwin Shelley — Margaret Carver Leighton

The Silver Sword — Ian Serraillier

Slaughterhouse Five — Kurt Vonnegut, Jr.

Smith — Leon Garfield

A Solitary Blue — Cynthia Voigt

The Soul Brothers and Sister Lou — Kristin Eggleston Hunter

Spunkwater, Spunkwater!: A Life of Mark Twain — James Playsted Wood

The Stone Book Quartet — Alan Garner

The Story of My Life — Helen Keller

Strawberry Girl — Lois Lenski

The Sun Also Rises — Ernest Hemingway

The Tale of Beatrix Potter — Margaret Lane

That Was Then, This is Now — S. E. Hinton

Thoreau of Walden Pond — Sterling North

To Kill a Mockingbird — Harper Lee

Tom Brown's Schooldays — Thomas Hughes

Traitor: The Case of Benedict Arnold — Jean Fritz

A Tree Grows in Brooklyn — Betty Smith

Viva Chicago — Frank Bonham

Walden — Henry David Thoreau

The Walls of Windy Troy — Marjorie Braymer

Walt Whitman: Builder for America — Babette Deutsch

Waterless Mountain — Laura Adams Armer

The Wheel on the School — Meindert DeJong

Where the Lilies Bloom — Vera and Bill Cleaver

Wild Animals I Have Known — Ernest Thompson Seton

William Blake — James Daugherty

William the Conquerer — Thomas B. Costain

Wind, Sand and Stars — Antoine de Saint-Exupery

Young Fu of the Upper Yangtze — Elizabeth Foreman Lewis

23. Just Good Reading for Teens

This list contains wholesome, engaging reading for teens and young adults. The books and stories are generally inspiring, uplifting, or thought-provoking.

Adams, Richard
  Shardik
  Watership Down

Adamson, Joy
  Born Free

Aiken, Joan
  Black Hearts in Battersea
  Bridle the Wind
  Go Saddle the Sea
  Nightbirds on Nantucket
  The Whispering Mountain
  The Wolves of Willoughby Chase

Arnosky, Jim
  Gray Boy

Austen, Jane
  Pride and Prejudice
  Emma

Beatty, Patricia
  Be Ever Hopeful, Hannalee
  Turn Homeward, Hannalee

Benchley, Nathaniel
  Bright Candles
  A Necessary End
  Only Earth and Sky Last Forever

Blakemore, Richard D.
  Lorna Doone

Blos, Joan W.
  Brothers of the Heart
  A Gathering of Days

Borland, Hal
  Editor's Boy

Boston, L. M.
  The Green Knowe (series)

Bronte, Charlotte
  Jane Eyre

Bronte, Emily
  Wuthering Heights

Brooks, Bruce
  The Move Makes the Man
  Midnight Hour Encores

Buchan, John
  Adventures of Richard Hannay (trilogy)

Burgess, Alan
  The Small Woman

Burnford, Sheila
  The Incredible Journey

Burns, Ann Olive
  Cold Sassy Tree

Byars, Betsy
  The Cybil War
  Midnight Fox
  The Summer of the Swans
  Trouble River

Cather, Willa
  My Antonia
  Death Comes for the Archbishop

Chesterton, G. K.
  Father Brown Mysteries

Clark, Ann Nolan
  Secret of the Andes

Cooper, James Fenimore
  The Deerslayer

Conrad, Joseph
  Lord Jim

Cooper, Susan
  The Dark Is Rising
  Greenwitch
  The Grey King
  Over Sea, Under Stone
  Silver on the Tree

Crane, Stephen
  Red Badge of Courage

Crichton, Michael
The Andromeda Strain

Defoe, Daniel
Robinson Crusoe

Dickens, Charles
David Copperfield
Great Expectations
Oliver Twist
A Tale of Two Cities

Douglas, Lloyd C.
The Robe

Doyle, Sir Arthur Conan
Adventures of Sherlock Holmes
Hound of the Baskervilles

Dumas, Alexandre
The Three Musketeers

Edgerton, Clyde
The Floatplane Notebooks

Fleming, Ian
Chitty-Chitty Bang-Bang

Forbes, Esther
Johnny Tremain

Fox, Paula
Lily and the Lost Boy
The Moonlight Man
One-Eyed Cat
The Slave Dancer

Gaines, Ernest
Autobiography of Miss Jane Pittman

George, Jean Craighead
The Cry of the Crow
Julie of the Wolves
My Side of the Mountain
Shark Beneath the Reef
The Talking Earth
Water Sky

Gilbreth, Frank and Ernestine Carey
Cheaper by the Dozen

Gipson, Fred
Old Yeller

Godden, Rumer
An Episode of Sparrows

Gordon, Ernest
Through the Valley of the Kwai

Gordon, Sheila
Waiting for the Rain: A Novel of South Africa

Goudge, Elizabeth
The Little White Horse

Green, Hannah
I Never Promised You a Rose Garden
In This Sign (under pseudonym)

Hamilton, Virginia
Anthony Burns: The Defeat and Triumph of a Fugitive Slave
Arilla Sun Down
House of Dies Drear
M. C. Higgins, The Great
The Mystery of Drear House
The People Could Fly
Zeely

Hautzig, Esther
The Endless Steppe: Growing Up in Siberia

Hemingway, Ernest
The Old Man and the Sea

Herriot, James
All Creatures Great and Small
All Things Bright and Beautiful
All Things Wise and Wonderful

Heyerdahl, Thor
Kon-tiki

Hickman, Janet
Valley of the Shadow

Hilton, James
Good-Bye, Mr. Chips
Lost Horizon

Holm, Anne
I Am David
North to Freedom

Hudson, William Henry
Green Mansions
A Little Boy Lost

Hugo, Victor
  Les Miserables

Hunt, Irene
  Across Five Aprils
  The Everlasting Hills
  Up a Road Slowly

Hunter, Mollie
  A Sound of Chariots

Irving, Washington
  The Legend of Sleepy Hollow

Irwin, Grace
  Andrew Connington
  Contend with Horses
  Least of All Saints
  In Little Place
  Servant of Slaves

James, Will
  Smoky, the Cowhorse

Janeway, Elizabeth
  Ivanov Seven
  Men of Iron

Jenkins, Peter
  The Walk Across America
  The Walk West

Kelly, Eric P.
  The Trumpeter of Krakow

Kerr, Judith
  When Hitler Stole Pink Rabbit

Kingsley, Charles
  Westward Ho!

Kipling, Rudyard
  Captain's Courageous
  Kim
  Puck of Pook's Hill

Kjelgaard, James A.
  Big Red
  Haunt Fox
  Irish Red: Son of Big Red
  Lion Hound
  Outlaw Red
  Trailing Trouble

Krumgold, Joseph
  ...and Now Miguel
  Onion John

Latham, Jean Lee
  Carry On, Mr. Bowditch

Lawhead, Stephen R.
  Dragon Trilogy
  Pendragon Cycle

Lee, Harper
  To Kill a Mockingbird

LeGuin, Ursula
  The Farthest Shore
  The Tombs of Atuan
  A Wizard of Earthsea

Levitin, Soni
  Journey to America
  Silver Days

Lewis, C. S.
  That Dark Tower and Other Stories
  That Hideous Strength
  Out of the Silent Planet
  Perelandra

Little, Jean
  Mama's Going to Buy You a Mockingbird

Llewellyn, Richard
  How Green Was My Valley

London, Jack
  Call of the Wild

Marshall, Catherine
  Christy
  Julie
  A Man Called Peter

Meader, Stephen
  Clear for Action
  Fish Hawk's Nest
  Red Horse Hill
  Shadow in the Pines
  Whaler 'round the Horn
  Who Rides in the Dark?

Melville, Herman
  Moby Dick

Montgomery, Lucy Maud
  Anne of Avonlea
  Anne of Green Gables
  Anne of the Island
  Emily of the New Moon

Morris, William
  The Well of the World's End
  Wood Beyond the World

Murphy, Robert
  The Pond
  Wild Geese Calling

North, Sterling
  Rascal
  So Dear to my Heart

O'Brien, Robert C.
  Mrs. Frisby and the Rats of NIMH

O'Dell, Scott
  Black Pearl
  The Dark Canoe
  Island of the Blue Dolphins
  The Road to Damietta
  The Serpent Never Sleeps
  Sing Down the Moon
  Streams to the River, River to the Sea: A Novel of Sacagawea
  Zia

O'Hara, Mary
  The Catch Colt
  The Green Grass of Wyoming
  My Friend Flicka
  Thunderhead

Oneal, Zibby
  A Formal Feeling
  In Summer Light
  The Language of Goldfish

Paterson, Katherine
  Bridge to Terabithia
  Come Sing, Jimmy Jo
  The Great Gilly Hopkins
  Jacob Have I Loved
  The Master Puppeteer

Patton, Frances Gray
  Good Morning, Miss Dove

Peck, Robert N.
  Soup

Porter, Gene Stratton
  A Girl of the Limberlost

Potok, Chaim
  The Chosen
  Davita's Harp
  In the Beginning
  My Name is Asher Lev
  The Promise

Pyle, Howard
  Otto of the Silver Hand

Rawlings, Marjorie
  The Yearling

Rawls, Wilson
  Where the Red Fern Grows

Richter, Conrad
  The Light in the Forest

Roberts, Kenneth
  Northwest Passage
  Rabble in Arms

Rolvaag, O. E.
  Giants in the Earth

Sampson, Fay
  Finnglas of the Horses
  Finnglas and the Stones of Choosing
  Pangur Ban, the White Cat
  Shape-Shifter, the Naming of Pangur Ban
  The Serpent of Senargo

Sherman, D. R.
  The Lion's Paw

Siegel, Robert
  Alpha Centauri
  Whalesong

Speare, Elizabeth George
  The Bronze Bow
  Calico Captive
  The Sign of the Beaver
  The Witch of Blackbird Pond

Sperry, Armstrong
Call It Courage
Danger to Windward
Frozen Fire
Thunder Country

Steele, William O.
The Buffalo Knife
Flaming Arrows
The Lone Hunt
The Perilous Road
Winter Danger

Steinbeck, John
The Red Pony

Stevenson, Robert Louis
The Black Arrow
David Balfour
Kidnapped
Treasure Island

Szabo, Tomas
Boy on the Rooftop

Taylor, Mildred
The Friendship
Let the Circle Be Unbroken
Roll of Thunder, Hear My Cry

Ten Boom, Corrie
The Hiding Place

Thurber, James
Thirteen Clocks

Tolstoy, Leo
Anna Karenina

Tolkien, J. R. R.
The Lord of the Rings
The Hobbit

Twain, Mark
The Adventures of Huckleberry Finn
A Connecticut Yankee in King Arthur's Court
The Prince and the Pauper

Verne, Jules
Around the World in Eighty Days
Journey to the Center of the Earth
20,000 Leagues Under the Sea

Voigt, Cynthia
The Callendar Papers
Dicey's Song
Homecoming
Izzy, Willy-Nilly
Jackaroo
Seventeen Against the Dealer

Wallace, Lew
Ben Hur

Wangerin, Walter
The Book of the Dun Cow

West, Jessamyn
Delahanty
The Massacre at Fall Creek

White, John
The Iron and the Scepter
The Swordbearer
The Tower of Geburah

Wiggin, Kate Douglas
Rebecca of Sunnybrook Farm

Wilder, Thornton
Bridge of San Luis Rey

Williams, Charles
Descent into Hell
Many Dimensions
The Place of the Lion
War in Heaven

Wilson, Dorothy Clarke
Ten Fingers for God

Wouk, Herman
This Is My God

24. POPULAR NONFICTION FOR YOUNG ADULTS

Often teens who don't particularly like to read will enjoy nonfiction. Even avid readers sometimes overlook nonfiction. This list of best-selling titles and reference books, many of which could be the beginnings of a great home library, is also appropriate to give parents as gift suggestions for young adults. Many are important older books that have been continuously popular; some are for mature teens or college students.

All the President's Men — Bob Woodward and Carl Bernstein

All Things Bright and Beautiful — James Herriot

America — Alistair Cook

The Ascent of Man — Jacob Bronowki

Backlash — Susan Faludi

Black Like Me — John H. Griffin

Body Language — Julius Fast

Cosmos — Carl Sagan

Debrett's Distinguished People of Today — Patricia Ellis, ed.

Diana: Her True Story — Andrew Morton

The Diary of a Young Girl — Anne Frank

Everything You Always Wanted to Know About Sex But Were Afraid to Ask — David Reuben

Four Days — United Press International and *American Heritage* magazine

Games People Play — Eric Berne

The Greatest Book Ever Written — Rochunga Pudaite and James C. Hefley

The Greatest Story Ever Told — Fulton Oursler

The Guinness Book of World Records (current year; various editors)

The Hidden Persuaders — Vance Packard

Hiroshima — John R. Hersey

Homesick: My Own Story — Jean Fritz

How to Stop Worrying and Start Living — Dale Carnegie

How to Be Your Own Best Friend — Mildred Newman and Bernard Berkowitz

How to Win Friends and Influence People — Dale Carnegie and Dorothy Carnegie, eds.

I'll Cry Tomorrow — Lillian Roth

I'm OK, You're OK — Thomas A. Harris

James Herriot's Yorkshire — James Herriot

Kon-Tiki — Thor Heyerdahl

Life on Earth — David Attenborough

The Living Planet — David Attenborough

The Lord God Made Them All — James Herriot

The New Oxford Book of Light Verse — Kingsley Amis, ed.

101 Famous Poems — Cook, compiler

The Outline of History: A Plain History of Life and Mankind (revised ed.) — H. G. Wells, ed.

Please Don't Eat the Daisies — Jean Kerr

The Power of Positive Thinking — Norman Vincent Peale

Profiles in Courage — John F. Kennedy

The Prophet — Kahlil Gibran

Soul on Ice — Eldridge Cleaver

30 Days to a More Powerful Vocabulary — Wilfred Funk and Norman Lewis

Walden Two — B. F. Skinner

The World at War — Mark Arnold-Forster

25. JUNIOR HIGH READING LIST: GIFTED STUDENTS

There are many lists for high interest/low reading levels, but sometimes gifted students are neglected. Here's an excellent, briefly annotated reading list for gifted students in their middle years, about ages 10 to 13, including both fiction and nonfiction.

Black Theater in America — James Haskins.
  Traces the history of black theater in America.

The Cat's Elbow and Other Secret Languages — Alvin Schwartz (ed.).
  Includes Pig Latin, Iggity, and Ku, "secret" languages of kids.

A Children's Almanac of Words at Play — William R. Espy.
  Challenging collection of wordplay riddles, poems, and other fun things to think about.

Cosmos — Carl Sagan.
  The cosmos illustrated and explained (as on Sagan's TV series).

The Crest and the Hide — Harold Courlander (ed.).
  Twenty short African tales expressing important human values.

The Cricket Sings: Poems and Songs for Children — Federico Garcia Lorca.
  Collection of twenty-five Spanish lyric poems with English translations.

Don't Forget to Fly: A Cycle of Modern Poems — Paul B. Janeczko (ed.).
  Collection of 130 poems arranged by theme.

Flight: A Panorama of Aviation — Melvin Zisfein.
  Traces the history of aviation.

Frankenstein's Aunt — Allan Rune Petterson.
  Humorous take-off on the Frankenstein/Dracula stories.

The Haunting — Margaret Mahy.
  Suspenseful story about an eight-year-old boy who receives messages from his supposedly deceased uncle.

History of Art for Young People — H. W. Janson.
  Overview of history of art with many illustrations.

The Ideas of Einstein — David E. Fisher.
  Informative discussion, with diagrams, of the basics of the theory of relativity.

The Kid's Whole Future Catalog — Paula Taylor.
  A catalog of sources of information about technology.

Man's Place in Evolution — British Museum of Natural History.
  Shows evolutionary cycle and admits "missing links."

National Geographic Book of Mammals — Donald J. Crump (ed.).
  Well-illustrated compendium of facts about mammals.

National Geographic Picture Atlas of Our Universe — Roy A. Gallant.
Paintings and photos of planets, their satellites, and other celestial bodies.

The Night Journey — Kathryn Lisky.
Story of a grandmother sharing her story of escape from Russia.

Rescue from Extinction — Joseph E. Brown.
Discusses how animals become extinct.

Scary Stories to Tell in the Dark: Collected from American Folklore — Alvin Schwartz.
Collection of psychic tales, stories of witches and ghosts, songs and legends.

The Secret Life of Hardware: A Science Experiment Book — Vicki Cobb.
Experiments in science using everyday objects.

The Sword and the Circle: King Arthur and the Knights of the Round Table — Rosemary Sutcliff.
A skillful retelling of Arthur, his knights, Excalibur (sword), and Merlin, the Magician.

Thorny Issues: How Ethics and Morality Affect the Way We Live — John Langone.
Discussion of questions that encourage values evaluation.

Thunder, Singing Sands, and Other Wonders: Sound in the Atmosphere — Kenneth Heuer
Discussion of reasons for the various sounds in nature.

Working Kids on Working — Sheila Cole.
Interviews of middle school children telling about their jobs.

26. HIGH SCHOOL READING LIST: OLDIES, BUT GOODIES

The books below were selected from a longer list, "Summertime Favorites," compiled by the National Endowment for the Humanities. Published before 1960, they commonly appear on book lists from public and private schools throughout the United States. This is recommended reading for grades 9-12. See also List 22, Literature for Young Adults; List 23, Just Good Reading for Teens; List 28, Reading List for the College Bound; List 38, Comic Format: Classics; List 39, Comic Format: Classics Translated into Spanish; List 64, The Novel Masters (American); and List 65, The Novel Masters (Other Than American).

Adam Bede — George Eliot

The American — Henry James

Black Boy — Richard Wright

Bleak House — Charles Dickens

Brideshead Revisited — Evelyn Waugh

Buddenbrooks — Thomas Mann

Candide — Voltaire

The Castle — Franz Kafka

The Cherry Orchard — Anton Chekhov

The Cruel Sea — Nicholas Monsarrat

Cyrano de Bergerac — Edmond Rostand

Darkness at Noon — Arthur Koestler

A Death in the Family — James Agee

The Divine Comedy — Dante

Far From the Madding Crowd — Thomas Hardy

Ghosts — Henrik Ibsen	(Plays and Sonnets) — William Shakespeare
Hard Times — Charles Dickens	(Poems) — Robert Browning
I, Claudius — Robert Graves	(Poems) — Emily Dickinson
Inherit the Wind — Jerome Lawrence and Robert E. Lee	(Poems) — Langston Hughes
J. B. — Archibald MacLeish	(Poems) — John Keats
The Jungle — Upton Sinclair	*The Power and the Glory* — Graham Greene
Light in August — William Faulkner	*Pudd'nhead Wilson* — Mark Twain
Look Homeward, Angel — Thomas Wolfe	*The Secret Sharer* — Joseph Conrad
The Magic Mountain — Thomas Mann	*Sense and Sensibility* — Jane Austen
A Man for All Seasons — Robert Bolt	(Short Stories) — O. Henry
The Mayor of Casterbridge — Thomas Hardy	(Short Stories) — Edgar A. Poe
Moll Flanders — Daniel Defoe	*Siddhartha* — Hermann Hesse
The Moonstone — Wilkie Collins	*Silas Marner* — George Eliot
Mythology — Edith Hamilton	*A Single Pebble* — John Hersey
The Nine Tailors — Dorothy Sayers	*Sons and Lovers* — D. H. Lawrence
Northanger Abbey — Jane Austen	*The Stranger* — Albert Camus
The Once and Future King — T. H. White	*Victory* — Joseph Conrad
On the Beach — Nevil Shute	*Waiting for Godot* — Samuel Beckett
On the Road — Jack Kerouac	*The Way of All Flesh* — Samuel Butler
Our Town — Thornton Wilder	*The Wild Duck* — Henrik Ibsen
Out of Africa — Isak Dinesen	*Wind, Sand, and Stars* — Antoine de Saint-Exupery
Pere Goriot — Honore de Balzac	*Winesburg, Ohio* — Sherwood Anderson
The Plague — Albert Camus	

27. HIGH SCHOOL READING LIST: GIFTED STUDENTS

There are many lists for high interest/low reading levels, but sometimes gifted students are neglected. Here's an excellent, briefly annotated reading list for gifted high school students, including both fiction and nonfiction. See also List 28, Reading List for the College-Bound; and List 30, Adult Great Books Reading Program.

The Assistant — Bernard Malamud.
   Novel about drifter who has difficulty changing.

Atlas Shrugged — Ayn Rand.
   Novel about technology and its impact in America.

Above Suspicion — Helen MacInnes.
   Suspense novel.

The Ambassadors — Henry James.
　　Novel of old and new world culture clashes.

Andersonville — MacKinlay Kantor.
　　Novel about life in a prison camp during Civil War.

Birdy — William Wharton.
　　Novel about Vietnam veteran and his buddy.

Black Dance in America: A History Through its People — James Haskins.
　　History of African-American dance.

Bonjour Tristesse — Francoise Sagan.
　　Novel about teenager who tries to block her father's marriage.

Call It Sleep — Henry Roth.
　　Novel set in New York about a Jewish child living in ghetto.

The Care of Time — Eric Ambler.
　　Story of CIA agent and Persian Gulf sheikh.

Christmas at Fontaines — William Kotzwinkle.
　　Novel about loneliness, set in New York.

A Concise History of Modern Painting — Herbert Reed.
　　History of modern painting.

Darkness Over the Valley — Wendelgard von Staden.
　　Biography of German girl who helps concentration camp victims.

A Death in China — William Montalbano and Carl Hiaasen.
　　Novel about an art teacher in China.

The Family of Women — Richard Peck.
　　Novel of six women from early days to World War II.

Fahrenheit 451 — Ray Bradbury.
　　Futuristic society where reading and thinking are crimes.

Fools of Fortune — William Trevor.
　　Twentieth-century historical novel about Ireland.

The French Lieutenant's Woman — John Fowles.
　　Historical fiction about woman in Victorian England.

Gabriela, Clove and Cinnamon — Jorge Amado.
　　Love story set in Brazil.

Gift from the Sea — Ann Morrow Lindbergh.
　　Collection of essays, mostly for women.

Going After Cacciato — Tim O'Brien.
Novel about Vietnam War defector.

The Gulag Archipelago — Aleksander Solzhenitsyn.
Novel about living in a Russian labor camp.

Hanta Yo — Ruth Beebe Hill.
Novel about two Indian families.

Helliconia Spring — Brian Aldiss.
Science fiction novel.

The History of Tom Jones — Henry Fielding.
Rags to riches story.

A House for Mr. Biswas — V. S. Naipaul.
Novel about a poor man in Trinidad.

I, Claudius — Robert Graves.
Historical fiction about stammering Claudius, Roman emperor.

The Joy Luck Club — Amy Tan.
Chinese-American woman understands how mother's early life separated them.

Just Looking: Essays on Art — John Updike.
Views on artists, art, and children's book illustrations.

Kristin Lavransdatter (3 volumes) — Sigrid Undset.
Three novels about woman and her family, set in Norway.

The Last of the Just — Andrè Schwarz-Bart.
Novel about persecution of Jews.

Learning to Look: A Handbook for the Visual Arts — Joshua Taylor.
Shows how to go about appreciating the visual arts.

Lie Down in Darkness — William Styron.
Novel about the descent of a southern family.

Lucky Jim — Kingsley Amis.
Novel about English teacher trying to better his position.

Man's Fate — Andre Malraux.
Novel about revolutionaries in Chinese uprising.

Messengers of God: Biblical Portraits and Legends — Elie Wiesel.
Accounts of Biblical characters from the Old Testament.

The Metamorphosis — Franz Kafka.
Allegorical story of man changed into an insect.

The Moon by the Water — Pamela Belle.
Romantic, historical fiction, set in Elizabethan England.

The Mosquito Coast — Paul Theroux.
Novel about a New England family resettling in Honduras.

My Place — Sally Morgan.
Biography of an aborigine from Australia.

The Name of the Rose — Umberto Eco.
Historical fiction about murder in a monastery.

Necessity — Brian Garfield.
Science fiction about woman on the run.

Nectar in a Sieve — Kamala Markandaya.
Novel about peasants and poverty in India.

One Hundred Years of Solitude — Gabriel Garcia Marquez.
Lives of Buendia family and beginning/end of the mythical town of Macondo.

Ordinary People — Judith Guest.
Novel about boy's life after trying to commit suicide.

Pilgrim at Tinker Creek — Annie Dillard.
Collection of essays.

Scent of Cloves — Norah Lofts.
Historical novel.

A Second Flowering: Works and Days of the Lost Generation — Malcolm Cowley.
Collection of essays by famous writers.

The Shadow Man — John Lutz.
Murder story about man with several personalities.

Slaughterhouse Five — Kurt Vonnegut, Jr.
Novel about World War II firebombing of Dresden and its effect on an American prisoner of war.

Sound-Shadows of the New World — Ved Mehta.
Biography of 15-year-old blind boy's adjustment to a new culture.

Steppenwolf — Hermann Hesse.
Novel revolving around man's conflict with materialism.

Stones for Ibarra — Harriet Doerr.
American Book Award Winner about Americans moving to Mexico.

The Story of Philosophy — Will Durant.
Philosophic ideas of prominent philosophers.

The Sword Is Forged — Evangeline Walton.
Historical novel.

The Tin Drum — Günther Grass.
Novel set before, during, and after WWII in Poland and Germany.

The Trial — Franz Kafka.
Novel about man arrested on unknown charges.

Ties of Blood and Silver — Joel Rosenberg.
Science fiction novel about a thief.

Under Thirty-Five: The New Generation of American Poets — Nicholas Christopher.
A varied collection of poems by young American poets.

The Wanderer — Henri Alain-Fournier.
French novel about first love.

War and Peace — Leo Tolstoy.
Novel about the Napoleonic War.

Welcome Chaos — Kate Wilhelm.
Science fiction story of espionage.

What to Listen for in Music — Aaron Copland.
Shows how to gain an understanding of what you hear.

The Woman in the Dunes — Kobo Abe.
Novel about woman battling encroaching sands.

A World of Strangers — Nadine Gordimer.
Novel about man from England and embittered South African.

A Wreath for Adam — Peter Abrahams.
Novel about man working for freedom against colonialism.

The Young Lions — Irwin Shaw.
Novel about two Americans and a Nazi during World War II.

Zen and the Art of Motorcycle Maintenance — Robert M. Pirsig.
Philosophic musings during motorcycle trip.

28. Reading List for the College-Bound

This reading list for college-bound students is a combination of many lists compiled by colleges and universities. Some college professors expect incoming students to be familiar with these works; in many cases they will be reread and studied in more depth at college.

POETRY

Beowulf

Chaucer, Geoffrey — *Canterbury Tales*

Dickinson, Emily — poems

Emerson, Ralph Waldo — poems

Frost, Robert — poems

Homer — *The Iliad; The Odyssey*

Milton, John — *Paradise Lost*

Virgil — *The Aeneid*

Whitman, Walt — *Leaves of Grass*

NONFICTION

Adams, Henry — *The Education of Henry Adams*

Aristotle — *Politics; Poetics*

Bible

Declaration of Independence

Douglass, Frederick — *Narrative of the Life of Frederick Douglass*

Didion, Joan — essays

Emerson, Ralph Waldo — essays

Freud, Sigmund — *Civilization and Its Discontents*

Franklin, Benjamin — *The Autobiography of Benjamin Franklin*

Johnson, James Weldon — *Autobiography of an Ex-Coloured Man*

Kingston, Maxine Hong — *The Woman Warrior*

King, Martin Luther — *I Have a Dream*

Machiavelli, Niccolo — *The Prince*

Marx, K. and F. Engels — *Communist Manifesto*

Montaigne, Michel de — Selected Essays

Plato — *The Republic*

Rousseau, Jean-Jacques — *Confessions* (selected)

St. Augustine — Confessions (selected)

Thoreau, Henry — *Walden*

Thurber, James — essays

Tocqueville, Alexis de — *Democracy in America*

FICTION (NOVELS AND SHORT STORIES)

Austen, Jane — *Pride and Prejudice*

Baldwin, James — *Go Tell It on the Mountain*

Bellow, Saul — *Humboldt's Gift*

Bronte, Emily — *Wuthering Heights*

Camus, Albert — *The Stranger*

Cervantes, Miguel de — *Don Quixote*

Conrad, Joseph — *Heart of Darkness*

Crane, Stephen — *The Red Badge of Courage*

Defoe, Daniel — *Robinson Crusoe*

Dickens, Charles — *David Copperfield; Tale of Two Cities*

Dostoyevsky, Fyodor — *Crime and Punishment*

Eliot, George — *Adam Bede*

Ellison, Ralph — *Invisible Man*

Faulkner, William — *The Unvanquished; Intruder in the Dust*

Fielding, Henry — *Joseph Andrews*

Fitzgerald, F. Scott — *The Great Gatsby*

Flaubert, Gustave — *Madame Bovary*

Fowles, John — *The French Lieutenant's Woman*

Golding, William — *Lord of the Flies*

Hardy, Thomas — *The Return of the Native*

Hawthorne, Nathaniel — *The Scarlet Letter*

Hemingway, Ernest — *A Farewell to Arms; The Nick Adams Stories*

James, Henry — *The Portrait of a Lady*

Joyce, James — *Dubliners*

Kafka, Franz — *The Trial*

Lewis, Sinclair — *Babbitt; Arrowsmith*

Malamud, Bernard — *The Magic Barrel*

Melville, Herman — *Moby Dick*

Orwell, George — *1984; Animal Farm*

Paton, Alan — *Cry, The Beloved Country*

Poe, Edgar Allan — *The Tell-Tale Heart; The Black Cat; The Pit and the Pendulum*

Salinger, J. D. — *The Catcher in the Rye*

Scott, Sir Walter — *Ivanhoe*

Steinbeck, John — *The Grapes of Wrath*

Stendhal — *The Red and the Black*

Stevenson, Robert Louis — *The Strange Case of Dr. Jekyll and Mr. Hyde*

Swift, Jonathan — *Gulliver's Travels*

Thackeray, William — *Vanity Fair*

Tolstoy, Leo — *War and Peace*

Twain, Mark — *Huckleberry Finn; The Adventures of Tom Sawyer; Innocents Abroad*

Vonnegut, Kurt — *Slaughterhouse Five*

Waugh, Evelyn — *A Handful of Dust*

Wright, Richard — *Native Son*

29. PUZZLE AND BRAINTEASER BOOKS

Many readers will enjoy teasing their brains with puzzles, games, and exercises in these books.

The Algonquin Literary Quiz Book — Louis D. Rubin, Jr.
Questions and answers about American and English literature and authors.

Annable's Treasury of Literary Teasers — H. D. Annable.
800 trivia questions on quotations, authors, and characters.

So You Think You're Smart: 150 Fun and Challenging Brain Teasers — Pat Battaglia.
General brainteasers to challenge and delight.

The World Almanac Real Puzzle Book — Don Rubin.
Over thirty-five graphic puzzles.

Brain Busters: The Most Challenging Puzzles You'll Ever Do — Abbie Salny.
Over 200 puzzles arranged by difficulty levels.

Brainbuilding in Just Twelve Weeks — Marilyn vos Savant and Leonore Fleischer.
150 playful exercises to help build brain skills.

Crime and Puzzlement (Volumes 1, 2, and 3) — Lawrence Treat.
Books of mysteries to solve that use your wits and logic.

Cryptograms and Spygrams — Norma Gleason.
More than 100 problems and puzzles.

Five-Minute Mysteries — Ken Weber.
  Add up clues and be logical to decide who committed crimes.

Games for the Super-Intelligent (**also** ***More Games for the Super-Intelligent***) — James Fixx.
  Two books of games using mathematics, language, and logic.

The Latin Riddle Book — Louis Phillips.
  Jokes and riddles with Latin, laughs, and puns.

The Mensa Think-Smart Book: Games and Puzzles to Develop a Sharper, Quicker Mind — Abbie F. Salny et al.
  Exercises in comprehension, memory, vocabulary, and logic.

Mind Puzzlers — George J. Summers.
  "Whodunit" word problems to test your skills.

Nutcrackers — Meg Wolitzer and Jesse Green.
  Crosswords, acrostics, word searches, and letter mazes.

30. ADULT GREAT BOOKS READING PROGRAM

The Great Books Foundation, founders of the Great Books programs, believed that it was important not only to read great books about Western civilization, but to discuss them in meaningful ways with others. They developed both a junior Great Books program and an adult program. Materials for study and discussion guides are available from The Great Books Foundation, 40 Huron Street, Chicago, Illinois 60611 (for a fee) or your local library. These books and writings, listed in alphabetical order by author, are recommended for study in the adult program.

Adams
  The Education of Henry Adams
Aeschylus
  Agememnon
Aristotle
  On Happiness
  On Tragedy
  Politics
Bible
  Ecclesiastes
  Exodus
  Genesis
  Job
  The Gospel of Mark
Burke
  Reflections on the Revolution in France

Chaucer
  The Canterbury Tales
Chekhov
  Rothschild's Fiddle
  Uncle Vanya
Clausewitz
  What Is War?
Conrad
  Heart of Darkness
Dante
  The Inferno
Darwin
  The Moral Sense of Man and the Lower Animals
Dewey
  Habits and Will
  The Virtues

Diderot
  Rameau's Nephew

Dostoyevsky
  Notes from the Underground

Euripides
  Iphigeneia at Aulis
  Medea

Flaubert
  A Simple Heart

Freud
  Civilization and Its Discontents
  On Dreams

Gibbon
  The Decline and Fall of the Roman Empire

Goethe
  Faust, Part One

Gogol
  The Overcoat

Hamilton, Jay, Madison
  The Federalist Papers

Herodotus
  The Persian Wars

Hobbes
  Origin of Government

Homer
  The Iliad

Hume
  Of Justice and Injustice
  Of Personal Identity

James
  The Beast in the Jungle

Kafka
  The Metamorphosis

Kant
  Conscience
  First Principles of Morals

Kierkegaard
  The Knight of Faith

Locke
  Of Civil Government

Machiavelli
  The Prince

Maimonides
  On Evil

Marx
  Alienated Labour

Melville
  Billy Budd, Sailor

Mill
  On Liberty
  Utilitarianism

Moliere
  The Misanthrope

Montaigne
  Of Experience

Montesquieu
  Principles of Government

Nietzsche
  Thus Spake Zarathustra

Plato
  The Apology
  The Crito
  The Republic
  Symposium

Rousseau
  The Social Contract

Schopenhauer
  The Indestructibility of Our Inner Nature

Shakespeare
  Antony and Cleopatra
  Hamlet
  King Lear
  Othello
  The Tempest

Shaw
  Caesar and Cleopatra

Simmel
  Individual Freedom

Smith
  Wealth of Nations

Sophocles
   Antigone
   Oedipus the King

St. Augustine
   The City of God

Swift
   Gulliver's Travels

Thoreau
   Civil Disobedience

Thucydides
   History of the Peloponnesian War

Tocqueville
   The Power of the Majority

Tolstoy
   The Death of Ivan Ilych

Weber
   The Spirit of Capitalism

S E C T I O N

3

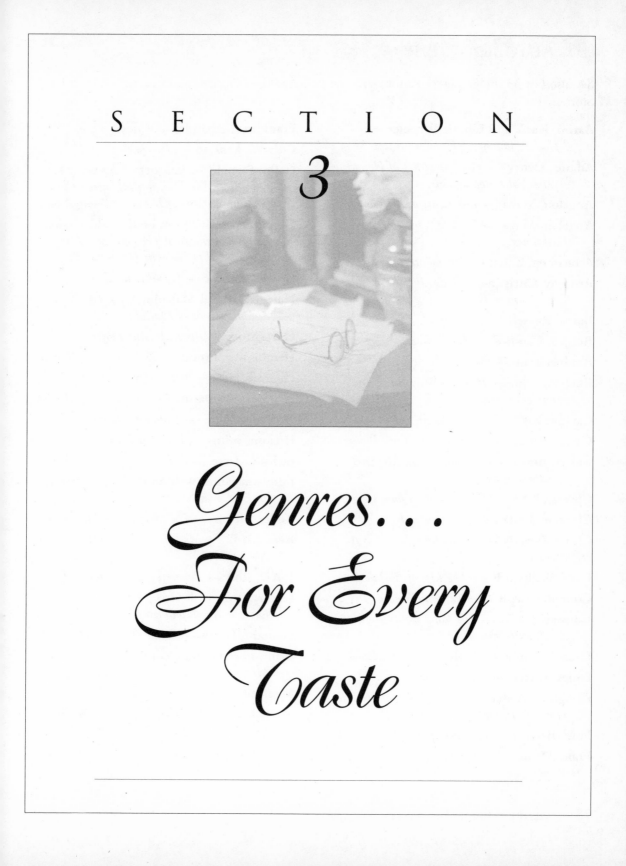

Genres...
For Every
Taste

31. Autobiography

See also List 33, Biography or Autobiography: Pulitzer Prize Winners, and List 125, Adventure Stories: True.

Aaron, Hank and Lonnie Wheeler — *I Had a Hammer: The Hank Aaron Story*

Adams, Henry — *The Education of Henry Adams: An Autobiography*

Angelou, Maya — *The Heart of the Woman*

Angelou, Maya — *I Know Why the Caged Bird Sings*

Armstrong, Karen — *Through the Narrow Gate*

Arnothy, Christine — *I Am Fifteen — and I Don't Want to Die*

Baker, Russell — *Growing Up*

Bergen, Candice — *Knock Wood*

Braden, Tom — *Eight Is Enough*

Buchan, John — *Pilgrim's Way: An Autobiography*

Carson, Kit — *Kit Carson's Autobiography*

Carter, Rosalynn — *First Lady from Plains*

Carter, Jimmy — *Keeping Faith: Memoirs of a President*

Cheever, John — *The Journals of John Cheever*

Christie, Agatha — *Autobiography*

Cleary, Beverly — *A Girl from Yamhill: A Memoir*

Cody, William F. — *The Life of Buffalo Bill*

Conrad, Joseph — *A Personal Record*

Conway, Jill K. — *The Road from Coorain: An Autobiography*

Dillard, Annie — *An American Childhood*

Dinesen, Isak — *Out of Africa*

Douglass, Frederick — *Narrative of the Life of Frederick Douglass*

Ford, Betty — *The Times of My Life*

Frank, Anne — *Anne Frank, the Diary of a Young Girl*

Franklin, Benjamin — *Autobiography*

Galarza, Ernesto — *Barrio Boy*

Gallo, Donald R. (editor) — *Speaking for Ourselves: Autobiographical Sketches by Notable Authors of Books for Young Adults*

Gies, Miep with Alison Leslie Gold — *Anne Frank Remembered: The Story of the Woman who Helped to Hide the Frank Family*

Graves, Robert — *Goodbye to All That*

Haley, Alex and Malcolm X — *The Autobiography of Malcolm X*

Hart, Moss — *Act I: An Autobiography*

Hemingway, Ernest — *The Dangerous Summer*

Hentoff, Nat — *Boston Boy*

Hepburn, Katharine — *Me: Stories of My Life*

Hunter, Mollie — *Hold on to Love*

Huston, John — *An Open Book*

Jackson, Jesse — *A Time to Speak*

Johnson, James Weldon — *Autobiography of an Ex-Coloured Man*

Keller, Helen — *The Story of My Life*

Kerr, M. E. — *Me, Me, Me, Me, Me: Not a Novel*

Kovic, Ron — *Born on the Fourth of July*

Landry, Tom with Gregg Lewis — *Tom Landry: An Autobiography*

Leonard, Hugh — *Home Before Night*

Lynn, Loretta and George Vecsey — *Coal Miner's Daughter*

MacNeil, Robert — *Wordstruck*

Mathabane, Mark — *Kaffir Boy: The True Story of a Black Youth's Coming of Age in Apartheid South Africa*

Mays, Willie with Lou Sahadi — *Say Hey: The Autobiography of Willie Mays*

Mead, Margaret — *Blackberry Winter*

Mehta, Ved — *The Ledge Between the Streams*

Mingus, Charles — *Beneath the Underdog*

Moody, Anne — *Coming of Age in Mississippi*

Nabokov, Vladimir — *Speak, Memory: An Autobiography Revisited*

O'Casey, Sean — *Autobiographies of Sean O'Casey (two volumes)*

Oliphant, Margaret — *The Autobiography of Mrs. Oliphant*

Parks, Gordon — *Voices in the Mirror: An Autobiography*

Poitier, Sidney — *This Life*

Rivera, Edward — *Family Installments*

Roth, Philip — *The Facts: A Novelist's Autobiography*

Rousseau, Jean Jacques — *Confessions*

Sakharov, Andrei — *Memoirs*

Salerno-Sonnenberg, Nadja — *Nadja on My Way*

Sandburg, Carl — *Prairie-Town Boy*

Sender, Ruth M. — *The Cage*

Singer, Isaac Bashevis — *In My Father's Court*

St. Augustine — *Confessions*

Sutcliff, Rosemary — *Blue Hills Remembered: A Recollection*

Taylor, Lawrence and Davic Falkner — *L. T.: Living on the Edge*

Von Trapp, Maria — *Story of the Trapp Family Singers*

Vonnegut, Kurt — *Palm Sunday: An Autobiographical Collage*

Washington, Booker T. — *Up from Slavery*

Waters, Ethel — *His Eye Is on the Sparrow*

Watson, James — *The Double Helix*

Welty, Eudora — *One Writer's Beginnings*

Wilkins, Roy — *Standing Fast: The Autobiography of Roy Wilkins*

Wolff, Tobias — *This Boy's Life: A Memoir*

Wright, Richard — *Black Boy: A Record of Childhood and Youth*

32. BIOGRAPHY

See also List 33, Biography or Autobiography: Pulitzer Prize Winners; and List 125, Adventure Stories: True.

Abraham Lincoln: The Man Behind the Myths — Stephen B. Oates

Afro-Americans, Seventy Six — Eugene Winslow (collection)

Agatha Christie: A Biography — Janet P. Morgan

Alan Alda: An Unauthorized Biography — Jason Bonderoff

American Caesar — William Manchester (about Douglas MacArthur)

American Dreams: Lost and Found — Studs Terkel (collection of mini-biographies)

Anne Sexton: A Biography — Diane Wood Middlebrook

Anne McCaffrey — Mary T. Brizzi

Abraham Lincoln — Ingri and Edgar D'Aulaire

Abraham Lincoln: The Prairie Years and the War Years — Carl Sandburg

Bessie — Chris Albertson (about Bessie Smith, blues musician)

Beyond the Myth: The Story of Joan of Arc —
Polly Schoyer Brooks

Billy the Kid — Edwin Corle

Bruce Springsteen — Peter Gambaccini

Carry On, Mr. Bowditch — Jean Lee Latham
(fictionalized)

C. S. Lewis: A Biography — An. N. Wilson

Churchill: A Life — Martin Gilbert

Columbus and the World Around Him —
Milton Meltzer

Crazy Horse: The Strange Man of the Oglalas
— Mari Sandoz

Damon Runyon, A Life — Jimmy Breslin

Daniel Boone — James Daugherty

Daniel Boone — John Mason Brown

Death of a President — William Manchester
(about John F. Kennedy)

Diana, Princess of Wales — Penny Junor

*Dorothy L. Sayers: The Life of a Courageous
Woman* — James Brabazon

E. B. White: A Biography — Scott Elledge

Edgar Allan Poe: His Writings and Influence
— Charles Haines

Einstein: His Life and Times — Robert Clark

*Eleanor Roosevelt: First Lady of American
Liberalism* — Lois Scharf

Elvis: The Final Years — Jerry Hopkins

*Entrepreneurs: The Men and Women Behind
Famous Brand Names* — Joseph J. Fucini
(collection)

Ernest Hemingway — Carlos Baker

Escalante: The Best Teacher in America —
Jay Mathews

The Fabulous Originals — Irving Wallace
(biographical sketches)

The Fabulous Showman — Irving Wallace
(about P. T. Barnum)

The Far Side of Paradise — Arthur Mitzener
(about F. Scott Fitzgerald)

The First Woman Doctor — Rachel Baker
(about Elizabeth Blackwell)

The Flying Scotsman — Sally Magnuson
(about Eric Liddell, Olympic runner)

Frank Herbert — Timothy O'Reilly

Franklin Delano Roosevelt — Russell
Freedman

F. Scott Fitzgerald — Howard Greenfeld

*Gandhi's Truth on the Origins of Militant
Nonviolence* — Erik Erikson

*The Gentle Barbarian: The Work and Life of
Turgenev* — V. S. Pritchett

Georgia O'Keefe: A Life — Roxana Robinson

Golda: The Romantic Years — Ralph Martin
(about Golda Meir)

Gorky: A Biography — Henry Troyat (about
Maxim Gorky)

Grandma Moses: The Artist Behind the Myth
— Jane Kallir

Great Negroes, Past and Present — Russell
Adams (collection)

*Laura Ingalls Wilder: Growing Up in the
Little House* — Patricia Riley Giff

Henry James — Leon Edel

Here I Stand: A Biography of Martin Luther
— Roland Bainton

Hitler: A Study in Tyranny — Alan Bullock

I'm Gonna Make You Love Me — James
Haskins (about Diana Ross)

*The Inklings: C. S. Lewis, J. R. R. Tolkien,
Charles Williams, and Their Friends* —
Humphrey Carpenter

In Search of J. D. Salinger — Ian Hamilton

*Isaac Bashevis Singer: The Story of a
Storyteller* — Paul Kresh

Jack Kerouac — Tom Clark

Jack: A Biography of Jack London — Andrew
Sinclair

Jack London: A Biography — Richard
O'Conner

James Joyce — John Donne

J. Edgar Hoover: The Man and the Secrets — Curt Gentry

Jim Beckwourth, Black Mountain Man and War Chief of the Crows — Elinor Wilson

Johann Sebastian Bach — Percy M. Young

John Cheever — Scott Donaldson

John F. Kennedy — Judie Mills

John Steinbeck — Richard O'Conner

Josephine Baker — Bryan Hammond and Patrick O'Connor

Judy Blume's Story — Betsy Lee

Kate, the Life of Katharine Hepburn — Charles Hingham

The Kennedys: An American Drama — Peter Collier and David Horowitz

The Last Algonquin — Theodore Kazimiroff (about Joe Two Trees)

Let the Trumpet Sound: The Life of Martin Luther King — Stephen B. Oates

The Last Lion — William Manchester (about Winston Churchill)

Laura: The Life of Laura Ingalls Wilder — Donald Zochert

A Life of Picasso, Vol. I, 1881–1906 — John Richardson

The Life and Adventures of John Muir — James Mitchell Clark

Life of Beethoven — Alexander Wheelock Thayer

The Life of Charlotte Bronte — Elizabeth Gaskell

Life of Johnson — James Bowell

Life of Milton — Samuel Johnson

The Life of Noel Coward — Lesley Cole

The Life of Raymond Chandler — Frank MacShane

The Life of Sir Arthur Conan Doyle — John Dickson Carr

Lone Star Rising: Lyndon Johnson and His Times, 1908–1960 — Robert Dallek

Lou Gehrig: An American Hero — Paul Gallico

The Love You Make: An Insider's Story of the Beatles — Peter Brown

Madame Curie: A Biography — Eve Curie

Maggie's American Dream: The Life and Times of a Black Family — James Comer (chronicles an African-American family's move from the South to the North)

Make Believe: The Story of Nancy and Ronald Reagan — Laurence Leamer

The Man Who Wrote Dracula: A Biography of Bram Stoker — Daniel Farson

Mark Twain and His World — Justin Kaplan

Martin Luther King, Jr.: To the Mountaintop — William R. Witherspoon

Mary Wollstonecraft Shelley: Romance and Reality — Emily W. Sunstein

Maus II — Art Spiegelman (about his father's experience surviving the Holocaust)

Means of Ascent: The Years of Lyndon Johnson — Robert A. Caro

Mornings on Horseback — David McCullough (about Theodore Roosevelt)

The New York Times Great Lives of the Twentieth Century — Arthur Gelb, ed. (50 biographies)

Nixon: Ruin and Recovery, 1973-1990 — Orlando Patterson

Oscar Wilde: The Dramatic Life and Fascinating Times of Oscar Wilde — Martin Fido

Pablo Picasso: The Man and the Image — Richard B. Lyttle

Particular Passions: Talks with Women Who Have Shaped our Time — Lynn Gilbert and Gaylen Moore (collection)

Paul Revere and the Minute Men — Dorothy Canfield Fisher

Patrimony — Philip Roth (about his father, Herman Roth)

Plain Speaking: An Oral Biography of Harry S. Truman — Merle Miller

Presenting S. E. Hinton — Jay Daly

President Reagan: The Role of a Lifetime — Lou Cannon

Private Demons: The Life of Shirley Jackson — Judy Oppenheimer

Queen Victoria — Lytton Strachey

Rachel Carson — Carol B. Gartner

Reagan — Lou Cannon

Rex Stout, a Biography — John L. McAleer

Richard Nixon: The Shaping of His Character — Fawn Brodie

The Right Stuff — Tom Wolfe (about early astronauts)

Roosevelt: The Lion and the Fox — James MacGregor Burns (about F. D. Roosevelt)

Roosevelt: The Soldier of Freedom — James MacGregor Burns (about F. D. Roosevelt)

Rough Magic: A Biography of Sylvia Plath — Paul Alexander

Saul Bellow: A Biography of the Imagination — Ruth Miller

The Sound of Wings: The Biography of Amelia Earhart — Mary S. Lovell

Sunday Nights at Seven: The Jack Benny Story — Joan Benny

Susan B. Anthony — A Biography: A Singular Feminist — Kathleen L. Barry

Susan B. Anthony: Rebel, Crusander, Humanitarian — Alma Lutz

Ten Fingers for God — Dorothy Clarke Wilson (about Dr. Paul Brand, missionary with the lepers in India)

Ten Saints — Eleanor Farjeon (collection of stories about lives of ten saints)

To All Gentleness: William Carlos Williams, the Doctor Poet — Neil Baldwin

Tolstoy — Martine de Courcel

Tom Selleck: An Unauthorized Biography — Jason Bonderoff

Touch of Light: The Story of Louis Braille — Anne E. Neimark

Traitor: The Case of Benedict Arnold — Jean Fritz

Truman — David McCullough

Truman Capote — Helen S. Garson

Uncommon Eloquence: A Biography of Angna Enters — Dorothy Mandel

Ursula K. LeGuin — Barbara Bucknall

The Voyages of Columbus — Armstrong Perry

Wanted! Frank and Jesse James — Margaret Baldwin and Pat O'Brien

Washington: The Indispensable Man — James Flexner

Weaver of Dreams: The Girlhood of Charlotte Bronte — Elfrida Vipont

When the Cheering Stopped: The Last Years of Woodrow Wilson — Gene Smith

The Whole World in His Hands: A Pictorial Biography of Paul Robeson — Susan Robeson

Wild Bill Hickok Tames the West — Stewart Holbrook

Willa: The Life of Willa Cather — Phyllis C. Robinson

With Malice Toward None — Stephen B. Oates (about Abraham Lincoln)

Woman in the Mists: The Story of Dian Fossey and the Mountain Gorillas of Africa — Farley Mowat

The Woman Warrior — Maxine H. Kingston (about author and her family)

The Young Hemingway — Michael S. Reynolds

Younger Days of Famous Writers — Katherine D. Cather

Zane Grey, a Biography — Frank Gruber

Zapata and the Mexican Revolution — John Womack

33. Biography or Autobiography: Pulitzer Prizewinners

The Pulitzer Prizes in this list were given for distinguished biography or autobiography by an American author. The prize has been given every year since 1917 (except 1962) from funds set aside by Joseph Pulitzer, a New York publisher. The prizewinners are listed in chronological order. Asterisks (*) mark joint awards.

Julia Ward Howe — Laura E. Richards and Maude Howe Elliott

Benjamin Franklin, Self-Revealed — William C. Bruce

The Education of Henry Adams — Henry Adams

The Life of John Marshall — Albert J. Beveridge

The Americanization of Edward Bok — Edward Bok

A Daughter of the Middle Border — Hamlin Garland

Life and Letters of Walter H. Page — Burton J. Henrick

From Immigrant to Inventor — Michael Pupin

Barrett Wendell and His Letters — DeWolfe Howe

Life of Sir William Osler — Harvey Cushing

Whitman: An Interpretation in Narrative — Emory Holloway

The American Orchestra and Theodore Thomas — Charles E. Russell

The Training of an American: The Earlier Life and Letters of Walter H. Page — Burton J. Hendrick

The Raven (Sam Houston) — Marquis James

Charles W. Eliot — Henry James

Theodore Roosevelt — Henry F. Pringle

Grover Cleveland — Allan Nevins

John Hay — Tyler Dennett

R. E. Lee — Douglas S. Freeman

The Thought and Character of William James — Ralph B. Perry

Hamilton Fish: The Inner History of the Grant Administration — Allan Nevins

Pedlar's Progress — Odell Shepard*

Andrew Jackson — Marquis James*

Benjamin Franklin — Carl Van Doren

Woodrow Wilson, Life and Letters — Ray S. Baker

Jonathan Edwards — Ola E. Winslow

Crusader in Crinoline — Forrest Wilson

Admiral of the Ocean Sea — Samuel E. Morison

The American Leonardo: The Life of Samuel F. B. Morse — Charleton Mabee

George Bancroft: Brahmin Rebel — Russell B. Nye

Son of the Wilderness — Linnie M. Wolfe

The Autobiography of William Allen White — William Allen White

Forgotten First Citizen: John Bigelow — Margaret Clapp

Roosevelt and Hopkins — Robert E. Sherwood

John Quincy Adams and the Foundations of American Foreign Policy — Samuel F. Bemis

John C. Calhoun: American Portrait — Margaret L. Colt

Charles Evans Hughes — Merlo J. Pusey

Edmund Pendleton, 1721–1803 — David J. Mays

The Spirit of St. Louis — Charles A. Lindbergh

The Taft Story — William S. White

Benjamin Henry Latrobe — Talbot F. Hamlin

Profiles in Courage — John F. Kennedy

George Washington, Vols. I–VI — Douglas S. Freeman*

George Washington, Vol. VII — John A. Carroll and Mary W. Ashworth*

Woodrow Wilson: American Prophet — Arthur Walworth

John Paul Jones — Samuel E. Morison

Charles Sumner and the Coming of the Civil War — David Donald

Henry James: Vol. II: The Conquest of London, 1870–1881 — Leon Edel*

Henry James: Vol. III: The Middle Years, 1881–1895 — Leon Edel*

John Keats — Walter J. Bate

Henry Adams — Ernest Samuels

A Thousand Days — Arthur M. Schlesinger, Jr.

Mr. Clemens and Mark Twain — Justin Kaplan

Memoirs (1925–1950) — George F. Kennan

The Man from New York: John Quinn and His Friends — B. L. Reid

Huey Long — T. Harry Williams

Robert Frost: The Years of Triumph, 1915–1938 — Lawrence Thompson

Eleanor and Franklin — Joseph P. Lash

Luce and His Empire — W. A. Swanberg

O'Neill, Son and Artist — Louis Sheaffer

The Power Broker: Robert Moses and the Fall of New York — Robert A. Caro

Edith Wharton: A Biography — R. W. B. Lewis

A Prince of Our Disorder: The Life of T. E. Lawrence — John E. Mack

Samuel Johnson — Walter J. Bate

Days of Sorrow and Pain: Leo Baeck and the Berlin Jews — Leonard Baker

The Rise of Theodore Roosevelt — Edmund Morris

Peter the Great: His Life and World — Robert K. Massie

Grant: A Biography — William S. McFeely

Growing Up — Russell Baker

Booker T. Washington — Louis R. Harlan

The Life and Times of Cotton Mather — Kenneth Silverman

Louise Bogan: A Portrait — Elizabeth Frank

Bearing the Cross: Martin Luther King, Jr. and the Southern Christian Leadership Conference — David J. Garrow

Look Homeward: A Life of Thomas Wolfe — David Herbert Donald

Oscar Wilde — Richard Ellmann

Machiavelli in Hell — Sebastian de Grazia

Jackson Pollock: An American Saga — Steven Naifeh and Gregory White Smith

Fortunate Son: The Healing of a Vietnam Vet — Lewis B. Puller, Jr.

Truman — David McCullough

W. E. B. DuBois: Biography of a Race, 1868–1919 — David Levering Lewis

Harriet Beecher Stowe: A Life — Joan D. Hedrick

God: A Biography — Jack Miles

34. Comics: Topics Of Study

Comics show human foibles; reflect history, society, and political attitudes; sometimes attempt to predict the future; and show changes in the ways we perceive ourselves. Hence, they are worthy of study as literature. Below are eight concepts that can serve as a framework for the study of comics. See also List 35, Comics: Picture Stories; List 36, Comics: Early Twentieth Century; List 37, Comics: Contemporary; List 38, Comic Format: Classics; List 39, Comic Format: Classics Translated to Spanish; List 40, Comic Format: Nonfiction; and List 41, Comic Format: Drama/History/Biography.

1. Stereotypes and Stereotypical Behavior
Female and male roles
Ethnic slant
Racial bias
"Ageless" characters
Exaggerated physical features
Exaggerated physical prowess
Exaggerated mental powers
Low brow versus high brow

2. Social Commentary
Ecological issues
Attitude toward war
Reflection of morals of era
Satire of human weaknesses
Family values
Attitude toward marriage
Relations between the sexes
Rearing children
Attitude toward technology
Sibling rivalry
Love and relationships
Man's inhumanity toward man

3. Political Commentary
Political parties
Corruption
Mistakes
Virtues
Ridicule of positions
Ridicule of personality traits
Caricatures of physical appearance

4. Aesthetic Value
Art
Story
Characterization
Humor
Imagery

5. Historical Value
Reflection of life
Reflection of mores
Depiction of societal changes
Tragedies
Fads
Universality of problems

6. Personal Value
Stress relief
Humor
Fantasy
Diversion
"Bubble-burster" (illusion-shatterer)
Identification with character/situation
Expectation/anticipation of next strip
Seeing others as perpetual victims

7. Influence
Future technology
Fashion and style
Manners
Language
Morals
Politics
Philosophy

8. TYPE OF HUMOR

Exaggeration and hyperbole
Slapstick
Irreverence
Tragicomedy
Mistakes
Clumsiness
"Poor soul"
Satire

Surprise
Incongruity
Irreverence for social or economic
   standing
Weirdness and bizarreness (off-the-wall)
Comeuppance and retribution
   (just deserts)

35. COMICS: PICTURE STORIES

The comic strip is a special creative form, combining art and writing. It often contains social commentary, reflects attitudes of the times, and uses humor. Comics are now studied in many universities as literature, as well as art and history.

Rodolphe Topffer of Switzerland is called the "father of comics" because he invented the picture story back in 1827 to amuse his students. Benjamin Franklin was the first American cartoonist, and along with Paul Revere drew cartoons about British tyranny. R. F. Outcault and Jimmy Swinnerton are credited with being the originators of the first real comic strips. Famous cartoon/comic creators are listed below, along with some of their most famous creations. By the way, Katzenjammer Kids, which debuted in 1897, is the longest-running comic strip.

VERY EARLY COMICS

Alphonse and Gaston — Frederick Burr Opper

And Her Name Was Maud — Frederick Burr Opper

Buster Brown — R. F. Outcault

Canyon Kids — Jimmy Swinnerton

Clarence the Cop — Charles Kahles

Foxy Grandpa — Charles Schultze

Hairbreadth Harry — Charles Kahles

Happy Holligan — Frederick Burr Opper

Katzenjammer Kids — Rudolph Dirks (later H. H. Knerr, John Dirks, and Joe Musial)

Little Nemo in Slumberland — Winsor McCary

Little Bears — Jimmy Swinnerton

Little Jimmy — Jimmy Swinnerton

Mutt and Jeff — Bud Fisher

Slim Jim — Raymond Ewer

The Upside Downs — Gustave Verbeck

Wee Willie Winkie's World — Lyonel Feininger

The Yellow Kid — R. F. Outcault

36. COMICS: EARLY TWENTIETH CENTURY

Barney Google — Billy DeBeck

Bringing Up Father — George McManus (later Vernon Greene, William Kavanaugh, Frank Fletcher, and Hamlet Campana)

Broom Hilda — Russell Myers

Cap Stubbs and Tippie (Tippie) — Edwina Dumm

Count Screwloose — Milt Gross

Desperate Desmond — Harry Hershfield

Dimples — Grace Drayton

Etta Kett — Paul Robinson

Felix the Cat — Pat Sullivan

For Better or Worse — Thomas "Tad" Dorgan (later Lynn Johnston)

Gasoline Alley — Dick Moores; Frank King

Gimple Beinsish the Matchmaker — Samuel Zagat

The Gumps — Sidney Smith

Harold Teen — Carol Ed

Hazel the Heartbreaker — Ted Key (later H. A. McGill)

Hem and Haw — Alfred Frugh

Krazy Kat — George Herriman

Little Elmer — Doc Winner

Little Orphan Annie — Harold Gray

Life's Little Jokes — Rueben "Rube" Goldberg

Maggie and Jiggs — George McManus

Moon Mullins — Frank Willard

The Newlyweds — George McManus

Positive Polly — Cliff Sterrett

Reg'lar Fellers — Gene Burns

Room and Board — Gene Ahern

Skippy — Percy Crosby

Toonerville Folks — Fontaine Fox

The Willetts — J. R. Williams

Winnie Winkle — A. E. Hayward

37. COMICS: CONTEMPORARY

Alley Oop — V. T. Hamlin

Andy Capp — Reginald Smythe

Apple Mary (later Mary Worth's Family and Mary Worth) — Martha Orr (later Dale Conner, Allen Saunders under the pseudonym Dale Allen)

Archie — Bob Montana

Arlo and Janis — Jimmy Johnson

B. C. — Johnny Hart

Beetle Bailey — Mort Walker

The Berrys — Carl Grubert

Betty — Charles Voight

Blondie — Murat "Chic" Young (later Dean Young, Jim Raymond, and Stan Drake)

Brenda Starr — Dale Messick (later Romona Fradon and Mary Schmich)

Buck Rogers — Richard Calkins and Philip Nowlan (later Rick Yager)

Buz Sawyer — Roy Crane (later Bill Crooks and Jim Lawrence)

Calvin and Hobbes — Bill Watterson

Cathy — Cathy Guisewite

Clarence — Weare Holbrook

Crankshaft — Batiuk and Ayers

Dennis the Menace — Hank Ketcham

Dick Tracy — Chester Gould

Donald Duck — Walt Disney logo; Bob Karp, Al Taliaferro, and Frank Grundeen

Doonesbury — Garry Trudeau

Dotty — Buford Tune

Drabble — Kevin Fagan

Eek and Meek — Howie Schneider

The Family Circus — Bil Keane

The Far Side — Gary Larson

Flash Gordon — Alex Raymond

The Flop Family — George Swanson

Frank and Ernest — Bob Thaves

Garfield — Jim Davis

Grandma — Charles Kuhn

The Green Hornet — Bert Whitman

Hagar the Horrible — Dik Browne (later Chris Browne)

Henry — Carl Anderson (later John Liney and Don Trachte)

Herb & Jamaal — Stephen Bentley

Herman — Jim Unger

Hi and Lois — Mort Walker and Dik Browne (later Greg and Brian Walker)

It's a Girl's Life (later Teena) — Hilda Terry

Joe Palooka — Ham Fisher

Kit 'n' Carlyle — Larry Wright

Li'l Abner — Al Capp

The Little King — Otto Soglow

The Lockhorns — Bill Hoest

The Lone Ranger — Charles Flanders and Paul Newman

Luann — Greg Evans

Mandrake the Magician — Lee Falk

Marmaduke — Brad Anderson

Marvin — Tom Armstrong

Mickey Mouse — Walt Disney and Ub Iwerks (later Floyd Gottfredson, Manuel Gonzales, Roy Williams, Del Connell)

The Middletons — Ralph Dunagin and Dana Summers

Nancy — Ernie Bushmiller

Our Bill — Harry Haenigsen

Peanuts — Charles Schulz

The Phantom — Lee Falk

Pogo — Walt Kelly (later Doyle and Sternecky)

Popeye — Elzie Segar

Prince Valiant — Harold "Hal" Foster (later John Cullen Murphy)

Priscilla's Pop — Al Vermeer

Sally Forth — Greg Howard

Shoe — Jeff MacNelly

Smokey Stover — Bill Holman

Spider-Man — Steve Ditko (later Stan Lee and Flor Dery)

Steve Canyon — Milton Caniff

Superman — Jerry Siegel and Joe Shuster

Tarzan — Harold "Hal" Foster (later Rex Maxon, Burne Hogarth, Russ Manning, and others)

Terry and the Pirates — Milton Caniff (later George Wunder)

The Treasury of Classic Tales — Frank Reilly

True Life Adventures — Dick Huemer and George Wheeler

Wash Tubs (later Captain Easy) — Roy Crane (later Leslie Turner)

The Wizard of Id — Johnny Hart (later also Brent Parker)

Ziggy — Tom Wilson

38. COMIC FORMAT: CLASSICS

This series of outstanding "illustrated format" booklets is similar to a comic book format in visual appeal, abridgment of plot, and exciting presentation. They differ from conventional comic books in that they are typeset in upper and lower case, have artistic page composition, and avoid sexist illustrations. They are obtainable by individual titles, in multiple copies, or by collection, with or without accompanying filmstrips, activity books, posters, and read-along cassettes, from American Guidance Service, P.O. Box 99, Circle Pines, MN 55014, 1-800-328-2560.

COLLECTION 1

Black Beauty
The Call of the Wild
Dr. Jekyll and Mr. Hyde
Dracula
Frankenstein
Huckleberry Finn
Moby Dick
The Red Badge of Courage
The Time Machine
Tom Sawyer
Treasure Island
20,000 Leagues Under the Sea

COLLECTION 2

The Great Adventures of Sherlock Holmes
Gulliver's Travels
The Hunchback of Notre Dame
The Invisible Man
Journey to the Center of the Earth
Kidnapped
The Mysterious Island
The Scarlet Letter
The Story of My Life
A Tale of Two Cities
The Three Musketeers
The War of the Worlds

COLLECTION 3

Around the World in Eighty Days
Captain's Courageous
*A Connecticut Yankee in King
    Arthur's Court*
The Hound of the Baskervilles
The House of the Seven Gables

Jane Eyre
The Last of the Mohicans
The Best of O. Henry
The Best of Poe
Two Years Before the Mast
White Fang
Wuthering Heights

COLLECTION 4

Ben Hur
A Christmas Carol
The Food of the Gods
Ivanhoe
The Man in the Iron Mask
The Prince and the Pauper
The Prisoner of Zenda
The Return of the Native
Robinson Crusoe
The Scarlet Pimpernel
The Sea Wolf
The Swiss Family Robinson

COLLECTION 5

Billy Budd
Crime and Punishment
Don Quixote
Great Expectations
Heidi
The Iliad
Lord Jim
The Mutiny on Board H. M. S. Bounty
The Odyssey
Oliver Twist
Pride and Prejudice
The Turn of the Screw

39. Comic Format: Classics Translated to Spanish

The following classics have been faithfully translated into beginning Spanish and illustrated with comic book pictures for visual impact and appeal.

Collection 1

Azabache
Dracula
*El extraño caso del Dr. Jekyll y
    Mister Hyde*
Frankenstein
El hombre invisible
Huckleberry Finn
La Isla del Tesoro
El llamado de la selva
Los mejores cuentos de O. Henry
Moby Dick
20,000 leguas de viaje submarino
Viaje al centro de la tierra

Collection 2

Las grandes aventuras de Sherlock Holmes
Cancion de Navidad
Cuento de dos cuidades
Don Quijote de la Mancha
La guerra de los mundos
Historia de mi vida
El Jorobado de Nuestra Señora de Paris
La maquina del tiempo
Los mejores cuentos de Poe
La Odisea
Tom Sawyer
Los tres mosqueteros

40. Comic Format: Nonfiction

These nonfiction books in comic book format explain complex topics clearly and informatively, in an entertaining manner.

Capitalism for Beginners — Robert Lekachman

Darwin for Beginners — Jonathan Miller

Ecology for Beginners — Stephen Croall

Economics for Beginners — Richard Caravan

Einstein for Beginners — Michael McGuinness and Joe Schwartz

Freud for Beginners — Richard Appignanesi

Lenin for Beginners — Richard Appignanesi

Mao for Beginners — Rius

Marx for Beginners — Rius

Marx's Kapital for Beginners — David Smith

Trotsky for Beginners — Tariq Ali

These other cartoon-type books of interest will instruct gleefully.

The Cartoon History of the Universe — Larry Gonick

The Cartoon History of the United States — Larry Gonick

The Cartoon Guide to Physics — Larry Gonick and Art Huffman

The Cartoon Guide to the Computer — Larry Gonick

The Cartoon Guide to Genetics — Larry Gonick

41. COMIC FORMAT: DRAMA/HISTORY/BIOGRAPHY

These books are obtainable in individual or multiple copies, with or without accompanying film-strips, cassettes, and activity books, in either hardcover or paperback, from Pendulum Press, Inc., 237 Saw Mill Road, Box 509, West Haven, Connecticut 06516.

SHAKESPEARE

As You Like It
Hamlet
Julius Caesar
King Lear
Macbeth
The Merchant of Venice
A Midsummer Night's Dream
Othello
Romeo and Juliet
The Taming of the Shrew
The Tempest
Twelfth Night

HISTORY OF THE U.S.

The New World
The Fight for Freedom
The United States Emerges
Problems of the New Nation
Americans Move Westward
Before the Civil War
The Civil War
The Industrial Era
America Becomes a World Power
The Roaring Twenties and the Great Depression
World War II
America Today

DUAL BIOGRAPHIES

Charles Lindbergh
Amelia Earhart

Houdini
Walt Disney

Davy Crockett
Daniel Boone

Elvis Presley
The Beatles

Benjamin Franklin
Martin Luther King, Jr.

Abraham Lincoln
Franklin Delano Roosevelt

George Washington
Thomas Jefferson

Madame Curie
Albert Einstein

Thomas Edison
Alexander Graham Bell

Vince Lombardi
Pele

Babe Ruth
Jackie Robinson

Jim Thorpe
Althea Gibson

42. DETECTIVE AND SPY STORIES/THRILLERS/MYSTERIES

Nearly everyone enjoys exciting mysteries, detectives, spying, espionage, and intrigue. British writers seem to excel in this field. Although not all of these stories are considered "great literature," many have found their way into the hearts of avid fans, and some are considered classics or prototypes of their genre. Authors are listed alphabetically, along with selected books or stories, recurring characters, and other comments. See also List 43, Detective Stories: Sherlock Holmes. For those authors who used pennames (*), see List 189, Pseudonyms of Famous Writers of the World.

Margery Allingham — *The Crime at Black Dudley; Mystery Mile; Police at the Funeral; Flowers for the Judge; The Fashion in Shrouds; Traitors Purse; Tiger in the Smoke; The China Governess; The Mind Readers, The Case of the White Elephant; The Care of Time; Dancers in Mourning; The White Cottage Mystery; Mr. Campion's Farthing*
 ◆ Prominent character: Albert Campion

Eric Ambler — *Checkmate* (TV series)*; A Coffin for Dimitrios; Journal into Fear; Dirty Story; The Levanter; The Care of Time; Here Lies: An Autobiography*

Evelyn Anthony — *Albatross; The Avenue of the Dead; The Company of Saints; The Defector; The Janus Imperative* (all spy stories with women protagonists)

Isaac Asimov — *Tales of the Black Widowers; The Best Mysteries of Isaac Asimov* (collection); *Asimov Mysteries* (collection)

John Dudley Ball — *In the Heat of the Night* (made into Academy Award movie; TV series); *Five Pieces of Jade; Then Came Violence; The Kiwi Target*
 ◆ Prominent character: Virgil Tibbs (one of first African-American sleuths)

Nathaniel Benchley — *Catch a Falling Spy* (humorous)

*Anthony Berkeley — *The Layton Court Mystery* (anonymously); *The Avenging Chance; The Poisoned Chocolates Case* (an expansion of the previous story); *Malice Aforethought; Before the Fact* (made into Hitchcock movie, *Suspicion*); *Trial and Error*
 ◆ Famous character: Roger Sheringham

Earl Derr Biggers — Charlie Chan series (movies made in the 1930s and 1940s)
 ◆ Prominent character: Charlie Chan

Malcolm Bosse — *The Man Who Loved Zoos* (woman-protagonist spy novel)

Christianna Brand — *Death in High Heels; Cat and Mouse; Fog of Doubt*

John Buchan — *The Thirty-Nine Steps* (classic 1915 spy novel; made into movie)
 ◆ Prominent character: Richard Hannay

William F. Buckley, Jr. — *High Jinx; See You Later Alligator; The Story of Henri Tod; Marco Polo, If You Can; Stained Glass; Saving the Queen*
 ◆ Prominent character: Blackford Oates

Michael Butterworth — *The Man in the Sopwith Camel; The Man who Broke the Bank at Monte Carlo; Remains to be Seen* (all humorous)

*John Dickson Carr — *Hag's Nook; The Bride of Newgate; The Dead Man's Knock; The Arabian Nights Murder; Case of the Constant Suicides; Crooked Hinge; The Man who Explained Miracles; The Incautious Burglar; Witch of the Low Tide; Papa La-Bas; The Curse of the Bronze Lamp; Punch and Judy Murders*
♦ Prominent characters: Sir Henry Merrivale; Dr. Gideon Fell
Note: Master of the locked-room mysteries.

Raymond Chandler — *The Big Sleep; Farewell, My Lovely; The Lady in the Lake; The Long Goodbye; Playback; The Pencil*
♦ Prominent character: Philip Marlowe
Note: Master of the hard-boiled detective story.

Leslie Charteris — *The Arrow of God*
♦ Famous character: The Saint

Gilbert Keith Chesterton — *Tremendous Trifles; The Innocence of Father Brown; Come To Think of It*
♦ Prominent character: Father Brown
Note: Called the Prince of Paradox because of the religious undertones he worked into his lighthearted writings.

Agatha Christie — *The Mysterious Affair at Styles; Murder at the Vicarage; The Secret Adversary; The Murder of Roger Ackroyd; Murder in the Calais Coach; The Mousetrap* (play); *Death on the Nile; And Then There Were None; Witness for the Prosecution* (play); *Dead Man's Folly; Sad Cypress; Towards Zero; Murder on the Orient Express*
♦ Prominent characters: Hercule Poirot and Miss Jane Marple
Note: Has sold hundreds of thousands of copies of books; play, *Mousetrap*, has run in London about forty years!

Manning Coles — *Drink to Yesterday; No Entry*
♦ Prominent character: Tommy Hambleton

Wilkie Collins — *The Woman in White; The Moonstone*
Note: Called first detective novel writer in English.

Richard Condon — *The Manchurian Candidate* (made into a movie); *A Talent for Loving; Arigato; The Star-Spangled Crunch; Winter Kills; Bandicoot; Prizzi's Honor* (made into movie); *Prizzi's Family*

Joseph Conrad — *The Secret Agent; Under Western Eyes* (classic spy novels from early twentieth century)

*John Creasey — Department Z series; The Toff series; Inspector West series; Dr. Palfrey series
Note: Wrote about 650 titles.

*Edmund Crispin — *Obsequies at Oxford; The Moving Toyshop; Buried for Pleasure*
♦ Prominent character: Gervase Fen

Freeman Willis Crofts — *The Cask; The Box Office Murders; The Mystery of the Sleeping Car Express*
   Note: Introduced police routine into detective stories; began new era in detective writing.

Len Deighton — *The Ipcress File; Funeral in Berlin; The Billion Dollar Brain; Spy Story; Goodbye, Mickey Mouse; Berlin Game; Spy Hook; Spy Line; Spy Sinker*
   Note: Master of espionage stories.

Gregory Dowling — *Double Take* (humorous)

Sir Arthur Conan Doyle — *A Study in Scarlet; The Sign of Four; Memoirs of Sherlock Holmes*
   ◆ Prominent characters: Sherlock Holmes and Dr. John Watson
   Note: See also List 43, Detective Stories: Sherlock Holmes

August Derleth — *The Solar Pons Omnibus* (two volumes/eight stories)
   ◆ Prominent character: Solar Pons

Ian Fleming — *Casino Royale; From Russia with Love; Dr. No; Goldfinger; Thunderball; Chitty-Chitty Bang-Bang*
   ◆ Prominent character: James Bond, 007 (secret agent)
   Note: Novels made into famous movies.

Kenneth Follett — *The Eye of the Needle; The Man from St. Petersburg; Lie Down with Lions*

Frederick Forsyth — *The Day of the Jackal; The Odessa File; The Dogs of War; The Fourth Protocol*

Dick Francis — *Dead Cert; Odds Against; Forfeit; High Stakes; In the Frame; Risk; Banker; Hot Money; Straight*
   Note: Famous jockey in England; wrote about jockeys and pilots.

Nicolas Freeling — *Love in Amsterdam; King of the Rainy Country*
   ◆ Prominent character: Inspector Van der Valk

Erle Stanley Gardner — *The Case of the Crimson Kiss; The Case of the Velvet Claws; The Case of the Crooked Candle*
   ◆ Prominent characters: Perry Mason, Della Street, Paul Drake
   Note: Wrote more than 100 books; TV series and movies based on his famous Perry Mason character.

Michael Gilbert — *The Claimant; A Clean Kill; Game without Rules; Amateur in Violence; Smallbone Deceased*

*Dorothy Gilman — *The Unexpected Mrs. Pollifax; The Amazing Mrs. Pollifax; The Elusive Mrs. Pollifax; Mrs. Pollifax on the China Station; Mrs. Pollifax and the Hong Kong Buddha*
   ◆ Prominent character: Mrs. Pollifax

Graham Greene — *Our Man in Havana* (humorous); *The Confidential Agent; The Quiet American*

Martha Grimes — *The Man with a Load of Mischief; The Old Fox Deceived; The Dirty Duck; The Five Bells and Bladebone*
   Note: Titles are names of British pubs.

P. N. Gwynne — *Pushkin Shove* (humorous)

Dashiell Hammett — *The Maltese Falcon: The Dain Curse; The Glass Key; The Thin Man; The Continental Op*
- ◆ Prominent characters: Nick and Nora Charles; Sam Spade

Note: His characters were basis for television and movie shows; invented hard-boiled private eye character Sam Spade.

Jack Higgins — *The Eagle Has Landed; Storm Warning; Day of Judgement; Exocet; Night of the Fox*

Patricia Highsmith — *Strangers on a Train* (made into movie); *Slowly Slowly in the Wind*

Tony Hillerman — *People of Darkness; The Dark Wind; Skinwalkers; A Thief of Time; Talking God; The Fly on the Wall*
Note: Native American settings.

Evan Hunter — *Every Little Crook and Nanny* (humorous)

*Michael Innes — *Hamlet, Revenge!; Lament for a Maker; The Secret Vanguard; Appleby on Ararat; The Journeying Boy; Operation Pax; The Man from the Sea; The Daffodil Affair; One Man Show; The Long Farewell; The Crabtree Affair*

P. D. James — *Cover her Face; Unnatural Causes; Shroud for a Nightingale; An Unsuitable Job for a Woman; A Taste for Death; Devices and Desires; A Mind for Murder; The Black Tower; Death of an Expert Witness*
- ◆ Prominent character: Adam Dalgliesh

Harry Kemelman — *Friday the Rabbi Slept Late; Wednesday the Rabbi Got Wet; Someday the Rabbi will Leave; One Fine Day, the Rabbi Bought a Cross*
- ◆ Prominent character: Rabbi David Small

Stephen King — *Carrie; The Shining; The Dark Half; Salem's Lot; The Dead Zone*
Note: Horror stories.

Rudyard Kipling — *Kim* (classic spy novel from 1901)

Jane Langton — *Dark Nantucket Noon; Emily Dickinson Is Dead; Murder at the Gardner*
- ◆ Prominent character: Homer Kelly

*Emma Lathen — *Death Shall Overcome; Murder to Go; Sweet and Low; By Hook or by Crook; Murder Makes the Wheels Go 'Round*
- ◆ Prominent character: John Putnam Thatcher

*John le Carre — *The Spy who Came in from the Cold; Tinker, Tailor, Soldier, Spy; The Honourable Schoolboy; The Little Drummer Girl; The Perfect Spy; Smiley's People*
Note: Realistic, older spies.

Joseph Sheridan le Fanu — *Uncle Silas: A Tale of Bartram Haugh; Wylder's Hand; Checkmate*
Note: Supernatural themes.

Gaston Leroux — *Phantom of the Opera; The Mystery of the Yellow Room; The Perfume of the Lady in Black*
Note: Phantom of the Opera made into movies and Broadway play.

*Cecil Day Lewis — *Overtures to Death*
Note: Also poet.

Richard Lockridge — *The Norths Meet Murder; Death on the Aisle; Murder within Murder; The Tenth Life; The Old Die Young*
◆ Prominent characters: Pam and Jerry North (husband and wife)
Note: Wrote with wife and separately; humorous.

Mark Lovell — *The Only Good Apple in a Barrel of Spies* (humorous)

*Robert Ludlum — *The Scarlatti Inheritance; The Osterman Weekend; The Rhinemann Exchange; The Holcroft Covenant; The Matarese Circle; The Bourne Identity; The Parsifal Mosaic; The Icarus Agenda; The Bourne Supremacy*

Nan and Ivan Lyons — *Someone Is Killing the Great Chefs of Europe; Champagne Blues*
Note: both humorous

John D. MacDonald — *The Damned; The Brass Cupcake; The Deep Blue Good-By; The Last One Left; The Dreadful Lemon Sky; Condominium; The Green Ripper;* Travis McGee series; *Dead Low Tide*

*Ross MacDonald — *The Dark Tunnel; The Moving Target; The Chill; The Far Side of the Dollar; The Goodbye Look; The Underground Man; The Blue Hammer; The Drowning Pool; The Dalton Case; The Way Some People Die*
◆ Famous character: Lew Archer

Helen Clark MacInnes — *Above Suspicion; While We Still Live; Decision at Delphi; The Snare of the Hunters; The Salzburg Connection; Ride a Pale Horse*
Note: Espionage; female spy.

Alistair MacLean — *The Guns of Navarone; Ice Station Zebra; Where Eagles Dare*
Note: Many of his books have been made into movies.

Ngaio Marsh — *I Can Find My Way Out; A Man Lay Dead; Overture to Death; Death of a Fool; Dead Water; Black as He's Painted; A Wreath for Rivera*
◆ Famous character: Roderick Alleyn

A. E. W. Mason — *House of the Arrow; At the Villa Rose; Prisoner in the Opal*
◆ Famous character: Hanaud

W. Somerset Maugham — *Ashenden, or, The British Agent*
Note: Classic spy novel.

Ed McBain — *Three Blind Mice; Death of a Nurse*
◆ Characters: Matthew Hope; Steve Carella

James McClure — *The Steam Pig; The Caterpillar Cop; The Gooseberry Fool; Rogue Eagle; The Sunday Hangman*
Note: South African.

*Herman Cyril McNeile — *Bulldog Drummond; The Adventures of a Demobilized Officer who Found Peace Dull; Bulldog Drummond Strikes Back*
◆ Prominent character: Bulldog Drummond
Note: Bulldog Drummond series continued by his friend Gerard Fairlie after author's death.

A. A. Milne — *The Red House Mystery*

Magdalen Nabb — *Death in Springtime; The Marshal and the Murderer; The Marshal and the Madwoman*
◆ Prominent character: Marshal Salvatore Guarnaccia

Peter O'Donnell — *Modesty Blaise* series
◆ Prominent character: Modesty Blaise
Note: Female James Bond–type character

Baroness Orczy — *The Scarlet Pimpernel*
Note: Classic spy novel.

Marco Page — *The Shadowy Third*
◆ Prominent character: Joel Glass (detective)
Note: Often had funny private eye.

Ellis Peters — *One Corpse Too Many; St. Peter's Fair; The Leper of St. Giles; The Sanctuary Sparrow; Dead Man's Ransom; The Confessions of Brother Haluin; The Pilgrim of Hate; The Heretic's Apprentice*
◆ Prominent character: Brother Cadfael

Edgar Allan Poe — *The Masque of the Red Death; The Fall of the House of Usher; The Pit and the Pendulum; The Tell-Tale Heart; The Murders in the Rue Morgue; The Mystery of Marie Roget; The Gold Bug; The Purloined Letter*
◆ Prominent character: C. Auguste Dupin
Note: Also wrote mysterious poems; see List 138, Poe: Complete Stories and Poems.

Joyce Porter — *Only with a Bargepole* (humorous)

Melville Post — *Nabath's Vineyard*
◆ Prominent character: Uncle Abner

Anthony Price — *The Labyrinth Makers; Our Man in Camelot; War Game*
Note: Historical mysteries.

*Ellery Queen — *The Lamp of God; The Roman Hat Mystery;* seventy anthologies
◆ Prominent character: Ellery Queen

*Ruth Rendell — *Live Flesh; Talking to Strange Men; The Veiled One; A Dark-Adapted Eye; A Fatal Inversion; A House of Stairs; A New Lease of Death*

Mary Roberts Rinehart — *The Circular Staircase; The Bat* (play); *The Amazing Adventures of Letitia Carbarry; Tish*
Note: Invented "had I but known" school of detective novels.

*Sax Rohmer — *Dr. Fu Manchu; Re-enter Fu Manchu; The Return of Fu;* thirteen-book series of mysteries.
◆ Prominent character: Fu Manchu

Lawrence Sanders — *The Anderson Tapes; The First Deadly Sin; The Sixth Commandment; The Case of Lucy Bending; The Fourth Deadly Sin; The Timothy Files*
Note: Some perversity.

Dorothy L. Sayers — *The Bone of Contention; Clouds of Witness; Murder Must Advertise; Suspicion; The Documents in the Case* (co-authored); *The Nine Tailors; Busman's Honeymoon; Strong Poison* (twelve novels, forty-five short stories); *Lord Peter* (twenty-one mystery stories)
◆ Prominent characters: Lord Peter Wimsey and wife, Harriet; Montague Egg

Mary Wollstonecraft Shelley — *Frankenstein, or the Modern Prometheus*
◆ Prominent character: Dr. Frankenstein
Note: Radical feminist; eloped with poet Percy Bysshe Shelley at age 18.

Georges Simenon — *The Strange Case of Peter the Lett; The Patience of Maigret; The Man Who Watched the Trains Go By; Maigret's Memoirs; The Girl with a Squint*
◆ Prominent character: Inspector Maigret
Note: Violent crimes.

Maj Sjöwall — *Roseanna; The Laughing Policeman; Murder at the Savoy; The Locked Room; The Terrorists*
◆ Prominent character: Martin Beck
Note: Wrote with husband, Per Wahlöö; police procedural novels.

Martin Cruz Smith — *Gorky Park; Stallion Gate; Nightwing; Polar Star*

Mickey Spillane — *The Girl Hunters; I, the Jury; My Gun Is Quick; The Big Kill*
◆ Prominent character: Mike Hammer
Note: One of originators of Captain Marvel and Captain America of comic book fame; starred in his own movie version of *Girl Hunters.*

Mary Stewart — *Nine Coaches Waiting; My Brother Michael; The Ivy Tree; The Moon-Spinners.*
Note: Romantic suspense novels.

Bram Stoker — *Dracula*

Rex Stout — *Instead of Evidence; Fer-de-Lance; Too Many Cooks; Some Buried Caesar; Black Orchids; The Black Mountain; The Doorbell Rang; Gambit*
◆ Prominent characters: Nero Wolfe and Archie Goodwin

*Edward Stratemeyer — Tom Swift series; Nancy Drew series; Bobbsey Twins series; Hardy Boys series; Dana Girls series
◆ Prominent characters: As shown in titles above
Note: Literature for youth

Julian Symons — *The Immaterial Murder Case; The Progress of a Crime; The Man who Killed Himself*

*Josephine Tey — *The Man in the Queue; A Shilling for Candles; Miss Pym Disposes; The Daughter of Time; The Singing Sands*
- ◆ Prominent character: Alan Grant

Robert Traver — *Anatomy of a Murder*

*S. S. Van Dine — *The Benson Murder Case; The Bishop Murder Case; The Gracie Allen Murder Case; The Winter Murder Case; The Dragon Murder Case*
- ◆ Prominent character: Philo Vance

Per Wahöö — *The Thirty-first Floor; The Steel Spring*
- ◆ Prominent character: Inspector Chief Jensen and Martin Beck
- *Note:* Wrote with his wife, Maj Sjöwall, and separately.

Edgar Wallace — *The Clue of the Twisted Candle; The Green Archer; On the Spot; My Hollywood Diary*

Joseph Wambaugh — *The Secrets of Harry Bright; Lines and Shadows*
- *Note:* See also List 64, The Novel Masters (American).

Hillary Waugh — *The Missing Man*

Patricia Wentworth — *Grey Mask; The Listening Eye; Beggar's Choice; Outrageous Fortune; Poison in the Pen; Mr. Zero*
- ◆ Prominent character: Miss Silver

*Donald Westlake — *Killing Time; The Fugitive Pigeon; The Hot Rock; Bank Shot; Jimmy the Kid; Nobody's Perfect; A Likely Story; Trust Me on This; Good Behavior* (humorous); *God Save the Mark* (humorous); *High Adventure* (humorous); *Why Me* (humorous)
- *Note:* Hard-boiled novels and humorous crime novels.

Phyllis Whitney — *Mystery of the Haunted Pool; Secret of the Emerald Star; Seven Tears for Apollo; The Winter People; Spindrift; Rainsong; Feather on the Moon*
- *Note:* Literature for youth.

P. G. Wodehouse — *Jeeves and the Tie That Binds; How Right You Are, Jeeves; Cat-Nappers; Stiff Upper Lip, Jeeves.*

43. Detective Stories: Sherlock Holmes

Considered by many to be the best detective fiction in English literature, the Sherlock Holmes stories, written by Sir Arthur Conan Doyle, were published in nine separate books. Below is a list of every Sherlock Holmes story written and the books in which they originally appeared. Want to become a Sherlock expert? You have your work cut out for you! For other detective stories, see List 42, Detective and Spy Stories/Thrillers/Mysteries.

A Study in Scarlet

The Sign of Four

Adventures of Sherlock Holmes
  A Scandal in Bohemia
  The Red-headed League
  A Case of Identity
  The Boscombe Valley Mystery
  The Five Orange Pips
  The Man with the Twisted Lip
  The Adventure of the Blue Carbuncle
  The Adventure of the Speckled Band
  The Adventure of the Engineer's Thumb
  The Adventure of the Noble Bachelor
  The Adventure of the Beryl Coronet
  The Adventure of the Copper Beeches

Memoirs of Sherlock Holmes
  Silver Blaze
  The Yellow Face
  The Stockbroker's Clerk
  The "Gloria Scott"
  The Musgrave Ritual
  The Reigate Squire
  The Crooked Man
  The Resident Patient
  The Greek Interpreter
  The Naval Treaty
  The Final Problem

The Return of Sherlock Holmes
  The Adventure of the Empty House
  The Adventure of the Norwood Builder
  The Adventure of the Dancing Men
  The Adventure of the Solitary Cyclist
  The Adventure of the Priory School
  The Adventure of Black Peter

  The Adventure of Charles Augustus
    Milverton
  The Adventure of the Six Napoleons
  The Adventure of the Three Students
  The Adventure of the Golden Pince-Nez
  The Adventure of the Missing Three-Quarter
  The Adventure of the Abbey Grange
  The Adventure of the Second Stain

The Hound of the Baskervilles

The Valley of Fear

His Last Bow
  The Adventure of Wisteria Lodge
  The Adventure of the Cardboard Box
  The Adventure of the Red Circle
  The Adventure of the Bruce-Partington
    Plans
  The Adventure of the Dying Detective
  The Disappearance of Lady Frances Carfax
  The Adventure of the Devil's Foot
  His Last Bow

The Case Book of Sherlock Holmes
  The Adventure of the Illustrious Client
  The Adventure of the Blanched Soldier
  The Adventure of the Mazarin Stone
  The Adventure of the Three Gables
  The Adventure of the Sussex Vampire
  The Adventure of the Three Garridebs
  The Problem of Thor Bridge
  The Adventure of the Creeping Man
  The Adventure of the Lion's Mane
  The Adventure of the Veiled Lodger
  The Adventure of Shoscombe Old Place
  The Adventure of the Retired Colourman

Other Works of Sir Arthur Conan Doyle
- A Duet
- A New Revelation (book on spiritualism)
- Beyond the City
- History of Spiritualism
- History of the British Campaign in France and Flanders
- Micah Clarke
- My Memories and Adventures (autobiography)
- Round the Red Lamp
- Sir Nigel
- The Captain of the Pole Star
- The Doings of Raffles Haw
- The Fires of Fate (play)
- The Firm of Girdlestone
- The Great Boer War
- The Poison Belt (play)
- The Refugees
- The Stark Munro Letters
- The War in South Africa: Its Causes and Conduct
- The White Company
- Uncle Bernac

44. DOCUMENTS: HISTORICAL AND QUASI-LITERARY

A number of important documents, some of high literary quality, have recorded and influenced the history of the world. Listed below are the documents everyone should at least recognize, along with their main themes and approximate dates of writing or official adoption. See also List 139, Religion: Bible; and List 143, Religious Documents and Holy Literature.

1750 B.C. **Code of Hammurabi** (oldest legal codes; Babylonian)

1000 B.C. **Old Testament** (religious teachings)

590 B.C. **Laws of Solon** (establishment of democracy in Athens)

100 A.D. **New Testament** (Christian teachings)

313 A.D. **Edict of Milan** (religious freedom to Christians)

640 A.D. **Koran** (Muhammad's teachings)

1215 A.D. **Magna Carta** (King John's guarantee of freedoms)

1517 A.D. **Martin Luther's Theses** (Protestant Reformation began)

1534 A.D. **Act of Supremacy** (Church of England established)

1566 A.D. **Catechism of the Council of Trent** (Catholic reforms)

1620 A.D. **The Mayflower Compact** (Pilgrims' first "constitution")

1776 A.D. **Declaration of Independence** (U.S. free from Great Britain)

1781 A.D. **Articles of Confederation** (thirteen original states' statement of rights and responsibilities)

1787 A.D. **Federalist Papers** (series of essays and pamphlets supporting ratification of U.S. Constitution)

1787 A.D. **Constitution of the United States** (beginning of the present U.S. system of government)

1791 A.D. **Bill of Rights** (first ten amendments to Constitution)

1804 A.D. **Code Napoleon** (French civil law)

1848 A.D. **Communist Manifesto** (communist philosophy by Marx and Engels)

1861 A.D. **Edict of Emancipation** (serfs given freedom in Russia)

1862 A.D. **Emancipation Proclamation** (freeing Confederate slaves)

1892 A.D. **Pledge of Allegiance** (Francis Bellamy)

1917 A.D. **The American's Creed** (William Tyler Page)

1918 A.D. **Fourteen Points** (President Wilson's peace plan after World War I)

1925 A.D. **Mein Kampf** (Hitler's Nazi philosophy)

1931 A.D. **Statute of Westminster** (colonies of Britain freed)

1941 A.D. **Atlantic Charter** (Roosevelt/Churchill peace plan)

1945 A.D. **United Nations Charter** (United Nations created)

1947 A.D. **Truman Doctrine** (Truman's Cold War policy began)

1948 A.D. **Universal Declaration of Human Rights** (United Nations)

1962 A.D. **Pastoral Constitution on the Church in the Modern World** (Second Vatican Council's views of Catholicism)

1978 A.D. **Camp David Accords** (Egypt/Israel peace agreements)

1979 A.D. **Panama Canal Treaties** (gradual ending of U.S. control of canal)

1979 A.D. **SALT II** (treaty between U.S.S.R and U.S. limiting strategic arms)

1990 A.D. **German Reunification Pact** (reuniting of East and West Germany)

1992 A.D. **Bush/Yeltsin Joint Statement** (formal end of Cold War)

1992 A.D. **Declaration of Commonwealth of Independent States** (end of Soviet Union; beginning of Soviet commonwealth)

45. EPICS

Epics are long works (poetry, prose, or drama) usually describing incidents in the lives of heroes and heroines, often figures from history or folklore who are portrayed as larger than life in their powers and emotions. The earliest epics were oral, and the epic as an oral art form continues to flourish in Africa. The following are famous epics of different types. (Some epics may be listed in more than one category.)

CLASSICAL EPICS

Aeneid — Virgil
Iliad — Homer
Odyssey — Homer

NATIONAL EPICS

Beowulf (Anglo-Saxon)
The Cid (Spanish)
Gilgamesh (Sumerian)
Kavevala (Finnish)
The Lusiad (Portuguese)
Mahabharata (Hindu)
Nibelungenlied (German)
The Song of Roland (French)
Sundiata (West African)
The Volsunga Saga (Scandinavian)

RENAISSANCE EPICS

Faerie Queen — Spenser
Gerusalemme Liberata — Tasso
Orlando Furioso — Ariosto
Paradise Lost — Milton
Paradise Regained — Milton

MOCK-HEROIC EPICS

The Battle of the Books — Swift
Don Juan — Byron
Don Quixote — Cervantes
The Dunciad — Pope
Hudibras — Butler
The Lectern — Boileau
Macflecknoe — Dryden
The Rape of the Lock — Pope
Sir Thopas — Chaucer (part of
    Canterbury Tales)
Tom Jones — Fielding

EPIC NOVELS

The Brothers Karamazov — Dostoyevsky
Doctor Zhivago — Pasternak
Don Quixote — Cervantes
*The Life and Opinions of Tristram
    Shandy, Gentleman* — Sterne
Moby Dick — Melville
Tom Jones — Fielding
Ulysses — Joyce
War and Peace — Tolstoy

EPIC DRAMAS

Faust — Goethe
Mother Courage — Brecht
Ten Days that Shook the World — Eisenstein

OTHER EPIC POEMS

The Anathemata — Jones
Cantos — Pound
Crow — Hughes
The Divine Comedy — Dante
Drake — Noyes
Four Quartets — Eliot
Hiawatha — Longfellow
John Brown's Body — Benet
Leaves of Grass — Whitman
Maximus — Olson
Metamorphoses — Ovid
Paterson — Williams
Prelude — Wordsworth
Ring and the Book — Browning

46. ESSAYS: COLLECTIONS

The following essays are quoted, imitated, and discussed by those well-versed in literature. All serious readers would do well to have at least a cursory acquaintance with them and their major premises. They are presented in approximate chronological order.

"The Defence of Poesie (An Apologie for Poetrie)" — Sir Philip Sidney (1595)
First English essay of literary criticism

"Areopagitica" — John Milton (1644)
Attacks censorship laws in England

"An Essay of Dramatic Poesy" — John Dryden (1668)
Critical essay

"Essay on Criticism" — Alexander Pope (1711)
Summary of neoclassical literary doctrine

"Essay on the Theater" — Oliver Goldsmith (eighteenth century)
Attacks sentimental comedies that stress the virtues of private life without showing the vices

"Moral Essays" — Alexander Pope (1731–35)
Four essays on ethics

"Essays on Crimes and Punishments" — Cesare Beccaria (1764)
Influenced criminal justice system; advocates punishment only when necessary to maintain order; against capital punishment

"Essay on the Nature and Immutability of Truth" — James Beattie (1770)
Disputes views of David Hume, who was skeptical of truth based on superstition or authority

"Essay on the Principle of Population" — Thomas Malthus (1798)
Analyzes the role of famine, disease, and other factors as natural limits of population growth; maintains that population growth is exponential and can outstrip the food supply

"On the Knocking at the Gate in Macbeth" — Thomas de Quincey (early nineteenth century)Literary criticism

"The Four Ages of Poetry" — Thomas Love Peacock (1820)
Ironic criticism of Romantic poetry; inspired Shelley's work

"A Defence of Poetry" — Percy Bysshe Shelley (1821)
Defends value of poets to civilization and the value of poets' imaginations.

"Table Talk" — William Hazlitt (1821–22)
Collection of critical and personal essays

"The Plain Speaker" — William Hazlitt (1826)
Collection of critical and personal essays

"On Hallam's Constitutional History" — Thomas Babington Macaulay (1828)
Refers to the press as a "fourth estate"

"Rural Rides" — William Cobbett (1830)
Essays on changes in rural life because of the Industrial Revolution

"The Defence of Poetry" — Henry Wadsworth Longfellow (1832)
Forerunner of Emerson's philosophy; condemns sentimentality and advocates intellectual freedom

"Nature" — Ralph Waldo Emerson (1836)
Says that transcendence can be found through self-knowledge, self-reliance, and contemplation of nature

"The American Scholar" — Ralph Waldo Emerson (1837)
Declares intellectual independence from Old World literature and the thought of England and Europe

"Essay on the Development of Christian Doctrine" — John Henry Newman (1845)
Expresses views on the development of Christian dogma

"Culture and Anarchy" — Matthew Arnold (1869)
Discussion of political and social issues in England and the role of literary culture in the life of the nation

"The Works of Max Beerbohm" — Max Beerbohm (1896)
Collection of humorous and satiric essays

"More" — Max Beerbohm (1899)
Collection of humorous and satiric essays

"Yet Again" — Max Beerbohm (1899)
Collection of humorous and satiric essays

"The Castilian Soul" — José Martinez Ruiz (a.k.a. Azorin) (1900)
Collection of essays by Spanish author

"Art in the Age of Mechanical Reproduction" — Walter Benjamin (early twentieth century)
Argues that technology that can reproduce art may also destroy art

"Essays" — Sir Rabindranath Tagore (late nineteenth and early twentieth century)
Forty volumes of essays mostly on man's search for God and truth

"Puritanism as a Literary Force" — H. L. Mencken (1917)
Identifies puritanism as the root of most American problems

"Shandygaff" — Christopher Morley (1918)
Essay and sketch collection

"Prejudices" — H. L. Mencken (1919–27)
Six volumes of essays

"The Sacred Wood" — T. S. Eliot (1920)
Collection of essays; rejects values of English Romantic poets (subjectivity and romanticism); champions modernism with its objectivity and tradition

"And Even Now" — Max Beerbohm (1920)
Collection of humorous and satiric essays

"The Strange Necessity" — Rebecca West (a.k.a. Dame Cicily Andrews) (1928)
Collection of essays

"Politics and the English Language" — George Orwell (1940)
Describes political jargon

"The Ironing Board" — Christopher Morley (1949)
Essay and sketch collection

"The Shores of Light" — Edmund Wilson (1952)
Collection of literary criticism

"Noblesse Oblige" — Nancy Mitford (1956)
Tongue-in-cheek essay about upper-class and lower-class usage

"Anatomy of Criticism: Four Essays" — Northrup Frye (1957)
Controversial analysis of literary Judeo-Christian archetypes

"Reflections of a Jacobite" — Louis Auchincloss (1961)
Collection of essays on Henry James

"The Fire Next Time" — James Baldwin (1963)
Exposes and condemns racial injustice in the United States

"Shadow and Act" — Ralph Ellison (1964)
Political, social, and critical essays exploring issues that affect the African-American artist

"The Literature of Exhaustion" — John Barth (1967)
Argues that literary forms of fiction have all been exhausted; authors have to rewrite work already written

"Essays of Four Decades" — Allen Tate (1969)
"Tension in Poetry" is statement of principles of the New Criticism (first expounded in 1938)

"Mystery and Manners" — Flannery O'Connor (1969)
Essay and lecture collection

"Notes on an Endangered Species" —
   Mordecai Richler (1974)
   Collection of essays

*"Spiritus Mundi: Essays on Literature, Myth,
   and Society"* — Northrup Frye (1976)
   Collection of essays

"Essays" — E. B. White (1977)
   Collection of essays

"The White Album" — Joan Didion (1979)
   Collection of essays of events of the times

"Joshua Then and Now" — Mordecai
   Richler (1980)
   Collection of essays

"The Gift of the Good Land" — Wendall
   Berry (1981)
   Expounds on agriculture's importance in
   the balance and structure of human life

"A Few Minutes with Andy Rooney" — Andy
   Rooney (1981)
   Collection of witty essays

"Cross Sections: From a Decade of Change" —
   Elizabeth Janeway (1982)
   About the women's movement and literature
   written by women from 1972 to 1982

"Second Words" — Margaret Atwood (1982)
   Critical essays

"The Second Life of Art" — Eugenio
   Montale (1982)
   Collection of essays

*"World Outside the Window: The Selected
   Essays of Kenneth Rexroth"* — Kenneth
   Rexroth (1987)
   Collection of essays

47. ESSAYS: INFORMAL

The following essays are called informal (or familiar) essays because their main purpose is to entertain and express ideas in a lighthearted manner, rather than to inform in a more serious way.

from *The Sketchbook* — Washington Irving
   "Philip of Pokanoket: An Indian Memoir"; "The Spectre Bridegroom"

"The Test" — James Milling Witherow

from *Life with Father* — Clarence Day
   "Father Opens My Mail"

from *You Know Charles* — Margaret Breuning
   "He Tries a Cafeteria"

"How to Make History Dates Stick" — Mark Twain

from *Essays of Elia* — Charles Lamb
   "A Dissertation on Roast Pig"; "Christ's Hospital Five and Thirty Years Ago";
   "On the Tragedies of Shakespeare…"

"The Fate of Melpomenus Jones" — Stephen Leacock

"Sir Roger at Church" — Joseph Addison

"Getting Up on Cold Mornings" — Leigh Hunt

"An Apology for Idlers" — Robert Louis Stevenson

"My Last Walk with the Schoolmistress" — Oliver Wendell Holmes

"The Newness of the Old" — Edward Verrall Lucas

"How to Live on Twenty-four Hours a Day" — Arnold Bennett

from *Americans and Others* — Agnes Repplier
"The Greatest of These is Charity"

from *Behind the Beyond* — Stephen Leacock
"Homer and Humbug"

from *The Comforts of Home* — Ralph Bergengren
"Furnace and I"

from *The Patient Observer* — Simeon Strunsky
"Interrogation"

from *Mince Pie* — Christopher Morley
"On Unanswering Letters"

"Why are Women Like That?" — Irvin S. Cobb

48. ESSAY MASTERS

Many of these authors wrote novels, short stories, or works in other genres, but all were masters of the essay. Their essays often provide surprising insights into their personalities and views, as well as reflecting the mores, philosophies, and changes taking place in the times in which they lived. See also List 46, Essays: Collections; and List 148, Transcendentalists.

SIXTEENTH- AND SEVENTEENTH-CENTURY ESSAYISTS

Michel de Montaigne — entertaining; (originator of essay form)
Sir Francis Bacon — didactic
Sir Thomas Browne — spiritual, quasi-scientific
Abraham Cowley — entertaining
Sir William Temple — literary

EIGHTEENTH-CENTURY ESSAYISTS

Alexander Pope — literary
John Dryden — literary criticism
Joseph Addison — humorous; satiric
Richard Steele — humorous; satiric
Samuel Johnson — serious
Oliver Goldsmith — lighthearted
Jonathan Swift — satiric

NINETEENTH-CENTURY ESSAYISTS

Charles Lamb — entertaining

Leigh Hunt — personal

William Hazlitt — personal

Washington Irving — story-like sketches

Thomas Babington Macaulay — serious; critical; historical

Thomas Carlyle — serious

Matthew Arnold — cultural

John Ruskin — theoretical

John Newman — about faith

Walter Pater — art critiques

Ralph Waldo Emerson — philosophical

Oliver Wendell Holmes — humorous

James Russell Lowell — humorous

Robert Louis Stevenson — entertaining

Thomas de Quincey — literary criticism; informal

Henry David Thoreau — about nature; critical

Agnes Repplier — informal; witty

Oscar Wilde — literary

Charles Augustin Sainte-Beuve — literary

TWENTIETH-CENTURY ESSAYISTS

James Thurber — informal; witty

Hilaire Belloc — informal

Christopher Morley — humorous; intimate; philosophical

Max Beerbohm — witty; satiric

David Grayson — narrative

John Galsworthy — about social change

Arnold Bennett — literary criticism; social life

Stephen Leacock — witty; nonsensical

Ralph Bergengren — humorous

Simeon Strunsky — humorous

Heywood Broun — caustic; humorous

Irvin S. Cobb — humorous

George Bernard Shaw — literary criticism

T. S. Eliot — literary criticism

Ezra Pound — literary

Jean-Paul Sartre — literary; existential

Norman Mailer — political; literary

Howard Nemerov — ironic

James Thurber — humorous; satiric

Garrison Keillor — humorous

Andy Rooney — humorous

Virginia Woolf — feminist; literary

49. FABLES: AESOP

The sheer number of fables attributed to Aesop is sufficient to ensure his everlasting fame, and the morals illustrated by his tales are still worthy of attention and study. Aesop's fables were first written down in the sixth century B.C., but not published until 2000 years later. Since then, they have been translated into almost every language and are perhaps the most widely read fables in world literature. Legends say Aesop was a Greek slave who told stories to his king to win his freedom. However, no one knows exactly how the fables originated. The following list provides the titles of Aesop's fables and the specific lessons they are meant to convey.

Androcles and the Lion
Gratitude is a quality not limited to man.

The Ant and the Dove
One good turn deserves another.

The Ant and the Grasshopper
Be thrifty and prepare today for what you need tomorrow.

The Arab and the Camel
A level path pleases the laden beast.

The Ass and His Driver
A willful beast must go his own way.

The Ass and His Masters
He who finds discontentment in one place is not likely to find happiness in another.

The Ass and the Grasshopper
Even a fool is wise when it is too late.

The Ass and the Lap Dog
It is better to be satisfied with your lot than to desire that for which you are not fit to receive.

The Ass Carrying Salt
An old trick may be played once too often.

The Ass Eating Thistles
One man's meat is another man's poison.

The Ass in the Lion's Skin
Clothes may disguise a fool, but his words will give him away.

The Ass's Shadow
Too many disagreements have nothing but a shadow for a basis.

The Ass, the Cock, and the Lion
False confidence is the forerunner of misfortune.

The Bald Knight
Your pride is but the prologue of your shame.

Belling the Cat
It is one thing to suggest a plan, but harder to carry it out.

The Belly and the Other Members
In the body and in the state, each member must work for the common good.

The Birds, the Beasts, and the Bat
He winds up friendless who plays both sides against the middle.

The Blind Man and the Whelp
The child is father to the man.

The Boasting Traveler
He who does a thing well does not need to boast.

The Boy and the Filberts
Half a loaf is better than none.

The Boy Bathing
There is a time and place for everything.

The Bull and the Goat
Those who take advantage of their neighbors' difficulties may live to regret it.

The Bundle of Sticks
In union there is strength.

The Cat and the Fox
One plan that works is better than a hundred doubtful ones.

The Cat and the Mice
He who is once deceived is doubly cautious.

The Cock and the Fox
The best liars often get caught in their own lies.

The Country Mouse and the Town Mouse
A crust eaten in peace is better than a banquet partaken in anxiety.

The Creaking Wheels
He who cries loudest is often the least hurt.

The Crow and the Pitcher
Necessity is the mother of invention.

The Dog and the Shadow
Grasp at the shadow and lose the substance.

The Dog in the Manger
Don't begrudge others what you yourself cannot use.

The Dog Invited to Supper
They who enter by the back stairs may expect to be shown out at the window.

The Eagle and the Arrow
We often supply our enemies with the means of our own destruction.

The Eagle and the Beetle
The laws of hospitality are not to be broken with impunity.

The Eagle and the Crow
It requires more than wings to be an eagle.

The Eagle and the Fox
Do unto others as you would have them do unto you.

The Eagle, the Wildcat, and the Sow
Gossips are to be seen and not heard.

The Falconer and the Partridge
Treachery is the worst crime of all.

The Farmer and his Dogs
When a neighbor's house is on fire, you better look at yours.

The Farmer and his Sons
Industry sometimes pays unexpected dividends.

The Farmer and the Nightingale
A bird in the cage is worth two on a branch.

The Farmer and the Snake
Don't expect gratitude from the wicked.

The Farmer and the Stork
You are judged by the company you keep.

The Farthing Rushlight
Know your place and keep it.

The Father and his Two Daughters
You can't please everybody.

The Fighting Cocks and the Eagle
Pride goes before a fall.

The Fir Tree and the Bramble
The humble are safe from many dangers to which the proud are subject.

The Fisherman Piping
To do the right thing at the right time is a great art.

The Fox and the Bramble
All are selfish to the selfish.

The Fox and the Crow
Don't trust flatterers.

The Fox and the Goat
Don't trust the advice of a man in difficulties.

The Fox and the Grapes
Don't trust the advice of a man in trouble.

The Fox and the Hedgehog
A needy thief steals more than one who enjoys plenty.

The Fox and the Lion
Familiarity breeds contempt.

The Fox and the Stork
Many go out for wool and come home shorn themselves.

The Fox and the Woodman
There is as much malice in a wink as in a word.

The Fox without a Tail
Misery loves company.

The Frog and the Ox
Conceit leads to destruction.

The Frogs Desiring a King
Let well enough alone.

The Gardener and his Dog
Don't bite the hand that feeds you.

The Gnat and the Bull
The smaller the mind, the greater the conceit.

The Goatherd and the Goats
People who neglect old friends for new justly lose both.

The Goose with the Golden Eggs
The over-greedy lose all.

The Hare and the Hound
Necessity is our strongest weapon.

The Hare and the Tortoise
Slow and steady wins the race.

The Hares and the Frogs
There is always someone who is worse off than you are.

The Hare with Many Friends
He who has many friends often has no friends.

The Hawk and the Farmer
Hypocrisy is the cloak of villainy.

The Hawk and the Pigeons
If you voluntarily put yourself under the power of a tyrant, you deserve whatever you get.

The Hedge and the Vineyard
They also serve who only stand and wait.

The Heifer and the Ox
He laughs best who laughs last.

The Hen and the Cat
Uninvited guests are often most welcome when they are gone.

The Hen and the Fox
Beware of an insincere friend.

Hercules and the Wagoner
The gods help them that help themselves.

The Horse and the Groom
A man may smile and still be a villain.

The Horse and the Laden Ass
A bad temper carries with it its own punishment.

The Horse and the Lion
The best laid-out scheme often has a kickback.

The Horse and the Stag
Liberty is too high a price to pay for revenge.

The House Dog and the Wolf
It is better to be thin and free than fat and a slave.

Jupiter, Neptune, Minerva, and Momus
It is time to criticize the works of others when you have done something good yourself.

Jupiter and the Bee
He who prays against others brings a curse upon himself.

The Kid and the Wolf
If you must criticize your neighbor, first be sure he can't reach you.

The Lark and her Young Ones
If you want a job well done, do it yourself.

The Lion and his Three Counselors
In dangerous times wise men say nothing.

The Lion and the Ass Go Hunting
Braggarts usually are laughed at in the end.

The Lion and the Bulls
United we stand; divided we fall.

The Lion and the Dolphin
When you choose allies, look to their power as well as their will to help you.

The Lion and the Goat
It's better to drink second at the spring than be food for the vultures.

The Lion and the Mouse
No act of kindness, however small, is ever wasted.

The Lion and the Other Beasts Go Hunting
Many may share in the labors, but not in the spoils.

The Lioness
Quality is more important than quantity.

The Lion in Love
Even the wildest beast can be tamed by love.

The Lion, the Ass, and the Fox
We learn by others' problems.

The Lion, the Bear, and the Fox
Only fools fight to exhaustion while a rogue runs off with the dinner.

The Man and his Two Wives
Yield to the whims of all and you soon will have nothing to yield at all.

The Man and the Lion
We are but sorry witnesses in our own cause.

The Man and the Satyr
Some men can blow hot and cold with the same breath.

The Mercury and the Sculptor
He who seeks a compliment sometimes discovers the truth.

The Mice in Council
It is one thing to propose something, another to execute it.

The Milkmaid and her Pail
Don't count your chickens before they're hatched.

The Miller, His Son, and their Donkey
If you try to please everyone, you end up pleasing none.

The Mischievous Dog
Men often mistake notoriety for fame.

The Miser
The true value of money is not in its possession, but in its use.

The Monkey and the Camel
Don't stretch your arm any farther than your sleeve will reach.

The Monkey and the Dolphin
Those who pretend to be what they aren't sooner or later find themselves in deep water.

The Mountain in Labor
Magnificent promises often end in paltry performances.

The Mountebank and the Farmer
Do not denounce the genuine only to applaud the imitation.

The Mouse and the Frog
He who plays to destroy his neighbor often is caught in his own snare.

The Mouse and the Weasel
Don't covet more than you can carry.

The Mule
Every truth has two sides.

The Nurse and the Wolf
Enemies' promises are made to be broken.

The Oak and the Reed
It is better to bend than to break.

The Old Man and Death
How sorry we would be if all our wishes were granted.

The Old Woman and her Maids
Too much cunning overreaches itself.

The Old Woman and the Physician
He who plays a trick must be prepared to take a joke.

The One-Eyed Doe
Trouble comes from the direction we least expect.

The Porcupine and the Snakes
It is safer to know your guest before offering hospitality.

The Quack Frog
Physician, heal thyself.

The Raven and the Swan
A change of scene doesn't change your character.

The Shepherd and the Sea
Trust not in him that seems a saint.

The Sick Lion
Don't believe all you hear.

The Stag and the Vine
Don't throw stones into the well that quenched your thirst.

The Stag at the Pool
Sometimes we despise the things that are most useful to us.

The Stag in the Ox Stall
There is no eye like the master's.

The Swallow's Advice
Unless the seed of evil is destroyed, it will grow up to destroy us.

The Shepherd Boy and the Wolf
Liars aren't believed even when they tell the truth.

The Thief and his Mother
Spare the rod and spoil the child.

The Thief and the Boy
He who tries to outsmart his neighbor winds up outsmarting himself.

The Thief and the Dog
A bribe in hand betrays mischief at heart.

The Three Tradesmen
It is hard to see beyond one's own nose.

The Tortoise and the Eagle
Vanity carries its own punishment.

The Travelers and the Bear
Don't trust a friend who is liable to desert you when trouble comes.

The Travelers and the Hatchet
He who won't allow his friend to share the prize must not expect him to share the danger.

The Trees and the Ax
They are foolish who give their enemies the means of destroying them.

The Trumpeter Taken Prisoner
He who incites to strife is worse than he who takes part in it.

The Two Crabs
Example is the best precept.

The Two Frogs
Think twice before you leap.

The Two Pots
Avoid too powerful neighbors.

The Vain Crow
Happiness is not found in borrowed finery.

Venus and the Cat
What is bred in the bone will not be absent in the flesh.

The Widow and the Hen
Figures don't lie, but they won't make a hen lay.

The Wild Boar and the Fox
It's too late to whet the sword when the trumpet sounds.

The Wind and the Sun
Persuasion is better than force.

The Wolf and the Crane
Those who live on expectation are sure to be disappointed.

The Wolf and the Goat
Beware of a friend with an ulterior motive.

The Wolf and the Lamb
Any excuse will serve a tyrant.

The Wolf and the Shepherds
Men are apt to condemn in others the very things they do themselves.

The Wolf in Sheep's Clothing
Appearances may deceive.

The Young Man and the Swallow
There is no profit in blaming your foolish mistakes on foolish advisers.

50. FAIRY TALES

Everyone should be familiar with the literary genre of fairy tales, because they are lively stories in themselves and also contain characters and situations that are alluded to in other literature. Fairy tales often contain fictional, supernatural creatures who intervene in human affairs through magic. Brownies, elves, goblins, trolls, dwarfs, pixies, and mythical royalty abound. See also List 51, Fairy Tales/Folktales/Myths/Legends: Collections.

MAJOR OLDER COLLECTIONS OF FAIRY TALES AND FOLKTALES

Charles Perrault's *Mother Goose's Fairy Tales*

Joseph Jacob's *English Fairy Tales*

Joseph Jacob's *More English Fairy Tales*

Joseph Jacob's *Celtic Fairy Tales*

Hans Christian Andersen's *Fairy Tales*

Grimm Brothers' *Fairy Tales*

Andrew Lang's *Blue, Red, Green (etc.) Fairy Books*

William Butler Yeats' *Irish Fairy Tales*

Thomas Croker's *Fairy Legends and Traditions of the South of Ireland*

Peter Asbjornsen and Jorgen Moe's *Popular Tales from the Norse*

Richard Chase's *The Jack Tales* (Appalachian)

Frances Olcott's *The Red Indian Fairy Book*

The Arabian Nights (The Thousand and One Nights), a collection of stories of unknown origin from India and the Middle East, often involving magic and imaginative adventures, is sometimes considered a collection of fairy tales.

ANNOTATED LIST OF FAMILIAR FAIRY TALES (AND A FEW LESS FAMOUS ONES)

The Adventures of a Brownie — Book about the mischievous adventures of a brownie, who lives in a coal cellar and becomes a friend to the children of the household.

Aladdin and the Wonderful Lamp — The story of the problems of a tailor's son, Aladdin, who was given a magic lamp and ring, married a princess, and finally ruled a kingdom.

The Ass, the Table, and the Stick — Fairy tale about Jack, an abused boy, and the magical objects that bring him a lovely wife.

Beauty and the Beast — Fairy tale about a beautiful girl, whose love for an ugly beast turns him into a handsome prince.

Boots and His Brothers — Fairy tale about curious Boots and his two brothers, who thought he wondered about things too much. By investigating an ax that chops by itself, a spade that digs by itself, and a walnut that yields water, Boots is able to win a kingdom and princess.

The Brownie of Blednock — Scottish fairy tale about a brownie named Aiken-Drum, who strenuously objects to being paid for his services, because he would then have to leave his friends.

Childe Rowland — Fairy tale about King Arthur's sons and his daughter, Burd Ellen. The youngest son, Childe Rowland, finally rescues Burd Ellen and her brothers from the Elf King, after slaying many adversaries along the way.

Cinderella — Fairy tale about an ill-treated girl, whose fairy godmother magically gets her to a dance where she loses her shoe, only to have it returned by a handsome prince who offers her marriage.

The Emperor's New Clothes — Story about an emperor who walks naked through the streets, assured by flatterers that his new clothes look wonderful, until a child blurts out the truth.

Farmer Tom and the Leprechaun — Irish fairy tale about the farmer's meeting with a leprechaun, who promises to bring him riches but deceives him instead.

The Golden Bird — Fairy tale of a boy, his brothers, and a wise fox, who keeps giving the boy advice (which he refuses to follow) to help him find a golden bird, a golden horse, and a princess. The boy finally does what the fox says and the story ends happily for all.

Goldilocks and the Three Bears — Story about a girl who visits the home of three bears, tries out their food, their chairs, and their beds, and is discovered sleeping in the little bear's bed.

Hansel and Gretel — Fairy tale about a wicked witch who tries to kill a young boy and girl, but whose plan is foiled by the children.

Henny-Penny (Chicken Little) — Fairy tale about a chicken who thought the sky was falling and set out with her friends to tell the king, but had to escape from a hungry fox instead.

Jack and the Beanstalk — Fairy tale about a boy who climbs up a magic beanstalk to the land of a giant, scurries back down, chops down the beanstalk, and kills the giant.

Little Red Riding Hood — Fairy tale about a girl and her grandmother who are tricked by a wolf who eats them; they are saved when a woodsman chops the wolf open.

The Old Woman and her Pig — Tale of a woman who bought a pig and was trying to get him home (with a little help from her friends).

The Princess and the Pea — Story about a prince who finds his true princess by testing her sensitive nature; she can't sleep because a pea is under the mattresses piled on her bed.

The Princess who Lived on a Glass Hill — Fairy tale about Boots and his brothers, who try to find the horses that are eating their grain. Boots, the underdog, captures the horse that is able to take him up the glass hill that everyone else slides down, and thereby wins the princess.

Puss in Boots — Fairy tale about a master who has good luck because of his clever cat.

Rapunzel — Fairy tale about a girl with extraordinarily long hair who is locked in a tower and can only be visited if someone says, "Rapunzel, Rapunzel, let down your hair."

Rumpelstiltskin — Fairy tale about a dwarf who helps a lady spin golden threads from straw in exchange for her firstborn baby; but she gets to keep the baby by guessing the man's name correctly.

The Sea Maiden — Irish fairy tale about a man who promises his son to a sea maiden who steals him away and hides his bride-to-be, a princess. The son, however, has befriended a dog, a hawk, and an otter, who end up saving his life and that of his princess.

The Shoemaker and the Elves — Fairy tale about a group of elves that finish the shoemaker's work every evening.

The Six Swans — Fairy tale of a king and a witch's daughter who turn the king's sons into swans, and of the swans' miraculous transformations many years later.

Sleeping Beauty — Tale of a princess under a spell that makes her sleep for 100 years. The spell is broken by the kiss of a handsome young prince.

Snow White — Fairy tale about a wicked stepmother who poisons a beautiful girl who has taken refuge with seven dwarfs. In the end, Snow White wakes up and marries a handsome prince.

The Sorcerer's Apprentice — Fairy tale about a sorcerer and his pupil, who unwittingly calls up Beelzebub while his master is away and has serious problems until the sorcerer returns and restores order.

Toads and Diamonds — Tale about a mother and two daughters (one kind and beautiful, the other ugly and impolite), who each are rewarded in kind by a fairy — one has toads come out her mouth when she speaks, the other, diamonds.

The Three Billy Goats Gruff — Norwegian tale about three goats and an ugly troll that lives under a bridge and causes them trouble.

The Traveling Musicians — Story about an unappreciated donkey who heads for the city to become a musician. He picks up an old dog, a cat, and rooster, and the three chase burglars from a house, where they live happily every after.

Three Little Pigs — Story about three pigs, each building a house of different materials, and of the wolf who blows the two weaker houses down.

Tom Thumb — Fairy tale set in the days of King Arthur and Merlin, about a woman who wants a child and has two-inch-high Tom Thumb; Tom has many misadventures but becomes a member of King Arthur's court.

The White Snake — Fairy tale about a king who learns the languages of the beasts and birds from a white snake. His servant acquires this wisdom, has many adventures, and is finally is saved by birds he has befriended; he marries the king's daughter.

The Widow's Son — Tale about a poor widow's son, whose curiosity helps him outwit a troll, turn a horse into a prince, and win the hand of a princess.

The Wild Swans — Tale about a princess and her eleven brothers, who turn into swans every night. The princess rescues her brothers by laboriously following the orders of a fairy and ends up marrying a king.

51. FAIRY TALES/FOLKTALES/MYTHS/LEGENDS: COLLECTIONS

This list contains valuable, readable collections. Names of selectors, editors, retellers, translators, introducers, or authors, if known, are provided. Items marked with an asterisk (*) are from the Pantheon Fairy Tale and Folklore Library, an outstanding series. See also List 50, Fairy Tales.

African Folktales: Traditional Stories of the Black World — Roger D. Abrahams*
Afro-American Folktales: Stories from Black Tradition in the New World — Roger D. Abrahams*
America in Legend: Folklore from the Colonial Period to the Present — Richard M. Dorson*
American Indian Myth and Legends — Richard Erdoes and Alfonso Artiz*
Arab Folktales — Inea Bushnaq*
Celtic Mythology — Proinsias MacCana
Chinese Fairy Tales and Fantasies — Moss Roberts*
The Complete Grimm's Fairy Tales — Padraic Colum*
Early Irish Myths and Sagas — Jeffrey Gantz
Egyptian Mythology — Veronica Ions
Eighty Fairy Tales — Hans Christian Andersen*
An Encyclopedia of Fairies: Hobgoblins, Brownies, Bogies, and Other Supernatural Creatures — Katharine Briggs*
English Myths and Legends — Henry Bett
Epics, Myths and Legends of India — P. Thomas
Favorite Folktales from around the World — Jane Yolen*
Folk Stories of the Hmong Peoples of Laos, Thailand, and Vietnam — Norma J. Livo and Dia Cha
Folktales of the British Isles — Keven Crossley-Holland*
French Folktales — Henri Pourrat, C. G. Bjurstrom, and Royall Tyler*
Gods and Heroes: Myths and Epics of Ancient Greece — Gustav Schwab*
Greek Mythology — John Pinsent
The Greek Myths — Robert Graves
Irish Folktales — Henry Glassie*
Italian Folktales — Italo Calvino*
Japanese Tales — Royall Tyler*
Legends of the Celts — Frank Delaney
The Mythology of North America — John Bierhorst (Native American)
Mythology of the British Isles — Geoffrey Ashe
The Norse Myths — Kevin Crossley-Holland*
Norwegian Folk Tales — Peter Christian Asbjornsen and Jorgen Moe*
North American Indian Mythology — Cottie Burland and Marion Wood
One Hundred and Fifty Folk Tales of India — Kanwarjit Singh and Kang Singh
Russian Fairy Tales — Aleksandr Afanas'ev*
Scottish Tradition: A Collection of Scottish Folk Literature — David Buchan
The Victorian Fairy Tale Book — Michael Patrick Hearn*
Yiddish Folktales — Beatrice Silverman Weinrich and Leonard Wolf*

52. FANTASY/HORROR/GHOSTS: STORIES

This list presents only a title or two by each author. Many of these authors have written numerous books in the genre. See also List 53, Fantasy/Horror/Ghosts: Collections; and List 54, Fantasy Series and King Arthur Stories.

Adams, Richard — *Watership Down*

Aiken, Joan — *The Stolen Lake*

Anderson, Poul — *Three Hearts and Three Lions; A Midsummer Tempest*

Beagle, Peter — *The Last Unicorn*

Blatty, William — *The Exorcist*

Blauer, Steven — *Satyrday*

Bradbury, Ray — *The October Country; Something Wicked This Way Comes*

Brooks, Terry — *Magic Kingdom for Sale — Sold!*

Cherryh, C. J. — *Gate of Ivrel; Well of Shiuan; Fires of Azeroth*

Crichton, Michael — *Eaters of the Dead*

Crowley, John — *Little, Big*

Dunsany, Lord — *The King of Elfland's Daughter*

Du Maurier, Daphne — *The Birds*

Eddison, E. R. — *The Worm Ouroboros*

Ende, Michael — *The Neverending Story*

Finney, Charles — *The Circus of Dr. Lao*

Finney, Jack — *Invasion of the Body Snatchers*

Ford, John M. — *The Dragon Waiting*

Ford, Richard — *Quest for the Faradawn*

Geare, Michael, and Michael Corby — *Dracula's Diary* (spoof)

Hales, E. E. Y. — *Chariots of Fire*

Heinlein, Robert A. — *Glory Road*

Holdstock, Robert — *Mythago Wood*

Helprin, Mark — *Winter's Tale*

Horwood, William — *Duncton Wood*

Hughart, Barry — *Bridge of Birds*

James, Henry — *The Turn of the Screw*

King, Stephen, and Peter Straub — *The Talisman*

Kipling, Rudyard — *Phantoms and Fantasies*

Lee, Tanith — *The Birthgrave; East of Midnight*

Lewis, C. S. — *The Lion, the Witch, and the Wardrobe*

L'Engle, Madeleine — *A Swiftly Tilting Planet*

MacAvoy, R. A. — *The Book of Kells*

Lovecraft, H. P. — *Dunwich Horror*

McKillip, Patricia A. — *The Forgotten Beasts of Eld*

Moorcock, Michael — *Lorian, or the Unfulfill'd Queen*

Myers, John — *Silverlock*

Piers, Anthony — *On a Pale Horse*

Powers, Tim — *The Anubis Gates*

Pratt, Fletcher — *The Well of the Universe*

Pratchett, Terry — *The Color of Magic* (parody)

Shea, Michael — *Nifft the Lean*

Shelley, Mary — *Frankenstein; or, the Modern Prometheus*

Stevenson, Robert Louis — *Dr. Jekyll and Mr. Hyde*

Stoker, Bram — *Dracula*

Swann, Thomas Burnett — *The Forest of Forever*

Tolkien, J. R. R. — *The Hobbit*

Wangerin, Walter — *The Book of the Dun Cow*

Warner, Sylvia Townsend — *Kingdom of Elfin*

Wells, H. G. — *The Sea Raiders*

Wilde, Oscar — *The Picture of Dorian Gray*

Williams, Tad — *Tailchaser's Song*

53. FANTASY/HORROR/GHOSTS: COLLECTIONS

Asimov, Isaac et al., eds., *Isaac Asimov Presents the Best Fantasy of the Nineteenth Century*, Beaufort, 1983.

Asimov, Isaac, et al., eds., *100 Great Fantasy Short Stories,* Doubleday, 1984.

Bierce, Ambrose, *Can Such Things Be?,* Citadel Press, 1977.

Bleiler, E. F., ed., *Ghost and Horror Stories of Ambrose Bierce*, Dover, 1964.

Boyer, Robert H. and Kenneth Zahorski, eds., *The Fantastic Imagination: An Anthology of High Fantasy*, Avon, 1977.

Bradley, Marion Zimmer, ed., *Sword and Sorceress: An Anthology of Heroic Fantasy*, DAW, 1984.

De La Mare, Walter, *The Wind Blows Over*, Ayer Co., 1936.

Doyle, Sir Arthur Conan, *Tales of Terror and Mystery, Buccaneer Books*, 1982; *Tales for a Winter's Night*, Academy Chi Publishers, 1989.

Du Maurier, Daphne, *Echoes from the Macabre: Selected Stories*, Aeonian Press, 1989.

Joshi, S. T., ed., *The Dunwich Horror and Others* (collected Lovecraft Fiction Series, Vol. 1), Arkham, 1985.

Lovecraft, H. P., *The Best of H. P. Lovecraft: Bloodcurdling Tales of Horror and the Macabre*, Ballantine, 1987.

Manguel, Alberto, *Black Water: The Book of Fantastic Literature*, Potter, 1984.

Onions, Oliver, *The First Book of Ghost Stories: Widdershins*, Dover, 1978.

Poe, Edgar Allan, *Tales of Terror: Ten Short Stories*, Prentice Hall, 1985; *Tales of Mystery and Terror*, Puffin Books, 1990.

Rabkin, Eric S., *Fantastic Worlds: Myths, Tales, and Stories*, Oxford University Press, 1979.

Schwartz, Susan, ed., *Moonsinger's Friends: An Anthology in Honor of Andre Norton*, Bluejay Books, 1985; *Whispers: An Anthology of Fantasy and Horror*, Doubleday, 1977.

Silverberg, Robert and Martin Harry Greenberg, *The Fantasy Hall of Fame*, Arbor House, 1983.

54. FANTASY SERIES AND KING ARTHUR STORIES

Let your imagination run wild and enjoy the world of fantasy. These authors did! See also List 52, Fantasy/Horror/Ghosts: Stories; and List 53, Fantasy/Horror/Ghosts: Collections.

CHRONICLES, SERIES, AND TRILOGIES

Alexander, Lloyd — *The Prydian Chronicles*

Akers, Alan Burt — *Davy Prescott* series

Anthony, Piers — *Magic of Zanth* series

Brackett, Leigh — *Stark* series

Brooks, Terry — *Shannara* series

Burroughs, Edgar Rice — *Barsoom* series

Cabell, James Branch — *Poictesme* series

Carter, Lin — *Thonger of Lemuria* series

Chalker, Jack L. — *Dancing Gods* series parody

Chant, Joy — *Vandarei* series

de Camp, L. Sprague — *Pusedian; Novaria; The Reluctant King* all series de Camp, L. Sprague and Fletcher Pratt — *The Compleat Enchanter: The Magical Misadventures of Harold Shea* four works

Delany, Samuel R. — *Neveryon* three stories

Donaldson, Stephen R. — *The Chronicles of Thomas Covenant, the Unbeliever*

Eddison, E. R. — *The Zimiamvian Trilogy*

Feist, Raymond E. — *Riftwar Trilogy*

Foster, Alan Dean — *The Spellsinger* series

Garrett, Randall, and Vicki Ann Heydron — *Ganalara Cycle* six stories

Gaskell, Jane — *Atlan Chronicles*

Haggard, H. Rider — *She* series

Howard, Robert E. — *Conan* series

Jakes, John — *Brak the Barbarian* trilogy

Kurtz, Katherine — *Deryni Saga* King Kelson series and more

Kuttner, Henry — *Elak of Atlantis* series

Lancour, Gene — *Dirshan the God-Killer* series

Le Guin, Ursula K. — *The Earthsea Trilogy*

Leiber, Fritz — *Fafhrd and the Gray Mouser* series

L'Engle, Madeleine — *The Unicorn Trilogy*

Lord, Jeffrey — *Richard Blade* series

Lewis, C. S. — *The Chronicles of Narnia* series; *The Space Triology*

MacAvoy, R. A. — *Damiano* series

McKillip, Patricia A. — *The Hed Trilogy*

Moorcock, Michael — *The Chronicle of Prince Corum and the Silver Hand; Elric of Melnibone* series; *Hawkmoon* series

Moore, C. L. — *Jirel of Joiry* series

Norman, John — *Gor* series

Norton, Andre — *Witch World* series

Peake, Mervyn — *The Gormenghast Triology*

Russ, Joanna — *Alyx* series

Silverberg, Robert — *Lord Valentine* series

Tarr, Judith — *The Hound and Falcon Trilogy*

Tolkien, J. R. R. — *The Lord of the Rings* trilogy; *The Hobbit*

Vance, Jack — *The Dying Earth; Lyonesse* series

Van Lustbader, Eric — *Sunset Warrior Trilogy*

Walton, Evangeline — *The Mabinogion* series

Watt-Evans, Lawrence — *The Lords of Dus* series

Wilson, Robert Anton — *The Schrodinger's Cat* series; *Illuminatus Trilogy*

Zelazny, Roger — *Amber* series

LEGENDS OF KING ARTHUR

(Note: Historians argue whether King Arthur's exploits are entirely legendary or partly true.)

Berger, Thomas — *Arthur Rex: A Legendary Novel*

Bradley, Marion Zimmer — *The Mists of Avalon*

Bradshaw, Gillian — *Hawk of May; Kingdom of Summer; In Winter's Shadow*

Godwin, Parke — *Firelord; Beloved Exile*

Kane, Gil, and John Jakes — *Excalibur!*

Malory, Thomas — *Morte d'Arthur*

MacLeod, Mary — *King Arthur and His Noble Knights*

Monaco, Richard — *Parsival, or, A Knight's Tale; The Grail War; The Final Quest*

Munn, H. Warner — *King of the World's Edge; Merlin's Godson; Merlin's Ring*

Newman, Sharan — *Guinevere; The Chessboard Queen; Guinevere Evermore*

Norton, Andre — *Merlin's Mirror*

Nye, Robert — *Merlin*

Stewart, Mary — *The Crystal Cave; The Hollow Hills; The Last Enchantment; The Wicked Day*

Tennyson, Alfred Lord — *Idylls of the King* poem

White, T. H. — *The Once and Future King; The Book of Merlin*

Wolfram (Von Eschenbach) — *Parsifal* poem

55. Fiction: Pulitzer Prize Winners

The Pulitzer Prize for Fiction has been awarded since 1918 for best fiction in book form by an American author, preferably dealing with American life. This list contains all the winning literature from 1918 through 1997. There are several years where no prize was awarded. The prize winners are arranged alphabetically, not chronologically, because whether old or new, none should be overlooked on the assumption they would be outdated or too recent to be assured of lasting value.

Note that only three authors managed to win the coveted prize twice: Booth Tarkington, William Faulkner, and John Updike. Also note that the prize was refused by Sinclair Lewis in 1926, though he is listed below. See also related lists: List 4, Nobel Prize Winners for Literature; and List 64, The Novel Masters (American).

The Able McLaughlins — Margaret Wilson

Advise and Consent — Allen Drury

The Age of Innocence — Edith Wharton

Alice Adams — Booth Tarkington

All the King's Men — Robert Penn Warren

Andersonville — MacKinlay Kantor

Angle of Repose — Wallace Stegner

Arrowsmith — Sinclair Lewis

A Bell for Adano — John Hersey

Beloved — Toni Morrison

Breathing Lessons — Anne Tyler

The Bridge of San Luis Rey — Thornton Wilder

The Caine Mutiny — Herman Wouk

Collected Stories — Jean Stafford

Collected Stories of Katherine Anne Porter — Katherine Anne Porter

The Color Purple — Alice Walker

A Confederacy of Dunces — John Kennedy Toole

Confessions of Nat Turner — William Styron

A Death in the Family — James Agee

Dragon's Teeth — Upton Sinclair

Early Autumn — Louis Bromfield

The Edge of Sadness — Edwin O'Connor

Elbow Room — James Alan McPherson

The Executioner's Song — Norman Mailer

A Fable — William Faulkner

The Fixer — Bernard Malamud

Foreign Affairs — Alison Lurie

Gone With the Wind — Margaret Mitchell

A Good Scent from a Strange Mountain — Robert Olen Butler

The Good Earth — Pearl S. Buck

The Grapes of Wrath — John Steinbeck

Guard of Honor — James Gould Cozzens

His Family — Ernest Poole

Honey in the Horn — Harold L. Davis

House Made of Dawn — M. Scott Momaday

Humboldt's Gift — Saul Bellow

Independence Day — Richard Ford

In This Our Life — Ellen Glasgow

Ironweed — William Kennedy

Journey in the Dark — Martin Flavin

The Keepers of the House — Shirley Ann Grau

The Killer Angels — Michael Shaara

Lamb in His Bosom — Caroline Miller

The Late George Apley — John P. Marquand

Laughing Boy — Oliver LaFarge

Lonesome Dove — Larry McMurtry

The Magnificent Ambersons — Booth Tarkington

The Mambo Kings Play Songs of Love — Oscar Hijuelos

Martin Dressler: The Tale of an American Dreamer—Steven Milhauser

Now in November — Josephine W. Johnson

The Old Man and the Sea — Ernest Hemingway

One of Ours — Willa Cather

The Optimist's Daughter — Eudora Welty

Rabbit at Rest — John Updike

Rabbit Is Rich — John Updike

The Reivers — William Faulkner

Scarlet Sister Mary — Julia Peterkin

The Shipping News — E. Annie Proulx

So Big — Edna Ferber

The Stone Diaries — Carol Shields

The Store — T. S. Stribling

The Stories of John Cheever — John Cheever

A Summons to Memphis — Peter Taylor

Tales of the South Pacific — James A. Michener

A Thousand Acres — Jane Smiley

To Kill a Mockingbird — Harper Lee

The Town — Conrad Richter

The Travels of Jaimie McPheeters — Robert Lewis Taylor

The Way West — A. B. Guthrie, Jr.

The Yearling — Marjorie Kinnan Rawlings

Years of Grace — Margaret Ayer Barnes

56. FOLKLORE (AMERICAN): IMAGINARY CHARACTERS

The Blue Lady — Traveled in Arizona, Texas, and New Mexico spreading Christianity in days before Spanish missionaries and explorers. Always dressed completely in blue.

Bowleg Bill — An extraordinarily tall cowboy who went to sea. Called his ship a "roundup wagon," and made trouble wherever he went.

Pecos Bill — Only man to be able to ride a horse named "Widow-Maker." Tamed a mountain lion and rode him like a horse, whipping him with a rattlesnake to make the lion run. Led the first cattle drive ever.

Paul Bunyan — A giant lumberjack who roamed the woods accompanied by his blue ox, Babe, performing superhuman feats.

Febold Feboldson — Swedish con man who sold sand from California's Death Valley to unsuspecting gold prospectors. Reportedly got $50 a bushel.

Big Frank — Worked in the wheat fields from Texas to North and South Dakota. Bragged that he could harvest a whole field of wheat in one day — and supposedly did.

Hank, the Freewheeler — Taught cows to ride bicycles from pastures to save time while he did his chores.

Old Jim — Grower and seller of world's largest potatoes. Had to sell at least 100 pounds at a time because otherwise he said he'd have to cut the potato in half.

John Henry — Black "steel-driving man" who made holes for dynamite using one 20-pound hammer in each hand and won a contest against a steam drill. Subject of numerous tales and ballads.

Slappy Hooper — World's biggest sign painter; reportedly painted a sign so big, people had to catch a train to go from one end of it to the other.

The Tommy Knawkers — Gnomes from Great Britain who came to Colorado to be with the miners. Told miners of best gold and silver veins and warned against danger by making sounds on the walls. Played tricks on miners.

Dan McGrew — Poet Robert W. Service told his story in "The Shooting of Dan McGrew." Dan, an Alaskan card player, was killed in a saloon after a disagreement with a miner.

Uncle Remus — Joel Chandler Harris, author, created this elderly black man to narrate animal legends to a young white boy in *Uncle Remus: His Songs and His Sayings.* Brer Rabbit wins out over Brer Fox in most of his tales.

Rip Van Winkle — In a story by Washington Irving, this Catskill mountain man went hunting to get away from his nagging wife. Met some strangers, drank their mountain drink, and went to sleep for 20 years. Later woke up and wondered why no one knew who he was.

Uncle Sam — Samuel "Uncle Sam" Wilson (1766–1854), a meat supplier to the U.S. Army, stamped his meat with the letters "U.S." Eventually Uncle Sam became a symbol for the United States.

Stackalee (Stagolee) — Lived in St. Louis and sold his soul to the devil. Could do magnificent feats and played a "mean" guitar. Shot Billy Lyons for stealing his magic hat. Stack O'Dollars, his girlfriend, smoked cigars and had diamond fillings in her teeth.

Old Stormalong — Alfred Bulltop Stormalong, Atlantic coast sailor, whose ship was so big he scraped the paint while passing through the English Channel, thus creating the White Cliffs of Dover.

57. FOLKLORE (AMERICAN): REAL CHARACTERS

Johnny Appleseed — John or Jonathan Chapman, a Massachusetts man who planted apple seeds to begin orchards all over Ohio and Indiana for forty years. Subject of ballads and poems.

P. T. Barnum — Famous circus man, Phineas Taylor Barnum, coined phrases "The greatest show on earth," and "There's a sucker born every minute." Displayed Jumbo the elephant, Tom Thumb the dwarf, and the original Siamese Twins.

Sam Bass — Cattle rustler and train robber operated in Texas. Supposedly buried gold in caves. Subject of ballads.

Judge Roy Bean — Lawman and gambler who operated out of the Jersey Lily Saloon in Texas. Famous quote, "Hear ye, hear ye, this honorable court is now in session, and if any galoot wants a snort before we start, step up to the bar and name your poison."

Billy the Kid — Henry McCarty, gunman and cattle rustler, supposedly killed twenty-one men by age twenty-one, when he was shot and killed by Sheriff Pat Garrett.

Black Caesar — Escaped slave who terrorized ships off Florida coast; joined pirate, Blackbeard; reputedly had harem of 100 women.

The Bloomer Girl — Amelia Bloomer founded a temperance magazine called *The Lily*. Was a women's rights worker, advocating trousers for women; "bloomers" were named for her.

Nellie Bly — Pen name of Elizabeth C. Seaman, a nineteenth-century reporter who traveled around the world in 72½ days, breaking the fictional 80-day record of Jules Verne's Phileas Fogg.

Bonnie and Clyde — Bonnie Parker and Clyde Barrow, outlaws and murderers in the Southwest.

Lizzie Borden — Tried and found not guilty of killing her stepmother and father with an ax. Preserved in doggerel poetry.

Daniel Boone — Blazed Wilderness Road trail through Kentucky's Cumberland Gap for pioneers. Built fort, founded Boonesboro, and helped defend Kentucky against Indians. Famous saying: "I want more elbow room."

Jim Bowie — Texas Revolution hero died defending the Alamo. Credited with inventing the Bowie knife.

James "Diamond Jim" Brady — Lived an extravagant lifestyle. Noted for eating too much and wearing lots of diamond jewelry.

Jim Bridger — First white man to see Great Salt Lake in Utah; built Fort Bridger; discovered Bridger Pass in Rocky Mountains. Told imaginative tales about Yellowstone and Grand Canyon.

William "Buffalo Bill" Cody — Hunter, Indian scout, and showman. Got his nickname because of large buffalo kills. Founded Cody, Wyoming, and Wild West Show in Nebraska.

John Brown — Led seizure of government arsenal at Harper's Ferry, Virginia, in attempt to spark a slave revolt. Was convicted of treason and hanged; became martyr for antislavery movement.

Christopher "Kit" Carson — Guide, scout, Indian agent. Guided John Fremont's expeditions to California and Wyoming. Helped occupy California during Mexican War; Civil War officer.

Martha Jane "Calamity Jane" Canary — Montana tomboy, dressed like a man. Rode for Pony Express. Called Calamity Jane because she said anyone who crossed her was headed for calamity. Heroine of popular nineteenth-century novels.

Davy Crockett — Frontiersman fought under Andrew Jackson in Creek War; served in Tennessee legislature and U.S. Congress. Died defending Alamo in Texas. Known for his coonskin cap. Subject of songs, stories, and television series.

The Dutchman — Referred to Jacob Walz or Wolz, gold prospector and murderer, whose Lost Dutchman Mine in Superstition Mountain was thought to be cursed.

Wyatt Earp — Officer of the law and gunfighter. Involved in shootout at the OK Corral in Tombstone, Arizona.

Mike Fink — Indian scout and flatboat pilot on the Ohio and Mississippi Rivers. Known as King of the Keelboatmen and Snapping Turtle of the Ohio.

Barbara Frietchie — Character created by John Greenleaf Whittier from traits of two women who lived during Civil War.

Hiawatha — Onondaga Indian chief who founded the Iroquois Confederacy. Subject of poem by Henry Wadsworth Longfellow.

James B. "Wild Bill" Hickock — Indian scout, expert marksman, Union Army officer, gold prospector, and frontier marshal. Murdered in Deadwood, South Dakota, by outlaw Jack McCall.

"Doc" Holliday — Friend of Wyatt Earp, famous Western gunfighter, came with Earp to Arizona in 1880.

Jesse James — Outlaw robbed banks and trains, supposedly taking from the rich and giving to the poor. Lived under false name of Thomas Howard. Murdered by own gang member, Robert Ford. Subject of songs and ballads.

John Luther "Casey" Jones — Railroad engineer, blew his train whistle in special way. Wrecked in Mississippi. Subject of folk songs.

Kamehameha — Hawaiian chief and first king of Hawaiian Islands. Born during thunderstorm. Killed by a tidal wave. Was said to be favored by Pele, mythical goddess.

Luther "Rattlesnake" King — Oregon man bitten by rattlesnake; lived to tell about it. Twenty years later the wound opened up, then healed. This went on for twelve years until his death.

Manteo — Indian helped British establish Lost Colony on Roanoke Island off North Carolina. Colony and Manteo vanished.

John Murrell — Outlaw who passed himself off as a preacher. During revivals meetings his gang stole the horses and slaves of those at the meeting.

Annie Oakley — Phoebe Anne Oakley Mozee, markswoman, appeared in Buffalo Bill's Wild West Show. Shot cigarettes out of people's mouths and hit targets while on a fast-moving horse. Now complimentary theater tickets are called "Annie Oakleys" because they have holes punched in them.

Mary "Molly Pitcher" Hays — Helped the wounded during the Revolutionary War in Monmouth, New Jersey, by carrying water to them in a pitcher.

Pocahontas — Indian woman reportedly saved Captain John Smith's life when her father, Chief Powhatan, threatened to kill him. Married John Rolfe, another colonist, who took her to England; treated as a princess.

Paul Revere — Boston silversmith and revolutionary; Henry Wadsworth Longfellow's poem tells of Revere's midnight ride in 1775, when he warned the American soldiers at Lexington that the British were coming.

Betsy Ross — Supposedly designed and sewed the first "Stars and Stripes" version of the American flag.

Sitting Bull — Sioux Indian chief defeated Gen. George Custer at Battle of Little Bighorn in 1876. Surrendered five years later at Fort Peck.

Jefferson Randolph "Soapy" Smith — Smooth-talking swindler. Called "Soapy" because he offered soap wrapped in five dollar bills, but gave his customers the soap with no money. Killed by Frank Reid in shootout in Alaska.

Squanto — Pawtuxet Indian kidnapped and taken to England by Capt. Thomas Hunt. Later, helped pilgrims by acting as interpreter and offering planting and fishing knowledge.

Belle Starr — Myra Belle Shirley led cattle rustlers and horse thieves in Oklahoma.

58. GOTHIC AND REGENCY ROMANCE

THE GOTHIC ROMANCE

The Gothic romance is a type of novel that first flourished in the 1700s. These works influenced later writers and Gothic novels are popular even today. This genre includes elements of mystery, romance, passion, and suspense. Typically, a female hero overcomes many obstacles and is rescued in the end by a handsome man. Often terror and the supernatural are involved. Some of the most famous early Gothic romances are listed below.

Caleb Williams — William Godwin

The Castle of Otrano — Horace Walpole

Frankenstein — Mary Shelley

The Heart of Midlothian — Sir Walter Scott

Ivanhoe — Sir Walter Scott

Melmoth the Wanderer — Charles Maturin

The Monk — Matthew Gregory Lewis

The Mysteries of Udolpho — Ann Radcliffe

Quentin Durward — Sir Walter Scott

Rob Roy — Sir Walter Scott

The Talisman — Sir Walter Scott

Vathek — William Beckford

Waverley — Sir Walter Scott

THE REGENCY ROMANCE

The Regency romance is a novel or story set in the Regency period of British history (1811–1820). At the time George III, the reigning king, was suffering from mental illness and his son had to act as regent. Literary romanticism reached its height during this time. Nevertheless, a modern-day writer, Georgette Heyer (1902–74) is regarded as the leading exponent of the Regency romance. Her books are filled with accurate historical details showing the customs, clothes, daily life, and speech of the Regency period. Among her many books are the following:

The Black Moth
Regency Buck

Friday's Child
The Reluctant Widow

Grand Sophie

59. HORROR STORY MASTERS

Some stories by these authors can be truly frightening and readers will proceed at their own risk. An asterisk (*) indicates the best known authors of this genre. See List 52, Fantasy/Horror/Ghosts: Stories; and List 53, Fantasy/Horror/Ghosts: Collections.

Robert Aickman	A. E. Coppard	Nathaniel Hawthorne*
Joan Aiken	Basil Copper*	James Herbert
V. C. Andrews	John Coyne*	Patricia Highsmith*
Piers Anthony	F. Marion Crawford*	Michael T. Hinkemeyer
Rosalind Ashe	Robertson Davies	Alfred Hitchcock*
Isaac Asimov*	Walter de la Mare*	William Hope Hodgson*
Ambrose Bierce*	August Derleth*	Geoffrey Household
Algernon Blackwood*	Charles Dickens*	Washington Irving*
William Blatty*	Isak Dinesen*	Shirley Jackson*
Robert Bloch*	Thomas M. Disch	Henry James*
Lawrence Block	Arthur Conan Doyle*	M. R. James*
Anthony Boucher*	Daphne du Maurier*	Stephen King*
Elizabeth Bowen	Lord Dunsany*	Francis King
Ray Bradbury*	Stanley Ellin	Rudyard Kipling*
Marion Zimmer Bradley	Dennis Etchison	Henry Kuttner*
Joseph Payne Brennan*	Anthea Fraser	Margharita Laski
John Buchan	Charles L. Grant	Tanith Lee
Ramsey Campbell*	Jessica Hamilton	J. S. Lefanu*
John Dickson Carr*	Marilyn Harris	Fritz Leiber*
John Collier*	L. P. Hartley	Ira Levin*
Wilkie Collins	W. F. Harvey*	John Linssen

Norah Lofts
Frank Belknap Long*
H. P. Lovecraft*
Richard Matheson*
Robert R. McCammon
Barbara Michaels
A. N. L. Munby
Joyce Carol Oates
Fitz-James O'Brien
Oliver Onions
Edgar Allan Poe*
Amanda Prantera

Herman Raucher
Simon Raven
Anne Rice
Berton Rouche
Fred Saberhagen*
Saki
Mary Shelley*
R. L. Stevenson*
Bram Stoker*
Whitley Strieber*
Theodore Sturgeon
Thomas Tessier*

Gene Thompson
Peter Tremayne
John Updike*
H. Russell Wakefield
Elizabeth Walter
Evangeline Walton
Manly Wade Wellman
H. G. Wells*
Oscar Wilde*
Tennessee Williams*
Chelsea Yarbro

60. JOURNALISM MASTERS

Journalistic style often differs from other writing; it tends to be more direct, factual, and terse. This genre includes master journalists as varied as war correspondents, gossip columnists, humorists, essayists, broadcasters, and sportswriters. Many were also involved in other aspects of literature.Some of their works contain much fine writing and therefore deserve careful study.

Shana Alexander
Joseph Alsop, Jr.
Jack Anderson
Russell Baker
Carl Bernstein
Jim Bishop
Erma Bombeck
Benjamin Bradlee
Jimmy Breslin
David Brinkley
Jane Brody
Tom Brokaw
Heywood Broun
Patrick Buchanan
Art Buchwald
William F. Buckley, Jr.
Bennett Cerf

Whittaker Chambers
Marquis Childs
Connie Chung
Robert Considine
Alistair Cooke
Howard Cosell
Walter Cronkite
Charlotte Curtis
Clifton Daniel, Jr.
Richard Davis
Frank DeFord
Sam Donaldson
Janet Flanner
Maz Frankel
Philip Freneau
Betty Furness
Elizabeth Gilmer

Sheilah Graham
Bryant Gumbel
John Gunther
David Halberstam
Marguerite Higgins
Hedda Hopper
Peter Jennings
Willard Kiplinger
Ted Koppel
Arthur Krock
Ann Landers
James Lehrer
Max Lerner
Anthony Lewis
Walter Lippmann
Donald Marquis
Robert MacNeil

Judith Martin
H. L. Mencken
Bill Moyers
Roger Mudd
Edward R. Murrow
Edwin Newman
Jane Pauley
Drew Pearson
Ernie Pyle
Jane Bryant Quinn
Dan Rather
John Reed
James Reston
Andrew Rooney
Louis Rukeyser
Mike Royko
William Safire

Adela St. Johns
Pierre Salinger
Harrison Salisbury
Diane Sawyer
Eric Sevareid
Bernard Shaw
William Shawn
William Shirer
Merriman Smith
Hedrick L. Smith
Howard K. Smith
Liz Smith
Lesley Stahl
John Cameron Swayze
Herbert Swope
Ida Tarbell
Helen Thomas

Lowell Thomas
Dorothy Thompson
Abigail Van Buren
Amy Vanderbilt
Oswald Villard
Mike Wallace
Barbara Walters
Theodore H. White
William Allen White
Thomas Wicker
George Will
Walter Winchell
Tom Wolfe
Robert Woodward
John Peter Zenger

61. LETTERS/DIARIES/JOURNALS

Letters, diaries, and journals are often written with eloquence and become part of the recognized literature of an era. They are important not only to provide historic facts but also to show the mores and ideas of a particular culture and to reveal the personality of the author. Below are several volumes worth serious reading time. (Note: Some might be out of print, but can be located in libraries and secondhand bookstores.)

Adams, Abigail — *Letters of Abigail Adams*

Browning, Robert and Elizabeth — *Letters*

Center, Stella S. and Lilian M. Saul, eds. — *Book of Letters for Young People*

Cheney, Ednah D., ed. — *Life, Letters, and Journals of Louisa M. Alcott*

Clark, Allen C., ed. — *Life and Letters of Dolly Madison*

Crevecoeur, Hector St. John de— *Letters of an American Farmer*

Dickinson, John — *A Farmer in Pennsylvania*

Emerson, Ralph W. — *The Heart of Emerson's Journals*

Evelyn, John — *His Diary*

Gilman, Russell D., ed. — *Letters of Charles Lamb*

Goldsmith, Oliver — *Letters from a Citizen of the World to his Friends in the East*

Ingpen, Roger — *Women as Letter Writers*

Johnson, Samuel — *Letter to Lord Chesterfield*

Kipling, Rudyard — *Letters of Travel*

Pepys, Samuel — *Diary*

Roosevelt, Theodore — *Letters to his Children*

Swift, Jonathan — *Journal to Stella*

Thoreau, Henry David — *Thoreau's Journals*

Woolf, Virginia — *The Diaries of Virginia Woolf 1915–1941, Volumes I–V*

Wordsworth, Dorothy — *Dorothy Wordsworth's Journals*

62. NONFICTION MASTERS: AMERICAN

See also List 46, Essays: Collections; List 47, Essays: Informal; List 48, Essay Masters; List 60, Journalism Masters; and List 63, Nonfiction: Pulitzer Prizewinners.

Conrad Aiken — *Ushant*

Richard Armour — *It All Started with Columbus; Twisted Tales from Shakespeare*

Robert Benchley — *From Bed to Worse; My Ten Years in a Quandary; Benchley Beside Himself; Chips off the Old Benchley*

Dale Carnegie — *How to Win Friends and Influence People; How to Stop Worrying and Start Living*

Clarence Day — *Life with Father; Life with Mother* (became plays)

Ralph Ellison — *Essays: Shadow and Act*

Ralph Waldo Emerson — *Nature; The American Scholar; Divinity School Address*

Susan Faludi — *Backlash*

Harry Golden — *Only in America; For Two Cents Plain; Mr. Kennedy and the Negroes; The Greatest Jewish City in the World*

Moss Hart — *Act I*

Oliver Wendell Holmes — *The Autocrat of the Breakfast Table; The Brahmin Caste of New England; The Professor's Story (Elsie Venner); The Guardian Angel; The Poet at the Breakfast Table; The Professor at the Breakfast Table*

Julia Ward Howe — *On Sex and Education; Modern Society; Reminiscences*

Washington Irving — *A History of New York; The Sketchbook of Geoffrey Crayon, Gent.*

Jonathan Kozol — *Savage Inequalities*

Garrison Keillor — *Happy to Be Here; Lake Wobegon Days; Leaving Home*

Jean Kerr — *How I Got to Be Perfect; Please Don't Eat the Daisies*

Ring Lardner — *Haircut; Lovenest; Alibi Ike*

Jack London — *John Barleycorn, or Alcoholic Memoirs*

William Manchester — *The Death of a President; The Arms of Krupp, 1587–1968; American Caesar: Biography of Douglas MacArthur; The Last Lion, Winston Spencer Churchill*

Edgar Lee Masters — *Across Spoon River*

Mary McCarthy — *Birds of America; How I Grew, Memories of a Catholic Girlhood; Venice Observed; The Company She Keeps; The Stones of Florence; Vietnam; Hanoi; Mask of State: Watergate Portraits; Occasional Prose*

Howard Nemerov — *New and Selected Essays*

Dorothy Parker — *Constant Reader: from The New Yorker, 1927–1933*

Philip Roth — *The Facts: A Novelist's Autobiography; Patrimony*

Gertrude Stein — *The Autobiography of Alice B. Toklas*

James Thurber — *Fables for Our Time; Further Fables for Our Time*

Mark Twain — *Roughing It; Sketches, New and Old; The Innocents Abroad; The Gilded Age* (co-authored)*; Life on the Mississippi*

Ayn Rand — *For the New Intellectual*

John Crowe Ransom — *The New Criticism; The World's Body*

Carl Sandburg — *Abraham Lincoln, the War Years; Abraham Lincoln, the Prairie Years*

William Saroyan — *My Name Is Aram; Places Where I've Done Time; Chance Meetings; My Name Is Saroyan*

Karl Shapiro — *Beyond Criticism; In Defense of Ignorance*

Robert Sherwood — *Roosevelt and Hopkins; An Intimate History*

Isaac Bashevis Singer — *In My Father's Court; A Little Boy in Search of God; A Young Man in Search of Love; Lost in America*

Lincoln Steffens — *The Shame of the Cities; The Struggle for Self-Government*

Allen Tate — *Stonewall Jackson, the Good Soldier*

Paul Theroux — *The Happy Isles of Oceania; Paddling the Pacific*

Henry David Thoreau — *Walden*

Calvin Trillin — *If You Can't Say Something Nice; An Education in Georgia; American Fried*

Irving Wallace — *The People's Almanac* (co-authored)

E. B. White — *Here is New York; The Elements of Style* (co-authored)*; One Man's Meat; Is Sex Necessary?* (co-authored)

Elie Wiesel — *Night; Dawn; The Jews of Silence: A Personal Report of Soviet Jewry; Souls on Fire; The Golem; The Accident*

63. NONFICTION: PULITZER PRIZEWINNERS

This award, named after Joseph Pulitzer, New York publisher, began in 1962 for the best general nonfiction by an American writer. It has been awarded every year. Below are the authors and their prizewinning works, arranged in alphabetical order by author. See also List 24, Popular Nonfiction for Young Adults; and List 62, Nonfiction Masters: American.

Becker, Ernest — *The Denial of Death*

Butler, Robert N. — *Why Survive? Being Old in America*

Coles, Robert — *Children of Crisis, Volumes II and III*

Davis, David Brian — *The Problem of Slavery in Western Culture*

Dillard, Annie — *Pilgrim at Tinker Creek*

Dubos, Rene Jules — *So Human an Animal: How We Are Shaped by Surroundings and Events*

Durant, Will and Ariel — *Rousseau and Revolution*

Erikson, Eric H. — *Gandhi's Truth*

FitzGerald, Frances — *Fire in the Lake: The Vietnamese and the Americans in Vietnam*

Hofstadter, Douglas R. — *Gödel, Escher, Bach: An Eternal Golden Braid*

Hofstadter, Richard — *Anti-intellectualism in American Life*

Holldobler, Bert, and Edward O. Wilson — *The Ants*

Jones, Howard Mumford — *O Strange New World*

Kidder, Tracy — *The Soul of a New Machine*

Kluger, Richard — *Ashes to Ashes: America's Hundred-Year Cigarette War, the Public Health, and the Unabashed Triumph of Philip Morris*

Lelyveld, Joseph — *Move Your Shadow*

Lukas, J. Anthony — *Common Ground*

Maharidge, Dale and Michael Williamson — *And Their Children after Them*

Mailer, Norman — *The Armies of the Night*

Remnick, David — *Lenin's Tomb: The Last Days of the Soviet Empire*

Rosenberg, Tina — *The Haunted Land: Facing Europe's Ghosts After Communism*

Rhodes, Richard — *The Making of the Atomic Bomb*

Sagan, Carl — *The Dragons of Eden*

Schorske, Carl E. — *Fin-de-Siècle Vienna: Politics and Culture*

Sheehan, Susan — *Is There No Place on Earth for Me?*

Sheehan, Neil — *A Bright Shining Lie: John Paul Vann and America in Vietnam*

Shipler, David K. — *Arab and Jew*

Starr, Paul — *Social Transformation of American Medicine*

Teal, Edwin Way — *Wandering Through Winter*

Terkel, Studs — *The Good War*

Toland, John — *The Rising Sun*

Tuchman, Barbara W. — *The Guns of August*

Tuchman, Barbara W. — *Stilwell and the American Experience in China, 1911–1945*

Warner, William W. — *Beautiful Swimmers*

Weiner, Jonathan — *The Beak of the Finch: A Story of Evolution in our Time*

White, Theodore — *The Making of the President 1960*

Wilson, Edward O. — *On Human Nature*

Yergin, Daniel — *The Prize: The Epic Quest for Oil*

64. THE NOVEL MASTERS (AMERICAN)

This list includes important and/or popular American novelists and representative works. Those novels marked with an asterisk became major movies, plays, or TV dramas. See also List 58, Gothic and Regency Romance; List 65, The Novel Masters (Other than American); List 66, Novelists and Storytellers: Women; and List 67, Novel: Picaresque

Alice Adams
  Careless Love
  Listening to Billie
  Second Chances

Conrad Aiken
  Blue Voyage

Louisa May Alcott (for youth)
  *Little Women**
  *Little Men**
  Eight Cousins
  Jo's Boys

Horatio Alger, Jr. (for youth)
  Ragged Dick
  Luck and Pluck
  Tattered Tom

Nelson Algren
  *The Man with the Golden Arm**
  *A Walk on the Wild Side**

Sholem Asch
  The Nazarene
  The Apostle
  Mary
  *Moses**

Jean M. Auel
  *The Clan of the Cave Bear**
  The Valley of Horses
  The Mammoth Hunters

Richard Bach
  *Jonathan Livingston Seagull**

James Baldwin
  Go Tell It on the Mountain
  Nobody Knows my Name
  *Another Country**
  *Notes of a Native Son**

John Barth
   The Sot-Weed Factor
   Giles Goat-Boy
   Chimera
   The Friday Book

L. Frank Baum (for young
   readers)
   *The Wonderful Wizard
      of Oz**

Saul Bellow
   *The Adventures of Augie
      March*
   Henderson the Rain King
   Herzog
   Mr. Sammler's Planet
   Humboldt's Gift
   Seize the Day*
   The Dean's December
   More Die of Heartbreak

Peter Benchley
   Jaws*

Ambrose Bierce
   *Cobwebs from an
      Empty Skull*

Judy Blume (for youth)
   Deenie
   Blubber
   Forever
   Wifey
   Superfudge
   Tiger Eyes

Barbara Taylor Bradford
   A Woman of Substance*
   Voice of the Heart
   To Be the Best

Max Brand (wrote over
   100 "pulp" books about
   the West)
   Destry Rides Again*

Louis Bromfield
   Escape tetrology
   The Green Bay Tree
   Early Autumn
   Possession*
   A Good Woman

Pearl S. Buck
   The Good Earth*
   A House Divided
   Fighting Angel
   The Exile
   Dragon Seed*

Ned Buntline (wrote over 400
   books; invented sensational
   "dime" novel genre)
   *Magdalena, the Beautiful
      Mexican Maid*
   The Black Avenger

Frances Hodgson Burnett
   (for young readers)
   Little Lord Fauntleroy*
   The Little Princess
   The Secret Garden*

Edgar Rice Burroughs
   Tarzan books, such as
   Tarzan of the Apes*

James M. Cain
   *The Postman Always
      Rings Twice**
   Double Indemnity*
   Mildred Pierce*

P. Erskine Caldwell
   Tobacco Road*
   God's Little Acre*
   You Have Seen Their Faces
      (co-authored)
   Trouble in July
   George Boy
   The Sure Hand of God

Hortense Calisher
   In the Absence of Angels
   Eagle Eye
   The Bobby-Soxer

Truman Capote
   Other Voices, Other Rooms
   Breakfast at Tiffany's*
      (novella)
   In Cold Blood*
      (nonfiction novel)

Willa Cather
   O, Pioneers!*
   One of Ours
   My Antonia
   *Death Comes for the
      Archbishop*

John Cheever
   The Wapshot Chronicle
   The Wapshot Scandal
   Bullet Park
   Falconer
   *Oh What a Paradise It
      Seems*

Kate Chopin
   The Awakening*

Walter Van Tilburg Clark
   The Ox-Bow Incident*

Tom Clancy
   The Hunt for Red October*
   Red Storm Rising
   Clear and Present Danger*
   Patriot Games*

James Clavell
   Taipan*
   King Rat*
   Shogun*
   Whirlwind

Beverly Cleary (for young
   readers)
   Henry Huggins
   Dear Mr. Henshaw
   The Girl from Yamhill

Pat Conroy
The Boo
*The Great Santini**
*The Lords of Discipline**
*Prince of Tides**
*The Water Is Wide**

Robin Cook
The Year of the Intern
*Coma**
Harmful Intent

James Fenimore Cooper (one
of first important American
novel writers)
Leatherstocking Tales:
The Pioneers
*The Last of the Mohicans**
The Prairie
The Pathfinder
*The Deerslayer**

James Gould Cozzens
Guard of Honor
SS San Pedro
*By Love Possessed**

Stephen Crane
*The Red Badge of Courage**
Maggie: A Girl of the Streets

Harry Crews
The Gospel Singer
Blood and Grits
All We Need of Hell

Michael Crichton
*The Andromeda Strain**
*The Terminal Man**
*The Great Train Robbery**
*Rising Sun**
*Jurassic Park**

Richard Henry Dana, Jr.
*Two Years Before the Mast**

Peter de Vries
The Tunnel of Love
*Reuben, Reuben**
Peckham's Marbles

James Dickey
*Deliverance**

Joan Didion
Play It as It Lays

E. L. Doctorow
Welcome to Hard Times
*The Book of Daniel**
*Ragtime**
Loon Lake
World's Fair

Mary Mapes Dodge (for
young readers)
*Hans Brinker (The Silver
Skates)**

John Dos Passos
Manhattan Transfer
U.S.A. trilogy

Theodore Dreiser
*Sister Carrie**
The Financier
The Titan
*An American Tragedy**
The Bulwark

Stanley Elkin
*Criers and Kibitzers,
Kibitzers and Criers*
The Sixties
The Coffee Room

Ralph Ellison
*The Invisible Man**

Nora Ephron
Wallflower at the Orgy
Scribble, Scribble
*Heartburn**

James T. Farrell
Trilogy:
Young Lonigan
*Young Manhood of Studs
Lonigan*
Judgment Day

Howard Fast
Citizen Tom Paine
The Immigrants
The Immigrant's Daughter
*Spartacus**
Trilogy:
The Establishment
Second Generation
*The Legacy**

William Faulkner
*The Sound and the Fury**
A Fable
*The Reivers**
Light in August
Soldier's Pay
Sanctuary
Absalom, Absalom!
The Hamlet
Intruder in the Dust
As I Lay Dying

Edna Ferber
*So Big**
*Show Boat**
*Cimarron**
*Giant!**

Rachel Field
*Hitty, Her First
Hundred Years*
*All This, and Heaven, Too**

Jack Finney
*Invasion of the Body
Snatchers**
*Time and Time Again**

F. Scott Fitzgerald
*The Great Gatsby**
This Side of Paradise
*The Beautiful and the
Damned*
Tender Is the Night
*The Last Tycoon**

Paul Gallico
*The Snow Goose**
Mrs. 'Arris Goes to Paris
*The Poseidon Adventure**

John Gardner
The Sunlight Dialogues
Jason and Medeia
Grendel
October Light

Ellen Glasgow
The Descendant
Barren Ground
In this our Life

Gail Godwin
The Perfectionists
The Odd Woman
A Southern Family

Mary Gordon
Final Payments
Company of Women
Men and Angels

Shirley Ann Grau
The Hard Blue Sky
The Keepers of the House

Andrew Greeley
The Cardinal Sins
Ascent into Hell
Thy Brother's Wife

Zane Grey
The Last of the Plainsmen
Riders of the Purple Sage

Arthur Hailey
*Airport**
*Hotel**
Wheels
The Moneychangers
Strong Medicine

Alex Haley
*Roots**

James Hall (co-authored)
Trilogy:
*Mutiny on the Bounty**
Men Against the Sea
Pitcairn Island

Thomas Harris
*The Silence of the Lambs**

John Hawkes
The Cannibal
Travesty
Innocence in Extremis

Nathaniel Hawthorne
*The Scarlet Letter**
*The House of the Seven Gables**
The Marble Faun

Joseph Heller
*Catch-22**
Something Happened
Good as Gold
God Knows

Ernest Hemingway
In Our Time
*The Sun Also Rises**
*A Farewell to Arms**
For Whom the Bell Tolls
*The Old Man and the Sea**

John Hersey
*A Bell for Adano**
Hiroshima
The Wall
*The War Lover**
The Child Buyer
The Algiers Motel Incident

Georgette Heyer
The Black Moth
Regency Buck
Friday's Child
The Reluctant Widow
The Grand Sophie

George Higgins
*The Friends of Eddie Coyle**
The Digger's Game
City on the Hill
Penance for Jerry Kennedy

S. E. Hinton (for young readers)
*That Was Then, This Is Now**
*Tex**
*Rumblefish**

Evan Hunter
*Blackboard Jungle**
*Strangers when we Meet**
Streets of Gold

Fannie Hurst
*Humoresque**
Back Street
*Imitation of Life**

Zora Neale Hurston
Their Eyes Were Watching God
Jonah's Gourd Vine

John Irving
*The World According to Garp**
*The Hotel New Hampshire**
Cider House Rules

Helen Hunt Jackson
*Ramona**

Rona Jaffe
*The Best of Everything**
Family Secrets
After the Reunion: A Novel

Henry James
*Daisy Miller**
*The Portrait of a Lady**
*Washington Square**
The Spoils of Poynton
*The Turn of the Screw**
The Ambassadors
*The Golden Bowl**
*The Bostonians**

James Jones
*From Here to Eternity**
*Some Came Running**
The Thin Red Line

Erica Jong
Fear of Flying
How to Save Your Own Life
Parachutes and Kisses
Fanny

MacKinlay Kantor
Long Remember
*Andersonville**
*The Voice of Bugle Ann**

William Kennedy
The Ink Truck
*Ironweed**
Quinn's Book

Ken Kesey
*One Flew Over the
Cuckoo's Nest**

John Knowles
*A Separate Peace**
Phineas
Peace Breaks Out

Judith Krantz
*Scruples**
*Princess Daisy**
*I'll Take Manhattan**

Maxine Kumin
Nightmare Factory
The Long Approach

Oliver La Farge
Laughing Boy
Sparks Fly Upward

Louis L'Amour
*Hondo**
*Shalako**
The Haunted Mesa

Harper Lee
*To Kill a Mockingbird**

Madeleine L'Engle
The Small Rain
A Wrinkle in Time
A Cry Like a Bell

Elmore Leonard
*Hombre**
City Primeval
*Bandits**

Ira Levin
*Rosemary's Baby**
*The Stepford Wives**

Sinclair Lewis
*Main Street**
*Babbitt**
*Arrowsmith**
*Elmer Gantry**
*Dodsworth**

Jack London
*The Call of the Wild**
*The Seawolf**
*White Fang**
Martin Eden
The Road

Anita Loos
*Gentlemen Prefer Blondes**

Alison Lurie
Love and Friendship
The War Between the Tates
Foreign Affairs

Norman Mailer
*The Naked and the Dead**
*Executioner's Song**

Bernard Malamud
*The Natural**
The Assistant
*A New Life**
God's Grace
*The Tenants**
Dubin's Lives

J. P. Marquand
*The Late George Apley**
Wickford Point
*H. M. Pulham, Esquire**

Mary McCarthy
A Charmed Life
Cannibals and Missionaries
*The Group**

Carson McCullers
*The Heart Is a Lonely
Hunter**
*A Member of the Wedding**
*Reflections in a Golden Eye**
Clock Without Hands

Jay McInerney
*Bright Lights, Big City**
Ransom

Larry McMurtry
Horseman, Pass By
*The Last Picture Show**
*Terms of Endearment**
*Lonesome Dove**

Herman Melville
*Moby Dick**
Typee
Omoo
White-Jacket
Pierre
*Billy Budd**
Benito Cereno

James Michener
*Tales of the South Pacific**
*Bridges at Toko-Ri**
*Sayonara**
*Hawaii**
The Source
Space
Alaska
Caribbean
*Centennial**

Margaret Mitchell
*Gone With the Wind**

Toni Morrison
The Bluest Eye
Tar Baby
Beloved
Sula

Vladimir Nabokov
Lolita*
The Real Life of Sebastian Knight
Bend Sinister
Pale Fire
Ada

Howard Nemerov
The Homecoming Game*

Joyce Carol Oates
Wonderland
Do with Me What You Will
Childwold
Unholy Love
A Bloodsmoor Romance
Solstice
Trilogy:
A Garden of Earthly Delights
Expensive People
Them

Edwin O'Conner
The Last Hurrah*
The Edge of Sadness

(Mary) Flannery O'Connor
Wise Blood*
The Violent Bear It Away

John O'Hara
Butterfield 8*
Appointment in Samarra
A Rage to Live*
Ten North Frederick*
From the Terrace*
Pal Joey (related stories)*

Walker Percy
The Moviegoer
The Last Gentleman
Love in the Ruins
Lancelot
The Second Coming

Marge Piercy
Dance the Eagle to Sleep
Fly Away Home

Katherine Anne Porter
Ship of Fools*

Chaim Potok
The Chosen*
The Promise
My Name Is Asher Lev
Davita's Harp

Edward Reynolds Price
A Long and Happy Life

Mario Puzo
The Fortunate Pilgrim
The Godfather*
The Sicilian*

Thomas Pynchon
The Crying of Lot 49
Gravity's Rainbow
Vineland
V*

Ayn Rand
The Fountainhead*
Atlas Shrugged

Margaret Rawlings (for young readers
The Yearling*
The Sojourner

Ishmael Reed
The Freelance Pallbearers
The Last Days of Louisiana Red
Cab Calloway Stands in for the Moon
Mumbo-Jumbo

Harold Robbins
Never Love a Stranger*
The Dream Merchants
A Stone for Danny Fisher
The Carpetbaggers*
The Adventurers*
The Betsy*
The Lonely Lady*
The Storyteller
79 Park Avenue

Kenneth Roberts
Arundel
Rabble in Arms
Northwest Passage*

Rosemary Rogers (romances)
Sweet Savage Love
Lost Love, Last Love
The Wanton

Ole E. Rolvaag
Giants in the Earth
Their Father's God
Peder Victorious

Henry Roth
Call It Sleep

Philip Roth
Portnoy's Complaint*
Letting Go
When She Was Good
The Great American Novel
The Professor of Desire
The Counterlife
Trilogy:
The Ghost Writer
Zuckerman Unbound
The Anatomy Lesson

J. D. Salinger
The Catcher in the Rye
Franny and Zooey
Raise High the Roof Beam, Carpenters
Seymour: An Introduction

William Saroyan
My Name Is Aram
The Human Comedy*

Budd Schulberg
What Makes Sammy Run?*
The Harder They Fall*
Everything that Moves

Erich Segal
Love Story*
Oliver's Story*

Irwin Shaw
  *The Young Lions**
  *Two Weeks in Another Town**
  *Rich Man, Poor Man**
  Evening in Byzantium
  Beggarman, Thief
  Acceptable Losses

Sidney Sheldon
  The Naked Face
  *The Other Side of Midnight**
  *Bloodline**
  A Stranger in the Mirror
  *Rage of Angels**
  *Master of the Game**
  If Tomorrow Comes

Upton Sinclair
  World's End
  Dragon's Teeth
  King Coal
  Oil!
  The Jungle

Isaac Bashevis Singer
  Satan in Goray
  *The Magician of Lublin**
  Old Love
  *Yentl, The Yeshiva Boy**
  Shosha
  Trilogy:
  The Family Moskat
  The Manor
  The Estate

Jane Smiley
  A Thousand Acres
  Moo
  Ordinary Love and Goodwill

Betty Smith
  *A Tree Grows in Brooklyn**
  Maggie — Now
  *Joy in the Morning**

Jean Stafford
  Mountain Lion
  A Mother in History
  Boston Adventure

Danielle Steel
  Passion's Promise
  *Remembrance**
  *Changes**
  Kaleidoscope

Wallace Stegner
  The Woman on the Wall
  Angle of Repose
  Crossing to Safety

Gertrude Stein
  Things as They Are
  Mrs. Reynolds

John Steinbeck
  Tortilla Flat
  In Dubious Battle
  *Of Mice and Men**
  *The Grapes of Wrath**
  *Cannery Row**
  *The Pearl**
  *East of Eden**
  The Winter of Our Discontent

Rex Stout
  (Nero Wolfe novels)
  Three at Wolfe's Door
  If Death Ever Slept
  A Family Affair
  *Gambit**
  Please Pass the Guilt
  Might as Well be Dead
  Silent Speaker

Harriet Beecher Stowe
  *Uncle Tom's Cabin**
  The Key to Uncle Tom's Cabin

William Styron
  The Confessions of Nat Turner
  Lie Down in Darkness
  Set this House on Fire
  *Sophie's Choice**

Booth Tarkington
  Seventeen
  *The Magnificent Ambersons**
  *Alice Adams**

Peter Taylor
  A Woman of Means
  The Widows of Thornton
  A Summons to Memphis

Paul Theroux
  Fong and the Indians
  Girls at Play
  Jungle Lovers
  *Saint Jack**
  The Family Arsenal
  *The Mosquito Coast**
  The Black House
  My Secret History
  Picture Palace

Kay Thompson
  Eloise
  Eloise in Paris

John Kennedy Toole
  A Confederacy of Dunces

Mark Twain
  *The Adventures of Tom Sawyer**
  *The Prince and the Pauper**
  *The Adventures of Huckleberry Finn**
  *A Connecticut Yankee in King Arthur's Court**
  *The Tragedy of Pudd'nhead Wilson**

Anne Tyler
If Morning Ever Comes
Earthly Possessions
*The Accidental Tourist**
Breathing Lessons

John Updike
*Rabbit, Run**
Rabbit Redux
Rabbit Is Rich
The Centaur
*The Music School**
Couples
The Coup
Too Far to Go
*The Witches of Eastwick**
A Month of Sundays
Roger's Versions
Saint Maybe

Leon Uris
*Battle Cry**
Armageddon
*Topaz**
*Exodus**
Mila Eighteen
Trinity
The Haj

Gore Vidal
Williwaw
The City and the Pillar
*Myra Breckinridge**
Lincoln: A Novel

Kurt Vonnegut, Jr.
Piano Player
Cat's Cradle
*Slaughterhouse Five**
Breakfast of Champions
Galapagos

Irving Wallace
The Chapman Report
*The Prize**
The Man
*The Seven Minutes**
The Fan Club
The Miracle

Alice Walker
*The Color Purple**
The Third Life of Grange Copeland
*Meridian**
The Temple of My Familiar
Horses Make a Landscape More Beautiful

Joseph Wambaugh
*The New Centurions**
*The Blue Knight**
*The Onion Field**
*The Choirboys**
*The Glitter Dome**
*The Black Marble**
*Echoes in the Darkness**

Robert Penn Warren
*All the King's Men**
A Place to Come To

Eudora Welty
Losing Battles
Delta Wedding
The Optimist's Daughter
A Curtain of Green
The Powder Heart

Nathanael West
The Dream Life of Balso Snell
Miss Lonelyhearts
A Cool Million
*The Day of the Locust**

Edith Warton
The House of Mirth
Ethan Frome
*The Age of Innocence**

E. B. White (for young readers)
Stuart Little
*Charlotte's Web**
The Trumpet of the Swan

Laura Ingalls Wilder (for young readers)
*Little House in the Big Woods**
Farmer Boy
*Little House on the Prairie**
On the Banks of Plum Creek

Thornton Wilder
*The Bridge of San Luis Rey**
The Cabela
The Woman of Andros
Heaven's My Destination

Owen Wister
*The Virginian** (western prototype)

Thomas Wolfe
You Can't Go Home Again
Look Homeward, Angel

Herman Wouk
*The Caine Mutiny**
*Marjorie Morningstar**
*The Winds of War**
*War and Remembrance**
Inside, Outside

Richard Wright
*Native Son**
The Outsider
The Long Dream

Paul Zindel (for young readers)
The Pigman
My Darling, My Hamburger
The Girl who Wanted a Boy
Pardon Me, You're Stepping on My Eyeball
To Take a Dare

65. The Novel Masters (Other Than American)

This list includes important novelists (other than American) and representative works. Novels marked with an asterisk became major movies, plays, or TV dramas. See also List 64, The Novel Masters (American); List 66, Novelists and Storytellers: Women; and List 67, Novel: Picaresque.

Jorge Amado (Brazilian)
Dona Flor and her Two Husbands

Yehuda Amichai (Israeli)
Not of This Time, Not of This Place

Jane Austen (British)
Pride and Prejudice*
Emma

Honorè de Balzac (French)
The Human Comedy

Simone de Beauvoir (French)
She Came to Stay
The Mandarins

Andrè Breton (French)
Nadja

Charlotte Bronte (British)
Jane Eyre*

Emily Bronte (British)
Wuthering Heights*

Ivan Bunin (Russian)
The Gentleman from San Francisco

Albert Camus (French)
The Stranger*

Miguel de Cervantes (Spanish)
Don Quixote*

François Chateaubriand (French)
Atala

(Sidonie) Colette (French)
The Cat*
Gigi*

Joseph Conrad (British)
Heart of Darkness
Lord Jim*

Daniel Defoe (British)
Robinson Crusoe*

Charles Dickens (British)
Great Expectations*
Oliver Twist*
The Tale of Two Cities*

Fyodor Dostoyevsky (Russian)
Crime and Punishment*
The Brothers Karamazov*

Alexander Dumas, Père (French)
The Count of Monte Cristo*
The Three Musketeers*

George Eliot (British)
The Mill on the Floss*
Middlemarch

Henry Fielding (British)
Tom Jones*
Joseph Andrews*

Gustave Flaubert (French)
Madame Bovary*

C. S. Forester (British)
Horatio Hornblower series
The African Queen*

E. M. Forster (British)
A Passage to India*
The Longest Journey
A Room with a View*
Where Angels Fear to Tread
Howard's End*

Anatole France (French)
The Crime of Sylvestre Bonnard

Carlos Fuentes (Mexican)
Aura
Birthdays

John Galsworthy (British)
The Forsyte Saga

Gabriel Garcia-Marquez (Colombian)
One Hundred Years of Solitude

Theophile Gautier (French)
Mademoiselle de Maupin

Jean Genet (French)
Our Lady of the Flowers

Andrè Gide (French)
The Counterfeiters

Jean Giraudoux (French)
My Friend from Limousin

William Golding (British)
Lord of the Flies*

Maxim Gorky (Russian)
The Artamanov Business

Günter Grass (German)
The Tin Drum*

Knut Hamsun (Norwegian)
Hunger

Thomas Hardy (British)
Tess of the D'Urbervilles*
The Return of the Native

Hermann Hesse (German)
Steppenwolf

Victor Hugo (French)
*The Hunchback of Notre Dame**
*Les Miserables**

Aldous Huxley (British)
Brave New World

James Joyce (Irish)
The Portrait of the Artist as a Young Man
Ulysses
Finnegan's Wake

Frankz Kafka (Czechoslovakian)
*The Trial**
*Metamorphosis**

Yasunari Kawabata (Japanese)
Snow Country
Thousand Cranes

Nikos Kazantzakis (Greek)
*Zorba the Greek**
*The Last Temptation of Christ**

Alexander Kielland (Norwegian)
Skipper Worse

Rudyard Kipling (British)
*Captain's Courageous**

Jerzy Kosinski (Polish)
The Painted Bird

Par Lagerkvist (Swedish)
Barabbas

Giuseppe di Lampedusa (Italian)
*The Leopard**

D. H. Lawrence (British)
Sons and Lovers
*Women in Love**

Alain Renè Lesage (French)
Adventures of Gil Blas of Santillane

J. Machado de Assis (Brazilian)
Dom Casmurro

Naguib Mahfouz (Egyptian)
Cairo Trilogy

Heinrich Mann (German)
*Professor Unrat**

Thomas Mann (German)
Buddenbrooks
Dr. Faustus
The Magic Mountain

Allesandro Manzoni (Italian)
The Betrothed

Roger Martin du Gard (French)
The World of the Thibaults

Harry Martinson (Swedish)
The Road
Cape Farewell

W. Somerset Maugham (British)
*Of Human Bondage**
The Moon and Sixpence
Ashendon
*The Razor's Edge**

Colleen McCullough (Australian)
The Thorn Birds

Vilhelm Moberg (Swedish)
*The Emigrants**

Alberto Moravia (Italian)
The Wheel of Fortune
The Time of Indifference

Shikibu Murasaki (Japanese)
Tales of Genji

George Orwell (British)
*Animal Farm**
*1984**

Baroness Orczy (Hungarian)
*The Scarlet Pimpernel**

Boris Pasternak (Russian)
*Doctor Zhivago**

Alan Paton (South African)
*Cry, the Beloved Country**

Marcel Proust (French)
Remembrance of Things Past

Francois Rabelais (French)
Gargantua and Pantagruel

Erich Maria Remarque (German)
*All Quiet on the Western Front**

Mordccai Richler (Canadian)
Joshua Then and Now
*The Apprenticeship of Duddy Kravitz**

Francoise Sagan (French)
A Certain Smile
Bonjour Tristesse

George Sand (French)
Lelia

Arthur Schnitzler (Austrian)
*Merry-Go-Round**

Frans Sillanpaa (Finnish)
Meek Heritage

Claude Simon (French)
The Flanders Road

Sir Walter Scott (British)
*Ivanhoe**
Heart of Midlothian

Mary Shelley (British)
*Frankenstein**

Mikhail Sholokhov (Russian)
The Quiet Don

Alexander Solzhenitsyn (Russian)
The Gulag Archipelago
One Day in the Life of Ivan Denisovich

Stendahl (French)
The Red and the Black
The Charterhouse of Parma

Jonathan Swift (British)
Gulliver's Travels*

William M. Thackeray
(British)
Vanity Fair*

J. R. R. Tolkien (British)
The Hobbit*
Lord of the Rings trilogy

Leo Tolstoy (Russian)
War and Peace*
Anna Karenina

Anthony Trollope (British)
Barchester Towers
Phineas Finn

Ivan Turgenev (Russian)
Fathers and Sons

Sigrid Undset (Norwegian)
Kristin Lavransdatter

Quevedo y Villegas (Spanish)
The Swindlers

H. G. Wells (British)
The Time Machine*

Morris West (Australian)
The Devil's Advocate

Virginia Woolf (British)
To the Lighthouse
Mrs. Dalloway
Jacob's Room

Emile Zola (French)
Nana*

66. NOVELISTS AND STORYTELLERS: WOMEN

In 1855, Nathaniel Hawthorne complained to his publisher that the American literary scene had been given over to a "damned mob of scribbling women." Here is a list of some of those female novelists that he felt were encroaching upon his territory, along with other outstanding women who have given the world important novels and stories. See also List 150, Women: Books/Stories with Female Emphasis; List 151, Women: Important Writers; and List 152, Women Writers: Women's Issues.

Louisa May Alcott — *Little Women; Little Men; Jo's Boys*

Jean M. Auel — *The Clan of the Cave Bear*

Judy Blume — (Prolific writer for teenagers)

Barbara Bradford — *A Woman of Substance*

Alice Brown — *The Country Road; Empire of Death*

Pearl Buck — *Dragon Seed; The Good Earth*

Frances Hodgson Burnett — *The Secret Garden; The Little Princess (for children)*

Willa Cather — *O, Pioneers!; Song of the Lark; My Antonia*

Mary Hartwell Catherwood — *Romance of Dollard*

Kate Chopin — *Bayou Folk; A Night in Acadie; The Awakening*

Beverly Cleary — (Prolific writer for teenagers)

Marie S. Cummins — *The Lamplighter*

Mary Maples Dodge — *Hans Brinker; or the Silver Skates*

Nora Ephron — *Heartburn*

Mary E. Wilkins Freeman — *A Humble Romance and Other Stories*

Alice French — *The Man of the Hour; Knitters in the Sun*

Ellen Glasgow — *The Descendant; In This Our Life; Barren Ground*

Gail Godwin — *A Southern Family; Battle Ground*

Mary Gordon — *Men and Angels; Final Payments*

Shirley Ann Grau — *The Keepers of the House*

Georgette Heyer — (Prolific writer of Regency romances)

Helen Hunt Jackson — *Ramona*

Sarah Orne Jewett — *The Country of the Pointed Firs*

Erica Jong — *Fear of Flying; Fanny*

Judith Krantz — *Scruples*

Maxine Kumin — *The Long Approach*

Madeleine L'Engle — (Prolific writer for teenagers)

Margaret Mitchell — *Gone with the Wind*

Toni Morrison — *Tar Baby; Beloved*

Marge Piercy — *Dance the Eagle to Sleep*

Katherine Ann Porter — *Ship of Fools*

Margaret Rawlings — *The Yearling*

Rosemary Rogers — (Prolific writer of romances)

Mary Shelley — *Frankenstein*

Betty Smith — *A Tree Grows in Brooklyn*

Danielle Steel — (Prolific writer of modern romances)

Harriet Beecher Stowe — *Uncle Tom's Cabin*

Anne Tyler — *The Accidental Tourist; Breathing Lessons*

Alice Walker — *The Color Purple*

Susan Warner — *The Wide, Wide World; Queechy*

Eudora Welty — *The Ponder Heart*

Edith Wharton — *The Custom of the Country; Ethan Frome; The Age of Innocence*

Laura Ingalls Wilder — (Prolific writer for teenagers)

Constance Fenimore Woolson — *Jupiter Lights, a Novel*

67. NOVEL: PICARESQUE

This special type of novel tells the story of a main character who is born with few advantages and is often a rogue. The protagonist usually wanders around, suffering many indignities and surviving one painful situation after another. Usually, the reader is meant to sympathize with the main character throughout his travails. Through cunning and adaptability, the hero or heroine ends up conforming to the harsh, cruel world and its demands. The works are often satiric. Examples are listed below.

Anonymous — *Estebanillo Gonzalez* (1646)

Anonymous — *Lazarillo de Tormes* (1554)

Mateo Aleman — *Guzman de Alfarache (The Rogue)* (1599–1604)

Saul Bellow — *The Adventures of Augie March* (1953)

Hugh Henry Brackenridge — *Modern Chivalry* (1792–1815)

Albert Camus — *The Stranger* (1942)

Louis Ferdinand Celine — *Journey to End of Night* (1932)

Miguel de Cervantes — *Don Quixote* (1605)

Daniel Defoe — *Moll Flanders* (1722)

Charles Dickens — *The Pickwick Papers* (1836–37)

Ralph Ellison — *The Invisible Man* (1952)

Henry Fielding — *Joseph Andrews* (1742); *Tom Jones* (1749)

Francisco Gomez de Quevedo — *El Buscon* (1626)

Joseph Heller — *Catch-22* (1961)

Alain Lesage — *The Adventures of Gil Blas* (1715–35)

Thomas Mann — *Confessions of Felix Krull, Confidence Man* (1954)

Thomas Nashe — *The Unfortunate Traveller* (1594)

Paul Scarron — *Comic Romance* (1651–57)

Tobias Smollett — *Roderick Random* (1748)

William Makepeace Thackeray — *Vanity Fair* (1847–48)

Mark Twain — *Adventures of Huckleberry Finn* (1884)

Christoffel von Grimmelshausen — *The Adventures of Simplicissimus* (1669)

Most people know at least the major nursery rhyme characters. Here are some of the most famous.

NAMED CHARACTERS

Bobby Shafto — went to sea

Billy Boy — charming boy gone to seek a wife

Doctor Fell — unpopular doctor

Doctor Foster — went to Gloucester in the rain

Georgie Porgie — kissed the girls and made them cry

Humpty Dumpty — tumbled off a wall

Jack — nimble and quick; jumped over a candlestick

Jack and Jill — went up a hill to fetch water and fell down

Jack Sprat — could eat no fat; had wife that ate no lean

Johnny Green — put a cat in the well

Knave of Hearts — stole some tarts, but learned his lesson

Little Bo Peep — lost her sheep

Little Boy Blue — shepherd boy who fell fast asleep

Little Jack Horner — sat in a corner eating a Christmas pie

Little Miss Muffet — frightened off her tuffet by a spider

Little Polly Flanders — sat among the cinders and got punished

Little Robin Redbreast — had an encounter with a cat

Margery Daw — went on the seesaw

Mary — quite contrary; had a garden

Mary — had a little lamb that followed her to school one day

Old King Cole — a merry old soul who called for his fiddlers three

Old Mother Hubbard — found a bare cupboard

Peter — pumpkin eater who kept his wife in a pumpkin shell

Peter Piper — picked a peck of pickled peppers

Polly — put the kettle on for tea

Queen of Hearts — made some tarts

Simple Simon — met a pieman going to the fair

Solomon Grundy — born on Monday, died on Sunday

Taffy — Welsh thief who stole some beef

Tom — piper's son who stole a pig

Tommy Snooks and Bessy Brooks — took a walk one Sunday

Tommy Stout — pulled a cat out of the well

Tommy Tucker — sang for his supper

Tweedledum and Tweedledee — were about to battle over a rattle

Wee Willie Winkie — ran through town in his nightgown

UNNAMED CHARACTERS

Barber — shaved a pig to get hairs for a wig

Black Hen — laid eggs for gentlemen

Black Sheep — are asked if they have any wool

A Crooked Man — walked a crooked mile, lived in a crooked house, and so on

Curly Locks — was proposed to and promised to be treated royally

King of France — marched up and down a hill

Ladybird — was admonished to fly away home

Lion and the Unicorn — fought for the crown, but were drummed out of town

Little Girl — had a little curl right in the middle of her forehead; was sometimes good, sometime horrid

Little Pussy — had a warm boat, was appreciated and well cared for

Old Woman — lived in a shoe with too many children

Pretty Maid — was asked to be married, then was rejected, but had a curt reply

Pussy Cat — wandered away and people wondered where she was

Ten O'Clock Scholar — came to school late

Three Men in a Tub — butcher, baker, and candlestick-maker rub-a-dub-dubbed until they were thrown out

Three Wise Men of Gotham — sank when they went to sea in a bowl

Three Little Kittens — cried when they lost their mittens

Two Cats of Kilkenny — fought until they killed each other

Wise Old Owl — spoke little, heard a lot, and knew much

69. SCIENCE FICTION MASTERS

Some of these works are books, others are individual stories. See the latest edition of *Annual World's Best Science Fiction*, edited by Donald A. Wollheim for excellent contributions to the genre. See also List 52, Fantasy/Horror/Ghosts; List 53, Fantasy/Horror/Ghosts: Collections; and List 54, Fantasy Series and King Arthur Stories.

Aldiss, Brian — Hot House; Greybeard; Frankenstein Unbound; Brotherhood of the Head; The Dark Light Years; Barefoot in the Head; The Long Afternoon of Earth; Helliconia trilogy (Helliconia Spring; Helliconia Summer; Helliconia Winter); Cyrptozoic!; The Eighty-Minute Hour: A Space Opera (parody)

Anderson, Poul — Trader to the Stars; Guardians of Time; Tau Zero; The Star Fox; Brain Wave; The Corridors of Time

Asimov, Isaac — Foundation (series); Nightfall; I, Robot; The Rest of the Robots; Caves of Steel; The Intelligent Man's Guide to Science (2 volumes); The Gods Themselves; The End of Eternity; A Subway Named Mobius; Pebble in the Sky; Opus 100

Benford, Gregory — Artifact

Bishop, Michael — No Enemy but Time

Blish, James — Cities in Flight (series); A Case of Conscience; A Torrent of Faces (co-authored); Jack of Eagles; Midsummer Century (Note: Wrote some episodes for Star Trek television series.)

Bova, Ben — Voyagers; Voyagers II; Privateers

Bradbury, Ray — The Illustrated Man; Fahrenheit 451; The Martian Chronicles; Dandelion Wine; The Halloween Tree; I Sing the Body Electric; (Note: Movies made of several books.)

Bradley, Marion Zimmer — Darkover (series)

Brin, David — The Postman; The Practice Effect; Startide Rising

Brown, Frederic — What Mad Universe; Martians, Go Home

Brunner, John — Stand on Zanzibar; The Sheep Look Up; Squares of the City; The Crucible of Time; The Atlantic Abomination; Times Without Number; Endless Shadow; The Whole Man

Burgess, Anthony — A Clockwork Orange; The Wanting Seed

Burroughs, Edgar Rice — At the Earth's Core

Burroughs, William S. — Nova Express

Campbell, John Wood — Who Goes There?; The Thing (movie) (Note: sci-fi magazine editor for nearly thirty-five years)

Cherryh, C. J. — Down Below Station; Cuckoo's Egg

Clarke, Arthur C. — Childhood's End; Sentinel; 2001: A Space Odyssey; Rendezvous with Rama; The Fountains of Paradise; Imperial Earth; Prelude to Space

Clement, Hal — Close to Critical; Needle; Mission of Gravity

Crichton, Michael — The Andromeda Strain

Decamp, Lyon Sprague — Viagens Interplanetarias (stories)

Delany, Samuel — Toromon trilogy; Nova; Dahlgren; Babel 17; The Einstein Intersection; Driftglass; Neveryona: Or, The Tale of Signs and Cities; Triton; The Fall of the Towers trilogy: Out of the Dead City; The Towers of Toron; City of a Thousand Suns

Del Rey, Lester — Nerves; The Eleventh Commandment

Dick, Philip K. — Time Out of Joint; Do Androids Dream of Electric Sheep? (movie); The Man who Jaded; The Man in the High Castle; Martian Time-Slip; The Three Stigmata of Palmer Eldritch; The Game-Players of Titan; Galactic Pot-Healer; Our Friends from Folix-B; Now Wait for Last Year; Eye in the Sky; Bloodmoney; We Can Build You; Counter-Clock World; Vulcan's Hammer

Dickson, Gordon — Dorsai trilogy; Soldier Ask Not; Delusion World; The Alien Way

Doyle, Sir Arthur Conan — The Lost World

Ellison, Harlan — A Boy and his Dog; I Have No Mouth and I Must Scream; Dark Visions; The Beast who Shouted Love at the Heart of the World; Ellison Wonderland; Alone Against Tomorrow; Dangerous Visions (Note: Wrote for Star Trek television series.)

Farmer, Philip J. — To Your Shattered Bodies Go; The Unreasoning Mask; Venus on the Half-Shell

Golding, William — The Inheritors

Harrison, Harry — Bill, the Galactic Hero; Make Room! Make Room!; War with the Robots; The Technicolor Time Machine; Planet Story (parody)

Heinlein, Robert — Farmer in the Sky; Stranger in a Strange Land; The Moon is a Harsh Mistress;…And he Built a Crooked House; I Will Fear No Evil; The Puppet Masters; A Citizen of the Galaxy; Have Spacesuit — Will Travel; The Door into Summer

Herbert, Frank — Dune; Dune Messiah; The Illustrated Dune; Hellstrom's Hive; Dragon in the Sea; Children of Dune; The God Makers; Heretics of Dune; Chapterhouse: Dune; Destination: Void

Huxley, Aldous — Brave New World; Island

Keyes, Daniel — Flowers for Algernon

Kornbluth, Cyril M. — (co-authored with Frederick Pohl) The Syndic

Kuttner, Henry — Mutant: The Dark World; Earth's Last Citadel; Fury

Le Guin, Ursula — The Left Hand of Darkness; The Lathe of Heaven; The Dispossessed; Always Coming Home

Leiber, Fritz — The Wanderer

Lem, Stanislaw — Solaris; The Invincible; Mortal Engines; The Cyberiad; One Human Minute; A Perfect Vacuum; Tales of Pirx the Pilot

Lewis, C. S. — Out of the Silent Planet; That Hideous Strength

McCaffrey, Anne — Dragonflight; Restoree; The Ship Who Sang; Crystal Singer; Killashandra; Dragonriders of Pern (series); To Ride Pegassus

Matheson, Richard — I am Legend; The Shrinking Man

Niven, Laurence von Cott — The Mote in God's Eye; Ringworld; Lucifer's Hammer; A Gift from Earth; Neutron Star; The Integral Trees; Footfall; Oath of Fealty; A World out of Time; World of Ptavvs (Note: Wrote sometimes with J. Pournelle.)

Orwell, George — 1984

Padgett, Lewis — Well of the Worlds; Mutant (Note: Wrote sometimes with wife C. L. Moore.)

Pohl, Frederick — The Space Merchants; Man Plus; Gateway; Drunkard's Walk; The Age of the Pussyfoot (Note: Sometimes wrote with Cyril M. Kornbluth)

Pronzini, Bill and Barry N. Malzberg — Prose Bowl (parody)

Silverberg, Robert — Nightwings; A Time of Changes; The Masks of Time

Simak, Clifford D. — Way Station; City; Here Gather the Stars; Ring Around the Sun; Time and Again; Time Is the Simplest Thing; A Choice of Gods

Smith, Cordwainer — The Planet Buyer; You Will Never be the Same; Space Lords; Norstrilia

Smith, Edward Elmer — Lensman series; Skylark series

Stapledon, William Olaf — Star Maker; Odd John; Last and First Men

Strugatsky, Arkady and Boris Strugatsky — Prisoners of Power; Roadside Picnic; Monday Begins on Saturday

Sturgeon, Theodore — More than Human; Cosmic Rape; The Dreaming Jewels (Note: Wrote for Star Trek television series.)

Vance, Jack — The Dying Earth; Eyes of the Overworld; To Live Forever

van Vogt, Alfred — Slan; The World of Null-A; The Weapon Shops of Isher; Voyage of the Space Beagle; The Weapon Makers; Mission to the Stars; Rogue Ship

Verne, Jules — Five Weeks in a Balloon; A Journey to the Center of the Earth; Twenty Thousand Leagues under the Sea; Around the World in Eighty Days; From the Earth to the Moon (Note: Writings described some scientific advancements that have since come to pass.)

Vinge, Joan D. — The Snow Queen; World's End

Vonnegut, Kurt, Jr. — Sirens of Titan; Slaughterhouse Five; Cat's Cradle; Player Piano

Wells, Herbert George — The Time Machine; The Invisible Man; The War of the Worlds; The First Men in the Moon; When the Sleeper Wakes

Wilhelm, Kate — Let the Fire Fall; Where Late the Sweet Birds Sang

Williamson, John (Jack) — The Humanoids; Reefs of Space (trilogy); Legion of Time; Darker than You Think (Note: Sometimes co-authored with Frederick Pohl.)

Wolfe, Gene — The Book of the New Sun: The Shadow of the Torturer; The Claw of the Conciliator; The Sword of the Loctor; The Citadel of the Autarch

Wyndham, John — The Midwich Cuckoos; The Village of the Damned (movie); Day of the Triffids; Rebirth

Zelazny, Roger — The Dream Master; And Call Me Conrad; Lord of Light; Isle of the Dead; This Immortal

70. THE SHORT STORY: CHARACTERISTICS

Short stories are not just abbreviated novels but have their own particular characteristics. Readers can use the following list of qualities to evaluate the short stories they read (or write).

1. All language is concise and necessary to the story.

2. A single emotion or impression is sustained throughout.

3. There is seldom a change of scene.

4. The opening sentence/paragraph arouses and hold attention.

5. One life experience is dealt with, rather than several.

6. The plot is simple.

7. Action takes place in the shortest amount of time possible.

8. Every character is essential.

9. The story creates one strong effect, instead of a series of effects.

10. The ending reflects the beginning and resolves what was begun.

11. The story ends when the author's purpose is fulfilled.

12. The story has the unities of one time, one place, one action.

13. Setting, character, or action is emphasized — not all three. The first paragraph should show which.

14. One could not add or detract from the story without destroying it.

15. The end may contain a twist or surprise to fulfill its author's purpose.

71. SHORT STORY COLLECTIONS

The following collections of short stories, listed by names of editors, provide a broad range of authors: men, women, black, white, Jewish, Christian, American, European, Canadian, Latin American, South African, Puerto Rican, classic, and modern.

Abrahams, William — *Prize Stories of the Seventies*

Angus, Douglas and Sylvia — *Great Modern European Short Stories*

Bellow, Saul — *Great Jewish Short Stories; Best American Short Stories of 19__* (annual collection)

Booth, Mark — *Christian Short Stories*

Cahill, Susan — *Women and Fiction*

Cerf, Bennett — *Great Modern Short Stories*

Clarke, John Henrik — *American Negro Short Stories*

Crane, Milton — *Fifty Great American Short Stories*

Gallo, Donald R. — *Sixteen: Short Stories by Outstanding Writers for Young Adults*

Goodman, Roger B. — *Seventy-five Short Masterpieces: Stories from the World's Literature*

Hughes, Langston — *The Best Short Stories by Negro Writers*

Lucas, Alex — *Great Canadian Short Stories*

Mancini, Pat McNees — *Contemporary Latin American Short Stories*

Raffel, Burton — *Signet Classic Book of Contemporary Short Stories*

Rosen, Kenneth — *The Man to Send Rain Clouds*

Rosenthal, Lucy — *Great American Love Stories*

Simmen, Edward — *The Chicano: From Caricature to Self-Portrait*

Stegner, Wallace and Margy Stegner — *Great American Short Stories*

Wagenheim, Kal — *Cuentos: An Anthology of Short Stories from Puerto Rico*

Warren, Robert Penn, and Albert Erskine — *Short Story Masterpieces*

72. THE SHORT STORY MASTERS

Some of the following titles are books containing short story collections. Others are important individual story titles. The authors and their works are divided into two sections: American Authors and Authors (Other Than Americans). See also List 70, The Short Story: Characteristics; List 71, Short Story Collections; and List 73, Short Works.

AMERICAN AUTHORS

Sherwood Anderson
"Winesburg" "Ohio"

James Baldwin
"Sonny's Blues"

Toni Cade Bambara
"My Man Bovanne"

Rick Bass
The Watch: Stories; "The Legend of Pig-Eye"

Ann Beattie
Secrets and Surprises

Saul Bellow
"A Father to Be"; "Mosby's Memoirs";
Him with His Foot in his Mouth and Other Stories

Stephen Vincent Benet
"The Devil and Daniel Webster"

Ambrose Bierce
"An Occurrence at Owl Creek Bridge";
"Jupiter Doke, Brigadier General";
"The Death of Halpin Frazer";
"The Moonlit Road"

Alice Brown
The Country Road

Raymond Carver
Will You Please Be Quiet, Please?

John Cheever
"The Five-Forty-Eight"; *The Stories of John Cheever*

Stephen Crane
"The Open Boat"; "The Blue Hotel";
"The Bride Comes to Yellow Sky"

Deborah Eisenberg
"The Custodian"

William Faulkner
"Barn Burning"; "Red Leaves";
"Wash, Old Man"; "A Rose for Emily"

Martha Finley
Elsie Dinsmore Stories (for young readers)

Mary Wilkins Freeman
*Humble Romance and Other Stories;
A New England Nun and Other Stories*

Kathryn Forbes (McLean)
"Mama's Bank Account"

Zona Gale
"The Charivari"

Mary Gordon
"At the Kirks'" "Separation"

Shirley Ann Grau
The Black Prince and Other Stories

Elizabeth Graver
"The Body Shop"

Edward Everett Hale
"The Man without a Country"

Bret Harte
"The Luck of Roaring Camp"; "The Outcasts of Poker Flat"

Nathaniel Hawthorne
Twice-told Tales; "Young Goodman Brown"; "Dr. Heidegger's Experiment"; "Mr. Higginbotham's Catastrophe"; "The Celestial Railroad"

Ernest Hemingway
"The Snows of Kilimanjaro"; "The Short Happy Life of Francis Macomber"; "The Killers"; "Indian Camp"; "The End of Something"; "Big Two-Hearted River"; "Fathers and Sons"; "Soldiers Home"

O. Henry
"The Adventures of Shamrock Jolnes"; "The Exact Science of Matrimony"; "The Gift of the Magi"; "Man About Town"; "The Ransom of Red Chief"; "A Retrieved Reformation"

Siri Hustvedt
"Houdini"

Washington Irving
"The Legend of Sleepy Hollow"; "Rip van Winkle"

Shirley Jackson
"The Lottery"

Henry James
"Europe"; "The Tree of Knowledge"; "The Turn of the Screw"

Sarah Orne Jewett
"Deep Haven"; *A White Heron and Other Stories*

Ring Lardner
"Haircut"; "Love Nest"; "Alibi Ike"; "You Know Me, Al"

Ursula Le Guin
"The Ones who Walk Away from Omelas"; *The Wind's Twelve Quarters*

Jack London
Tales of the Fish Patrol; "The Son of the Wolf"; "The Apostate"; "Children of the Frost"; "To Build a Fire"

Bernard Malamud
"The Prison"; "The Magic Barrel"; "Pictures of Fidelman"; "Idiot's First"

Mary McCarthy
Cast a Cold Eye

Herman Melville
"Bartleby, the Scrivener"

Alice Munro
"Friend of My Youth"

Joyce Carol Oates
A Sentimental Education; Raven's Wing; "Wheel of Love"; "Where Are You Going, Where Have You Been?"; "Upon the Sweeping Flood"

(Mary) Flannery O'Connor
"A Good Man is Hard to Find"; "Everything that Rises Must Converge"; *Flannery O'Connor: The Complete Stories*

John O'Hara
The Doctor's Son and Other Stories; The Cape Cod Lighter; The Hat on the Bed; The Horse Knows the Way

Tillie Olsen
Tell Me a Riddle

Grace Paley
The Little Disturbances of Man; Enormous Changes at the Last Minute; "Later the Same Day"

Dorothy Parker
Laments for the Living; After Such Pleasures; "The Big Blonde"

Edgar Allan Poe
"The Black Cat"; "The Cask of Amontillado"; "The Fall of the House of Usher"; "The Gold Bug"; "Ligeia"; "The Masque of the Red Death"; "Murders in the Rue Morgue"; "The Mystery of Marie Roget"; "The Pit and the Pendulum"; "The Purloined Letter"; "William Wilson"

Katherine Anne Porter
Flowering Judas; Pale Horse, Pale Rider; "The Leaning Tower"; "The Jilting of Granny Weatherall"; "Rope"; "Noon Wine"; "Old Mortality"; "Theft"; "Hacienda"; *The Collected Stories of Katherine Anne Porter*

Philip Roth
Good Bye, Columbus

J. D. Salinger
Nine Stories; "A Perfect Day for Banana Fish"

William Saroyan
"The Daring Young Man on the Flying Trapeze"; "Fifty Yard Dash"

Delmore Schwartz
The World Is a Wedding; Successful Love and Other Stories

Jean Stafford
Collected Stories; Children are Bored on Sunday; Bad Characters

Wilbur Daniel Steele
"Footfalls"

John Steinbeck
"Flight"; *The Long Valley;* "The Red Pony"

Frank R. Stockton
"The Lady or the Tiger?"

Peter Taylor
"Miss Leonora Last Seen"; "In the Miro District"; "The Old Forest"; *The Collected Stories*

Paul Theroux
Sinning with Annie and Other Stories; The Consul's File

James Thurber
"The Secret Life of Walter Mitty"; "The Night the Bed Fell": "The Catbird Seat"

Mark Twain
"The Celebrated Jumping Frog of Calaveras County"; "Mysterious Stranger"

John Updike
Pigeon Feathers and Other Stories; Too Far to Go: The Maples Stories

Alice Walker
In Love and Trouble

Eudora Welty
"The Golden Apples"; "The Bride of Innisfallen"; "Why I Live at the Po"; "The Worn Path"; "The Petrified Man"; The Collected Stories of Eudora Welty

Edith Wharton
"Roman Fever"

Owen Wister
"The Jimmyjohn Boss"; "Lin McLean"

AUTHORS (OTHER THAN AMERICANS)

Sholom Aleichem (Russian)
The Best of Sholom Aleichem

Yehuda Amichai (German)
The World Is a Room and Other Stories

Isaac Babel (Russian)
Odessa Tales; Red Cavalry

Henri de Balzac (French)
"A Passion in the Desert"

Bjornstjerne Bjornson (Norwegian)
A Happy Boy

Anton Chekhov (Russian)
"The Kiss"; "Misery"; "The Lady with the Dog"; "The Bishop"; "The Bet"

Joseph Conrad (British)
"The Secret Sharer"

Coppee (French)
"The Substitute"

Alphonse Daudet (French)
Monday Tales

Arthur Conan Doyle (British)
"The Red-Headed League"; "A Study in Scarlet"; "Hound of the Baskervilles"

Anatole France (French)
The Mother-of-Pearl Box

Nadine Gordimer (South African)
Selected Stories

William W. Jacobs (British)
"The Monkey's Paw"; *Many Cargoes;* "Captains All"; *Night Watches*

James Joyce (Irish)
Dubliners; "Araby"; "The Boarding House"

Franz Kafka (German)
"The Hunter Gracchus"; "Metamorphosis"; "The Hunger Artist"

Rudyard Kipling (British)
"The Man who would Be King"; "The Strange Ride of Morrowbie Jukes"; "Baa, Baa, Black Sheep"; "The Village that Voted the Earth was Flat"; *The Jungle Book*

Selma Lagerlof (Swedish)
The Wonderful Adventures of Nils (for young readers)

D. H. Lawrence (British)
"The Odour of Chrysanthemums"; "The Fox"; "The Blind Man"; "The Horse Dealer's Daughter"; "The Rocking Horse Winner"

Doris Lessing (British)
African Stories

Hugh Lofting (British/American)
The Story of Dr. Doolittle; The Voyages of Dr. Doolittle; Dr. Doolittle and the Secret Lake (all for young readers)

Thomas Mann (German/American)
"Disorder and Early Sorrow"; *Death in Venice and Other Stories*

Katherine Mansfield (British)
"Her First Ball"; *The Garden Party and Other Stories; Bliss and Other Stories*

Gabriel Garcia Marquez (Colombian)
"Very Old Man with Enormous Wings"

W. Somerset Maugham (British)
"Miss Thompson"; "Rain"

Guy de Maupassant (French)
"A Piece of String"; "The Necklace"; "Ball of Fat (Ball of Tallow)"; "The House of Mlle. Fifi"; "The Mask"

Prosper Merimèe (French)
"Carmen"

Alice Munro (Canadian)
Dance of the Happy Shades; Something I've Been Meaning to Tell You; The Progress of Love; Friend of My Youth

Edna O'Brien (Irish)
A Rose in the Heart

Frank O'Connor (Irish)
Guests of the Nation; Crab Apple Jelly; Domestic Relations

Sean O'Faolain (Irish)
Midsummer Night Madness and Other Stories; The Heat of the Sun

Saki (British)
"The Open Window"; *Reginald*

Isaac Singer (Polish/American)
Gimpel the Fool and Other Stories; "The Spinoza of Market Street"; *Collected Stories of Isaac Bashevis Singer; Death of Methuselah and Other Stories;* "The Dead Fiddler"; "A Crown of Feathers"

Leo Tolstoy (Russian)
"Where Love Is, there God is Also"

Ivan Turgenev (Russian)
A Sportsman's Sketches

OTHER CLASSIC SHORT STORY WRITERS (GREAT BRITAIN)

English

H. E. Bates
C. S. Forester
Graham Greene
Nigel Kneale
William Plomer
V. S. Pritchett
William Sansom
Christopher Sykes
Frances Tower
Evelyn Waugh

Irish

Daniel Corkery
Eric Cross
Mary Lavin
Bryan MacMahon
George Moore
Liam O'Flaherty
James Plunkett

Scottish

Sir James Barrie
Samuel Rutherford Crockett
Ian Hamilton Finlay
Thomas Gillespie
Dorothy Haynes
George MacDonald
Ian Macpherson
M. M. Reid
Sir Walter Scott

73. SHORT WORKS

Readers who want to encounter great authors but do not have time, inclination, or patience for longer works, can turn to this list of outstanding short literature. These works, ranging from a few pages to novella length, are well worth making time for. See also List 71, Short Story Collections; and List 72, The Short Story Masters

Martin Armstrong — "The Poets and the Housewife"

Isaac Asimov — "The Fun They Had"

Saul Bellow — *Seize the Day*

Bible — "David and Goliath"

Ray Bradbury — "Embroidery"

Lewis Carroll — *Alice's Adventures in Wonderland*

Willa Cather — "Old Mrs. Harris"; "Uncle Valentine"; "Neighbour Rosicky"; "The Enchanted Bluff"; "The Bohemian Girl"; *A Wagner Matinee;* "Paul's Case"; "Eric Hermannson's Soul"

Anton Chekhov — "The Slanderer"

Fyodor Dostoyevsky — "A Gentle Creature"; *The Dream of a Ridiculous Man; Notes from the Underground; The Gambler;* "A Disgraceful Affair"; *The Double; White Nights; The Eternal Husband*

Lord Dunsany — "The Speech"

Oliver Goldsmith — "The Soldier's Story"

Nathaniel Hawthorne — *The Scarlet Letter;* "The Minister's Black Veil";
   "Rappacini's Daughter"; "Ethan Brand"; "The Birthmark"; "Roger Malvin's Burial";
   "Major Molineaux"

O. Henry — "The Courier"; "The Ransom of Mack"; "Jimmy Hayes and Muriel"; "Two
   Thanksgiving Day Gentlemen"; "Mammon and the Archer"

Henry James — *Washington Square; Daisy Miller; The Aspern Papers;* "The Pupil"; "The
   Beast in the Jungle"

Wolf Mankowitz — "A Handful of Earth"

John Masefield — "The Yarn of Happy Jack"

Herman Melville — *Billy Budd, Sailor;* "Benito Cereno"; "The Bell Tower"; "Poor Man's
   Pudding and Rich Man's Crumbs"; "The Encantadas"; "The Town-Ho's Story"

Hguyen-Du — "The Abandoned Pagoda"

George Orwell — *Animal Farm*

Edgar Allan Poe — "The Tell-Tale Heart"

Saki — "Mrs. Packletide's Tiger"

William Saroyan — "One of Our Future Poets, You Might Say"

Susan Sontag and Howard Hodgkin — "The Way We Live Now"

Dorothy Stevens — "The Priceless Gift"

Leo Tolstoy — "Master and Man"; "Father Sergius"; *Jadji Murad;* "Alyosha the Pot"; *The
   Death of Ivan Ilych; The Devil; The Kreutzer Sonata;* "The Cossacks"; *Family Happiness;*
   "Children May Be Wiser than their Elders"

Mark Twain — "Jim Baker's Bluejay Yarn"; "A True Story"; "The Man that Corrupted
   Hadleyburg"; "The Mysterious Stranger"; "Old Times on the Mississippi"; "The Man
   who put up at Gadsby's"

Fred Urquhart — "Two Ladies"

Voltaire — *Candide*

Roger Zelazny — *Horseman!*

74. Speech Masters

Those who like history often enjoy the texts of eloquent speeches made by famous people who have shaped world events. Some of these speeches are listed here, in chronological order with the topic or occasion noted. You may want to read the speech and try to pick out the theme as shown in a phrase, sentence, or paragraph.

SPEAKER	OCCASION/TOPIC	DATE
Moses	Presenting the Ten Commandments	c. 1250 B.C.
Marcus Cicero	After an attempt on his life by Catiline	63 B.C.
Julius Caesar	Objecting to execution of Catiline	63 B.C.
Marcus Cato, the Younger	Demanding execution of Catiline	63 B.C.
Jesus Christ	Sermon on the Mount	33 A.D.
Girolamo Savonarola	Feast of the Ascension (asking people to repent)	May 12, 1496
Martin Luther	Defending himself at Diet of Worms	April 18, 1521
Queen Elizabeth	Visiting her troops (facing the Spanish Armada)	July 29, 1588
Andrew Hamilton	Defending Zenger in freedom of press trial	August 4, 1735
James Otis	Arguing against illegal search and seizure	February 24, 1761
William Pitt, the Elder	Arguing against taxation without representation	January 14, 1766
Patrick Henry	Arguing for American independence	March 23, 1775
Benjamin Franklin	Constitutional Convention (just before the signing of Declaration of Independence)	September 17, 1787
William Wilberforce	Arguing against slave trade	May 12, 1789
Honoré Mirabeau	Arguing for the right of King of France to wage war	May 22, 1790
Thomas Erskine	Arguing for the rights of man, as declared by Thomas Paine	December 18, 1792
Maximilien de Robespierre	Arguing for morality and tyranny	February 5, 1794
Napoleon Bonaparte	Speaking to his victorious troops	April 26, 1796

SPEAKER	OCCASION/TOPIC	DATE
Henry Gratton	Speaking in Irish parliament to defend himself	February 14, 1800
Lord Byron	Arguing for the rights of the working class	February 27, 1812
Frances (Fanny) Wright	Fourth of July celebration at New Harmony, Indiana	July 4, 1828
Thomas Macaulay	Speaking in Parliament for Jewish emancipation	April 17, 1833
Ralph Waldo Emerson	Arguing for the right to intellectual freedom	August 31, 1837
Wendell Phillips	At Faneuil Hall, arguing for abolition of slavery	December 8, 1837
Henry Highland Garnet	At National Negro Convention	August 1843
Alexis de Tocqueville	Speaking at the French Chamber of Deputies warning that revolution was soon to come	January 29, 1848
Elizabeth Cady Stanton	Arguing for women's rights at convention	July 19, 1848
Daniel Webster	Speaking in Senate about slavery	March 7, 1850
Frederick Douglass	Former slave speaks on Independence Day in New York	July 4, 1852
Louis Pasteur	Lecturing on science at a university	December 7, 1854
John Brown	Defending himself in court against treason charges	November 2, 1859
Abraham Lincoln	At dedication of National Cemetery at Gettysburg	November 19, 1863
Abraham Lincoln	Second inaugural speech	March 4, 1865
John Ruskin	Lengthy speech called "The Mystery of Life and its Arts"	May 13, 1868
Henry George	Speech on progress and poverty (December 8, 1837 relationship)	June 1878
Fyodor Dostoyevsky	Centennial of Pushkin's birth and celebration of Russian literature	June 8, 1880
Henry Grady	Speech to heal New South after Civil War	December 22, 1886
Booker T. Washington	At Atlanta on role of African-Americans	September 18, 1893

SPEAKER	OCCASION/TOPIC	DATE
William Jennings Bryan	"Cross of Gold" speech at Democratic National Convention	July 8, 1896
Woodrow Wilson	First political speech	September 15, 1910
Woodrow Wilson	Speech to Congress to declare war on Germany	April 2, 1917
Nikolai Lenin	Speaking about the workers' rebellion	November 7, 1917
Mohandas K. Gandhi	Speaking at his trial for sedition	March 23, 1922
Clarence Darrow	Plea to Detroit court involving justice for blacks	May 19, 1926
F. D. Roosevelt	First inaugural speech	March 4, 1933
Adolph Hitler	Justification of his bloody purge	July 13, 1934
Edward VIII	Giving up his royal position to marry an American divorcèe	December 11, 1936
Winston Churchill	House of Commons, vote of confidence	May 13, 1940
Winston Churchill	House of Commons, vowing all-out war effort	June 18, 1940
Joseph Stalin	To his people about the war	July 3, 1941
F. D. Roosevelt	Asking Congress for declaration of war	December 8, 1941
Dwight D. Eisenhower	After victory in Europe	June 12, 1945
W. E. B. DuBois	On life in the South	October 20, 1946
David Lilienthal	Defining democracy	February 3, 1947
Jawaharlal Nehru	Speaking to the people after Gandhi's murder	January 30, 1948
William Faulkner	Accepting Nobel Prize for Literature	December 10, 1950
Douglas MacArthur	Defending himself with "Old soldiers never die..." talk	April 19, 1951
Dwight D. Eisenhower	Inaugural address	January 20, 1953
Harry Truman	Powers of President	May 8, 1954
John F. Kennedy	Inaugural address	January 20, 1961

SPEAKER	OCCASION/TOPIC	DATE
Martin Luther King, Jr.	"I have a dream…" speech	August 28, 1963
John F. Kennedy	Poetry and Power	October 26, 1963
Malcolm X	Black revolution	January 21, 1965
Lyndon Johnson	Vietnam war and decision not to run for reelection	March 31, 1968
Jimmy Carter	Inaugural speech	January 12, 1971
Richard Nixon	Watergate Case	April 30, 1973
Mario Cuomo	Democratic National Convention keynote speech	July 16, 1984
Jesse Jackson	"Keep hope alive!" Democratic National Convention speech	July 19, 1988

75. STORY-TELLING FRAMEWORK

This list contains works built around the narration of a series of tales. Though each author treats the theme differently, basically the characters are in the same place at the same time for a unified purpose, and the work unfolds as they tell stories to each other.

Arabian Nights Entertainment (The Thousand and One Nights; The Arabian Nights) — Author Unknown (Antoine Galland, translator; Richard Burton, translator, English version). Stories told by Scheherazade in order to save her life, notably "The History of Ali Baba and the Forty Thieves," "The History of Sinbad the Sailor," and "The History of Aladdin, or the Wonderful Lamp."

The Canterbury Tales — Geoffrey Chaucer. Pilgrims on horseback tell tales on their way to Canterbury, England, each revealing interesting facets of their personalities and social status. See List 165, England in the Fourteenth Century (Chaucer's *Canterbury Tales*).

Decameron — Giovanni Boccaccio. Ten people flee the city of Florence for the countryside to escape the plague; each tells one story a day for ten days, resulting in one hundred stories in all

The Earthly Paradise — William Morris. These five volumes of poetry are about a group of Norsemen fleeing from unfortunate circumstances and heading across the sea to a fabled earthly paradise. They fail to find it and return to a city where twice a month they hold a feast and tell tales. Of the twenty-four stories told, half are classical Greek tales and half are medieval romances.

Metamorphoses — Ovid (Ovidius Naso). A series of fifteen books of classical myths, mostly about humans changing into animals, plants, and other forms.

Tales of a Wayside Inn — Henry Wadsworth Longfellow. This series of poems consists of tales supposedly told at the Red Horse Tavern in Sudbury, Massachusetts, in 1863. Perhaps the opening poem, "Paul Revere's Ride" is the most famous work in the volume.

76. THE WESTERN MASTERS

The appeal of Westerns as a literary genre has stood the test of time. They are full of action, adventure, and self-reliant people; good triumphs over evil, and readers can experience in their imagination the simple, unrestrained life of the Wild West. Here are some of the most popular westerns, both classic and modern, including many prototypes of basic themes. Asterisks (*) denote humorous parodies of the western genre. They are arranged alphabetically by author. See also List 150, Women: Books/Stories with Female Emphasis.

Adams, Andy — *The Log of a Cowboy*

Adams, Clifton — *Shorty**

Atherton, Gertrude — *Before the Gringo Came; The Californians*

Barr, Amelia — *Remember the Alamo*

Bass, Milton — *Jory*

Berger, Thomas — *Little Big Man*

Bickham, Jack — *The Apple Dumpling Gang**

Bradford, Richard — *Red Sky at Morning; So Far from Heaven*

Brand, Max — *Destry Rides Again; The Gentle Desperado*; Fightin' Fool; Singing Guns; The Untamed*

Brown, Dee — *Action at Beecher Island; The Girl from Fort Wicked*

Burnett, W. R. — *Adobe Walls; Bitter Ground*

Burroughs, Edgar Rice — *Apache Devil; The War Chief; The Bandit of Hill's Bend; Sheriff of Comanche County*

Capps, Benjamin — *The Trail to Ogallala; The White Man's Road; A Woman of the People; White Apache*

Clark, Walter Van Tilburg — *The Oxbow Incident*

Comfort, Will — *Apache*

Condon, Richard — *A Talent for Loving; or, The Great Cowboy Race**

Cook, Will — *The Drifter; The Apache Fighter; Two Rode Together*

Decker, William — *To Be a Man*

Durham, Marilyn — *The Man Who Loved Cat Dancing*

Erdman, Louella — *The Year of the Locust*

Evans, Max — *The Rounders*; The Hi Lo Country; The One-Eyed Sky*

Ferber, Edna — *Cimarron*

Fergusson, Harvey — *Wolf Song; Blood of the Conquerors; In Those Days*

Fisher, Clay — *Nino*

Fisher, Vardis — *Mountain Man*

Giles, Janice Holt — *Six-Horse Hitch*

Grey, Zane — *Riders of the Purple Sage; U. P. Trail; Trail Driver; Wilderness Trek; The Lone Star Ranger; The Light of Western Stars; Forlorn River; The Vanishing American; To the Last Man; The Spirit of the Border; The Last of the Plainsmen* (Note: Wrote nearly one hundred Westerns.)

Greenberg, Alvin — *The Invention of the West**

Gulick, Bill — *Liveliest Town in the West*; They Came to a Valley*

Guthrie, Jr., A. B. — *The Big Sky; Fair Land, Fair Land; The Way West; These Thousand Hills; The Big H. and Other Stories*

Hall, Oakley — *Warlock*

Harte, Bret — *The Luck of Roaring Camp; The Outcasts of Poker Flat*

Haycox, Ernest — *Canyon Passage; The Earthbreakers; The Adventurers; Troubleshooter; Free Grass; Trail Town; Rawhide Range; Bugles in the Afternoon; Man in the Saddle; The Border Trumpet; Stage to Lordsburg*

Henry, Will — *McKenna's Gold; From Where the Sun Now Stands; One More River to Cross; Death of a Legend*

Hough, Emerson — *The Covered Wagon*

Jakes, John — *The Kent Family Chronicles*

Johnson, M. — *The Man Who Shot Liberty Valance*

Johnson, Dorothy M. — *Indian Country; The Hanging Tree*

Kantor, MacKinlay — *Gentle Annie*

Knibbs, H. H. — *The Ridin' Kid from Powder River*

L'Amour, Louis — *The Empty Land; Hondo; Chancy; Down the Long Hills; Sackett Family Series; Dutchman's Flat; Four-Card Draw; Riding for the Brand; His Brother's Debt*

La Farge, Oliver — *Laughing Boy*

Lea, Tom — *The Wonderful Country; The Brave Bulls*

LeMay, Alan — *The Searchers; The Unforgiven; Useless Cowboy*; The Smokey Years*

Leonard, Elmore — *Valdez Is Coming*

Lott, Milton — *Back Track*

MacLeod, Robert — *The Muleskinner; The Californio*

Manfred, Frederick — *Conquering Horse; This Is the Year*

Matthews, Jack — *Sassafras**

Matthews, John Joseph — *Sundown*

McMurtry, Larry — *Lonesome Dove; Horseman, Pass By; Leaving Cheyenne*

Miller, Arthur — *The Misfits*

Mulford, Clarence E. — *Hopalong Cassidy*

Myers, John — *Dead Warrior**

Nye, Nelson — *Wolf Trap*

O'Rourke, Frank — *The Bride Stealer*; The Swift Runner; The Last Ride*

Purdom, Herbert — *A Hero for Henry**

Reese, John — *My Brother John; Jesus on Horseback; Horses, Honor, and Women*; Singalee; Sure Shot Shapiro*

Rhodes, Eugene Manlove — *Paso por Aqui; Good Men and True*

Richter, Conrad — *The Sea of Grass*

Santee, Ross — *Cowboy*

Schaefer, Jack — *Shane; Monte Walsh*

Shelley, John and David Shelley — *Hell-for-Leather Jones**

Short, Luke — *Ride the Man Down; Debt of Honor; Ambush*

Spearman, Frank — *Whispering Smith*

Striker, Fran — *The Lone Ranger*

Taylor, Robert Lewis — *The Travels of Jaimie McPheeters*

Turner, William — *Destination Doubtful**

Twain, Mark — *The Celebrated Jumping Frog of Calaveras County; Roughing It*

White, Stewart Edward — *Arizona Nights; The Story of California*

Will, Henry — *One More River to Cross; Death of a Legend; The Gates of the Mountains*

Williams, Jeanne — *The Valiant Women*

Wister, Owen — *The Virginian*

SECTION

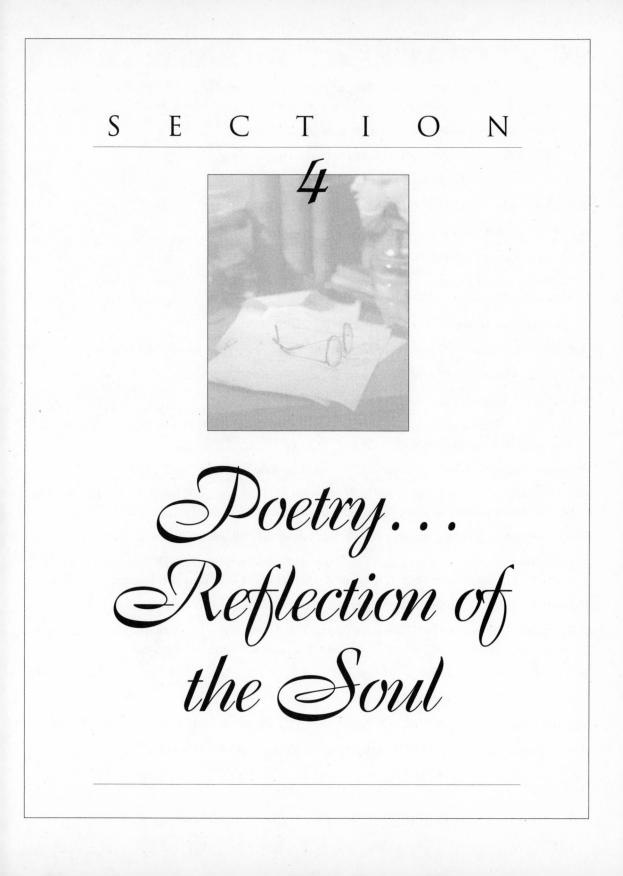

4

Poetry...
Reflection of
the Soul

77. MASTER AMERICAN POETS

Note: ▲ Pulitzer prizewinners; ◆ Bollingen prizewinners. See also List 78, Poets Laureate of England and the United States; and List 138, Poe: Complete Stories and Poems.

◆ **Leonie Adams** — Collected Poems (with Louise Bogan)

▲◆ **Conrad Aiken** — The Charnel Rose; Selected Poems

◆ **Archie Randolph Ammons** — Collected Poems

▲◆ **John Ashbery** — Self-Portrait in a Convex Mirror

▲◆ **W. H. Auden** — The Age of Anxiety

▲ **Leonard Bacon** — Sunderland Capture

▲ **Stephen Vincent Benet** — "John Brown's Body"; "Western Star"; "Thomas Jefferson 1743–1826" (written with Rosemary Benet)

▲ **William Rose Benet** — The Dust Which Is God

▲◆ **John Berryman** — "Homage to Mistress Bradstreet"; Seventy-Seven Dream Songs

▲ **Elizabeth Bishop** — Poems, North and South

John Peale Bishop — Now with His Love; Minute Particulars

Robert Bly — Silence in the Snowy Fields; The Light Around the Body; Point Reyes Poems; Loving a Woman in Two Worlds

◆ **Louise Bogan** — Collected Poems: 1923–53; The Blue Estuaries

Anne Bradstreet — The Tenth Muse Lately Sprung Up in America; "The Author to Her Book"; In Reference to her Children; "Upon the Burning of Our House"

Joseph Brodsky — Short and Long Poems; "A Halt in the Wilderness"; "The End of a Lovely Era"

▲ **Gwendolyn Brooks** — Annie Allen; The World of Gwendolyn Brooks; "We Real Cool"; Sadie and Maud; The Lovers of the Poor; A Bronzeville Mother Loiter in Mississippi; Boy Breaking Glass

Raymond Carver — Ultramarine; Where the Water Comes Together with Other Water

John Ciardi — Homeward to America; I Marry You; How Does a Poem Mean? (an introduction to poetry); Thirty-Nine Poems; "For Instance"; Echoes: Poems Left Behind

▲ **Robert P. Tristram Coffin** — Strange Holiness

Hart Crane — The Bridge; White Buildings; Collected Verse

Stephen Crane — "War Is Kind"; "A Newspaper"; "In the Night"; "I Wonder"; "Black Riders"

◆ **e. e. cummings** (sic) — Fifty Poems; Poems; Is Five; Ninety-Five Poems

James Dickey — Buckdancer's Choice; Stone and Other Poems; "The Zodiac"

Emily Dickinson — Collected Poems; Further Poems of Emily Dickinson; "The Lost Jewel"; "Fringed Gentian"; "Called Back"; "The Martyrs"; "Time's Healing"; "Hope"; "Disenchantment"; "The Past"; "Much Madness Is Divinest Sense"; "Because I Could not Stop for Death"; "I Heard a Fly Buzz"; "I Felt a Funeral in My Brain"; "I Taste a Liquor Never Brewed"; "I'm Nobody! Who Are You?"; "My Life Closed Twice Before Its Close"; "I Never Saw a Moor"; "He Ate and Drank the Precious Words"; "I'll Tell You How the Sun Rose"; "What's O'Clock"

▲ **George Dillon** — "The Flowering Stone"

Hilda Doolittle — Sea Garden; Hymen; Red Shores for Bronze; Helen in Egypt

▲ **Rita Dove** — "Thomas and Beulah"

▲ **Alan Dugan** — Poems

Paul Dunbar — Lyrics of Lowly Life; Folks from Dixie

▲◆ **Richard Eberhart** — Selected Poems; Collected Poems

Eliot, T. S. — The Waste Land

Ralph Waldo Emerson — "Brahma"; "The Problem"; "The Concord Hymn"

Lawrence Ferlinghetti — A Coney Island of the Mind; "Starting from San Francisco"; "Pictures of a Gone World"

Eugene Field — "Little Boy Blue"; "Wynken, Blynken, and Nod"; "A Little Book of Western Verse"

▲ **John Gould Fletcher** — Selected Poems

▲◆ **Robert Frost** — "New Hampshire: A Poem with Notes and Grace Notes"; Collected Poems; "A Further Range"; "A Witness Tree"; "The Death of the Hired Man"; "Stopping by Woods on a Snowy Evening"; "The Mending Wall"; "The Road not Taken"

Allen Ginsberg — Howl and Other Poems; "Kaddish"; "Planet News"; "Reality Sandwiches"; Mind Breaths: Collected Poems, 1947–80; White Shroud: Poems, 1980–1985

Albert Goldbarth — "Heaven and Earth: A Cosmology"

◆ **Horace Gregory** — Collected Poems; "Chelsea Rooming House"

Edgar Guest — "A Heap o' Livin"; "Just Folks"; "Life's Highway"

Fitz-Greene Halleck — "Croaker Papers" (co-authored); "Marco Bozzarius"

Bret Harte — "Plain Language from Truthful James (The Heathen Chinee)"

▲◆ **Anthony Hecht** — "The Hard Hours"

▲ **Robert Hillyer** — Collected Verse

Oliver Wendell Holmes — "Old Ironsides"; "The Moral Bully"; "The Chambered Nautilus"; "The Deacon's Masterpiece, or the Wonderful 'One Horse Shay'"

▲ **Richard Howard** — "Untitled Subjects"

Langston Hughes — "The Negro Sings of Rivers"; "The Weary Blues"; "Fine Clothes to the Jew"; Lament for Dark People and Other Poems

Randall Jarrell — "Blood for a Stranger"; "Little Friend, Little Friend"; "Losses"; "Pictures from an Institution"; "The Lost World"; "The Woman at the Washington Zoo"

Robinson Jeffers — "Tamar"; "The Woman at Point Sur"; "Medea"; Hungerfield and Other Poems

Erica Jong — "Loveroot"; "Fruits and Vegetables"

▲ **Donald Justice** — Selected Poems

Francis Scott Key — "The Star-Spangled Banner"

Joyce Kilmer — "Trees"

▲ **Galway Kinnell** — Selected Poems

▲ **Carolyn Kizer** — "Yin"

▲ **Maxine Kumin** — "Up Country"; "Our Ground Time Here will be Brief"

▲◆ **Stanley Kunitz** — "Intellectual Things"; Selected Poems: 1928–1958; "Next-to-Last Things"

Sidney Lanier — "Corn"; "The Symphony"; "Song of a Chattahoochee"; "The Marshes of Glynn"

Emma Lazarus — "The New Colossus"; Admetus and Other Poems

Denise Levertov — "Here and Now"; "The Jacob's Ladder"; "The Sorrow Dance"; "Oblique Prayers"

Anne Morrow Lindbergh — The Unicorn and Other Poems

Vachel Lindsay — General William Booth Enters into Heaven and Other Poems; "The Congo"; "The Chinese Nightingale"

Henry Wadsworth Longfellow — Ballads and Other Poems; "Evangeline"; "The Song of Hiawatha"; "The Courtship of Miles Standish"; "Paul Revere's Ride"; "The Village Blacksmith"

▲ **Amy Lowell** — Some Imagist Poems; "Dome of Many-Colored Glass

James Russell Lowell — "The Bigelow Papers"; "A Fable for Critics'; "The Vision of Sir Launfal"

▲ **Robert Lowell** — "Lord Weary's Castle"; "The Mills of the Kavanaughs"; "Life Studies"; "For the Union Dead"; "The Dolphin"

▲◆ **Archibald MacLeish** — "Conquistador"; Collected Poems: 1917–1952

Edwin Markham — Lincoln and Other Poems; "The Man with the Hoe"

Edgar Lee Masters — Spoon River Anthology

▲ **Phyllis McGinley** — Love Letters of Phyllis McGinley; Times Three: Selected Verse from Three Decades; "Sixpence in Her Shoe"

Rod McKuen — "Stanyan Street and Other Sorrows"; "Listen to the Warm"; "Come to Me in Silence"

▲ **William Meredith** — Partial Accounts: New and Selected Poems

▲◆ **James Merrill** — "Divine Comedies"

▲◆ **William S. Merwin** — "The Carrier of Ladders"

*****Edna St. Vincent Millay** — "Renascence"; "A Few Figs from Thistles"; "The Harp Weaver"; Eight Sonnets in American Poetry, 1922; A Miscellany

Joaquin Miller — Pacific Poems; Songs of the Sierras; Songs of the Sunlands

Clement Moore — "A Visit from St. Nicholas"

▲◆ **Marianne Moore** — "The Pangolin"; "To a Steam Roller"; "When I Buy Pictures"; "Poetry"; "Poems"; "Observations"; "What Are Years?"; Collected Poems

Ogden Nash — "One Touch of Venus" (co-authored); "I'm a Stranger Here Myself"; "Everyone but Thee and Me"

▲◆ **Howard Nemerov** — "The Image and the Law"; "Mirrors and Windows"; "The Blue Swallows"; "The Western Approaches"; Collected Poems; "Inside the Onion"

▲ **Mary Oliver** — "American Primitive"

▲ **George Oppen** — "Of Being Numerous"

Dorothy Parker — "Enough Rope"; "Sunset Gun"; "Death and Taxes"

Marge Piercy — "Breaking Camp"; "Circles on the Water"

▲ **Sylvia Plath** — "Ariel"; The Collected Poems

◆ **Ezra Pound** — Cantos

◆ **John Crowe Ransom** — "Bells for John Whiteside's Daughter"; Selected Poems; "Chills and Fever"

Ishmael Reed — Conjure: Selected Poems 1963–70

James Whitcomb Riley — The Old Swimmin' Hole and 'Leven More Poems; "Home Folks"

▲ **Edward Arlington Robinson** — "Richard Cory"; "Miniver Cheevy"; Collected Poems; "The Man Who Died Twice"; "Tristram"

▲◆ **Theodore Roethke** — "Open House"; The Lost Son and Other Poems; "The Waking"; "Words for the Wind"

Philip Roth — "What Work Is"

Muriel Rukeyser — "Waterlily Fire"; "Gates"; Collected Poems

Carl Sandburg — Chicago Poems; Complete Poems; "Breathing Tokens"; "Good Morning, America"; "The People, Yes"

▲ **James Schuyler** — "The Morning of the Poem"

◆ **Delmore Schwartz** — "In Dreams Begin Responsibilities"; "Genesis"; Summer Knowledge: New and Selected Poems 1938–58

▲ **Anne Sexton** — "To Bedlam and Part Way Back"; "All My Pretty Ones"; "Live or Die"; Love Poems; "The Awful Rowing Toward God"

▲◆ **Karl Shapiro** — "Poem, Place and Thing"; V-Letter and Other Poems; Poems of a Jew; "Auto Wreck"; "The Fly"; "Adult Book Store"; "The Piano Tuner's Wife"; "Elegy for a Dead Soldier"

▲ **Charles Simic** — "The World Doesn't End"

▲ **Louis Simpson** — The Arrivistes: Poems 1940–48; "At the End of the Open Road"; "North of Jamaica"; "Caviare at the Funeral"

▲ **W. D. Snodgrass** — "Heart's Needle"; "After Experience"

▲ **Gary Snyder** — "Turtle Island"

▲ **Leonora Speyer** — "Fiddler's Farewell"

▲◆ **Wallace Stevens** — "Sunday Morning"; "Le Monocle de Mon Oncle"; "Quince at the Clavier"; "The Comedian as the Letter C"; "Harmonium"; "Ideas of Order"; "The Man with the Blue Guitar"; Collected Poems

May Swenson — "Another Animal"; "A Cage of Spines"; Poems to Solve

◆ **Allen Tate** — Collected Poems: 1919–1976

▲ **Henry Taylor** — "The Flying Change"

Sara Teasdale — "Rivers to the Sea"; "Love Songs"; "Flame and Shadow"; "Strange Victory"

▲ **Mark Van Doren** — Collected Poems; Morning Worship and Other Poems

▲ **Peter Viereck** — "Terror and Decorum"

Julia Ward — "The Battle Hymn of the Republic"

▲◆ **Robert Penn Warren** — Promises: Poems 1954–1956; Now and Then: 1976–1978

Phillis Wheatley — Poems on Various Subjects, Religious and Moral, by Phillis Wheatley, Negro Servant to Mr. John Wheatley of Boston, in New England; Memoir and Poems of Phillis Wheatley; The Letters of Phillis Wheatley, The Negro Slave-Poet of Boston

Walt Whitman — "Song of Myself"; "Out of the Cradle Endlessly Rocking"; "When Lilacs Last in the Dooryard Bloom'd"; "O, Captain! My Captain"; Leaves of Grass

John Greenleaf Whittier — "Snow-Bound"; "Barbara Frietchie"; "The Barefoot Boy"

Michael Wigglesworth — "The Day of Doom: Or, A Poetical Description of the Great and Last Judgment"; "God's Controversy with New England"

▲◆ **Richard Wilbur** — The Beautiful Changes; Things of This World; The Poems of Richard Wilbur; "Walking to Sleep"; New and Collected Poems

▲◆ **William Carlos Williams** — Paterson; Al Que Quierre? Sour Grapes; Journey to Love; Pictures from Brueghel, and Other Poems; Collected Poems, Volume I: 1909–1939; Collected Poems, Volume II: 1939–1962

◆ **Yvor Winters** — Poems

James Wright — Collected Poems

▲ **Audrey Wurdemann** — Bright Ambush

▲ **Marya Zaturenska** — Cold Morning Sky

78. Poets Laureate of England and the United States

Poet Laureate is a title bestowed on an outstanding poet by a government. In England, poets laureate have been around since Chaucer and are appointed for their lifetimes. In the United States, the first poet laureate was appointed in 1986 by the Library of Congress. The following men and women, listed in chronological order by country, have held this coveted position. See also List 77, Master American Poets; and List 79, Master British Poets.

GREAT BRITAIN

"Unofficial" Poets Laureate:

Geoffrey Chaucer (1340)

John Kay (1461)

Andrew Bernard (1485)

John Skelton (1509)

Edmund Spencer (1547)

Samuel Daniel (1599)

Ben Jonson (1619)

Sir William D'Avenant (1637)

Official Poets Laureate:

John Dryden (1670)

Thomas Shadwell (1688)

Nahum Tate (1692)

Nicholas Rowe (1715)

Laurence Eusden (1718)

Colley Cibber (1730)

William Whitehead (1757)

Thomas Warton (1785)

Henry Pye (1790)

Robert Southey (1813)

William Wordsworth (1843)

Alfred, Lord Tennyson (1850)

Alfred Austin (1896)

Robert Bridges (1913)

John Masefield (1930)

Cecil Day-Lewis (1967)

Sir John Betjeman (1972)

Ted Hughes (1984)

Note: The following British poets refused to accept the honor of poet laureate of England, and others were appointed in their places:

Thomas Gray (1757)

William Mason (1785)

Sir Walter Scott (1813)

UNITED STATES

Robert Penn Warren (1986)

Richard Wilbur (1987)

Howard Nemerov (1988)

Mark Strand (1990)

Joseph Brodsky (1991)

Mona Van Duyn (1992)

Rita Dove (1993)

Robert Hass (1995)

See also List 78, Poets Laureate of England and the United States; List 117, Shakespeare: Complete Plays and Poems; List 165, England in the Fourteenth Century (Chaucer's Canterbury Tales); List 166, The Romantic Period (1786–1832).

Arnold Matthew — "Dover Beach"

Barker, George — Songs of Innocence

Blake, William — "Laughing Song"

Bridges, Robert — "The Idle Life I Lead"

Brooke, Rupert — "The Soldier"

Browning, Elizabeth Barrett — Sonnets from the Portuguese

Browning, Robert — "The Pied Piper of Hamelin"

Bruns, Robert — "To a Louse"

Butler, Samuel — "Hudibras"

Byron, George Gordon — "She Walks in Beauty"

Carew, Thomas — "Ask Me No More Where Jove Bestows"

Coleridge, Samuel Taylor — "Rime of the Ancient Mariner"

Cowley, Abraham — "The Wish"

Cowper, William — "John Gilpin's Ride"

Day-Lewis, Cecil — "Pegasus"

de la Mare, Walter — "The Listeners"

Donne, John — "Good Morrow"

Dryden, John — "Alexander's Feast"

Gay, John — "Black-Eyed Susan"

Goldsmith, Oliver — "The Traveller"

Graves, Robert — "Flying Crooked"

Gray, Thomas — "Hymn to Adversity"

Hardy, Thomas — "In Time of the Breaking of Nations"

Henley, William Ernest — "Invictus"

Herbert, George — "Easter Wings"

Herrick, Robert — "Gather Ye Rosebuds While Ye May"

Hodgson, Ralph — "Stupidity Street"

Hopkins, Gerard Manley — "Pied Beauty"

Houseman, A. E. — "When I was One-and-Twenty"

Hughes, Ted — Crow

Keats, John — "Ode to a Nightingale"

Kipling, Rudyard — "Gunga Din"

Jonson, Ben — "Inviting a Friend to Supper"

Langland, William — Piers Plowman

Larkin, Philip — Philip Larkin: Collected Poems

Lawrence, D. H. — "How Beastly the Bourgeois Is"

Lovelace, Richard — "To Althea from Prison"

Lyly, John — "Spring's Welcome"

MacNeice, Louis — "Snow"

Marlowe, Christopher — Hero and Leander

Masefield, John — "Sea-Fever"

Milton, John — "The Hymn"

Moore, Thomas — "Believe Me, If All Those Endearing Young Charms"

Muir, Edwin — "The Gate"

Noyes, Alfred — "The Highwayman"

Owen, Wilfred — "From My Diary, July, 1914"

Pope, Alexander — "The Universal Prayer"

Raleigh, Sir Walter — "The Nymph's Reply to the Shepherd"

Rodgers, W. R. — "White Christmas"

Rossetti, Dante Gabriel — Sonnet 86, "Lost Days"

Rossetti, Christina — "Up-Hill"

Scott, Sir Walter — "The Solitary Reaper"

Shakespeare, William — Sonnets
Shelley, Sir Philip — "The Nightingale"
Spender, Stephen — "After They Have Tired"
Spenser, Edmund — The Fairie Queen
Southey, Robert — "The Battle of Blenheim"
Suckling, Sir John — "Ballad upon a Wedding"
Swinburne, Algernon Charles — "The Salt of the Earth"

Tennyson, Alfred, Lord — "The Revenge"
Thomas, Dylan — "In My Craft or Sullen Art"
Watkins, Vernon — "The Fire in the Snow"
Wilde, Oscar — "The Ballad of Reading Gaol"
Wordsworth, William — "My Heart Leaps Up"
Yeats, William Butler — "The Song of the Old Mother"

80. Major Poets from Other Lands

Akhmatova, Anna *(Russian)*
Alexandre y Merlo, Vincente *(Spanish)*
Alighieri, Dante *(Italian)*
Aragon, Louis *(French)*
Asturias, Miguel *(Guatemalan)*
Atwood, Margaret *(Canadian)*
Basho, Matsuo *(Japanese)*
Baudelaire, Charles *(French)*
Benn, Gottfried *(German)*
Bjornson, Bjornstjerne *(Norwegian)*
Blok, Aleksandr *(Soviet)*
Boccaccio, Giovanni *(Italian)*
Boileau-Despreaux, Nicolas *(French)*
Camoens/Canies *(Portuguese)*
Carducci, Giosue *(Italian)*
Catullus, Gaius Valerius *(Roman)*
Celan, Paul *(Romanian-French)*
Cocteau, Jean *(French)*
de Bellay, Joachim *(French)*
Ekelof, Gunnar *(Swedish)*
Elytis, Odysseus *(Greek)*
Firdousi *(Persian)*
Garcia Lorca, Federico *(Spanish)*
Gautier, Thèophile *(French)*

Hafiz *(Persian)*
Heidenstam, Vernor von *(Swedish)*
Heine, Heinrich *(German)*
Heredia, Josè Maria *(Cuban)*
Hölderlin, Friedrich *(German)*
Holub, Miroslav *(Czechoslovakian)*
Homer *(Greek)*
Horace *(Roman)*
Hugo, Victor *(French)*
Jimenez, Juan Ramon *(Spanish)*
La Fontaine, Jean de *(French)*
Li Po/Li T'ai-Po *(Chinese)*
Louw, N. P. van Wky *(South African)*
Machado de Assis, Joachim Maria *(Brazilian)*
Marinetti, Filippo Tommaso *(Italian)*
Mayakovsky, Vladimir *(Russian)*
Mickiewicz, Adam *(Polish)*
Milosz, Czeslaw *(Polish)*
Mistral, Gabriela *(Chilean)*
Mistral, Frèdèric *(French)*
Montale, Eugenio *(Italian)*
Nekrasov, Nikolai *(Russian)*
Neruda, Pablo *(Chilean)*
Oehlenschlager, Adam Gottlieb *(Danish)*

Ovid *(Roman)*	Sappho *(Greek)*
Paz, Octavio *(Mexican)*	Seferis, Giorgos *(Greek)*
Perse, St. John *(French)*	Senghor, Leopold Sedar *(Senegalese)*
Pessoa, Fernando *(Portuguese)*	Service, Robert *(Canadian)*
Petrarch *(Italian)*	Tu Fu *(Chinese)*
Pindar *(Greek)*	Tzara, Tristan/Samuel Rosenfeld *(Romanian-French)*
Popa, Vasco *(Yugoslavic)*	Verlaine, Paul *(French)*
Pushkin, Alexander *(Russian)*	Virgil *(Roman)*
Quasimodo, Salvatore *(Italian)*	Voznesensky, Andrei *(Russian)*
Rimbaud, Arthur *(French)*	Yevtushenko, Yevgeny *(Russian)*
Ronsard, Pierre de *(French)*	
Saint-Exupery, Antoine de *(French)*	

81. POETRY GLOSSARY

Items marked with an asterisk (*) are explained more fully (with examples) in other lists as noted in parentheses at the end of the definition. Pronunciation aids are given immediately after the entry word. See also List 95, Figures of Speech.

*alliteration (uh-lit-er-RAY-shun) — Repetition of consonant sounds, usually at the beginnings of words, to create smoothness and effect. (See List 96, Alliteration from A to Z.)

alexandrine (al-uhks-ZAN-dreen) — One line of six iambic feet. Ex: Sustains it from beneath, and kindles it above. (Shelley, *Adonais*)

*assonance (ASS-uh-nuhns) — Repetition of internal vowel sounds for aural effect. (See List 97, Assonance.)

*ballad (BAL-luhd) — Songlike, narrative poetry; usually simple, rhyming verse using *a b c b* rhyme scheme. (See List 82, Ballad.)

*ballade (buh-LAHD) — French poetic form, usually having three stanzas and concluding with an *envoy*. Do not confuse with *ballad* above. (See List 85, French Verse Forms.)

caesura/cesura (si-ZUHR-uh) — Pause in a line of poetry before the end of the line.

cinquain (SEEN-kayn) — Five-line poetic form, with twenty-two total syllables divided according to a set pattern. (See List 100, Stanza Type and Typical Arrangement.)

*couplet — Two consecutive rhymed lines of poetry; rhyme pattern: *a a.* (See List 100, Stanza Type and Typical Arrangement.)

couplet, heroic — Two consecutive rhymed lines of poetry written in iambic pentameter. Ex: "But I have told them, 'Since you will be true,/You shall be true to them, who're false to you." — Donne

dramatic poem — Play written in verse. Ex: *Prometheus Bound* — Percy Bysshe Shelley.

***elegy** (El-uh-gee) — Poetic form lamenting the death of a person or decline of a situation. (See List 84, Elegy.)

enjambment (in-JAMB-muhnt) — Continuation of meaning from one poetry line to the next; run-on lines.

***envoy/envoi** (EN-voy) — Conclusion in last stanza or lines in certain verse forms. (See List 93, Sestina.)

***epic** — Long narrative poem, usually telling of heroic deeds, events of historic importance, or religious or mythological subjects. Examples: *Iliad; Odyssey; Beowulf.* (See List 45, Epics.)

***figure of speech** — Use or arrangement of words for specific effects. (See List 95, Figures of Speech.)

***foot** — Smallest unit of poetic measurement; lines are divided into metrical groups (feet), with from one to three syllables in each. (See List 101, Versification: Foot.)

***grue** (GROO) — Short, simple, *gruesome* rhyme, originated by writers such as Robert Louis Stevenson. (See List 86, Grue.)

***haiku** (heye-KOO) — Japanese unrhymed poetic form with one observation in three lines, seventeen syllables. (See List 87, Haiku and Tanka.)

***limerick** — Poem (often humorous) with five lines and sing-song rhythm of three beats in first, second, and fifth lines, and two in the remainder; typical rhyme pattern: *a a b b a.* (See List 88, Limerick.)

***metaphysical** (met-uh-FIZ-uh-kuhl) — Refers to seventeenth-century English poets who employed exalted imagery, spiritual topics, and witty arrogance. (See List 129, Authors by Group.)

***meter** — Rhythm of poetry; stressed and unstressed syllables in the lines. (See List 102, Versification: Meter.)

ode — Form of lyric poetry characterized by giving praise or showing appreciation. (See List 90, Ode.)

***onomatopoeia** (on-uh-mah-tuh-PEE-uh) — Words that sound like what they represent. Ex: *buzz.* (See List 98, Onomatopoeia.)

***pantoum** (pan-TOOM) — Malayan rhymed poetic form with stanzas of four lines each, according to a set pattern. A "modified" pantoum is an unrhymed pantoum. (See List 91, Pantoum.)

pastoral — Poem about country life (originally about shepherds).

***pentameter, iambic** (pen-TAM-uh-ter, eye-AM-bik) — Poetic meter; ten syllable lines, stressed on every second beat. (See List 101, Versification: Feet; and List 102, Versification: Meter.)

***pictogram, poetic** — Poetry arranged in lines that form a shape or make a picture about the subject; sometimes called "shaped poem." Ex: Christmas poem in the shape of a Christmas tree. (See List 92, Pictogram and Parallel Poem.)

poem — Literature other than prose, often with rhythm, rhyme, and lines forming stanzas.

*poem, parallel — Poem with each line starting or ending with same word or phrase. Example: I remember... (See List 92, Pictogram and Parallel Poem.)

poetry, dramatic — Poetry with characters who speak and act. Ex: Shakespearian plays.

*poetry, lyric — Short poetry usually expressing one emotion. Ex: sonnets, elegies, odes, songs. (See List 89, Lyric Poetry.)

poetry, narrative — Poetry that tells a story. Included in this category are ballads, epic poetry, and metrical romances.

poetry, occasional — Poetry written for a particular occasion.

*prosody (PRAH-suh-dee) — The study of versification: meter, rhyme, and stanza form. (See List 100, Stanza Type and Typical Arrangement; List 101, Versification: Feet; and List 102, Versification: Meter.)

*quatrain (KWAH-trayn) — Poem or stanza containing four lines. (See List 100, Stanza Type and Typical Arrangement.)

*refrain — Repetition of words or phrases at the end of each stanza in poetry or song. (See List 99, Repetition.)

rhyme — Words that sound like another word or have similar sounding parts; often used in poetry. Example: *should/could.*

romance, metrical — Poetry dealing with chivalry, love, romance, and religion. Ex: *Idylls of the King* — Tennyson.

*rondeau (RAHN-doh) — French verse form with set pattern of fifteen lines. (See List 85, French Verse Forms.)

*rondel (rahn-duhl) — French verse form with set pattern of thirteen lines. (See List 85, French Verse Forms.)

*sestina (ses-TEEN-uh) — Six-stanza poetic form plus a three-line envoy, arranged in a specific pattern. (See List 93, Sestina.)

*sonnet — Lyric poem expressing one idea, containing fourteen lines of iambic pentameter and set rhyme scheme. (See List 94, Sonnet.)

*sonnet, Petrarchan (Italian Sonnet) — Sonnet with an octave (eight lines) expressing the main theme and a sestet (six lines) expanding or contradicting the main theme. (See List 94, Sonnet.)

*sonnet, Shakespearian — Sonnet with three quatrains (stanzas of four lines each) and ending with a couplet. (See List 94, Sonnet.)

*stanza — Group of lines of poetry, usually with a common form and spaced apart from each other; commonly called a *verse.* (See List 100, Stanza Type and Typical Arrangement.)

*tanka (TAHN-kuh) — Japanese poetic form with a total of thirty-one syllables divided into five lines. (See List 87, Haiku and Tanka.)

*triolet (TREE-uh-LAY) — French poetic form with two rhymes in eight short lines, with set pattern. (See List 85, French Verse Forms.)

*verse, blank — Unrhymed iambic pentameter. Ex: Shakespeare's tragedies. (See List 83, Blank Verse and Free Verse.)

*verse, free — Also called vers libre (ver-LEE-bruh). Poetry without standard meter or rhyme, but rhythmical arrangement of lines for effect. Ex: Walt Whitman's *Leaves of Grass*. (See List 83, Blank Verse and Free Verse.)

*villanelle (VIL-uh-NEL) — French poetic form; two rhymes and six stanzas in a set pattern. (See List 85, French Verse Forms.)

82. BALLAD

Ballads, in literary usage, are short narrative poems and one of the earliest poetic forms. Many were handed down by word of mouth long before they were written. They are suitable for singing and sometimes are danced to because of their simple rhythm. Ballads usually consist of four lines per stanza. Typically, the first and third lines of each verse have four metrical feet (sometimes rhyming), and the second and fourth lines have three feet (almost always rhyming). Not all ballads have this pattern. See also List 108, War and Antiwar Poems/Songs.

IMPORTANT BALLAD COLLECTIONS

The following collections gave legitimacy to the ballad as a true poetic art form. Ballads are now accepted as literature.

Reliques of Ancient English Poetry (Thomas Percy, editor)

Minstrelsy of the Scottish Border (Sir Walter Scott, editor)

English and Scottish Popular Ballads (Francis James Child, editor)

Barrack Room Ballads (Rudyard Kipling)

Salt Water Ballads (John Masefield)

American Songbag (Carl Sandburg)

POPULAR FOLK AND/OR MINSTREL BALLADS OF ENGLAND AND SCOTLAND

Heroic (Robin Hood)
Robin Hood and the Monk
A Lytell Geste of Robyn Hode
Robin Hood's Death and Burial
Robin Hood and Allen-a-Dale

Historical
The Battle of Otterburn
Hugh of Lincoln
Johnie Armstrong
Sir Patrick Spens

Tragic
   Bonny Barbara Allan
   The Cruel Brother
   The Twa Sisters
   Young Waters (Child Waters)
   Edward

Humorous
   The Gardener
   The Farmer's Curst Wife
   Get Up and Bar the Door

Mournful (lament; coronach)
   The Twa Corbies
   Bonnie George Campbell

Supernatural
   The Wife of Usher's Well
   Kemp Owyne
   Sweet William's Ghost
   Thomas Rymer

LITERARY BALLADS (BRITISH)

The Rime of the Ancient Mariner (Samuel Taylor Coleridge)

La Belle Dame sans Merci (John Keats)

The Lady of Shalott (Alfred Lord Tennyson)

The White Ship (D. G. Rosetti)

The King's Tragedy (D. G. Rosetti)

Sister Helen (D. G. Rosetti)

Tommy (Rudyard Kipling)

The Ballad of Father Gilligan (William Butler Yeats)

Lochinvar (Sir Walter Scott)

POPULAR BALLADS OF AMERICA

Occupations
   Casey Jones
   Git Along, Little Dogies
   The Roving Gambler

War
   Yankee Doodle
   The Battle of Shiloh Hill
   The Blue and the Gray (Francis Miles
      Finch)
   Lovewell's Fight
   Nathan Hale
   Soldier Song
   The Liberty Song (John Dickinson)

"Characters"
   Billy the Kid
   Frankie and Johnny
   John Henry

Literary Ballads (American)

The Skeleton in Armor (Henry Wadsworth Longfellow)

Skipper Ireson's Ride (John Greenleaf Whittier)

The Chinese Nightingale (Vachel Lindsay)

The Night Before Christmas (Clement C. Moore)

The Wreck of the Hesperus (Henry Wadsworth Longfellow)

The Singing Leaves (James Russell Lowell)

Ballad of the Oysterman (Oliver Wendell Holmes)

Maud Miller (John Greenleaf Whittier)

Ballad Example (first verse only)

The Fate of John Burgoyne

When Jack the King's commander
  Was going to his duty,
Through all the crowd he smiled and bow'd
  To every blooming beauty.

— **Author Unknown**

83. Blank Verse and Free Verse

Blank verse is composed of unrhymed iambic pentameter. (There are five feet or stressed syllables in each line, and each foot sounds like tuh-TAH.) This verse form was popular in England in the sixteenth century and beyond, and was used by such major poets as Marlowe, Shakespeare, Keats, Milton, and Tennyson. (/ marks stressed syllables; x marks unstressed syllables.)

Example of Blank Verse:

```
x    /   x    /   x     /  x / x   /
But, soft! What light through yonder window breaks?
x / x  /    x   / x / x  /
It is the east, and Juliet is the sun.
x /   x   /   x    /   x  /x     /
Arise, fair sun, and kill the envious moon,
x    / x / x  /  x    /   x    /
Who is already sick and pale with grief
x    /    x   /    x  / x   /   x    /
That thou, her maid, art far more fair than she.
```

— **William Shakespeare,** *Romeo and Juliet*

Free verse has no set meter, line, or rhyme patterns, but has rhythm and balance. It usually uses alliteration, assonance, and imagery. Free verse is very much like prose, as illustrated in certain Bible passages from Psalms and Job. Dryden, Coleridge, and Whitman were masters of free verse.

EXAMPLES OF FREE VERSE:

"I Hear America Singing"

I hear America singing, the varied carols I hear,
Those of mechanics, each one singing his as it should be blithe
    and strong,
The carpenter singing his as he measures his plank or beam,
The mason singing his as he makes ready for work, or leaves off
    work,
The boatman singing what belongs to him in his boat, the deckhand
    singing on the steamboat deck,
The shoemaker singing as he sits on his bench, the hatter singing
    as he stands,
The wood-cutter's song, the ploughboy's on his way in the morning,
    or at noon intermission or at sundown,
The delicious singing of the mother, or of the young wife at work,
    or of the girl sewing or washing,
Each singing what belongs to him or her and to none else,
The day what belongs to the day — at night the part of young
    fellows, robust, friendly,
Singing with open mouths their strong melodious songs.

                     — **Walt Whitman,** *Leaves of Grass*

84. ELEGY

An elegy is a lyric poem about death. Elegies can be sonnets, odes, or songs, depending on the metrical form they take. Following are famous elegies listed alphabetically by poet. See also List 89, Lyric Poetry; List 90, Ode; List 94, Sonnet; and List 108, War and Antiwar Poems/Songs.

Matthew Arnold — "Thyrsis"
Mary Hunter Austin — "The Paiute Lament of a Man for His Son"
Arlo Bates — "In Paradise"
Rupert Brooke — "The Dead"
Elizabeth Barrett Browning — "On Cowper's Grave"
William Cullen Bryant — "Thanatopsis"
Robert Burns — "A Bard's Epitaph"
George Gordon Byron — "Elegy on Thurza"
William Cowper — "The Loss of the Royal George"
Walter de la Mare — "How Sleep the Brave"
Thomas Gray — "Elegy Written in a Country Churchyard"
Fitz-Greene Halleck — "On the Death of Joseph Rodman Drake"
William Ernest Henley — "Margaritae Sorori"
Oliver Wendell Holmes — "Under the Violets"
Alfred Edward Housman — "With Rue my Heart Is Laden"
Henry Wadsworth Longfellow — "Footsteps of Angels"
John Masefield — "The Island of Skyros"
Edgar Lee Masters — "Anne Rutledge"
John McCrae — "In Flanders Fields"
John Milton — "Lycidas"
Edgar Allan Poe — "Annabel Lee"
James Whitcomb Riley — "Bereaved"
Alan Seeger — "I Have a Rendezvous with Death"
William Shakespeare — "Elegy" (from *Cymbeline*)
Percy Bysshe Shelley — "Adonais"
Robert Louis Stevenson — "Requiem"
Alfred, Lord Tennyson — "In Memoriam"
Walt Whitman — "O Captain, My Captain"
Oscar Wilde — "Requiescat"
Thomas Wolfe — "The Burial of Sir John Moore"
William Wordsworth — "She Dwelt Among the Untrodden Ways"
Edward Young — "Night Thoughts"

85. FRENCH VERSE FORMS

The main early French poetic verse forms are the villanelle, rondeau, rondel, ballade, and triolet. Though complex and exacting in their specific requirements, they are delightful to read and to compose. Each is described in the list below. Explore Chaucer, W. E. Henley, Austin Dobson, and Algernon Swinburne for fine examples of these forms. See also List 81, Poetry Glossary.

VILLANELLE

6 total stanzas

2 rhymes throughout poem

first stanza
>   3 lines
>   rhyme scheme: *a b a*

second stanza
>   3 lines
>   rhyme scheme: *a b a*
>   last line: identical to first line of first stanza

third stanza
>   3 lines
>   rhyme scheme: *a b a*
>   last line: identical to last line of first stanza

fourth stanza
>   3 lines
>   rhyme scheme: *a b a*
>   last line: identical to first line of first stanza

fifth stanza
>   3 lines
>   rhyme scheme: *a b a*
>   last line: identical to last line of first stanza

sixth stanza
>   4 lines
>   rhyme scheme: *a b a a*
>   3rd line: identical to first line of first stanza
>   last line: identical to last line of first stanza

RONDEAU*

15 lines

3 stanzas

2 rhymes throughout poem

first stanza
>5 lines
>
>rhyme scheme: *a a b b a*

second stanza
>4 lines
>
>rhyme scheme: *a a b* plus refrain (see below)
>
>last line: refrain from first half, first line, first stanza

third stanza
>6 lines
>
>rhyme scheme: *a a b b a* plus refrain (same as above)
>
>last line: same refrain as in second stanza

RONDEL*

13 lines

3 stanzas

2 rhymes throughout poem

rhyme scheme: *a b b a   a b a b   a b b a a*

first stanza
>4 lines
>
>rhyme scheme: *a b b a*

second stanza
>4 lines
>
>rhyme scheme: *a b a b*
>
>last two lines: identical to first two lines of first stanza

third stanza
>5 lines
>
>rhyme scheme: *a b b a a*
>
>last line: identical to first line of first stanza (or)
>
>last two lines: identical to first two lines of first stanza

BALLADE

3 stanzas (8 lines each stanza)

envoy (4 lines)

3 rhymes with no rhyming word repeated

rhyme scheme for each stanza: *a b a b b c b c*

rhyme scheme for envoy: *b c b c*

variations

    10 lines per stanza

    4 rhymes

    6 lines in envoy

    double and triple ballades (multiples of the basic form)

TRIOLET

8 short lines

2 rhymes throughout poem

    lines 1, 3, and 5 rhyme

    lines 2 and 6 rhyme

rhyme scheme: *a b a a a b a b*

first, fourth, and seventh lines are identical

second and last lines are identical

Note: The *roundeau, rondel,* and *roundel* are variant forms of a similar pattern. The descriptions here show only two possibilities, but there are other variations.

86. GRUE

Grues are short, humorous, gruesome poems, not to be taken literally. They are fun to read and even more fun to write. A few examples follow.

Billy, in one of his nice new sashes,
Fell in the fire and was burned to ashes;
Now, although the room grows chilly,
I haven't the heart to poke poor Billy.

    — Harry Graham

Little Willie from his mirror
Licked every bit of mercury off,
Wishing, thinking, in his error,
That it would cure his whooping cough.
But when his funeral came around,
His mother said to Mrs. Brown,
"T'was a cold day for our Willie
When the mercury went down!"

    — Anonymous

When with my little daughter, Blanche,
I climbed the Alps last summer
I saw a dreadful avalanche
About to overcome her.
And as the stones came hurtling down
I vaguely wondered whether
It would be wise to cut the rope
Which bound us twain together.
I must confess I'm glad I did —
And yet I miss the child, poor kid.

      — Harry Graham

Lizzie Borden with an axe,
Hit her father forty whacks;
When she saw what she had done,
She hit her mother forty-one.

      — Anonymous

87. Haiku and Tanka

The Haiku form of Japanese poetry has three unrhymed lines of five, seven, and five syllables respectively, with a total of seventeen syllables. Originally the poems referred to one of the seasons of the year, but now they are written on various topics. The Tanka is similar, except has five lines of five, seven, five, seven, and seven syllables, with a total of thirty-one syllables. This is an enjoyable way to get started writing poetry.

Examples of Haiku

So lonely ... lovely...
The exquisite pure-white fan
of the girl I lost.

      —Buson
        (Trans. Peter Beilenson)

If things were better
for me, flies, I'd invite you
to share my supper.

      —Issa
        (Trans. Harry Behm)

Examples of Tanka

"Autumn"
Autumn comes moistly,
As frost, rain, snow vie for leaves.
Each mixes jointly
To crisscross its imprint and
Pattern its death knell for all.

      — Judie Strouf

Ah, the peasant who
   Is watching over rice field
   Seems to listen, too,
With a pensive wistful sigh,
   To the deer's receding cry.

      — Hosokawa Yusai
        (Trans. Richard Lewis)

88. LIMERICK

One successful way to get into poetry is to begin with limericks. They are quick to read, simple to understand, and often humorous. Readers are encouraged to try making up a few of their own.

"A Young Lady of Spain"

There was a young lady of Spain
Who was dreadfully sick in a train,
*   Not once, but again*
*   And again and again,*
And again and again and again.

(Note: *Again* is pronounced so it rhymes with *Spain* in this poem.)

"An Epicure"

An epicure, dining at Crewe,
Found quite a large mouse in his stew.
*   Said the waiter, "Don't shout,*
*   And wave it about,*
Or the rest will be wanting one, too!"

"An Old Man From Peru"

There was an old man from Peru
Who dreamed he was eating his shoe,
*   He woke up in a fright*
*   In the middle of the night*
And found it was perfectly true!

"A Happy Time"

There was a young fellow named Hall,
Who fell in the spring in the fall;
*   'Twould have been a sad thing*
*   If he'd died in the spring,*
But he didn't — he died in the fall.

"A Limerick"

There was a young man from Japan
Whose limericks never would scan;
*   When they said it was so,*
*   He replied, "Yes, I know,*
But I always try to get as many words into the
*   last line as I can."*

"Not Just for the Ride"

There was a young lady of Niger
Who smiled as she rode on a tiger:
*   They came back from the ride*
*   With the lady inside*
And the smile on the face of the tiger!

89. LYRIC POETRY

Lyric poetry usually expresses a single emotion. In addition to odes, elegies, and sonnets, lyric poems can have many varieties of form and rhythm. The famous lyric poetry below is listed alphabetically by poet. See also List 84, Elegy; List 90, Ode; and List 94, Sonnet.

Rosemary and Stephen Vincent Benet — "Nancy Hanks"

Bible — "King Solomon" (from *The Song of Songs*)

William Blake — "The Tyger"

William Blake — "To the Muses"

Elizabeth Barrett Browning — "The Cry of the Children"

Robert Browning — "Home Thoughts from the Sea"

Robert Burns — "A Man's a Man for A' That"

George Gordon Byron — "When we two Parted"

Thomas Campbell — "The Soldier's Dream"

Geoffrey Chaucer — "The Complaint to his Empty Purse"

Chiyo — "Hunter of the Dragonfly"

William Cowper — "On Receipt of my Mother's Picture"

Walter de la Mare — "Silver"

Emily Dickinson — "Chartless"

Robert Frost — "Snow Dust"

Johann Wolfgang Goethe — "The Erl-King"

Thomas Hardy — "Weathers"

Thomas Hood — "Past and Present"

Horace — "A Winter Party"

Alfred Edward Housman — "When I was One-and-Twenty"

Langston Hughes — "Mother to Son"

John Keats — "When I Have Fears that I may Cease to Be"

Rudyard Kipling — "If"

Edwin Markham — "Victory in Defeat"

John Masefield — "Tewkesbury Road"

Edna St. Vincent Millay — "Afternoon on a Hill"

John Milton — "Il Penseroso"

Frèdèric Mistral — "In the Mulberry Leaves"

Thomas Moore — "The Journey Onward"

Edward Arllington Robinson — "The House on the Hill"

Carl Sandburg — "Prayers of Steel"

Johann Schiller — "Three Words of Strength"

Percy Bysshe Shelley — "The Recollection"

Robert Louis Stevenson — "Lost Youth"

Algernon Charles Swinburne — "The Salt of the Earth"

Sara Teasdale — "Clear Evening"

Alfred, Lord Tennyson — "Merlin and the Gleam"

William Wordsworth — "The Daffodils"

William Butler Yeats — "The Lake Isle of Innisfree"

90. ODE

An ode is a type of lyric poem. Odes are written to commemorate special occasions, both glorious and horrendous, or to praise someone or something. This list includes famous poets, along with some of their well-known odes. See also List 89, Lyric Poetry.

Samuel Taylor Coleridge — "Dejection: An Ode"

George Gordon Byron — "Ode: O Venice! O Venice!"

Abraham Cowley — "To the Royal Society"

John Dryden — "Alexander's Feast; or, the Power of Music: An Ode in Honor of St. Cecilia's Day"

Thomas Gray — "Ode on the Death of a Favorite Cat, On Being Drowned in a Tub of Fishes"; "Ode to Spring"

Robert Herrick — "An Ode for Ben Jonson"

Gerard Manley Hopkins — "The Wreck of the Deutschland"

Horace — "Ode I"

Ben Jonson — "To the Memory of my Beloved Master, William Shakespeare"

John Keats — "Ode on a Grecian Urn"; "Ode to a Nightingale"; "Ode to Autumn"

Edwin Markham — "Lincoln, the Man of the People"

Andrew Marvell — "An Horatian Ode upon Cromwell's Return from Ireland"

Edgar Lee Masters — "O Glorious France"

John Milton — "On the Morning of Christ's Nativity"

Pindar — "Epinicea" (ancient Greek odes celebrating athletic victories)

John Crowe Ransom — "Bells for John Whiteside's Daughter"

Percy Bysshe Shelley — "Ode to the West Wind"

Allen Tate — "Ode to the Confederate Dead"

William Wordsworth — "Ode: Intimations of Immortality from Recollections of Early Childhood"; "Ode to Duty"

91. PANTOUM

Pantoums are fairly easy and fun to write. Pantoums can be rhymed or unrhymed. The unique line pattern is 1234, 2546, 5768, 7183. The rhyme scheme is *a b a b, b c b c, c d c d, d a d a.* Begin with a basic idea and fit it into the scheme. This example shows the patterns at the beginnings of the lines.

"The Cat"

1	a	Cat sleeping lazily on the bed,
2	b	Chest throbs in heaving beats.
3	a	He doesn't raise a paw or head;
4	b	He loves my warm, green sheets.
2	b	Chest throbs in heaving beats;
5	c	Orpheus creeps upon his soul.
4	b	He loves my warm, green sheets;
6	c	His night of wandering takes its toll.
5	c	Orpheus creeps upon his soul;
7	d	He dreams his tender dreams.
6	c	His night of wandering takes its toll;
8	d	Life isn't what it seems.
7	d	He dreams his tender dreams,
1	a	Cat sleeping lazily on the bed.
8	d	Life isn't what it seems —
3	a	He doesn't raise a paw or head.

— Judie Strouf

A Poet is...

"a person passionately in love with language";
>—W. H. Auden

"a man who lives ... by watching his moods";
>—Henry David Thoreau

"one who utters great and wise things which he does not himself understand";
>—Plato

"one who can survive anything but a misprint";
>—Oscar Wilde

"one whose business is not to save the soul of a man, but to make it worth saving."
>—James E. Fletcher

92. Pictogram and Parallel Poem

Two interesting verse forms are pictograms and parallel poems. A pictogram is a poem written in a relevant shape; parallel poems are poems using repetitive lines. These poems are easy to understand, enjoyable to write, and need not rhyme.

Examples of Pictogram Shapes:

Christmas tree
Angel
Square
Circle
Diamond
Mountains
Telephone pole
Heart
Diagonal
Triangle

Example of Pictogram Poem:

I
wish
everyone
could see my
Christmas tree
and have the fun
and feel the childish
glee that comes to me when
decorating it for all my friends
to see.

>— Judie Strouf

I can…

I can run;

I can try;

I can dream;

I can fly;

I can do anything if I aim for the sky.

— **Judie Strouf**

…Is Like… (Similes)

The sun is like an orange;

The moon is like cheese;

The lake is like blue crepe waving in
breeze;

Trees are like octopi grasping for air;

Grass is like carpet before it gets bare;

Flowers are like rainbows,

And clouds are like cotton;

Nature's gifts are like presents not soon
forgotten.

— **Judie Strouf**

I can…

I wish I could…

I always…

I remember…

You might think I…, but really I…

…is like… (similes)

…is a… (metaphors)

When I grow up, I…

I think I should have been a…

I used to think…, but now I know that…

93. SESTINA

A sestina has six unrhymed stanzas of six lines each; repeat end words with these patterns — first stanza: 123456; second stanza: 615243; third stanza: 364125; fourth stanza: 532614; fifth stanza: 451362; sixth stanza: 246531; three-line envoy: end words as middle and end words.

"Kenyan Train"

1   I think I see a long, black train

2   Snaking through the wilderness,

3   But upon closer inspection discover a herd

4   Of wildebeasts foraging for sustenance

5   On the Serengeti Plain:

6   Thin, bony animals on their annual journey.

6   Ebony flesh, lumbering along, making their journey
1   In a wavy, endless train
5   Along the arid, dusty plain
2   In ever-changing wilderness,
4   Searching, searching for sustenance
3   As connected parts of one giant herd.

3   Who is leading the herd
6   On this lonely, long journey?
4   Who tells them where their sustenance
1   Is to be found? Does this zig-zag train
2   Have an engine to pull it through the wilderness
5   And across the lifeless plain?

5   The barren, treeless plain
3   Kills and defiles weaklings in the herd
2   As they shuffle slowly across wilderness:
6   Will they finish their journey —
1   This chugging, puffing train,
4   Lapping up mile after mile for its sustenance?

4   And what is needed for sustenance?
5   Will it find enough food and water on this plain
1   As it inches along methodically, this train —
3   This pathetic, tragic herd,
6   Heading north and further north upon its journey
2   Through the wilderness?

2   Please be kind, oh, wilderness;
4   Provide these beasts their sustenance.
6   Supply the tracks they need to follow on their journey
5   Through the hot and hostile plain.
3   Guide this hapless, hopeless herd;
1   Provide the engine for their train.

1–2 The engine of this train in the wilderness
3–4 Is the leader of the herd, driving toward sustenance.
5–6 His crew plunder the plain before ending their jagged journey.

                                       — Judie Strouf

94. SONNET

All sonnets have fourteen lines of iambic pentameter (x / x / x / x / x /), though there are three main variations. The first is named after Petrarch (Francesco Petrarca), an Italian poet of the fourteenth century; the second is named after William Shakespeare; the third is named after Edmund Spencer, English poet of the sixteenth century. See also List 89, Lyric Poetry.

ITALIAN SONNET (PETRARCHAN)

Usual rhyme schemes: *a b b a   a b b a   c d e   c d e*
a b b a   a b b a   c d   c d   c d

"On his Blindness"
When I consider how my light is spent,
E're half my days, in this dark world and wide,
And that one talent which is death to hide,
Lodg'd with me useless, though my Soul more bent
To serve therewith my Maker, and present
My true account, lest He returning chide,
"Doth God exact day-labour, light deny'd?"
I fondly ask. But patience, to prevent
That murmur, soon replies, "God doth not need
Either man's work or his own gifts. Who best
Bear his mild yoke, they serve him best. His State
Is kingly: Thousands at his bidding speed,
And post o'er land and ocean without rest;
They also serve who only stand and wait."

— **John Milton,** *Sonnets*

"On his Deceased Wife"

Methought I saw my late espoused Saint
  Brought to me like Alcestis from the grave,
  Whom Jove's great son to her glad husband gave,
Rescu'd from death by force though pale and faint.
Mine as whom washed from spot of child-bed taint,
  Purification in the old law did save,
  And such, as yet once more I trust to have
Full sight of her in Heaven without restraint,
Came vested all in white, pure as her mind:
  Her face was veil'd, yet to my fancied sight,
  Love, sweetness, goodness, in her person shin'd
So clear, as in no face with more delight.
  But O, as to embrace me she inclin'd
  I wak'd, she fled, and day brought back my night.

— John Milton, *Sonnets*

SHAKESPEARIAN SONNET (ENGLISH)

Usual rhyme scheme: *a b a b   c d c d   e f e f   g g*

Sonnet 18

Shall I compare thee to a summer's day?
  Thou art more lovely and more temperate:
Rough winds do shake the darling buds of May,
  And summer's lease hath all too short a date:
Sometime too hot the eye of heaven shines,
  And often is his gold complexion dimmed,
And every fair from fair sometime declines,
  By chance, or nature's changing course untrimmed:
But the eternal summer shall not fade,
  Nor lose possession of that fair thou ow'st,
Nor shall death brag thou wand'rest in his shade,
  When in eternal lines to time thou grow'st,
So long as men can breathe or eyes can see,
So long lives this, and this gives life to thee.

— William Shakespeare, *Sonnets*

SPENSERIAN SONNET

Usual rhyme scheme: *a b a b   b c b c   c d c d   e e*

Sonnet 79

Men call you fair, and you do credit it,
*   For that yourself ye daily such do see:*
But the true fair, that is the gentle wit
*   And virtuous mind, is much more praised of me:*
*   For all the rest, however fair it be,*
Shall turn to nought and lose that glorious hue;
*   But only that is permanent and free*
From frail corruption that doth flesh ensue.
That is true beauty; that doth argue you
*   To be divine, and borne of heavenly seed;*
Derived from that fair Spirit from whom all true
And perfect beauty did at first proceed:
*   He only fair, and what he fair hath made;*
*   All other fair, like flowers, untimely fade.*

— **Spenser,** *Amoretti*

95. FIGURES OF SPEECH

In an inclusive sense, a figure of speech is intentional use or arrangement of words to produce a specific, expressive, and striking effect by departing from customary language. There are over 250 of these devices used by writers. In a narrow sense, a figure of speech is an expression that has meanings beyond or different from its literal meaning. Figures of speech in both categories are listed and defined below with examples. See also List 5, Literary Terminology; List 81, Poetry Glossary; and List 96, Alliteration from A to Z.

alliteration — repetition of beginning consonant sounds in words (righteous rapture; singsong syllable; sing a song of sixpense; big, black bear)

antithesis — contrasted ideas in parallel form (Give me liberty or give me death.)

apostrophe — speaking to someone or something that cannot answer (Death, hear me cry and tell me you will spare me now.)

contractions — shortening words by leaving out letters for poetic or other effect (o'er = over; 'tis = it is)

hyperbole — overstatement and exaggeration (I died laughing.)

litotes — understatement; using words that deliberately say less than meant (She had not a few regrets.)

metaphor — implied comparison between things basically not alike, but not using comparison words such as *like* or *as* (Her eyes were saucers; rodents scurrying into their underground subway; Harry, the brightly dressed peacock)

metonymy — using a word to substitute for something else closely associated with it (the *White House* for the *President*)

paradox — using words and phrases that seem contradictory, but actually are true (Love and hate were intertwined.)

personification — giving human characteristics to nonhuman things (Love held James in her arms; fear grabbed her tightly; death peered over my shoulder.)

repetition — repetition of sounds, rhyme, word, or phrase (Beat, drums, beat!)

rhyme — using words that end in similar vowel and consonant sounds (round, sound)

simile — comparison between things basically not alike, and using the word *like* or *as* (Her lips were soft as rose petals.)

synecdoche — using part of something to represent the whole ("I don't have a penny" means "I don't have any money.")

symbolism — means using a person, object, situation, setting, or action to stand for something different or more than it is (Is your glass half empty or half full?)

verbal irony — saying the opposite of what is really meant (Dropping in on someone unexpectedly, finding them in a mess, and saying, "I can see you expected company.")

96. ALLITERATION FROM A TO Z

Alliteration consists of recurring sounds, often consonants, at the beginnings of adjacent or nearby words. Some are just fun; others create special effects for an author by evoking a mood corresponding to the particular sound. Here are examples. See also List 95, Figures of Speech.

awful argument	jumbled jargon	slimy, slithering snake
beastly bulls	kinky kangaroo	tight and taut
cheerful cherubs	lion's lair	uselessly Utopian
dull and dim	mother's milk	vim and vigor
easily eaten	never so numb	wend our way
full of fun	onerous odor	xeroxed xylophones
ghastly ghoul	portly paunch	yin and yang
hit, hurt, and harm	quaint and quiet	zany zebras
icy island	rest and recuperation	

97. ASSONANCE

Assonance is the use of vowel sounds in stressed syllables to create a desired effect. Examples:

GLOOM OR MYSTERY	SHARPNESS OR HARSHNESS	SOFTNESS OR FLUIDITY	JOVIALITY OR LIGHTNESS
bassoon	beat	azure	dippy
boo	bite	cotton	ditty
bowel	blight	demure	fibbing
croon	cleat	fog	filly
doom	cleaver	fur	flitty
dragoon	fate	hollow	frilly
festoon	fight	masseur	giddy
foul	fright	meadow	giggle
ghoul	gloat	mellow	happy
gloom	goat	narrow	hippie
goon	grate	pleasure	jiggle
growl	hate	purr	nitty-gritty
howl	ignite	sallow	peppy
lagoon	mote	satin	preppy
loon	night	shadow	sappy
moon	plight	smog	silly
owl	sleight	sparrow	squiggle
prowl	smite	swallow	tipsy
swoon	spite	velour	wiggle
voodoo	tight	velvet	witty
yowl	wait	wallow	wriggle

98. ONOMATOPOEIA

Onomatopoeia is the use of words in poetry or prose that sound like what they represent. Words like these are called onomatopoeic, or onomatopoetic words.

arf	clip-clop	kerplunk	smack
bang	clippety-clop	meow	snarl
bark	clomp	mew	snort
beep	cluck	moan	spit
bing bong	coo	moo	splash
bleat	crash	neigh	splat
blip	creak	nip	splunk
bobwhite	crunch	oink	squeak
bong	ding-a-ling	ouch	squeal
boom	ding dong	ping	squish
bop	drip	ping pong	swish
bow-wow	drop	plod	tap
bray	drum	plop	thud
bump	fizz	plunk	thump
bumpity-bump- bump	fling	pop	tick-tock
burp	flush	purr	tinkle
buzz	flutter	quack	twang
caw	gargle	ruff-ruff	tweet
cheep	glug	rumble	wail
chirp	gong	rum-te-tum-tum	whack
chomp	groan	rustle	whine
chortle	growl	screech	whinny
chug	grunt	shriek	whir
clang	gurgle	shush	whisper
clap	gusher	sh	whiz
clash	guzzle	sip	woof
clatter	hiss	sizzle	zap
click	honk	slap	zing
clickety-clack	howl	slosh	zip
clink	hum	slurp	zoom
	hush	slush	

99. REPETITION

Repetition is a device used in poetry for effect. It can involve repeating (or almost repeating) a word, phrase, line, refrain, or entire stanza. Examples:

WORD REPETITION

Read, read, read, 'til your
eyes are weak and blurred;
Talk, talk, talk, 'til your
speech is slow and slurred.
— Judie Strouf

PHRASE REPETITION

Into the heart, into the heart,
Into the heart it came,
Piercing and probing,
And setting aflame.
— Judie Strouf

LINE REPETITION

"When Life Is Done"

When life is done,
And shadows fall,
Pray do not weep,
Just let me sleep.

When life is done,
I've no regrets,
I've done my best,
And now — I rest.

When life is done
I shall be free,
The battle's won
When life is done.

— **Alida Federspiel Hockey**

Bumbling, fumbling, mumbling —
HE never got it right.
Mumbling, fumbling, bumbling —
Such a pathetic sight!
But love walked in adroitly
And wrapped HER in its glow
And his bumbling, fumbling, mumbling
Ceased ere again to show.
— Judie Strouf

REFRAIN REPETITION

Over land and over sea
In his thoughts he came to me.
With a hey, hey, ho,
and a fiddle dee dee,
My true love thought of me.

He went to war to set men free;
He struggled hard, with dignity.
With a hey, hey, ho,
And a fiddle dee dee,
My true love fought for me.

He sought in vain for liberty
He tried, but died so valiantly,
With a hey, hey, ho,
And a fiddle dee dee,
My true love sought for me.

— Judie Strouf

STANZA REPETITION

"So Little Time"

So little time
To say and do the things we should;
So little time
To play the game we wish we could.

Life fleets and flits
Along her merry way,
Dancing, darting, here and there —
Everywhere.

She zigs, then zags,
And never seems to stay
Silent, stagnant, here or there —
Anywhere.

So little time
To say and do the things we should;
So little time
To play the game we wish we could.

— Judie Strouf

100. STANZA TYPE AND TYPICAL ARRANGEMENT

Modern stanzas can be almost any length and pattern, but older poetry had typical patterns. When innovations were made, the stanza was often named after the poet who first used the scheme. Rhyme schemes are denoted *a* for the first rhyme, *b* for the next rhyme, and so on. The examples should make this clear. This list shows the most common stanza forms.

COUPLET — TWO RHYMING LINES *(a a)*

Give me courage; give me hope;
Then I won't be taking dope.

— Judie Strouf

(*a a* rhyme scheme)

TERCET — THREE LINES *(a a a; or a b a, b c b, c d c, etc.)*

Oh, the lovely wind does blow
The autumn leaves around
And covers them with frost and snow.

The colored leaves upon the ground
Come peeking through the white
And make a rainbow hue abound.

— Judie Strouf

(*a b a, b c b* rhyme scheme)

QUATRAIN

Four lines that can contain many variations of rhyme patterns
(*a b c b, a b a b, a b b a, a a b b, or a a a a*), line lengths, and rhythms.

> Oh, come to me on bended knee,
> And make your wishes clear.
> Ply me with your earnest plea,
> And I will wed you, dear.
>
>   — **Judie Strouf**

(*a b a b* rhyme scheme)

CINQUAIN

Five lines, unrhymed, specifically the Japanese cinquain with twenty-two total syllables divided
as follows: first line (2); second line (4); third line (6); fourth line (8); fifth line (2).

> Kitty
> Fluffy, furry,
> Always ready to pounce.
> He makes me a youngster again.
> Purr-fect!
>
>   — **Judie Strouf**

(unrhymed)

BURNS STANZA

Six lines containing two miniature or short lines, according to a set pattern (also called Tail-Rhyme
because of the short tail lines). In this example, the fourth and last lines are the "tails."

> O wad some Power the giftie gie us
> To see oursels as others see us!
> It wad frae monie a blunder free us,
>   An' foolish notion:
> What airs in dress an' gait and wad lea'e us,
>   An' ev'n devotion.
>
>   — **Robert Burns, "To a Louse"**

(*a a a b a b* rhyme scheme)

CHAUCERIAN STANZA (RIME ROYAL)

Seven lines of iambic pentameter with *a b a b b c c* rhyme scheme.

> A great gray sea was running up the sky,
> Desolate birds flew past; their mewings came
> As that lone water's spiritual cry,
> Its forlorn voice, its essence, its soul's name.
> The ship limped in the water as if lame,
> Then in the forenoon watch to a great shout
> More sail was made, the reefs were shaken out.
>
> — John Masefield, "Dauber"

OCTAVE (OCTAVIA RIME)

Eight lines of iambic pentameter with *a b a b a b c c* rhyme scheme.

> The coast — I think it was the coast that I
>   Was just describing — Yes, it was the coast —
> Lay at this period quiet as the sky,
>   The sands untumbled, the blue waves untost,
> And all was stillness, save the sea-bird's cry,
>   And dolphin's leap, and little billow crost
> By some low rock or shelve, that made it fret
> Against the boundary it scarcely wet.
>
> — Lord Byron, "Don Juan"

SPENSERIAN STANZA

Nine lines (eight lines of iambic pentameter, followed by a ninth line of iambic hexameter) with *a b a b b c b c c* rhyme scheme.

> He is made one with Nature: there is heard
>   His voice in all her music, from the moan
> Of thunder, to the song of night's sweet bird;
>   He is a presence to be felt and known
>   In darkness and in light, from herb and stone,
> Spreading itself where'er that power may move
>   Which has withdrawn his being to its own:
> Which wields the world with never wearied love,
> Sustains it from beneath, and kindles it above.
>
> — Percy Bysshe Shelley, "Adonais"

101. VERSIFICATION: FEET

The number of feet in a line of poetry contributes to its rhythm and thereby to the feeling the poem imparts. Short lines convey an impression of speed; long lines take us on a more leisurely journey. All types of meter can be used with any number of feet per line. See related List 102, Versification: Meter.

Determining the number of syllables and feet per line and how they are accented is called *scansion*. Below are listed the various names used depending on the number of feet per line. (This is a good review of Greek prefixes.)

1 foot per line = monometer

2 feet per line = dimeter

3 feet per line = trimeter

4 feet per line = tetrameter

5 feet per line = pentameter

6 feet per line = hexameter

7 feet per line = heptameter

8 feet per line = octameter

The most common meter/foot combinations are iambic pentameter and iambic tetrameter.

EXAMPLE OF IAMBIC PENTAMETER:

x /   x   / x   /   x / x   /
It gives me won der great as my con tent
      — Shakespeare, *Othello*

EXAMPLE OF IAMBIC TETRAMETER:

```
x /   x  /  x /  x /
```
A bout the year of one B. C.
```
x / x  /  x /  x /
```
A gallant ship set out to sea,
```
x /   x /   x  /  x /
```
To catch a whale and salt his tail

        — **Author Unknown,** *Jonah and the Whale*

102. VERSIFICATION: METER

Readers generally enjoy and appreciate poetry more if they understand (and therefore can admire) the techniques used. Basic techniques used are rhythm (meter), rhyme, and astute word choice and groupings. This list shows the most common types of rhythm. Though most poets change meter within lines and switch back and forth for effect, these examples show pure meters. Each group of syllables containing one accented syllable is called a foot. (See related List 101, Versification: Feet.)

COMMON TYPES OF METER (RHYTHM):

(*x* represents *un*stressed syllable; / shows stressed syllable)

IAMBIC — two syllables; first syllable *un*stressed; second syllable stressed. Example:
```
x / x /
```
If you but knew
```
x  / x /  x   / x /   x /
```
How all my days seemed filled with dreams of you.

    — **Author Unknown**

```
x / x /  x /  x /x /
```
Mnemonic device: Am I the one of whom the poet dreams?

TROCHAIC — two syllables; first syllable stressed; second syllable unstressed. Example:
```
/  x / x / x  / x
```
Once upon a midnight dreary

    — **Poe, "The Raven"**

Mnemonic device: Poe is Tro(chaic)

ANAPESTIC — three syllables; first two syllables unaccented; last syllable accented. Example

x x / $x\,x$ / x

'Twas the night before Christmas,

> — Clement Moore, "A Visit from St. Nicholas"

Mnemonic device: Santa is contained in *ANApeSTic.*

DACTYLIC — three syllables; first syllable accented; last two syllables unaccented. Example:

/ x x / $x\,x$ / x x / $x\,x$

Cannon to right of them, cannon to left of them

> — Tennyson, "The Charge of the Light Brigade"

/ xx

Mnemonic device: Tennyson's name has dactylic meter.

103. HUMOROUS POETRY (SHORT)

Almost everyone enjoys short, humorous poetry. See also List 86, Grue; List 88, Limerick; and List 104, Humorous Poetry (Longer).

"The Purple Cow"

I never saw a Purple Cow,
*   I never hope to see one;*

But I can tell you, anyhow,
*   I'd rather see than be one.*

> — Gelett Burgess

"A Case"

As I was going up the stair
I met a man who wasn't there.
He wasn't there again today —
I wish to God he'd go away!

> — Anonymous

It Isn't The Cough

It isn't the cough
That carries you off;
It's the coffin
They carry you off in.

> — Anonymous

"Cruel Clever Cat"

Sally, having swallowed cheese,
Directs down holes the scented breeze,
Enticing thus with baited breath
Nice mice to an untimely death.

> — Geoffrey Taylor

"The Turtle"

The turtle lives 'twixt plated decks
Which practically conceal its sex.
I think it clever of the turtle
In such a fix to be so fertile.

    — Ogden Nash

"A Maxim Revised"

Ladies, to this advice give heed —
In controlling men:
If at first you don't succeed,
Why, cry, cry again.

    — Anonymous

"The Optimist"

The optimist fell ten stories.
  At each window bar

He shouted to his friend:
  "All right so far!"

    — Anonymous

"Judged By the Company One Keeps"

One night in late October, when
  I was far from sober,

Returning with my load with
  manly pride,

My feet began to stutter, so I
  lay down in the gutter,

And a pig came near and lay
  down by my side;

A nice lady passing by, said
  quite sadly with a sigh,

"You can tell a man who boozes,
  by the company he chooses,"

And the pig got up and slowly
  walked away.

    — Anonymous

104. Humorous Poems (Longer)

Here is a list of humorous poems that are readily available from a variety of collections. They are listed in alphabetical order according to poet. See related List 86, Grue; List 88, Limerick; List 103, Humorous Poetry (Short).

Anonymous — "To Be or Not to Be"
Anonymous — "I Had But Fifty Cents"
Anonymous — "Dried Apple Pies"
Robert Burns — "To a Louse"
Bliss Carman — "Hem and Haw"
Lewis Carroll — "The Walrus and the Carpenter"
Guy Wetmore Carryl — "The Sycophantic Fox and the Gullible Raven"
William Crosswell Doane — "The Modern Baby"
e. e. cummings — "Nobody Loses All the Time"
T. S. Eliot — "Macavity, the Mystery Cat"

Eugene Field — "The Duel"

James T. Fields — "The Owl Critic"

Rose Fyleman — "Bingo Has an Enemy"

W. S. Gilbert — "Nightmare"

Oliver Goldsmith — "Elegy on the Death of a Mad Dog"

Arthur Guiterman — "Strictly Germ-Proof"

Bret Harte — "Plain Language from Truthful James (The Heathen Chinee)"

Oliver Wendell Holmes — "A Parody on a Psalm of Life"

Wallace Irwin — "The Worried Skipper"

Don Marquis — "The Tom-Cat"

Ogden Nash — "The Tale of Custard, the Dragon"

Luther Patrick — "Sleepin' at the Foot o' the Bed"

Edwin Milton Royle — "Doan't You Be What You Ain't"

Carl Sandburg — "Phizzog"

John Godfrey Saxe — "The Blind Men and the Elephant"

Ernest Lawrence Thayer — "Casey at the Bat"

Carolyn Wells — "An Overworked Elocutionist"

105. Poems: Early British History

Poetry is often written to express political feelings, narrate historical events, or describe reactions to these events. Listed below are several poets who wrote about incidents in British history. For other historical poetry, see List 90, Ode; List 108, War and Antiwar Poems/Songs; and List 117, Shakespeare: Complete Plays and Poems (historical Shakespearian dramas).

Elizabeth Barrett Browning
"The Cry of the Children"
"Crowned and Wedded"

Robert Browning
"Strafford"
"Cavalier Tunes"

Robert Burns
"The Battle of Bannockburn: Bruce's
     Address to his Men"
"Lament of Mary, Queen of Scots, on the
     Approach of Spring"
"Lament for Culloden"

Lord Byron
Childe Harold's Pilgrimage

Michael Drayton
"The Battle of Agincourt"

Thomas Heywood
"King Edward the Fourth"
"A Praise of Princess Mary"

John Keats
"King Stephen"

Richard Lovelace
"To Althea from Prison"

Christopher Marlowe
"King Edward the Second"

Gerald Massey
"Nelson"

John Milton
  "To the Lord General Cromwell"

Alexander Pope
  "The Age of Queen Anne" (from "The Rape of the Lock")

Dante Rossetti
  "Raleigh's Cell in the Tower"
  "The King's Tragedy"
  "The White Ship"

Sir Walter Scott
  "Flodden Field" (from *Marmion*)
  "Pitt and Fox" (from *Marmion*)
  "Bannockburn" (from *Lord of the Isles*)
  "The Field of Waterloo"

Robert Southey
  "The Death of Wallace"
  "After Blenheim"
  "Wat Tyler"
  "At Coruna"
  "King Henry V and the Hermit of Dreux"

Alfred, Lord Tennyson
  "The Passing of Arthur"
  "Harold"
  "Becket"
  "The Forresters"
  "Queen Mary"
  "The Revenge: A Battle of the Fleet"
  "Ode on the Death of the Duke of Wellington"
  "To the Memory of Prince Albert" (Dedication to *Idylls of the King*)
  "To the Queen"

William Wordsworth
  "Glad Tidings"
  "Alfred and his Descendants"
  "King Henry the Eighth"
  "George III"
  "Charles the Second"
  "The Pilgrim Fathers"

106. POETRY ON GREAT WRITERS

Here are some of the more famous poets who immortalized or defamed other writers in poetry. (A few even conducted running feuds through their poems!) Names of poems are listed first; the poet's names are listed second. If it is not obvious whom the poem is about, the name of the subject is in parentheses.

"**Burns**" — Ebenezer Elliott

"**Burns**" — John Greenleaf Whittier

"**Byron**" — Robert Pollok

"**Carlyle and Emerson**" — Montgomery Schuyler

"**Dickens**" — Algernon Charles Swinburne

"**Dickens in Camp**" — Bret Harte

"**Emerson**" — Sarah Chauncy Woolsey

"**An Epitaph on the Admirable Dramatic Poet, W. Shakespeare**" — John Milton

"**Fitz-Greene Halleck**" — John Greenleaf Whittier

"**From Wordsworth's Grave**" — William Watson

"**George Sand**" — Elizabeth Barrett Browning

"**Guilielmus Rex**" — Thomas Bailey Aldrich (William Shakespeare)

"Hans Christian Andersen" — Edmund Gosse

"Harriet Beecher Stowe" — Paul Lawrence Dunbar

"Hawthorne" — Edmund Clarence Stedman

"Hawthorne" — Henry Wadsworth Longfellow

"Hierarchy of Angels" — Thomas Heywood (William Shakespeare)

"In Memory of Walter Savage Landor" — Algernon Charles Swinburne

"Joseph Rodman Drake" — Fitz-Greene Halleck

"The Lost Leader" — Robert Browning (William Wordsworth)

"Macaulay As Poet" — Walter Savage Landor

"Memorabilia" — Robert Browning (Percy Bysshe Shelley)

"Myself" — Walt Whitman

"Ode to Ben Jonson" — Robert Herrick

"On a Portrait of Wordsworth by B. R. Haydon" — Elizabeth Barrett Browning

"On the Death of Thomas Carlyle and George Eliot" — Algernon Charles Swinburne

"On the Departure of Sir Walter Scott from Abbotsford, for Naples" — William Wordsworth

"On the Portrait of Shakespeare" — Ben Jonson

"Robert Browning" — Walter Savage Landor

"Shelley" — Alexander Hay Japp

"Tennyson" — Thomas Bailey Aldrich

"To Benjamin Robert Haydon" — John Keats

"To Henry Wadsworth Longfellow" — James Russell Lowell

"To Milton" — William Wordsworth

"To the Memory of My Beloved Master, William Shakespeare, and What He Has Left Us"
    — Ben Jonson

"To the Memory of Ben Jonson" — John Cleveland

"To the Memory of Thomas Hood" — Bartholomew Simmons

"To Thomas More" — Lord Byron

"To Victor Hugo" — Alfred, Lord Tennyson

"Under the Portrait of John Milton" — John Dryden

"A Welcome to 'Boz'" — H. Venable (Charles Dickens)

107. POETS ON POETRY

Several poets have written about poetry itself. It can be enlightening to study what these masters say about poetry and to observe the poetic forms they use to express themselves. See also List 106, Poetry on Great Writers.

Auden, W. H. ("In Memory of W. B. Yeats")

Barker, George ("Resolution of Dependence")

Bishop, John P. ("Speaking of Poetry")

Empson, William ("Just a Smack at Auden")

Graves, Robert ("The Bards")

Henley, William Ernest ("The Triolet")

Henley, William Ernest ("The Villanelle")

Lawrence, D. H. ("Song of a Man Who Has Come Through")

MacLeish, Archibald ("Ars Poetics")

Moore, Marianne ("Poetry")

Muir, Edwin ("In Love for Long")

Pound, Ezra ("E. P. 'Ode pour l'election de son sepulchre'")

Reed, Henry ("Chard Whitlow")

Swinburne, Algernon Charles ("The Roundel")

Thomas, Dylan ("In My Craft or Sullen Art")

Williams, Oscar ("I Sing an Old Song")

Yeats, William Butler ("A Coat")

"…people are exasperated by poetry which they do not understand and contemptuous of poetry which they understand without effort."

> — **T. S. Eliot**

"A poet is one who announced that which no man has foretold."

> — **Ralph Waldo Emerson**

"A poet is one who simply tells the most hearteasing things."

> — **John Keats**

"A poet is a nightingale, who sits in darkness and sings to cheer its own solitude with sweet sounds."

> — **Percy Bysshe Shelley**

"A poet is the painter of the soul."

> — **Isaac Disraeli**

108. WAR AND ANTIWAR POEMS/SONGS

Note: For prose on this theme, see List 149, War. See also List 84, Elegy; List 90, Ode; and List 105, Poems: Early British History.

TROJAN WAR

Homer
Iliad
Odyssey

CRIMEAN WAR

Tennyson, Alfred Lord
"The Charge of the Light Brigade at Balaclava"

REVOLUTIONARY WAR

Bryant, William Cullen
"The Green Mountain Boys"
"Seventy-Six"

Calvert, George Henry
"Bunker Hill"

Dickinson, John
"The Liberty Song"

Emerson, Ralph Waldo
"The Concord Hymn"

Finch, Francis Miles
"Nathan Hale"

Freneau, Philip
"The Northern Soldier"
"To The Memory of the Brave Americans"
"Arnold's Departure"

Hale, Edward Everett
"New England's Chevy Chase"

Longfellow, Henry Wadsworth
"Paul Revere's Ride"

Odell, Jonathan
"The Old Year and the New: A Prophecy"

Pierpont, John
"Warren's Address at Bunker Hill"

Sherwood, Kate Brownlee
"Molly Pitcher"

Simms, William Gilmore
"The Swamp Fox"

Stansbury, Joseph
"Loyalist Song"

Unknown
"Lovewell's Fight"

WAR OF 1812

Browning, Robert
"How They Brought the Good News from Ghent to Aix"

Key, Francis Scott
"The Star-Spangled Banner"

Unknown
"The Banks of Champlain"
"The Battle of Bridgewater"
"The Battle of New Orleans"

MEXICAN WAR

Lowell, James Russell
The Bigelow Papers

CIVIL WAR

Boker, George Henry
Poems of the War

Finch, Francis Miles
"The Blue and the Grey"

Foss, Sam Walter
"House by the Side of the Road"

Gilmore, Patrick
"When Johnny Comes Marching Home"

Howe, Julia Ward
"Battle-Hymn of the Republic"

Longfellow, Henry Wadsworth
"Killed at the Ford"

Lowell, James Russell
"Once to Every Man and Nation"
"For the Union Dead"

Melville, Herman
"Shiloh: A Requiem"
"Malvern Hill"
"Dirge for McPherson"

Meredith, William Tucker
"Farragut"

Read, Thomas
"Sheridan's Ride"

Root, George F.
"Tramp, Tramp, Tramp!"
"Just Before the Battle, Mother"
"The Battle Cry of Freedom"

Ryan, Abram
"The Conquered Banner"

Tate, Allen
"Ode to the Confederate Dead"
"To the Lacedemonians"

Ticknor, Francis
"Little Giffen"

Whitman, Walt
Drum Taps

Whittier, John Greenleaf
"Maud Muller"
"Barbara Frietchie"
"The Barefoot Boy"

WORLD WAR I

Blunden, Edmund Charles
Poems
Pastorals: A Book of Verses

Brooke, Rupert (killed during WWI)
"The Soldier"

Cammaerts, Emile
Belgian Poems
New Belgian Poems

Cummings, e. e.
"I Sing of Olaf Glad and Big"
"My Sweet Old Etcetera"

Eliot, T. S.
"Triumphal March"

Frost, Robert
"The Soldier"

Graves, Robert
"Recalling War"

Grenfell, Julian
"Into Battle"

Hardy, Thomas
"In Time of 'The Breaking of Nations'"
"And There Was a Great Calm"
"Channel Firing"

Hopkins, Gerald Manley
"The Soldier"

Kilmer, Joyce
"Rouge Bouquet"

McCrae, John
"In Flanders Fields"

Owen, Wilfred (killed in WWI)
"Greater Love"
"Strange Meeting"
"Insensibility"
"Anthem for Doomed Youth"
"Dulce et decorum est"
"The Show"
"Arms and the Boy"
"À terre"
"Futility"

Pound, Ezra
"They Fought in Any Case"

Rilke, Rainer Maria
"The Last Evening"

Rosenberg, Isaac (killed in action)
"Dead Man's Dump"
"Break of Day in the Trenches"

Sandburg, Carl
"Smoke"
"Gargoyle"
"Grass"
"A. E. F."

Sassoon, Siegfried
Collected War Poems, 1919
"Counter-Attack"
"The Dug-Out"

Seeger, Alan
"I Have a Rendezvous with Death"
"Champagne, 1914–15"

WORLD WAR II

Aiken, Conrad
"The Soldier"

Armstrong, J. A.
"Another Reply to In Flanders Fields"

Auden, W. H.
"September 1, 1939"
Journey to a War
"Far from the Heart of Culture"

Barker, George
"Munich Elegy No. 1"

Cèlan, Paul
"Death Fugue"

Day-Lewis, Cecil
Poems in Wartime

Derwood, Gene
"Elegy on the Death of Gordon Barber"

Douglas, Keith
"Dead Men"
"Gallantry"

Fuller, Roy
"Soliloquy in an Air-Raid"
"A Wry Smile"
"Spring 1942"

Jeffers, Robinson
"May–June 1940"
"I Shall Laugh Purely"
"Rearmament"

Keyes, Sidney
"Elegy"
"Time Will Not Grant"
"The Foreign Gate"

Lewis, Alun
"The Soldier"
"Postscript: For Gweno"
"After Dunkirk"

Lilliard, R. W.
"America's Answer"

Lowell, Robert, Jr. (wrote about several wars)
"The Quaker Graveyard at Nantucket"
"Mother Marie Therese"
"Skunk Hour"
"Christmas Eve Under Hooker's Statue"
"The Bomber"
"On the Eve of the Feast of the
    Immaculate Conception: 1942"

MacNeice, Louis
"Brother Fire"

Manifold, John
"The Tomb of Lieutenant John
    Learmonth, AIF"

Mitchell, John
"Reply to In Flanders Fields"

Moore, Marianne
"In Distrust of Merits"

Neruda, Pablo
"The Battle of Jarama"

Nemerov, Howard
"Redeployment"
"A Fable of the War"
"The War in the Air"

Read, Herbert
"To a Conscript of 1940"

Reed, Henry
"Naming of Parts"

Reilly, Catherine W. (ed.)
*Chaos of the Night, Women's Poetry and
    Verse of the Second World War*

Rose, Billy
"The Unknown Soldier"

Shapiro, Karl
"Nostalgia"
"Troop Train"
"Elegy for a Dead Soldier"

Sitwell, Edith
"Still Falls the Rain"

Slessor, Kenneth
"Beach Burial"

Spender, Stephen
"Ultima Ratio Regum"

Stevens, Wallace
"The Soldier's Wound"

Thomas, Dylan
"A Refusal to Mourn the Death, by Fire, of a Child in London"

Thompson, Dunstan
"Largo"

Wilbur, Richard
"Mined Country"
"First Snow in Alsace"

KOREAN WAR

Carruth, Hayden
"On a Certain Engagement South of Seoul"

Dickey, James
"The Performance"
"The Firebombing"

McGrath, Thomas
"Ode for the American Dead in Korea"
"The Odor of Blood"
"Night"

Sardar J'afre, Ali
"The Final Night"

VIETNAM WAR

Appleman, Philip
"Waiting for the Fire"

Bly, Robert
"War and Silence"
"At a March Against the Vietnam War"
"Counting Small-Boned Bodies"

Duncan, Robert
"Uprising"

Ginsberg, Allen
Reality Sandwiches
Planet News

Levertov, Denise
"What Were They Like"
"Staying Alive"

Major, Clarence
"Vietnam #4"

5

Drama...
Thereby Hangs
a Tale

109. DRAMA MASTERS

Readers who wish to comprehend the full range of drama will need to become acquainted with the following dramatists. Each had a special talent which propelled drama along its way. The list presents the playwright's name, nationality, and a representative work, and it is organized alphabetically within general time periods to provide historical perspective. See also List 110, Twentieth-Century Master American Dramatists; List 111, Drama: Pulitzer Prizewinners; List 112, Drama Critics' Circle Awards; and List 117, Shakespeare: Complete Plays and Poems.

CLASSICAL ERA

Aeschylus — Greek *(Agamemnon)*

Aristophanes — Greek *(The Frogs)*

Euripides — Greek *(Medea)*

Menander — Greek *(The Bad-Tempered Man)*

Plautus — Roman *(The Captives)*

Sophocles — Greek *(Oedipus Rex)*

Terence — Roman *(Phormio)*

FIRST THROUGH FIFTEENTH CENTURIES

Mimes; spectacles; tropes; church and religious dramas; mysteries; "paternoster" plays; morality plays; passion plays; farces; Noh plays; puppet theatres

Anon. — English *(Everyman)*

Anon. — Chinese *(The Circle of Chalk)*

Kalidasa — Indian *(Shakuntala)*

Kwanami — Japanese *(Sotoba Komachi)*

Motokiyo Seami — Japanese *(Atsumori)*

Shudraka — Indian *(The Little Clay Cart)*

SIXTEENTH CENTURY

Lodovico Ariosto — Italian *(Pretenders)*

Thomas Dekker — English *(The Shoemaker's Holiday)*

Robert Greene — English *(James IV)*

Ben Jonson — English *(Every Man in His Humour)*

Thomas Kyd — English *(The Spanish Tragedy)*

Christopher Marlowe — English *(Doctor Faustus)*

Torquato Tasso — Italian *(Aminta)*

SEVENTEENTH CENTURY

Pietro Aretino — Italian *(Cortiagana)*

Francis Beaumont — English *(The Woman-Hater)* Note: Often collaborated with John Fletcher

Pedro Calderón de la Barca — Spanish *(Life Is a Dream)*

Paul Claudel — French *(The Satin Slipper)*

William Congreve — English *(The Way of the World)*

Pierre Corneille — French *(The Cid)*

Lope de Vega — Spanish *(The Sheep Well)*

George Etherege — English *(Love in a Tub)*

John Fletcher — English *(The Faithful Shepherdess)* Note: Often collaborated with Francis Beaumont

John Ford — English *('tis Pity She's a Whore)*

Battista Guarini — Italian *(The Faithful Shepherd)*

Niccolo Machiavelli — Italian *(Mandragola)*

John Milton — English *(Samson Agonistes)*

Jean Molière — French *(The Misanthrope)*

Jean Racine — French *(Phèdre)*

William Shakespeare — English *(Romeo and Juliet)*

Nicholas Udall — English *(Ralph Roister Doister)*

John Webster — English *(The White Devil)*

EIGHTEENTH CENTURY

Joseph Addison — English *(Rosamund)*

Pierre-Augustin Beaumarchais — French *(The Barber of Seville)*

George Farquhar — English *(The Recruiting Officer)*

John Gay — English *(The Beggar's Opera)*

Carlo Goldoni — Italian *(The Mistress of the Inn)*

Oliver Goldsmith — Irish/English *(She Stoops to Conquer)*

Ludvig Holberg — Danish *(Rasmus Montanus)*

Gotthold Lessing — German *(Minna von Barnhelm)*

Richard Sheridan — Irish *(The School for Scandal)*

NINETEENTH CENTURY

Alexandre Dumas (fils) — French *(The Lady of the Camelias)*

Johann Wolfgang von Goethe — German *(Faust, Parts I and II)*

Maxim Gorky — Russian *(The Lower Depths)*

Franz Grillparzer — Austrian *(The Jewess of Toledo)*

Gerhart Hauptmann — German *(The Weavers)*

Friedrich Hebbel — German *(Maria Magdalena)*

Victor Hugo — French *(Hernani)*

Henrik Ibsen — Norwegian *(A Doll's House)*

Eugene Ionesco — French *(The Bald Soprano)*

Heinrich von Kleist — German *(The Prince of Homburg)*

Alfred de Musset — French *(The Follies of Marianne)*

Alexander Pushkin — Russian *(Boris Godunov)*

Edmond Rostand — French *(Cyrano de Bergerac)*

Friedrich von Shiller — German *(The Maid of Orleans)*

August Strindberg — Swedish *(Miss Julie)*

Leo Tolstoy — Russian *(The Power of Darkness)*

Oscar Wilde — Irish/English *(The Importance of Being Earnest)*

William Butler Yeats — Irish *(The Countess Cathleen)*

TWENTIETH CENTURY

Jean Anouilh — French *(Antigone)*

Alan Ayckbourn — English *(The Norman Conquests)*

James M. Barrie — Scottish *(Peter Pan)*

Bertolt Brecht — German *(Mother Courage and her Children)*

Anton Chekhov — Russian *(The Three Sisters)*

Noel Coward — English *(Blithe Spirit)*

Friedrich Dürrenmatt — Swiss *(The Marriage of Mr. Mississippi)*

T. S. Eliot — English, born in U.S. *(Murder in the Cathedral)*

George Feydeau — French *(The Lady from Maxims)*

Christopher Fry — English *(The Lady's not for Burning)*

Athol Fugard — South African *(Master Harold and the Boys)*

Jean Genet — French *(The Blacks)*

Vaclav Havel — Czechoslovakian *(The Garden Party)*

Jean Giraudoux — French *(The Madwoman of Chaillot)*

Georg Kaiser — German *(The Burghers of Calais)*

Ferenc Molnar — Hungarian *(Liliom)*

Sean O'Casey — Irish *(Cock-a-Doodle Dandy)*

John Osborne — English *(Look Back in Anger)*

Harold Pinter — English *(The Homecoming)*

Luigi Pirandello — Italian *(Six Characters in Search of an Author)*

Terrence Rattigan — English *(Separate Tables)*

Jean-Paul Sartre — French *(The Files)*

Peter Shaffer — English *(Equus)*

George Bernard Shaw — Irish *(Pygmalion)*

Tom Stoppard — English *(The Real Thing)*

John Synge — Irish *(The Playboy of the Western World)*

Peter Weiss — German *(The Investigation)*

110. TWENTIETH-CENTURY MASTER AMERICAN DRAMATISTS

Zoe Akins — *A Royal Fandango; The Greeks Had a Word for It; The Old Maid*

Edward Albee — *The Zoo Story and Other Plays; Who's Afraid of Virginia Woolf?; Tiny Alice; A Delicate Balance; Seascape*

Maxwell Anderson — *What Price Glory?* (with Laurence Stallings)*; Both Your Houses; Winterset; Knickerbocker Holiday* (with Kurt Weill); *Anne of a Thousand Days; The Bad Seed*

James Baldwin — *Amen Corner; Blues for Mister Charlie*

Philip Barry — *Holiday; The Philadelphia Story*

Abe Burrows — *Guys and Dolls; How to Succeed in Business Without Really Trying; Cactus Flower*

Mary Chase — *Harvey*

Paddy Chayefsky — *Marty; Network*

Marc Connelly — *The Green Pastures; Dulcy* (with George S. Kaufman)*; Merton of the Movies* (with George S. Kaufman); *To the Ladies* (with George S. Kaufman)*; Beggar on Horseback* (with George S. Kaufman)

Russel Crouse — *Life With Father* (with Howard Lindsay)*; State of the Union; Call Me Madam; The Sound of Music* (with Rodgers and Hammerstein)

Edna Ferber — *Show Boat; The Royal Family* (with George S. Kaufman)

Charles Fuller — *Perfect Party; The Brownsville Raid; A Soldier's Play*

William Gibson — *Two for the Seesaw; The Miracle Worker; Handy Dandy*

Frank Gilroy — *Who'll Save the Plowboy?; The Subject Was Roses; Last Licks*

John Guare — *Muzeeka; House of Blue Leaves; Women and Water*

Lorraine Hansberry — *Raisin in the Sun; The Sign in Sidney Brustein's Window; To Be Young, Gifted, and Black*

Moss Hart — *You Can't Take It With You* (with George S. Kaufman)*; The Man Who Came to Dinner* (with George S. Kaufman)*; Lady in the Dark* (with Kurt Weill and Ira Gershwin)

Ben Hecht — *The Front Page* (with Charles MacArthur); *Twentieth Century* (with Charles MacArthur)

Lillian Hellman — *The Children's Hour; Watch on the Rhine; Another Part of the Forest; The Little Foxes*

William Inge — *Come Back, Little Sheba; Picnic; The Dark at the Top of the Stairs*

George S. Kaufman — *You Can't Take It With You* (with Moss Hart)*; The Man Who Came to Dinner* (with Moss Hart)*; Of Thee I Sing* (with Morrie Ryskind)

Jean Kerr — *Mary, Mary*

Ira Levin — *No Time for Sergeants; Deathtrap*

Howard Lindsay — *Life with Father* (with Russel Crouse)*; Anything Goes* (with Russel Crouse); *State of the Union* (with Russel Crouse); *Call Me Madam* (with Russel Crouse)

Charles MacArthur — *The Front Page* (with Ben Hecht); *Twentieth Century* (with Ben Hecht)

Archibald MacLeish — *J. B.*

David Mamet — *Sexual Perversity in Chicago; Glengarry Glen Ross; Speed-the-Plow*

Arthur Miller — *Death of a Salesman; All My Sons; The Crucible; After the Fall; The Price; The American Clock*

Joyce Carol Oates — *The Triumph of the Spider Monkey*

Clifford Odets — *Waiting for Lefty; Awake and Sing; Paradise Lost; Golden Boy; The Big Knife; The Country Girl*

Eugene O'Neill — *Beyond the Horizon; Anna Christie; Strange Interlute; A Long Day's Journey into Night; The Emperor Jones; Desire Under the Elms; Mourning Becomes Electra; Ah, Wilderness!; The Iceman Cometh*

David Rabe — *The Basic Training of Pavlo Hummel; Streamers; Hurlyburly*

Elmer Rice — *The Adding Machine; Street Scene; Counsellor-at-Law; We, the People*

Nelly Sachs — *A Mystery Play of the Sufferings of Israel*

William Saroyan — *The Time of Your Life; My Heart's in the Highlands*

Sidney Sheldon — *The Bachelor and the Bobby Soxer* (movie); *Redhead* (musical)

Sam Shepard — *Chicago; Buried Child; A Lie of the Mind; The Tooth of Crime; True West*

Robert Sherwood — *The Petrified Forest; Idiot's Delight; Abe Lincoln in Illinois; There Shall Be No Night*

Neil Simon — *The Odd Couple; Barefoot in the Park; The Sunshine Boys; Biloxi Blues; Broadway Bound; Sweet Charity; Come Blow Your Horn; Chapter Two*

Laurence Stallings — *What Price Glory?* (with Maxwell Anderson); *First Flight* (with Maxwell Anderson); *The Buccaneer* (with Maxwell Anderson)

James Thurber — *The Male Animal* (with Elliot Nugent)

Gore Vidal — *Visit to a Small Planet; The Best Man*

Thornton Wilder — *The Merchant of Yonkers* (later revised and called *The Matchmaker* and still later a musical, *Hello, Dolly!*); *Our Town**; *The Skin of Our Teeth*; *The Long Christmas Dinner*

Tennessee Williams — *The Glass Menagerie; A Streetcar Named Desire; Cat on a Hot Tin Roof; The Night of the Iguana; Suddenly Last Summer; Sweet Bird of Youth*

August Wilson — *Ma Rainey's Black Bottom; Fences; Joe Turner's Come and Gone*

Lanford Wilson — *So Long at the Fair; The Hot L Baltimore; Talley's Folly*

Paul Zindel — *The Effect of Gamma Rays on Man-in-the-Moon Marigolds; And Miss Reardon Drinks a Little; The Secret Affairs of Mildred Wild; Ladies at the Alamo; Amulets Against the Dragon Forces*

111. DRAMA: PULITZER PRIZEWINNERS

The Pulitzer Prize for Drama is awarded annually for an American play having to do with life in the United States. The following dramatists and the drama for which they were honored are listed below. Note: Eugene O'Neill is the only four-time winner of this coveted prize. See also List 115, Drama Critics' Circle Awards.

1918	Jesse Williams	*Why Marry?*
1920	Eugene O'Neill	*Beyond the Horizon*
1921	Zona Gale	*Miss Lulu Bett*
1922	Eugene O'Neill	*Anna Christie*
1923	Owen Davis	*Icebound*
1924	Hatcher Hughes	*Hell-Bent for Heaven*
1925	Sidney Howard	*They Knew What They Wanted*
1926	George Kelly	*Craig's Wife*
1927	Paul Green	*In Abraham's Bosom*
1928	Eugene O'Neill	*Strange Interlude*
1929	Elmer Rice	*Street Scene*
1930	Marc Connelly	*The Green Pastures*
1931	Susan Glaspell	*Alison's House*
1932	Kaufman/Ryskind/Gershwin	*Of Thee I Sing*
1933	Maxwell Anderson	*Both Your Houses*
1934	Sidney Kingsley	*Men in White*
1935	Zoe Akins	*The Old Maid*
1936	Robert Sherwood	*Idiot's Delight*
1937	George Kaufman/Moss Hart	*You Can't Take It With You*
1938	Thornton Wilder	*Our Town*
1939	Robert Sherwood	*Abe Lincoln in Illinois*

1940	William Saroyan	*The Time of Your Life*
1941	Robert Sherwood	*There Shall Be No Night*
1943	Thornton Wilder	*The Skin of Our Teeth*
1945	Mary Chase	*Harvey*
1946	R. Crouse/H. Lindsay	*State of the Union*
1948	Tennessee Williams	*A Streetcar Named Desire*
1949	Arthur Miller	*Death of a Salesman*
1950	Rodgers/Hammerstein/Logan	*South Pacific*
1952	Joseph Kramm	*The Shrike*
1953	William Inge	*Picnic*
1954	John Patrick	*Teahouse of the August Moon*
1955	Tennessee Williams	*Cat on a Hot Tin Roof*
1956	Goodrich/Hackett	*The Diary of Anne Frank*
1957	Eugene O'Neill	*Long Day's Journey Into Night*
1958	Ketti Frings	*Look Homeward, Angel*
1959	Archibald MacLeish	*J. B.*
1960	Abbott/Weidman/Hamick/Bock	*Fiorello*
1961	Tad Mosel	*All the Way Home*
1962	Frank Loesser/Abe Burrows	*How To Succeed in Business Without Really Trying*
1965	Frank Gilroy	*The Subject Was Roses*
1967	Edward Albee	*A Delicate Balance*
1969	Howard Sackler	*The Great White Hope*
1970	Charles Gordone	*No Place to Be Somebody*
1971	Paul Zindel	*The Effect of Gamma Rays on Man-in-the-Moon Marigolds*
1973	Jason Miller	*That Championship Season*
1975	Edward Albee	*Seascape*
1976	Bennett/Kirkwood/Dante/ Hamlisch/Kleban	*A Chorus Line*
1977	Michael Cristofer	*The Shadow Box*
1978	Donald Coburn	*The Gin Game*
1979	Sam Shepard	*Buried Child*
1980	Lanford Wilson	*Talley's Folly*
1981	Beth Henley	*Crimes of the Heart*
1982	Charles Fuller	*A Soldier's Play*
1983	Marsha Norman	*'night, Mother*

1984	David Mamet	*Glengarry Glen Ross*
1985	Stephen Sondheim/James Lapine	*Sunday in the Park with George*
1987	August Wilson	*Fences*
1988	Alfred Uhry	*Driving Miss Daisy*
1989	Wendy Wasserstein	*The Heidi Chronicles*
1990	August Wilson	*The Piano Lesson*
1991	Neil Simon	*Lost in Yonkers*
1992	Robert Schenkkan	*The Kentucky Cycle*
1993	Tony Kushner	*Angels in America: Millennium Approaches*
1994	Edward Albee	*Three Tall Women*
1995	Horton Foote	*The Young Man from Atlanta*
1996	Jonathan Larson	*Rent*

112. DRAMA CRITICS' CIRCLE AWARDS

The following American playwrights, listed alphabetically, have been awarded the New York Drama Critics' Circle Award. The award has been given annually since 1935 for plays and musicals, both American and foreign. This list does not include musicals. An asterisk (*) indicates those who have been recognized for more than one play. Those with (C) after their names indicate co-authors of a winning work. See also List 111, Drama: Pulitzer Prizewinners.

Albee, Edward*
Anderson, Maxwell*
Bullins, Ed
Frings, Ketti
Fuller, Charles
Gilroy, Frank
Goodrich, Frances (C)
Guare, John*
Hackett, Albert (C)
Hansberry, Lorraine
Hellman, Lillian*
Henley, Beth
Kingsley, Sidney*

Kushner, Tony
Mamet, David*
McCullers, Carson
Miller, Arthur*
Miller, Jason
Mosel, Tad
O'Neill, Eugene
Patrick, John
Piñero, Miguel
Pomerance, Bernard
Rabe, David
Sackler, Howard
Saroyan, William

Simon, Neil
Steinbeck, John
Shepard, Sam
Tomlin, Lily (C)
Van Druten, John
Wagner, Jane (C)
Wasserstein, Wendy
Williams, Tennessee*
Wilson, Lanford
Wilson, August*
Zindel, Paul

113. ELEMENTS OF DRAMA

The first list shows the essential elements of drama as a literary form. Familiarity with the techniques dramatists employ in putting plays together will increase a readers' appreciation of this literary form. The last list includes classic devices dramatists use to obtain special effects.

THE FIVE PARTS OF A DRAMA

1. **Introduction** — situation and characters introduced.
2. **Rising action** — conflict becomes clear and action rises as obstacles are presented.
3. **Climax** — high point of interest; turning point of play.
4. **Falling action** — conflict is worked out.
5. **Conclusion** — ending, resolution.

CLASSIC DEVICES USED BY DRAMATISTS

1. **Contrast** — alternating humor and pathos, song and dialogue, tense and tranquil scenes.
2. **Irony** — lines having one meaning for the audience and another for the character to whom they are spoken.
3. **Suspense** — the experience of uncertainty about what will happen next, accompanied by anticipation.
4. **Surprise** — unexpected twist or turn.
5. **Soliloquy** — character speaking to the world in general with no other characters in the scene.
6. **Aside** — character speaking confidentially to the audience (often humorously) as if other characters cannot hear what is said.
7. **Disguise** — props to change the appearance of the character to fool other characters in the play.
8. **Pause** — an incident introduced just before the climax to mislead the audience.
9. **Poetic Justice** — letting the villain be punished and the hero reap reward.

114. Stage Diagram

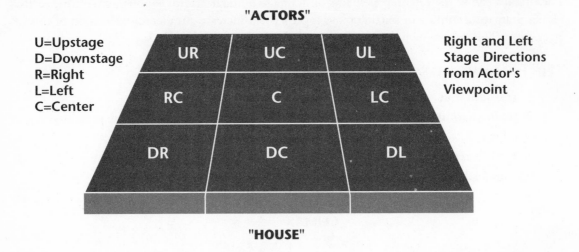

"ACTORS"

U=Upstage
D=Downstage
R=Right
L=Left
C=Center

Right and Left Stage Directions from Actor's Viewpoint

UR	UC	UL
RC	C	LC
DR	DC	DL

"HOUSE"

115. Drama Glossary

acoustics — Structural qualities of a theater that affect the transmission of sounds from the stage to an audience.

act — Major portion or segment of a play.

aside — See List 113, Elements of Drama

at rise — Refers to the action taking place as the curtain rises.

cast (verb) — To assign parts to the actors in a play.

cast (noun) — Group of characters in a play.

casting call — Notice to actors of an audition for parts in a play.

character — Person being played by an actor in a play.

comedy — Light and amusing drama, usually with a happy ending

costume — Clothing, jewelry, and other paraphernalia used to help the actor portray a character.

curtain — End of a scene; closing of the curtain to depict the end of an act or scene.

curtain call — The tradition of actors taking their bows, receiving applause, and/or being reintroduced to the audience at the end of a play.

dialogue — Conversation; spoken words between two or more people.

downstage — The part of a traditional stage closest to the audience. See List 114, Stage Diagram.

drama — Story created for performance on a stage by actors; contains dialogue and stage directions; play.

dramatis personae — Cast of characters in a drama, or more generally, participants in an event.

exeunt — Stage direction meaning "they exit."

exit — Stage direction telling the actor to leave the stage.

Freytag's pyramid — Three elements of drama, according to Gustav Freytag, German drama critic: rising action, climax, falling action. See List 113, Elements of Drama.

ghost writer — Author who writes a work that another person takes credit for. See List 116, Shakespeare's Ghost Writers?

house — The audience or the theatrical building.

makeup — Cosmetics, wigs, hair colorings, or other items applied to the actors and actresses to change or enhance their appearance.

melodrama — Play with exaggerated plot and emotion.

monologue — Speech delivered by one character as if he is speaking to himself, but is overheard by and for the benefit of the audience.

playwright — Person who writes a play.

proscenium — In ancient theater, the stage; in modern theater, the foreground or part of stage in front of the curtain.

proscenium arch — Opening in the proscenium through which the audience sees the stage.

props — Properties; objects or articles used in a play to add to the characters' portrayals (other than costumes and the set).

rehearsals — Practice sessions that take place before a play is presrented to an audience.

scene — Subdivision of an act of a play, where action takes place in one stage setting.

scenery — Painted scenes and accessories used to depict the setting of a play.

set — Artificial setting for a scene in a play, including furniture, scenery, and other items to create an illusion of another time and place.

soliloquy — See List 113, Elements of Drama.

stage directions — Directions to the actors written in the script of a play to tell them where to go or how to speak their lines.

stage left — Left side of stage as actor faces audience. See List 114, Stage Diagram.

stage right — Right side of stage as actor faces audience. See List 114, Stage Diagram.

tragedy — Drama characterized by an unhappy or disastrous ending for the main characters.

upstage — The part of a traditional stage farthest back from the audience. Also, to steal the scene away from another actor by moving upstage, forcing the downstage actor to turn his or her back on the audience. See List 114, Stage Diagram.

119. SHAKESPEARE'S GHOST WRITERS?

Since the middle of the eighteenth century, commentators have periodically suggested that some or all of Shakespeare's works were actually written by other authors. Orthodox Shakespearian scholars have steadfastly rejected these claims, but champions of one or another candidate have not been deterred. Readers interested in exploring this controversy might delve into a work by a writer on this list (where available) and compare the style, vocabulary, and themes to those in a work by Shakespeare.

Francis Bacon (main contender)

Robert Burton

Edward DeVere

John Donne

Anne Hathaway (Shakespeare's wife)

King James I

Ben Jonson

Roger Manners

Christopher Marlowe

Sir Walter Raleigh

William Seymour

Thomas Wolsey

Edmund Spenser

117. SHAKESPEARE: COMPLETE PLAYS AND POEMS

The plays of William Shakespeare have been immensely popular from the time they were written until the present because they encompass life's fundamental problems and the struggles of men and women to resolve them. His language and poetic style have seldom been equaled, and he is considered one of the greatest dramatists of all time, not only in his native England but in other countries as well. This full title list contains all Shakespeare's known works categorized by type. (Some plays are tragi-comedies, and can be classified differently.) See also List 118, Getting a Line on Shakespeare.

COMEDIES

All's Well That Ends Well

As You Like It

The Comedy of Errors

Cymbeline

Love's Labour's Lost

Measure for Measure

The Merchant of Venice

The Merry Wives of Windsor

A Midsummer Night's Dream

Much Ado About Nothing

Pericles, Prince of Tyre

The Taming of the Shrew

The Tempest

Twelfth Night; or, What You Will

The Two Gentlemen of Verona

The Two Noble Kinsmen

The Winter's Tale

TRAGEDIES

The Life of Timon of Athens
The Tragedy of Antony and Cleopatra
The Tragedy of Coriolanus
The Tragedy of Hamlet, Prince of Denmark
The Tragedy of Julius Caesar
The Tragedy of King Lear
The Tragedy of Macbeth
The Tragedy of Othello, the Moor of Venice
The Tragedy of Romeo and Juliet
The Tragedy of Titus Andronicus
The Tragedy of Troilus and Cressida

HISTORIES

The First Part of King Henry IV
The Second Part of King Henry IV
The Life of King Henry V
The First Part of King Henry VI
The Second Part of King Henry VI

The Third Part of King Henry VI
The Famous History of the Life of King
    Henry VIII
The Life and Death of King John
The Tragedy of King Richard II
The Tragedy of King Richard III

POEMS

"A Lover's Complaint"
"The Passionate Pilgrim"
"The Rape of Lucrece"
"Venus and Adonis"
154 untitled sonnets (Sonnets were
    numbered in Roman numerals from
    I to CLIV.)

Note: *The Two Noble Kinsmen* and King
Henry VIII were probably co-authored with
John Fletcher.

118. GETTING A LINE ON SHAKESPEARE

These one-liners give quick hints of the subject matter of most of William Shakespeare's plays. He apparently wrote the works from 1590 to 1611, a span of about twenty-one years, when he was between the ages of twenty-six and forty-seven. (He died when he was in his early fifties.) You will notice recurring themes. The plays are in alphabetical, not chronological order. See also List 117, Shakespeare: Complete Plays and Poems.

All's Well That Ends Well — Woman finally wins love of her husband.

As You Like It — Rosalind and her family in the Forest of Arden.

Antony and Cleopatra — Tragic story of queen and her Roman lover.

Comedy of Errors — Twins separated in youth search for each other.

Coriolanus — Tragic life and experiences of Coriolanus.

Cymbeline — Story of King of England and his family.

Hamlet — Hamlet seeks revenge for father's death.

Henry IV (Part I) — Henry's son saves his life.

Henry IV (Part II) — Henry's son defeats his foes and becomes king.

Henry V — Henry, King of England, seeks the throne of France.

Henry VI (Part I) — John and Humphrey, uncles, rule over Henry.

Henry VI (Part II) — Tale of early years of War of the Roses.

Henry VI (Part III) — Tale of Henry VI's downfall.

Henry VIII — Henry's plan to abandon his wife and remarry.

Julius Caesar — Assassination of Caesar and its bloody aftermath.

King John — Feuds between John and Duke Arthur end in John's poisoning.

King Lear — Conflict between king and three daughters unfolds.

Love's Labour's Lost — King tries to avoid women but succumbs.

Macbeth — Macbeth's ambition leads to his destruction.

Measure for Measure — Deputy tries to enforce law against fornication.

Merchant of Venice — Money-lender confronts his enemies.

Merry Wives of Windsor — Man foiled trying to dupe women out of money.

Midsummer Night's Dream — One wedding ends up as three weddings.

Much Ado About Nothing — Two couples and their tales of marriage.

Othello — Jealousy results in vengeful plot against Othello.

Pericles — Prince thinks wife and daughter dead, but they are reunited.

Richard II — Henry IV becomes king after having Richard killed.

Richard III — Richard will do anything (even kill) to become king.

Romeo and Juliet — Feuding families' children fall in love.

Taming of the Shrew — Sisters and their matrimonies.

The Tempest — Magician endures hardships as exiled ruler of an island.

Timon of Athens — Timon loses wealth but recaptures it.

Titus Andronicus — Titus seizes queen during war, but she gains revenge.

Troilus and Cressida — Prince finds out his true love is unfaithful.

Twelfth Night — Shipwrecked twins believe one another dead.

Two Gentlemen of Verona — Friends are rivals over a woman's love.

Winter's Tale — Two kings and their families survive misfortunes.

119. SHAKESPEARE GLOSSARY

Many words common in Shakespeare's time are now unfamiliar. Here is a glossary to help decipher and add meaning to Shakespearean plays. See also List 117, Shakespeare: Complete Plays and Poems; and List 120, Allusions: Shakespearean.

all-thing — wholly

an't — if it

auger-hole — tiny spot

augures — prophecies

bechanc'd — happened

beholding — indebted

benison — blessing

betimes — quickly

blow our nails together — wait patiently

bodements — omens

bootless — in vain

breech'd — covered

brooch'd — adorned

brindl'd — spotted

broad words — speaking freely

bruited — reported

buzzard — worthless person

chare — chore

check — rebuke

clept — called

closet — room

cloudy — sullen

coign — corner

complexion — disposition

conceit — thought

corporal agent — muscle

counters — coins

coz — cousin; relative

cozen — cheat

daff't — doff it; take it off

dearest chuck — term of endearment

ducat — gold coin

dudgeon — dagger hilt

enow — enough

estate — social position; condition

ewer — jug

eyne — eyes

fain — willingly

father — old man

fay — faith

fil'd — defiled

firstling — first

foison — plenty

forebear — leave

free hearts — true feelings

full of lead — in low spirits

ghosted — haunted

God 'ild us — God reward us

golden round — crown

graff — graft

graymalkin — gray cat

groom — servant

habiliments — attire

half a soul — halfwit

hand — handwriting

haply — per chance

hart — male deer

hilding — nasty beast or wretch

hind — deer

hipp'd — lame

ho — halt

hurlyburly — tumult

I'll do — do him harm

in a few — briefly

in compt — brought to account

incarnadine — turn red

insane root — hemlock

is't call'd — is it

Jack — name used in contempt; servant; drinking utensil

jade — tired horse

Jill — maid, drinking utensil

keep counsel — keep a secret

lank'd — thin

lethe — death

levell'd at — guessed

loose — let go

lover — friend

make boot — take advantage

make to — approach

maw and gulf — gullet and stomach

meed — reward

meetly — pretty good

mew her up — confine her

milch-kine — milking cows

moe — more

moiety — part

mortified — deadened

napkins — handkerchiefs

nave to the chops — navel to the throat

near'st of life — vital organs

noddle — head

outface it — bluff it out

ow'd — owned

owe — own

paddock — toad

parlous — dangerous

patch — fool

poke — pocket

posts — messengers

prime — spring

priser — prizefighter

proper — handsome

raise the waters — start things moving

rate — scold; rebuke

roundly — directly

roynish — mangy

rudesby — rough young man

scanted — limited

scape — escape

scarf up — blindfold

seated in the mean — living comfortably

second cock — 3:00 a.m.

signs well — good omen

sith — since

skirr — scour

sooth — true

spaniel'd me — followed me

speak me fair — speak well of me

spoiled — plundered

spot — blemish

stay — keep

stay'd her — let her stay

stomach — resentment; courage; inclination

striding the blast — riding out the storm

suborn'd — bribed

sufferance — permission

supp'd — had your fill

swounded — swooned; fainted

ta'en you napping — caught you in the act

thorough — through

thrall'd — enthralled

travelling lamp — sun

trusted home — trusted all the way

unlineal — not kin

unrough — no beard

usance — interest

weet — know

wis — know

younker — young man

120. ALLUSIONS: SHAKESPEAREAN

See also List 117, Shakespeare: Complete Plays and Poems; List 118, Getting a Line on Shakespeare; and List 119, Shakespeare Glossary.

"**Age cannot wither her, nor custom stale her infinite variety.**" *Antony and Cleopatra.* Said by a friend of Antony about Cleopatra.

"**A horse! A horse! My kingdom for a horse!**" *King Richard III* King Richard says this after his horse is killed while he is in the middle of a battle.

"**Alas, Poor Yorick!**" *Hamlet.* Hamlet laments the inevitability of death as he looks at his friend's skull.

"**All the world's a stage and all the men and women merely players…**" *As You Like It.* Describes the Seven Ages of Man from infancy to old age, illustrating how each age plays its distinctive part as people go through their lives.

"**A pound of flesh.**" *The Merchant of Venice.* Spoken by Shylock, the money-lender, as what he wants in return for Antonio's loan. This now refers to any high price or sacrifice one must pay, especially when beholden to someone else.

"As flies to wanton boys, are we to the gods; they kill us for their sport." *King Lear,* spoken by the Earl of Gloucester, friend of Lear, illustrating the harshness and futility of life.

"A tale told by an idiot, full of sound and fury, signifying nothing." *Macbeth.* Macbeth laments life's insignificance.

Banquo's ghost. The ghost of Banquo, who was murdered under Macbeth's guidance, appears only to Macbeth at a dinner party. Anyone appearing uninvited or unexpectedly is called Banquo's ghost.

"Beware the ides of March." *Julius Caesar.* The ides of March are March 15. This warning is given Caesar by a fortuneteller and proves to be well-founded.

"Brutus is an honorable man." *Julius Caesar.* Spoken by Mark Antony as he is ironically discrediting Brutus and his fellow conspirators.

"The die is cast." Plutarch's *Lives* and Shakespeare's *Richard III.* This gambling term indicated the die was thrown and the consequences must be lived with. The saying is used now when something, once done, cannot be taken back but will continue to its inevitable conclusion.

"Double, double, toil and trouble; fire burn, and cauldron bubble." *Macbeth.* A witches' chant.

"Et tu Brute?" (Latin: And you, Brutus?) *Julius Caesar.* Spoken by Caesar when he realizes that Brutus, one of his dearest friends, has betrayed him and is participating in his assassination.

"Every inch a king." *King Lear.* Ironically spoken by Lear to the Earl of Gloucester about himself.

Falstaffian. Falstaff was an obese and self-indulgent but appealing character who appears in several of Shakespeare's histories. Anyone resembling Falstaff is called Falstaffian.

"Fear not till Birnam Wood do come to Dunsinane." *Macbeth.* Prophecy made by witches to Macbeth.

"Frailty, thy name is woman." *Hamlet.*

"Friends, Romans, countrymen, lend me your ears." *Julius Caesar.* Spoken by Mark Antony as he speaks to the people at Caesar's funeral, when he wants everyone to listen well.

"Get thee to a nunnery." *Hamlet.* Hamlet's advice to Ophelia.

"How sharper than a serpent's tooth it is to have a thankless child." *King Lear.* Spoken by Lear about the pain of his daughters' betrayals.

Iago. *Othello.* Iago is Othello's cunning, manipulative aide, who causes Othello to kill his wife and himself. Iago has become the personification of a spiteful, scheming person.

"I am a Jew. Hath not a Jew eyes? Hath not a Jew hands, organs, dimensions, senses, affections, passions?" *The Merchant of Venice.* Spoken by Shylock, the money-lender, in defense of his own humanity.

"If music be the food of love, play on." *Twelfth Night.*

"Lay on, MacDuff." *Macbeth.* Spoken as Macbeth begins a single combat with MacDuff.

"**Let me not to the marriage of true minds admit impediments.**" Shakespeare's Sonnet CXVI, which maintains that nothing can come between two people who really love one another.

"**Lord, what fools these mortals be!**" *A Midsummer Night's Dream.* Refers to the foolishness of people entering Puck's enchanted forest.

"**More sinned against than sinning.**" *King Lear.*

"**Neither a borrower nor a lender be.**" *Hamlet.* Advice from Polonius to his son.

"**Once more unto the breach, dear friends.**" *King Henry V.* Henry inspires his troops to storm an enemy stronghold.

"**One that loved not wisely but too well.**" *Othello.* Spoken by Othello after killing his wife.

"**Out, damned spot.**" *Macbeth.* Spoken by Lady Macbeth, who feels guilty about persuading her husband to commit murder. She dreams her hand is stained with the blood of their victim, the king.

"**Parting is such sweet sorrow.**" *Romeo and Juliet.* Juliet means it is sad to part, but it will be sublime when she sees Romeo again.

"**Romeo, Romeo! Wherefore art thou Romeo?**" *Romeo and Juliet.* Juliet laments the difficulties facing her and her lover.

"**Shall I compare thee to a summer's day?**" Opening line of Sonnet XVIII.

"**Something is rotten in the state of Denmark.**" *Hamlet.* Spoken by guard of the palace when he sees the king's ghost, meaning that evil forces are afoot.

"**That way madness lies.**" *King Lear.* Refers to the idea that if you dwell too long on unpleasantness, you will go crazy.

"**The lady doth protest too much.**" *Hamlet.* Spoken by Gertrude.

"**The noblest Roman of them all.**" *Julius Caesar.* Mark Antony describing Brutus, after his former enemy's death.

"**The quality of mercy is not strained.**" *The Merchant of Venice.* "Strained" here means "forced" (constrained), referring to the idea that mercy should be given freely, even if it is not required.

"**The winter of our discontent.**" *King Richard III.* Refers to the Wars of the Roses in England.

"**There are more things in heaven and earth, Horatio, than are dreamt of in your philosophy.**" *Hamlet.* Hamlet tells his friend that any given person's knowledge is limited.

"**There is a tide in the affairs of men which, taken at the flood, leads on to fortune.**" *Julius Caesar.* Brutus urges his friends to take advantage of their golden opportunity.

"**There's a divinity that shapes our ends.**" *Hamlet.* A divine power controls human destiny.

"**There's a special providence in the fall of a sparrow.**" *Hamlet.* Refers to the Biblical idea that God observes even small events like the fall of a sparrow.

"To be or not to be: that is the question." *Hamlet.* Hamlet contemplates suicide but draws back.

"Tomorrow, and tomorrow, and tomorrow creeps in this petty pace from day to day to the last syllable of recorded time ..." *Macbeth.* Spoken by Macbeth on his wife's death.

"We are such stuff as dreams are made on." *The Tempest.* Spoken by Prospero, the magician, telling his daughter that just like the spirits he made disappear, life can also vanish quickly.

"What's in a name: that which we call a rose by any other name would smell as sweet." *Romeo and Juliet.* Spoken by Juliet, referring to the fact Romeo's family name is keeping them apart.

"Yon Cassius has a lean and hungry look." *Julius Caesar.* Spoken by Caesar about Cassius, who Caesar thinks is hungry for power.

121. POPULAR HIGH SCHOOL PRODUCTIONS

The following plays are among the most popular high school productions. Many readers may remember haveing played a role in one or more of them. See also List 122, Long-Running Broadway Plays.

Adaptation
Antigone
Anything Goes
Arsenic and Old Lace
Bye Bye Birdie
The Comedy of Errors
Dark of the Moon
Fiddler on the Roof
Fools
God
Godspell
Gorey Stories
Grease
Guys and Dolls

I Know I Saw Gypsies
I Never Saw Another Butterfly
Joseph and the Amazing Technicolor Dreamcoat
Little Shop of Horrors
Mask of Hiroshima
A Midsummer Night's Dream
The Music Man
The Nerd
Oklahoma!
Once Upon a Mattress
Our Town
Rashomon

The Roar of the Greasepaint, the Smell of the Crowd
Romance Romance
Runaways
Steel Magnolias
Strider
Up the Down Staircase
Waiting for the Parade
Wedding Band
The Wizard of Oz
You Can't Take It With You
You're a Good Man, Charlie Brown

These plays have stood the test of time, having enjoyed at least 1,000 performances on Broadway. Many are based on books by the same or a different name. Many readers find the books even more interesting, because they can use their own imaginations to create the characters and settings. Often the play is appreciated more fully after the book is read. See also List 121, Popular High School Productions.

Abie's Irish Rose
Ain't Misbehavin'
Amadeus
Angel Street
Annie
Annie Get Your Gun
Arsenic and Old Lace
Barefoot in the Park
Best Little Whorehouse in Texas
Born Yesterday
Brighton Beach Memoirs
Butterflies Are Free
Cabaret
Cactus Flower
Cats
Chorus Line
Dancin'
Deathtrap
Dreamgirls
Equus
Evita
Fiddler on the Roof

Forty-Second Street
Funny Girl
Gemini
Grease
Guys and Dolls
Hair
Harvey
Hello Dolly!
Hellzapoppin'
How to Succeed in Business
    Without Really Trying
The King and I
La Cage aux Folles
Les Miserables
Life with Father
Lightnin'
Magic Show
Mame
Man of La Mancha
Mary, Mary
Me and My Girl
Miss Saigon

Mister Roberts
Mummenschanz
The Music Man
My Fair Lady
Oh, Calcutta
Oklahoma!
Pins and Needles
Pippin
Phantom of the Opera
Promises, Promises
Same Time, Next Year
"1776"
Seven-Year Itch
Sleuth
The Sound of Music
South Pacific
Sugar Babies
Tobacco Road
Torch Song Trilogy
Voice of the Turtle
The Wiz

123. ACADEMY AWARDS (OSCARS)

These movies won the "best picture" award from the Motion Picture Academy in the years shown. Many books or plays from which screenplays are adapted are even better than the corresponding movies. It is fun to pick a movie that was in book or play form first and compare and contrast the book with the movie. Note: Cinderella was the most-often made movie (58 times) but it never won any Academy Awards. See also List 124, Films Preserved by Act of Congress.

1928 — *Wings*
1929 — *Broadway Melody*
1930 — *All Quiet on the Western Front*
1931 — *Cimarron*
1932 — *Grand Hotel*
1933 — *Cavalcade*
1934 — *It Happened One Night*
1935 — *Mutiny on the Bounty*
1936 — *The Great Ziegfeld*
1937 — *Life of Emile Zola*
1938 — *You Can't Take It With You*
1939 — *Gone With the Wind*
1940 — *Rebecca*
1941 — *How Green Was My Valley*
1942 — *Mrs. Miniver*
1943 — *Casablanca*
1944 — *Going My Way*
1945 — *The Lost Weekend*
1946 — *The Best Years of Our Lives*
1947 — *Gentleman's Agreement*
1948 — *Hamlet*
1949 — *All the King's Men*
1950 — *All About Eve*
1951 — *An American in Paris*
1952 — *Greatest Show on Earth*
1953 — *From Here to Eternity*
1954 — *On the Waterfront*
1955 — *Marty*
1956 — *Around the World in 80 Days*

1957 — *The Bridge on the River Kwai*
1958 — *Gigi*
1959 — *Ben-Hur*
1960 — *The Apartment*
1961 — *West Side Story*
1962 — *Lawrence of Arabia*
1963 — *Tom Jones*
1964 — *My Fair Lady*
1965 — *The Sound of Music*
1966 — *A Man for all Seasons*
1967 — *In the Heat of the Night*
1968 — *Oliver!*
1969 — *Midnight Cowboy*
1970 — *Patton*
1971 — *The French Connection*
1972 — *The Godfather*
1973 — *The Sting*
1974 — *The Godfather, Part II*
1975 — *One Flew Over the Cuckoo's Nest*
1976 — *Rocky*
1977 — *Annie Hall*
1978 — *The Deer Hunter*
1979 — *Kramer vs. Kramer*
1980 — *Ordinary People*
1981 — *Chariots of Fire*
1982 — *Gandhi*
1983 — *Terms of Endearment*
1984 — *Amadeus*
1985 — *Out of Africa*

1986 — *Platoon*
1987 — *The Last Emperor*
1988 — *Rain Man*
1989 — *Driving Miss Daisy*
1990 — *Dances with Wolves*
1991 — *The Silence of the Lambs*

1992 — *Unforgiven*
1993 — *Schindler's List*
1994 — *Forrest Gump*
1995 — *Braveheart*
1996 — *The English Patient*
1997 — *Titanic*

FAMOUS WRITERS ON FILM

Maxwell Anderson
Raymond Chandler
Theodore Dreiser
William Faulkner
F. Scott Fitzgerald
Dashiell Hammett
Ben Hecht

Lillian Hellman
Ernest Hemingway
James Hilton
Aldous Huxley
Christopher Isherwood
Clifford Odets
Dorothy Parker

S. J. Perelman
Ayn Rand
George Bernard Shaw
John Steinbeck
Nathaniel West
Thornton Wilder
Tennessee Williams

124. FILMS PRESERVED BY ACT OF CONGRESS

The following American films have been placed on the National Film Registry to be preserved in accordance with the National Film Preservation Act of 1988. They have been designated as culturally, historically, or aesthetically significant. Many have been adapted from notable books that are at least as interesting as the movies. The one hundred films are listed in alphabetical order. See also List 123, Academy Awards (Oscars).

Adam's Rib
All Above Eve
All Quiet on the Western Front
Annie Hall
The Bank Dick
The Battle of San Pietro
The Best Years of Our Lives
Big Business
The Big Parade
The Birth of a Nation
The Blood of Jesus

Bonnie and Clyde
Bringing Up Baby
Carmen Jones
Casablanca
Castro Street
Chinatown
Citizen Kane
City Lights
The Crowd
David Holzman's Diary
Detour

Dodsworth
Dog Star Man
Double Indemnity
Dr. Strangelove
Duck Soup
Fantasia
Footlight Parade
Frankenstein
The Freshman
The General
Gertie the Dinosaur

Gigi

The Godfather

The Gold Rush

Gone With the Wind

The Grapes of Wrath

The Great Train Robbery

Greed

Harlan County, U. S. A.

High Noon

High School

How Green Was My Valley

I Am a Fugitive From a Chain
    Gang

Intolerance

The Italian

It's a Wonderful Life

Killer of Sheep

King Kong

Lawrence of Arabia

The Learning Tree

Letter From an Unknown
    Woman

Love Me Tonight

The Magnificent Ambersons

The Maltese Falcon

Meshes of the Afternoon

Mr. Smith Goes to Washington

Modern Times

Morocco

My Darling Clementine

Nashville

Nanook of the North

The Night of the Hunter

Ninotchka

On the Waterfront

Out of the Past

Paths of Glory

A Place in the Sun

The Poor Little Rich Girl

Primary

The Prisoner of Zenda

Psycho

Raging Bull

Rebel Without a Cause

Red River

Ride the High Country

The River

Salesman

Salt of the Earth

The Searchers

Shadow of a Doubt

Sherlock, Jr.

Singin' in the Rain

Snow White and the Seven
    Dwarfs

Some Like It Hot

Star Wars

Sullivan's Travels

Sunrise

Sunset Boulevard

Tevya

Top Hat

The Treasure of the Sierra
    Madre

Trouble in Paradise

2001: A Space Odyssey

Vertigo

What's Opera, Doc?

Within Our Gates

A Woman Under the Influence

The Wizard of Oz

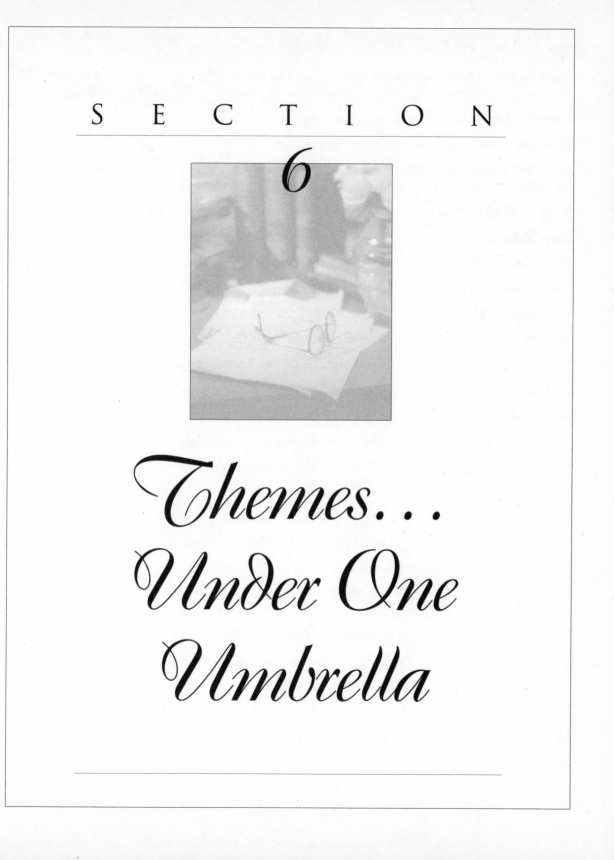

Themes...
Under One
Umbrella

125. ADVENTURE STORIES: TRUE

It is often said that truth is stranger than fiction. The following authors relate a variety of true-life adventures. Topics are in parentheses. See also List 31, Autobiography, and List 32, Biography.

Adamson, Joy — *Born Free* (adopted lion cub)

Anderson, Scott — *Distant Fires* (1700-mile canoe trip)

Antekeier, Kristopher and Greg Aunapu — *Ringmaster! My Year on the Road with "The Greatest Show on Earth"* (ringmaster for Ringling Brothers Barnum and Bailey Circus)

Bligh, William — *Mutiny on Board the HMS Bounty* (South Seas mutiny)

Blum, Arlene — *Annapurna, a Woman's Place* (women climb a mountain)

Charriere, Henri — *Papillon* (imprisonment, escape of innocent man)

Cheng, Nien — *Life and Death in Shanghai* (experiences during China's Cultural Revolution)

Cookridge, E. H. — *The Orient Express* (experiences on train)

Davidson, Robyn — *Tracks* (crossing Australia by camel)

Emert, Phyllis Raybin — *Mysteries of Ships and Planes* (strange disappearances and happenings)

Graham, Robin Lee — *Dove* (sailing voyage in South Pacific)

Heyerdahl, Thor — *Kon-Tiki* (rafting across the Pacific)

Heyerdahl, Thor — *The Ra Expeditions* (small boat across Atlantic)

Hillaby, John — *Journey to the Jade Sea* (walking through Kenya)

Hood, William — *Mole* (Russian and American spy)

Hyde, H. Montgomery — *The Atom Bomb Spies* (Russian defection)

Jenkins, Peter — *Walk Across America* (New Orleans/New York walk)

La Bastille, Anne — *Woodswoman* (woman lives like Thoreau)

Lane, Rose Wilder and Roger Lea MacBride — *Rose Wilder Lane: Her Story* (adventures of Laura Ingalls Wilder's daughter)

Leslie, Robert Franklin — *In the Shadow of a Rainbow* (friendship between man and wolf)

Lindbergh, Charles A. — *The Spirit of St. Louis* (trans-Atlantic flight)

Lord, Walter — *A Night to Remember* (sinking of Titanic)

Marton, Kati — *Wallenberg* (rescue of Jews during WWII)

Matthiesson, Peter — *The Snow Leopard* (walking from Nepal to Tibet)

McDonald, John J. — *Howard Hughes and the Spruce Goose* (building a huge wooden airplane)

McPhee, John A. — *Coming into the Country* (encounters in Alaska)

Mitts, Michael H. and Carl Larsen — *Only a Gringo Would Die for an Anteater* (veterinarian adventures)

Mowat, Farley — *The Boat Who Wouldn't Float* (sailing across the Atlantic)

Olsen, Jack — *Night of the Grizzlies* (bears in Glacier National Park)

Polo, Marco — *The Travels of Marco Polo* (travels in Asia)

Read, Piers Paul — *Alive: The Story of the Andes Survivors* (aftermath of plane crash)

Reader's Digest — *They Beat the Odds* (collection of adventures)

Robertson, Dougal — *Survive the Savage Sea* (family at sea on raft)

Roth, Arthur — *Against Incredible Odds* (collection of adventures)

Saint-Exupèry, Antoine de — *Wind, Sand, and Stars* (aviation stories)

Simpson, Colin — *The Lusitania* (German U-boat sinks ocean liner in WWI)

Spierling, Frank — *Lizzie* (story of Lizzie Borden)

Stoll, Cliff — *The Cuckoo's Egg: Tracking a Spy Through the Maze of Computer Espionage* (tracking a rogue computer hacker)

126. ALLEGORIES

Poetry or prose may contain an allegory, a second or deeper meaning than the story alone suggests. An allegory usually includes events and characters that, taken as a whole, symbolically represent truths or generalizations about the human condition or the state of society. These examples of allegories include brief explanations of symbolic meanings. See also List 10, Famous Characters from Literature; List 13, Famous Places from Literature; List 146, Symbolism in Literature; and List 147, Symbols.

Absalom and Achitophel — John Dryden
  In this satirical political poem based on the Biblical story of King David and Absalom, Absalom symbolizes the Duke of Monmouth (son of Charles II); Achitophel, the Earl of Shaftsbury; and Zimri, the Duke of Buckingham. In the Bible, Absalom was King David's son and Achitophel was a counselor to King David.

An American Dream — Norman Mailer
  The comic novel concerns sex, violence, and death and is meant to be a parody and allegory of contemporary American life.

Animal Farm — George Orwell

In this allegorical beast fable the domesticated animals rebel against their masters but soon find themselves under the dictatorship of the pigs, who have formed a new ruling class. The animals represent those who overthrew the tsars in Russia only to be repressed by the totalitarianism of Josef Stalin during the Soviet era.

Bible (Abounds with allegory and symbolism throughout)

The Book of Ezekiel contains Ezekiel's symbolic acts of eating the scroll, shaving his beard and hair, and the allegorical story of the rusty pot. The Song of Solomon, a collection of love songs, has come to represent either God's love for his church and people (Christian interpretation); the relationship between God and Israel (Jewish interpretation); or the love and union of a man and woman.

Cato (play) — Joseph Addison

This tragedy about Cato, a Roman patriot, is an allegory of contemporary politics in the 1800s.

A Connecticut Yankee in King Arthur's Court — Mark Twain

This allegorical satire is an indictment of political and social injustices.

Death in Venice — Thomas Mann

The allegorical novella is about an aging author who risks everything when he becomes infatuated with a young boy who represents artistic perfection. The city of Venice is slowly sinking into the sea and cholera is killing the population, but the author finds it impossible to leave.

The Divine Comedy (La Divina Commedia) — Dante Alighieri

The three-sectioned, allegorical epic poem traces the poet's journey through hell, purgatory, and paradise, representing every person's life on Earth.

Erewhon — Samuel Butler

This Utopian romance's hero ventures to Erewhon (anagram of "nowhere"). In his description of Erewhon, Butler satirizes the schools, churches, legal systems, and social values of Victorian England.

Everyman — (author unknown)

In this play, the protagonist, Everyman, faces and fears death. Everyman represents every man and this universal fear.

The Fairie Queene — Edmund Spenser

This unfinished epic poem considers the virtues of Holiness, Temperance, Chastity, Friendship, Justice, Courtesy, and Constancy, which represent England in general, and Queen Elizabeth I in particular.

Gulliver's Travels — Jonathan Swift

Gulliver goes on four journeys: Lilliput (home of tiny people); Brobdingnag (home of giants); Laputa (flying island of scientists, sorcerers, and immortals); and Houyhnhnm (place where horses rule humans). Swift satirizes pride, selfishness, avarice, and dishonesty.

Love in the Ruins — Walker Percy

This is an allegory of human failure in a civilization that is trying to cope with the collapse of technology.

Penguin Island — Anatole France

A satirical allegory of civilization in general.

Pilgrim's Progress — John Bunyan

The hero, Christian, and other characters, such as Faithful and Mr. Worldly Wisdom, are all symbolic figures as are the names of places, such as the Valley of the Shadow of Death and Celestial City. The allegory deals with the salvation of the individual, though on the surface it is just the story of a man's travels.

Pincher Martin — William Golding

This modern fable, a shorter allegorical story, tells of Pincher, a shipwrecked sailor, stranded on a barren rock, who reflects on the selfishness and greed of his past existence as he struggles to survive. His experience represents self-discovery along the road of life.

The Plague — Albert Camus

This story, in which bubonic plague descends upon the Algerian city of Oran, is an allegory of the human condition, in which people are trapped by external circumstances but can nevertheless preserve their humanity and dignity.

Purple Island — Phineas Fletcher

This allegorical poem is about the human body and mind.

The Republic — Plato

Socrates and others debate justice, government, and the ideal state. In Book Seven, the Allegory of the Cave, Plato portrays how the majority of people mistake illusory shadows for the truth, while only philosophers are able to see clearly and perceive the ideal forms of justice.

Roman de la Rose (Romance of the Rose) — Guillaume de Lorris and Jean de Meun

This two-part allegorical poem uses a rose to represent love. The first part (by Guillaume de Lorris) is an idealistic story of a lover trying to pluck the rose of love; the second (by Jean de Meun) is a satirical attack on love, women, and the church.

Ship of Fools — Katherine Anne Porter

This novel is based on the work of Sebastian Brant of the same name and uses the same theme. See below.

Ship of Fools — Sebastian Brant

This allegorical poem, about a ship that never gets to its destination, employs the passengers to represent a catalogue of human weaknesses.

The Spell — Hermann Broch

This novel, which chronicles the moral disintegration of a town, is an allegory for the Nazis' corruption of Germany.

The Spire — William Golding

The hero's obsession with building a cathedral spire despite all obstacles and regardless of consequences is an allegory of obsessive behavior.

The Vision of William Concerning Piers the Plowman (Piers Plowman) — William Langland

This allegorical religious poem, containing a series of dreams and visions, depicts the social life of medieval England. The work attacks the greed of unscrupulous clergymen, depicts the hardships of common Christian people, and promotes the ideals of justice and spiritual salvation.

White Fang — Jack London

This tale of a sled dog's survival in the wild is an allegory contrasting the ways of civilization with the savage laws of nature.

A Winter's Tale — William Shakespeare

This play has been said to symbolize the regenerative process of nature or human belief in salvation and immortality.

127. Animals: Books and Stories

See also List 128, Animals: Poems.

Bear

The Bear — William Faulkner

A Bear Called Paddington — Michael Bond

The Bears on Hemlock Mountain — Alice Dalgliesh

Gentle Ben — Walt Morey

Gloomy Gus — Walt Morey

Little Bear — Else Holmelund Minarik

Track of the Grizzly — Frank C. Craighead, Jr.

Bird

Birds, Beasts and Relatives — Gerald Durrell

The Cry of the Crow — Jean Craighead George

Gay-Neck, the Story of a Pigeon — Dhan Ghopal Mukerji

Hawkmistress! — Marion Zinner Bradley

Owls in the Family — Farley Mowat

A Time to Fly Free — Stephanie S. Tolan

Cat

All I Need to Know I Learned from My Cat — Susie Becker

The Black Cat — Edgar Allan Poe

A Book of Cats: Poems in Prose — Michael Joseph

The Cat — Sidonie Colette

Cat-a-log — Purrcy B. Shelley

The Cat and Mrs. Cary — Doris Gates

The Cat and the Curmudgeon — Cleveland Amory

The Cat by the Fire — Leigh Hunt

The Cat that Wasn't There — Stella Whitelaw

Cathletics: Ways to Amuse and Exercise Your Cat — Jo and Paul Loeb

The Cat in the Hat — Dr. Seuss

Catlore — Desmond Morris

The Cat Psychologist — Mardie MacDonald

Cats — Philip Gilbert Hamerton

Cat Scan: All the Best from the Literature of Cats — Robert Byrne

The Cat That Walked by Himself — Rudyard Kipling

Catwatching — Desmond Morris

The Cat Who Came for Christmas — Cleveland Amory

The Cat Who Lived in a Drainpipe — Joan Aiken

The Cat Who Went to Heaven — Elizabeth Coatsworth

The Cat Who Went to Paris — Peter Gethers

Catwings — Ursula K. LeGuin

The Christmas Day Kitten — James Herriot

The Cricket in Times Square — George Selden

The Cyprian Cat — Dorothy L. Sayers

Dick Baker's Cat — Mark Twain

Do Cats Think? — Paul Corey

The Fur Person — May Sarton

The Game of Rat and Dragon — Cordwainer Smith

Great Cat Tales — Leslie O'Mara (Collection of stories by Colette, Twain, Zola, Lessing, Highsmith, Kipling)

Harry's Cat's Pet Puppy — George Selden

How to Get Your Cat to Do What You Want — Warren and Fay Eckstein

How to Live with a Neurotic Cat — Stephen Baker

The Incredible Journey — Sheila Burnford

Jennie's Lessons to Peter on How to Behave Like a Cat — Paul Gallico

The King of the Cats — Stephen Vincent Benet

The Last Little Cat — Meindert DeJong

The Literary Cat — Jean-Claude Suares

The Lives and Times of Archie and Mehitabel — Don Marquis

Magicats! — Jack Dann and Gardner Dozois, eds.

The Mind of the Cat — Gary Brodsky

Moses the Kitten — James Herriot

Nine Lives: The Folklore of Cats — Katharine M. Briggs

One-Eyed Cat — Paula Fox

Oscar, Cat-About-Town — James Herriot

Particularly Cats… and Rufus — Doris Lessing

The Philanthropist and the Happy Cat — Saki

Simon and Schuster's Guide to Cats — Gino Pugnetti

Socks — Beverly Cleary

The Solar Cat Book — James Augustyn

The Story of Serapina — Anne H. White

The Story of Webster — P. G. Wodehouse

Tailchaser's Song — Tad Williams

Thomasino — Paul Gallico

Tobermory — Saki

Tricks Your Cat Can Do — Gilbert W. Langley

Uncle Whiskers — Phillip Brown

When in Doubt — Wash! — Paul Gallico

The White Cat — W. W. Jacobs

COYOTE

Don Coyote: The Good Times and Bad of a Maligned American Original — Dayton O. Hyde

Skywater — Melinda Worth Popham

CRANE/STORK/GOOSE/DUCK/SWAN/PENGUIN

Cranes in My Corral — Dayton O. Hyde

Make Way for Ducklings — Robert McCloskey

Mr. Popper's Penguins — Richard and Florence Atwater

The Snow Goose — Paul Gallico

The Trumpet of the Swan — E. B. White

The Wheel on the School — Meindert DeJong

Wild Geese Calling — Robert Murphy

Deer

Bambi: A Life in the Woods — Felix Salten

The Yearling — Margaret Rawlings

Dog

An Adventure with a Dog — Stephen Crane

Along Came a Dog — Meindert DeJong

Big Red — James A. Kjelgaard

Black Star, Bright Dawn — Scott O'Dell

The Blind Dog — R. K. Narayan

Blue Milk — Booth Tarkington

Bruce — Albert Terhune

Call of the Wild — Jack London

A Dog's Night — Francoise Sagan

A Dog's Tale — Mark Twain

The Dog Who Wouldn't Be — Farley Mowat

Don — Zane Grey

The Emissary — Ray Bradbury

The Faithful — Lester Del Rey

The Farewell Kid — Barbara Wersba

For the Love of a Man — Jack London

Good-Bye My Lady — James Street

The Grudge — Albert Payson Terhune

Harry's Cat's Pet Puppy — George Selden

Harry the Dirty Dog — Gene Zion

The Heart of a Dog — Albert Terhune

Henry Huggins — Beverly Cleary

The Incredible Journey — Sheila Burnford

Irish Red: Son of Big Red — James A. Kjelgaard

Kavik the Wolf Dog — Walt Morey

Lad, a Dog — Albert Terhune

Lad of Sunnybank — Albert Terhune

Lassie Come Home — Eric Knight

Literary Dog: Contemporary Dog Stories — Jeanne Shinto

The Market Square Dog — James Herriot

Max, the Dog That Refused to Die — Kyra Petrovskaya Wayne

Memoirs of a Yellow Dog — O. Henry

Millie's Book — Barbara Bush

Mumu — Ivan Turgenev

The Old Meadow — George Selden

Old Yeller — Fred Gipso

Otto and the Magic Potatoes — William Pene du Bois

Outlaw Red — James A. Kjelgaard

Puppy Love — Barbara Steiner

Rabchik, A Jewish Dog — Sholom Aleichem

Rex — D. H. Lawrence

Silver Chief: Dog of the North — Kurt Wiese

Simon and Schuster's Guide to Dogs — Gino Pugnetti

Slipstream — Corey Ford

Sounder — William H. Armstrong

Stone Fox — John Reynolds Gardiner

That Spot — Jack London

The Voice of Bugle Ann — Mackinlay Cantor

Wanted, Mud Blossom — Betsy Byars

The Way of a Dog — Albert Terhune

Where the Red Fern Grows — Wilson Rawls

White Fang — Jack London

Woodsong — Gary Paulsen

Dolphin/Whale/Shark/Fish/Seal

The Book of Shark — Keith Bannister

The Cry of the Seals — Larry Weinberg

Island of the Blue Dolphins — Scott O'Dell

Jaws — Peter Benchley

Moby Dick — Herman Melville

The Old Man and the Sea — Ernest Hemingway

A Ring of Endless Light — Madeleine L'Engle

Shark Beneath the Reef — Jean Craighead George

Water Sky — Jean Craighead George

A Whale for the Killing — Farley Mowat

Whale Nation — Heathcote Williams

Whalesong — Robert Siegel

Whale Watch — Ada Graham and Frank Graham

The White Seal — Rudyard Kipling

DRAGON

Dealing with Dragons — Patricia Wrede

The Dragon Trilogy — Stephen R. Lawhead

The Dragons of Blueland — Ruth S. Gannett

Elmer and the Dragon — Ruth S. Gannett

My Father's Dragon — Ruth S. Gannett

The Reluctant Dragon — Kenneth Grahame

FOX

Fantastic Mr. Fox — Roald Dahl

The Foxes of Firstdark — Garry Kilworth

The Midnight Fox — Betsy Byars

HORSE

Alpha Centauri — Robert Siegel

Black Beauty — Anna Sewell

Black Gold — Marguerite Henry

Black Horses — Luigi Pirandello

The Black Stallion — Walter Farley

The Black Stallion and Satan — Walter Farley

The Blind Colt — Glen Rounds

Bonny's Big Day — James Herriot

Born to Trot — Marguerite Henry

Brighty of the Grand Canyon — Marguerite Henry

The Catch Colt — Mary O'Hara

Danza — Lynn Hall

An Expensive Operation — James Herriot

The Family Horse: How to Choose, Care for, Train and Work Your Horse — Jackie Spaulding

First Money — Will James

The 500-Mile Race from Deadwood to Omaha — Jack Schaefer

Flowers of Anger — Lynn Hall

A Genuine Mexican Plug — Mark Twain

The Gymkhana — Enid Bagnold

A Happy Ending — Anna Sewell

Herds of Thunder, Manes of Gold — Bruce Coville

The Horse in the Camel Suit — William Pene du Bois

The Horse Show — Clare Leighton

How Mr. Pickwick Undertook to Drive and Mr. Winkle to Ride — Charles Dickens

Hunted Horses — Glen Rounds

The Island Stallion — Walter Farley

Justin Morgan Had a Horse — Marguerite Henry

King of the Wind — Marguerite Henry

Lost in the Moors — Diana Pullein-Thompson

The Maltese Cat — Rudyard Kipling

Misty of Chincoteague — Marguerite Henry

Misty's Twilight — Marguerite Henry

Mr. Carteret and His Fellow Americans Abroad — David Grey

My First Wild Horse — Barbara Woodhouse

My Friend Flicka — Mary O'Hara

National Velvet — Enid Bagnold

The Red Pony — John Steinbeck

Ride a Wild Dream — Lynn Hall

Runaway Stallion — Walt Morey

Sea Star — Marguerite Henry

The Singing Hill — Meindert DeJong

Smokey, the Cowhorse — Will James

The Snowbird — Patricia Calvert

Son of the Black Stallion — Walter Farley

Stormy, Misty's Foal — Marguerite Henry

A Stranger to the Wild — Charles G. D. Roberts

Sugar for the Horse — H. E. Bates

Tale of the Gipsy Horse — Donn Byrne

Throw a Hungry Loop — Dona Schenker

Thunderhead — Mary O'Hara

White Stallion Of Lipizza — Marguerite Henry

LAMB/LION

Born Free: A Lioness of Two Worlds — Joy Adamson

The Lion's Paw — D. R. Sherman

Smudge, the Little Lost Lamb — James Herriot

MONKEY/CHIMPANZEE/GORILLA

Friend Monkey — Pamela Travers

Gorillas in the Mist — Jane Goodall

In the Shadow of Man — Jane Goodall

Summer of the Monkeys — Wilson Rawls

MOUSE

Ben and Me — Robert Lawson

The Cricket in Times Square — George Selden

Mossflower — Brian Jacques

The Mouse and the Motorcycle — Beverly Cleary

Stuart Little — E. B. White

RABBIT/HAMSTER

Bunnicula: A Rabbit Tale of Mystery — Deborah and James Howe

I, Houdini — Lynne Reid Banks

Shadrach — Meindert DeJong

The Tale of Peter Rabbit — Beatrix Potter

The Velveteen Rabbit — Margery Williams

Watership Down — Richard Adams

RACCOON/BADGER

Incident at Hawk's Hill — Allan Eckert

Rascal — Sterling North

Rascal: A Memoir of a Better Era — Sterling North

WOLF

Call of the Wild — Jack London

Dance of the Wolves — Roger Peters

Flight of the White Wolf — Mel Ellis

Julie of the Wolves — Jean Craighead George

The Jungle Books — Rudyard Kipling

Secret Go the Wolves — R. D. Lawrence

The Whispering Mountain — Joan Aiken

The Wolves of Willoughby Chase — Joan Aiken

GENERAL

All Things Wise and Wonderful; All Creatures Great and Small; All Things Bright and Beautiful; The Lord God Made Them All; Every Living Thing — James Herriot

Dr. Wildlife: The Crusade of a Northwoods Veterinarian — Rory C. Foster

Living Wonders: Mysteries and Curiosities of the Animal World — John Michell And Robert J. M. Rickard

Sherlock Bones — John Keane

Simon and Schuster Guide to Mammals — Luigi Boitani and Stefania Bartoli

The Wolf Tracker and Other Animal Tales — Zane Grey

A Zoo for All Seasons — Smithsonian Exposition Books

The Zoo That Never Was: The Reluctant Zoo Keeper — R. D. Lawrence

128. ANIMALS: POEMS

See also List 127, Animals: Books and Stories

DOG

"Bishop Doane on His Dog" — George Washington Doane

"Bum" — W. Dayton Wedgefarth

"The Curate Thinks You Have No Soul" — St. John Lucas

"Epitaph to a Dog" — Lord Byron

"A Malemute Dog" — Pat O'Cotter

"My Dog" — John Kendrick Bangs

"The Owner of the Dog" — Rudyard Kipling

"Rags" — Edmond Vance Cooke

"Supplication of the Black Aberdeen" — Rudyard Kipling

"To a Dog" — Josephine Preston Peabody

"To My Setter, Scout" — Frank H. Seldon

CAT

"Cruel Clever Cat" — Jeffrey Taylor

"I Am the Cat" — Leila Usher

"In Memoriam — Leo: A Yellow Cat" — Margaret Sherwood

"Leo to His Mistress (Answer)" — Henry Dwight Sedgwick

"The Little Cat Angel" — Leontine Stanfield

"Macavity: The Mystery Cat" — T. S. Eliot

HORSE

"The Arab's Farewell to His Horse" — Caroline Norton

"The Broncho That Would Not Be Broken" — Vachel Lindsay

MISCELLANEOUS

"The Blinded Bird" — Thomas Hardy

"The Bull" — Ralph Hodgson

"The Darkling Thrush" — Thomas Hardy

"I Heard a Linnet Courting" — Robert Bridges

"The Purple Cow" — Gelett Burgess

"The Redbreast" — Charlotte Richardson

"The Sea-Gull" — Ogden Nash

"Sheep" — W. H. Davies

"The Thrush" — Timothy Corsellis

"The Turtle" — Ogden Nash

129. AUTHORS BY GROUP

Literature can be approached by studying authors in specific categories. The writers listed below all had something in common that caused critics or scholars to group them together under a convenient label: philosophical outlook, writing style, or simply friendship. They are listed in no particular order. (Nationality of group: ✖ = American; ★ = British)

✖ THE KNICKERBOCKERS

Washington Irving

James Fenimore Cooper

William Cullen Bryant

George Pope Morris

Thomas Dun English

Phoebe Cary

Stephen Collins Foster
Donald Grant Mitchell
John Howard Payne
Samuel Woodworth
James K. Paulding
Nathaniel Parker Willis
Fitz-Greene Halleck
Joseph Rodman Drake
John James Audubon
George William Curtis

*THE CONCORD GROUP
Ralph Waldo Emerson
Nathaniel Hawthorne
Henry David Thoreau
Bronson Alcott
Margaret Fuller
William Ellery Channing

*THE FUGITIVES (AGRARIANS)
John Crowe Ransom
Allen Tate
Robert Penn Warren

*THE NEW YORK POETS
John Ashbery
Kenneth Koch
Frank O'Hara

*THE LOST GENERATION
Ezra Pound
Gertrude Stein
T. S. Eliot
e. e. Cummings
Ernest Hemingway
John Dos Passos
William Faulkner
F. Scott Fitzgerald

*THE BEAT WRITERS
Allen Ginsburg
Gregory Corso
Lawrence Ferlinghetti
William Burroughs
Jack Kerouac
Gary Snyder
Michael McClure
Philip Whalen
John Clellon Holmes

*THE NEW YORK INTELLECTUALS
Philip Rahv
Alfred Kazin
Irving Howe

*THE CAMBRIDGE SCHOLARS
Henry Wadsworth Longfellow
Oliver Wendell Holmes
James Russell Lowell

*THE CONNECTICUT WITS (HARTFORD WITS; PLEIADES OF CONNECTICUT)
John Trumbull
Joel Barlow
Timothy Dwight
David Humphreys

*ALGONQUIAN ROUND TABLE
Franklin P. Adams
Robert Benchley
Heywood Broun
Frank Case
Edna Ferber
George S. Kaufman
Harpo Marx
Neysa McMein

Dorothy Parker

Harold Ross

Robert E. Sherwood

Alexander Woollcott

✱THE FIRESIDE POETS

Henry Wadsworth Longfellow

John Greenleaf Whittier

Oliver Wendell Holmes

✱THE BLACK MOUNTAIN POETS

Charles Olson

John Ashbery

Robert Bly

James Merrill

James Wright

Robert Creeley

✱LOCAL COLOR AUTHORS (REGIONALISTS)

Ambrose Bierce

William Wells Brown

George Washington Cable

Willa Cather

Charles Chestnutt

Kate Chopin

Mary E. Wilkins Freeman

Hamlin Garland

Ellen Glasgow

Henry W. Grady

Joel Chandler Harris

Bret Harte

John Hay

Helen Hunt Jackson

Sarah Orne Jewett

Joaquin Miller

Mark Twain

Edith Wharton

★THE GEORGIAN POETS

Rupert Brooke

Walter de la Mare

Ralph Hodgson

W. H. Davies

G. K. Chesterton

D. H. Lawrence

★THE CAVALIER POETS

Richard Lovelace

Sir John Suckling

Thomas Carew

Robert Herrick

★THE VICTORIAN POETS

Alfred Lord Tennyson

Matthew Arnold

Robert Browning

Elizabeth Barrett Browning

★THE ROMANTIC POETS

See list 166, The Romantic Period.

★THE PURITANS

John Donne

John Milton

John Bunyan

★THE NEO-CLASSICISTS

John Dryden

Samuel Pepys

Daniel DeFoe

Joseph Addison

Richard Steele

Jonathan Swift

John Gay

Alexander Pope

★THE GRAVEYARD POETS

Thomas Gray

Robert Blair

Edward Young

Thomas Parnell

★THE PRE-RAPHAELITES

Dante Gabriel Rossetti

Christina Rossetti

William Morris

Algernon Swinburne

John Masefield

★THE METAPHYSICAL POETS

John Donne

George Herbert

Richard Crashaw

Henry Vaughan

Thomas Traherne

Andrew Marvell

Henry King

Abraham Cowley

★THE BLOOMSBURY GROUP

Lytton Strachey

E. M. Forster

Leonard Woolf

Virginia Woolf

John Maynard Keynes

★THE UNIVERSITY WITS

Robert Greene

Thomas Lodge

Thomas Nashe

George Peele

130. BLACK (AFRICAN-AMERICAN) WRITERS OF NOTE

See also List 131, Black (African-American) Literature

Maya Angelou — novelist, poet

James Baldwin — novelist; playwright; essayist; nonfiction writer

Imamu Amiri Baraka (LeRoi Jones) — poet; playwright

Gwendolyn Brooks — novelist; poet; first African-American to win the Pulitzer Prize

Sterling A. Brown — poet

William Wells Brown — novelist; playwright; first African-American to publish a novel

Charles Waddell Chesnutt — short story writer; novelist

Eldridge Cleaver — poet; autobiographer

Countee Cullen — poet

Frederick Douglass — author; orator

William E. B. DuBois — author

Paul Laurence Dunbar — novelist; poet

Ralph Ellison — novelist; essayist

Mari Evans — poet

Charles Fuller — playwright

Ernest J. Gaines — novelist, short story writer

Nikki Giovanni — poet

Charles Gordone — playwright

Nicholas Guillen — poet

Alex Haley — author; winner of Pulitzer Prize

Jupiter Hammond — poet; first African-American to have poetry published

Lorraine Hansberry — playwright; winner of Drama Critics' Circle Award; poet

Chester Himes — novelist

Langston Hughes — poet; writer of song lyrics; short story writer

Zora Neale Hurston — novelist; folklorist

James Weldon Johnson — poet; novelist

Don L. Lee — poet

Alain Locke — editor of essays

Claude McKay — Jamaican poet

Henry T. Moore — author

Toni Morrison — novelist; winner of Pulitzer Prize and Nobel Prize

Willard Motley — novelist

Benjamin Quarles — author; historian

Sonia Sanchez — poet

Ntozake Shange — nonfiction writer

Mildred Taylor — novelist for juveniles

Jean Toomer — author

Alice Walker — novelist; essayist

Phillis Wheatley — poet; first African-American woman to have poetry published

August Wilson — playwrght; winner of two Pulitzer Prizes

Richard Wright — novelist

Frank Yerby — novelist

131. Black (African-American) Literature

The following works of fiction and nonfiction, by or about Africans or African-Americans, are listed in alphabetical order. Words in parentheses describe the main character, author, or book. See also List 130, Black (African-American) Writers of Note.

All American Women — Johnnetta B. Cole, ed. (African-American culture)

Arilla Sun Down — Virginia Hamilton (girl who is part Indian and part black girl)

The Autobiography of Malcolm X — Alex Haley (African-American leader)

The Autobiography of Miss Jane Pittman — Ernest J. Gaines (novel about black life in the South)

Baby of the Family — Tina McElroy Ansa (African-American girl)

Barbara Jordan: Congresswoman — Linda Carlson Johnson (biography)

The Best of Simple — Langston Hughes (humorous sketches)

Black Americans: A History in Their Own Words — Milton Meltzer, ed. (anthology)

Black Boy — Richard Wright (memoir of segregated South)

Black Dance in America — James Haskins

Black in Selma: The Uncommon Life of J. L. Chestnut, Jr. — J. L. Chestnut

Black Like Me — John Howard Griffin (white man poses as black to experience racism)

Black Music In America: A History Through Its People — James Haskins

Black Odyssey — Nathan Irvin Huggins (history of slavery)

Black Theater in America — James Haskins

Blues People — Imamu Amiri Baraka (African-American culture)

Booker T. Washington: The Making of a Black Leader, 1856–1901 — Louis R. Harlan

Booker T. Washington: The Wizard of Tuskegee, 1901–1915 — Louis R. Harlan

Breaking the Chains: African-American Slave Resistance — William Loren Katz

Bright April — Marguerite de Angeli (African-American girl)

Chain of Fire — Beverley Naidoo (South African experience)

The Changelings — Jo Sinclair (African-American girls)

Clover — Dori Sanders (race relations)

The Complete Poems of Paul Laurence Dunbar — Paul Laurence Dunbar

Conjure Woman and Other Tales — Charles W. Chesnutt (slavery)

Cry, the Beloved Country — Alan Paton (South African experience)

Durango Street — Frank Bonham (African-American teenager)

Duke Ellington — James Lincoln Collier (musician)

Edith Jackson — Rosa Guy (African-American family)

The Fire Next Time — James Baldwin (racism and African-American culture)

*For Colored Girls Who Have Considered Suicide When the Rainbow Is Enuf;
   A Choreopoem* — Ntozake Shange (African-American culture)

Freedom Road — Howard Fast (slavery)

Freedom Train — Dorothy Sterling (story of Harriet Tubman, escaped slave)

The Friends — Rosa Guy (African-American girl)

The Friendship — Mildred D. Taylor (interracial friendship)

From Slavery to Freedom — John Hope Franklin (history of African Americans)

A Gathering of Days — Joan W. Blos (runaway slave)

A Gathering of Old Men — Ernest J. Gaines (racial conflict in the South)

George Washington Carver — Linda O. McMurry (biography of scientist)

Go Tell it on the Mountain — James Baldwin (coming-of-age novel)

Great Slave Narratives — Arna Bontemps (autobiographies of slaves)

Guests in the Promised Land — Kristin Hunter (stories)

A Hero Ain't Nothin' But a Sandwich — Alice Childress (drug use)

The Horse Trader — Wade Everett (cowboy story)

If Beale Street Could Talk — James Baldwin (novel of black experience)

I Know Why the Caged Bird Sings — Maya Angelou (autobiography)

Invented Lives: Narratives of Black Women 1860–1960 — Mary Helen Washington

The Invisible Man — Ralph Ellison (allegory of the black experience)

Judith Jamison: Aspects of a Dancer — Olga Maynard

Jump Ship to Freedom — James L. and Christopher Collier (son of slave)

Kareem — Kareem Abdul-Jabbar and Mignon McCarthy (memoirs of an athlete)

Leroy and the Old Man — W. E. Butterworth (African-American youth)

Letters of Phillis Wheatley, the Negro Slave — Poet of Boston, 1864 — Phillis Wheatley

Let the Circle Be Unbroken — Mildred D. Taylor (family novel)

The Life of Langston Hughes: I Dream a World, 1941–1967 — Arnold Rampersad

The Life of Langston Hughes: I, Too, sing America, 1902–1941 — Arnold Rampersad

Listen for the Fig Tree — Sharon Bell Mathis (inspiration for young readers)

Little Vic — Doris Gates (stable boy)

Louis Armstrong: An American Genius — James Lincoln Collier (musician)

Ludell — Brenda Wilkinson (African-American girl)

Ludell and Willie — Brenda Wilkinson (historical novel for young readers)

Ludell's New York Time — Brenda Wilkinson (historical novel for young readers)

Luke Was There — Eleanor Clymer (Social worker)

M. C. Higgins, the Great — Virginia Hamilton (African-American boy)

Manchild in the Promised Land — Claude Brown (memoir)

Mary McLeod Bethune: Voice of Black Hope — Milton Meltzer (civil rights leader)

Memoirs and Poems of Phillis Wheatley, 1834 — Phillis Wheatley

The Me Nobody Knows — Steven M. Joseph, ed. (children's writings)

Meridian — Alice Walker (African-American culture)

The Mis-Education Of the Negro — Carter G. Woodson

Mojo and the Russians — Walter Dean Myers (street gangs)

The Move Makes the Man — Bruce Brooks (basketball player)

Move Your Shadow: South Africa Black and White — Joseph Lelyveld

Narrative of the Life of Frederick Douglass — Frederick Douglass

Native Son — Richard Wright (novel)

Negro Servant to Mr. John Wheatley of Boston, in New England, 1773 — Phillis Wheatley

The New Negro — Alain Locke (essays)

One More River to Cross — Will Henry (cowboy story)

One-Way Ticket — Langston Hughes (poems)

The Outsider — Richard Wright (novel)

The People Could Fly: American Black Folktales — Virginia Hamilton, ed.

Pickel and Price — Pieter van Raven (race relations)

Poems on Various Subjects, Religious and Moral — Phillis Wheatley

Prince Among Slaves — Terry Alford

The Promised Land: The Great Black Migration and How It Changed America — Nicholas Lemann

Rainbow Jordan — Alice Childress (African-American women)

Raisin in the Sun — Lorraine Hansberry (first Broadway play by a black woman)

The Road to Memphis — Mildred D. Taylor (race relations)

Roll of Thunder, Hear My Cry — Mildred D. Taylor (family story)

Roots — Alex Haley (family heritage)

Servant of Slaves — Grace Irwin (slave trade)

Shakespeare in Harlem — Langston Hughes (poems)

The Sign in Sidney Brustein's Window — Lorraine Hansberry (play)

Simple Speaks His Mind — Langston Hughes (humorous sketches)

The Slave Dancer — Paula Fox (slave trade)

Sorrow's Kitchen: The Life and Folklore of Zora Neale Hurston — Mary E. Lyons

Soul on Ice — Eldridge Cleaver

The Souls of Black Folk — W. E. B. Dubois (essays on the black experience)

Sounder — William H. Armstrong (man and dog)

South African Dispatches: Letters to My Countrymen — Donald Wood

Stop the Violence: Overcoming Self-Destruction — Nelson George, ed.

The Tales of Uncle Remus — Julius Lester (retold by an African-American)

Thank You, Jackie Robinson — Barbara Cohen (baseball player)

Their Eyes Were Watching God — Zora Neale Hurston (novel of African-American culture)

A Time to Ride — Ray Gaulden (cowboy story)

To Be a Slave — Julius Lester (slave life)

To Be Young, Gifted, and Black — Lorraine Hansberry (self-portrait)

To Kill a Mockingbird — Lee Harper (race relations)

Top Hand — Wade Everett (cowboy story)

Tripwire — Brian Garfield (cowboy story)

Uncle Tom's Cabin — Harriet Beecher Stowe (novel condemning slavery)

Voices in the Mirror: An Autobiography — Gordon Parks

Voices of South Africa: Growing Up in a Troubled Land — Carolyn Meyer

Waiting for the Rain: A Novel of South Africa — Sheila Gordon

War Comes to Willie Freeman — James L. and Christopher Collier (son of slave)

The Weary Blues — Langston Hughes (poems)

When and Where I Enter: The Impact of Black Women on Race and Sex in America — Paula J. Giddings

White Man, Listen! — Richard Wright

Why We Can't Wait — Martin Luther King, Jr.

Wole Soyinka: Collection Plays 1 — Wole Soyinka (plays by Nobel Prize-winning Nigerian playwright)

The Words of Martin Luther King, Jr. — Coretta Scott King, compiler

132. CHRISTIAN NONFICTION

See also List 139, Religion: Bible; and List 143, Religious Documents and Holy Literature.

BIOGRAPHY/AUTOBIOGRAPHY

Apologia pro Vita Sua—John Henry Cardinal Newman

Apostle: A Life of Paul — John Pollock

Beyond Death's Door — Maurice Rawlings

Born Again — Charles Colson

Boy Who Sailed 'Round the World Alone — Robin Graham

Breaking Points — Jack and Jo Ann Hinckley

Confessions of St. Augustine — Saint Augustine

From Ashes to Glory — William McCartney

James: Apostle of Practical Christianity — Robert P. Lightner

John: Apostle of Love — Earl P. McQuay

John Wesley, His Life and Theology — Robert Tuttle

Michelle — Carolyn Phillips

Moody: The Biography; To All the Nations; The Billy Graham Story — John Pollock

Moses; Paul; Peter; Abraham; David — F. B. Meyer

Paul: Apostle of Steel and Velvet; Peter: Apostle of Contrasts — James Dyet

Tough Times Never Last... — Robert Schuller

Trevor's Place — Frank Ferrell

Walking with the Giants — Warren Wiersbe

CHILDREN'S REFERENCES ON THE BIBLE

Bible Almanac; A Comprehensive Handbook of the People of the Bible and How They Lived
 — James I. Packer, et al.

Bible Atlas — Orrin Root

Bible Dictionary for Young Readers — William N. McElrath

Bible Panorama — Terry Hall

Christian Theology in Plain Language — Bruce Shelley

The Dictionary of Biblical Literacy — Oliver Nelson

Fun with Bible Geography — Marie Chapman

*Handbook of Scriptures to Grow On: Selected Bible Verses to Equip Children
 and Teens for Everyday Living* — Lois Schmitt and Joyce Price

International Children's Bible Handbook — Larry Richards

The Picture Bible — C. Elvan Omstead, ed.

133. HUMOR

Humor is never out of place in literature, no matter how profound the issues it deals with—Shakespeare, for one, rarely lost sight of this. The following list contains books that were written primarily to amuse and entertain. See also List 86, Grue; List 88, Limerick; List 103, Humorous Poetry (Short); and List 104, Humorous Poems (Longer).

Ace Hits the Big Time — Barbara Beasley Murphy and Judie Wolkoff

The Adventures of Huckleberry Finn — Mark Twain

The Adventures of Tom Sawyer — Mark Twain

All Things Bright and Beautiful — James Herriot

All Things Wise and Wonderful — James Herriot

Belles on Their Toes — Frank B. Gilbreth, Jr. and E. G. Carey

The Best Christmas Pageant Ever — Barbara Robinson

The Big Garage on Clear Shot — Tom Bodett

The Boat Who Wouldn't Float — Farley Mowat

Can You Sue Your Parents for Malpractice? — Paula Danziger

The Cat Ate My Gymsuit — Paula Danziger

Cheaper by the Dozen — Frank B. Gilbreth, Jr., and E. G. Carey

Chucklebait — Margaret C. Scroggin, Collector

A Connecticut Yankee in King Arthur's Court — Mark Twain

Discontinued — Julian E. Thompson

The Dog Who Wouldn't Be — Farley Mowat

Enter Three Witches — Kate Gillmore

Fables for Our Time — James Thurber

A Five-Color Buick and a Blue-Eyed Cat — Phyllis Anderson Wood

Fox Trot — Bill Amend

Freaky Friday — Mary Rodgers

From the Mixed-up Files of Mrs. Basil E. Frankweiler — E. L. Konigsburg

The Grass Is Always Greener over the Septic Tank — Erma Bombeck

Growing Up Catholic: An Infinitely Funny Guide for the Faithful, the Fallen, and Everyone In-Between — Mary Jane Francis, Cavolina Meara, Maureen Anne Teresa Elly, et al.

Half Nelson, Full Nelson — Bruce Stone

The Heroic Life of Al Capsella — J. Clarke

Homer Price — Robert McCloskey

How to Eat Fried Worms — Thomas Rockwell

It's an Aardvark-Eat-Turtle World — Paula Danziger

It Was a Dark and Stormy Night: The Best (?) from the Bulwer-Lytton Contest — Scot Rice (compiler)

Laid Back in Washington — Art Buchwald

The Lord God Made Them All — James Herriot

Losing Joe's Place — Gordon Korman

Maniac Magee — Jerry Spinelli

Murder in a Pig's Eye — Lynn Hall

My Life and Hard Times — James Thurber

The Not-Just-Anybody Family — Betsy Byars

The Pistachio Prescription — Paula Danziger

Rascal: A Memoir of a Better Era — Sterling North

Skinny Malinky Leads the War for Kidness — Stanley Kiesel

The Snarkout Boys and the Avocado of Death — Daniel Pinkwater

The Snarkout Boys and the Baconburg Horror — Daniel Pinkwater

S.O.R. Losers — Avi

Soup — Robert N. Peck

The Swiss Family Perelman — S. J. Perelman

Teenage Romance: Or How to Die of Embarrassment — Delia Ephron

There's a Bat in Bunk Five — Paula Danziger

Three Men in a Boat — Jerome K. Jerome

The Thurber Carnival — James Thurber

Time to Laugh — Phyllis Fenner

Twisted Tales from Shakespeare — Richard Armour

The War Between the Pitiful Teachers and the Splendid Kids — Stanley Kiesel

Who Put that Hair in My Toothbrush? — Jerry Spinelli

Without Feathers — Woody Allen

134. NATIVE AMERICAN AUTHORS/CHARACTERS

See also List 136, Native American Literature; and List 137, Native American-American Relations: Westerns.

Battle of the Little Big Horn — Marl Sandoz (Army versus Sioux)

Black Star, Bright Dawn — Scott O'Dell (Inuit girl)

The Blessing Way — Tony Hillerman (Navaho detective)

Brother Eagle, Sister Sky — Susan Jeffers (Chief Seattle)

Call It Courage — Sperry Armstrong (Indian boy)

The Ceremony of Innocence — Jamake Highwater (Indian boy)

Cheyenne Autumn — Marl Sandoz (Cheyenne)

A Circle Unbroken — Sollace Hotze (Sioux-U.S. relations)

Columbus and the World Around Him — Milton Meltzer

Dancehall of the Dead — Tony Hillerman (Navaho detective)

Dawn Rider — Jan Hudson (Blackfoot girl)

Eyes of Darkness — Jamake Highwater (Indian life)

Flaming Arrows — William O. Steele (not from Native American point of view)

Fox Running — R. R. Knudson (Indian girl)

Geronimo: His Own Story — S. M. Barrett, editor (Apache warrior)

The Girl from Limbo — Robert Bedding (mixed Indian/white girl)

The Green Stone — Susanne Blanc (Indian detective)

Halfbreed — Maria Campbell (part-Indian girl)

Hatter Fox — Marilyn Harris (Navajo girl)

I Wear the Morning Star — Jamake Highwater (Indian boy)

I Will Fight No More Forever — Merrill D. Beal (Chief Joseph)

Indian Chiefs — Russell Freedman

Island of the Blue Dolphins — Scott O'Dell (Indian girl)

Julie of the Wolves — Jean Craighead George (Inuit girl)

The Last Algonquin — Theodore L. Kazimiroff

Leatherstocking Tales — James Fenimore Cooper (Native American and pioneer life in New York)

Legend Days — Jamake Highwater (Indian boy)

The Light in the Forest — Conrad Richter (Indian/American ties)

The Massacre at Fall Creek — Jessamyn West

The Matchlock Gun — Walter D. Edmonds (not Native American point of view)

Mother Earth Father Sky — Sue Harrison (Aleut woman)

North Against the Sioux — Kenneth Ulyatt (Chief Red Cloud)

Paddle-to-the-Sea — Honing C. Holling (Indian boy)

Ramona — Helen Hunt Jackson (sympathetic toward Native Americans)

Red Power — Alvin M. Josephy, Jr. (fight for freedom)

Sacajawea — Donna Lee Waldo (Shoshoni girl)

The Shadow Brothers — A. E. Cannon (Navajo boy)

Sign of the Beaver — Elizabeth George Speare (chief and son)

Sing Down the Moon — Scott O'Dell (Navaho girl)

Sing for a Gentle Rain — James J. Alison (Indian girl)

The Spider, the Cave and the Pottery Bowl — Eleanor Clymer (Native Americans)

A Thief of Time — Tony Hillerman (Navajo detective)

To Kill an Eagle — Edward Kadlecek (Crazy Horse)

Trouble River — Betsy Byars (not Native American point of view)

War Clouds in the West — Albert Marrin (Native American)

Water Sky — Jean Craighead George (Inuit)

When the Legends Die — Hal Borland (Indian boy)

135. NATIVE AMERICAN LITERATURE

The literature of Native Americans has its origins in rituals, ceremonies, story-telling, oratory, and autobiographical and historical accounts of the various tribes. Not until the twentieth century did this literature come into its own with a variety of genres, such as poetry, drama, novels, and short stories.

Listed below are selected Native American writers, their tribal ancestry, and writings, gleaned from *Literatures of the American Indian* by A. Lavonne Brown Ruoff and other sources.

See also List 135, Native American Authors/Characters; and List 137, Native American-American Relations: Westerns.

NINETEENTH CENTURY

William Apes (Pequot). *A Son of the Forest* (autobiography)

David Cusick. *Sketches of Ancient History of the Six Nations*

George Copway (Ojibwa). *Traditional History and Characteristic Sketches of the Ojibway Nation; Running Sketches of Men and Places, in England, France, Germany, Belgium, and Scotland; Life, History, and Travels of Kah-Ge-Ga-Gah-Bowh* (autobiography)

Peter Jones (Kahkewaquonaby). *History of the Ojibway*

Charles Warren (Ojibwa). *History of the Ojibways, Based Upon Traditions and Oral Statements*

Peter Dooyentate Clarke (Wyandot). *Origin and Traditional History of the Wyandotts and Other Indian Tribes in North America*

Elias Johnson (Tuscarora). *Legends, Traditions and Laws of the Iroquois, or Six Nations, and History of Tuscarora Indians*

Andrew J. Blackbird (Ottawa). *History of the Ottawa and Chippewa Indians of Michigan; A Grammar of their Language, and Personal and Family History of the Author George Henry* (Ojibwa). *An Account of the Chippewa Indians, who have been travelling among the Whites, in the United States, England, Ireland, Scotland, France, and Belgium*

Rollin Ridge (Cherokee). *Life and Adventures of Joaquin Murieta* (novel)*; Poems; A Trumpet of Our Own* (essays)

Sarah Winnemucca Hopkins (Piute). *Life Among the Piutes* (autobiography)

Simon Pokagon (Potawatomi). *Queen of the Woods* (novel attributed to Pokagon)

EARLY TWENTIETH CENTURY

Emily Pauline Johnson (part Mohawk). *White Wampum* (poetry); *Canadian Born* (poetry); *Flint and Feather* (poetry); *The Moccasin Maker* (short stories)

Alexander Posey (Creek). *Indian Journal* (editor); *The Poems of Alexander Posey*

Charles Eastman. *Soul of the Indian* (nonfiction); *The Indian Today* (history); *Indian Heroes and Great Chieftains* (nonfiction); *Indian Boyhood* (autobiography to age fifteen); *From the Deep Woods to Civilization* (autobiography)

Charles and Elaine Eastman. *Red Hunters and the Animal People* (animal stories); *Old Indian Days* (stories); *Wigwam Evenings: Sioux Folktales Retold*

Luther Standing Bear (Sioux). *My People, the Sioux* (coauthored, nonfiction); *Land of the Spotted Eagle* (coauthored, nonfiction); *My Indian Boyhood* (for children)

Gertrude Bonnin (Sioux). *American Indian Stories* (autobiographical essays)

Francis LaFlesche (Omaha). *The Middle Five* (autobiography)

John G. Neihardt (Sioux). *Black Elk Speaks* (autobiography)

Will Rogers (Cherokee descent). *Roger-isms: The Cowboy Philosopher on the Peace Conference; Roger-isms: The Cowboy Philosopher on Prohibition; Illiterate Digest; Letters of a Self-Made Diplomat to His President; There's Not a Bathing Suit in Russia; Ether and Me*

John Milton Oskison (part Cherokee). *Wild Harvest* (novel); *Black Jack Davy* (novel); *Brothers Three* (novel); *Tecumseh and His Times* (biography)

John Joseph Mathews (Osage). *Wah' Kontah* (nonfiction); *Sundown* (novel); *Life and Death of an Oilman: The Career of E. W. Harland* (biography); *The Osages: Children of the Middle Waters*

D'Arcy McNickle (Cree ancestry). *The Surrounded* (novel); *The Runner in the Sun* (novel for middle schoolers); *Wind from an Enemy Sky* (novel); *They Came Here First; The Indian Tribes of the United States; Indians and Other Americans; Native American Tribalism; Indian Man* (biography)

Lynn Riggs (Cherokee). *The Iron Dish* (poetry); *Big Lake* (drama); *Borned in Texas* (folk drama produced as *Roadside*); *Green Grow the Lilacs* (folk drama produced as *Oklahoma!*); *Cherokee Night* (drama)

Ella C. Deloria (part Sioux). *Dakota Texts; Dakota Grammar; Speaking of Indians; Waterlily* (novel)

MIDDLE AND LATE TWENTIETH CENTURY

John Fire (Sioux). *Lame Deer, Seeker of Visions* (autobiography)

Christine Quintasket (part Colville) published posthumously. *Co-Gen-We-A, the Half Blood* (novel, coauthored); *Mourning Dove: A Salish Autobiography* (co-authored)

N. Scott Momaday (Kiowa). *House Made of Dawn* (novel); *The Way to Rainy Mountain* (autobiography); *Ancient Child* (novel); *Names* (autobiography); *The Gourd Dancer* (poetry)

Leslie Marmon Silko (part Laguna ancestry). *Ceremony* (novel); *Storyteller* (short stories and poetry)

James Welch (Blackfoot/Gros Ventre). *Winter in the Blood* (novel); *The Death of Jim Loney* (novel); *Fools Crow* (novel)

Gerald Vizenor (Ojibwa). *Twin Citian* (contributing editor); *Interior Landscapes* (autobiography); *Wordarrows* (fiction/nonfiction); *Earthdivers* (fiction/nonfiction); *The People Named the Chippewa* (fiction/nonfiction); *Darkness in Saint Louis Bearheart* (novel); *Griever: An American Money King in China* (novel); *The Trickster of Liberty: Tribal Heirs to a Wild Baronage at Petronia* (novel)

Louise Erdrich (Ojibwa). *Love Medicine* (novel); *The Beet Queen* (novel); *Tracks* (novel); *Jacklight* (poetry)

Michael Dorris (Modoc). *A Yellow Raft on Blue Water* (novel); *The Broken Cord: A Family's Ongoing Struggle with Fetal Alcohol Syndrome* (nonfiction)

Louise Erdrich (Ojibwa) and **Michael Dorris**. *The Crown of Columbus*

Martin Cruz Smith (Senecu del Sur/Yaqui). *Nightwing* (mystery); *Stallion Gate* (mystery); *Gorky Park* (mystery); *Polar Star* (mystery)

Thomas King (Cherokee). *Medicine River* (novel)

Anna Walters (Otoe/Pawnee). *Ghost Singer* (novel)

Paula Gunn Allen (part Laguna/Sioux). *The Woman Who Owned the Shadows* (novel); *Skins and Bones: Poems 1979–81*

Janet Campbell Hale (Coeur d'AIene/Kootenai). *The Jailing of Cecelia Capture* (novel); *Owl's Song* (novel)

Forest Carter (Cherokee). *The Education of Little Tree* (autobiographical fiction for teenagers); *Rebel Outlaw, Josey Wales* (western); *The Vengeance Trail of Josey Wales* (western); *Watch for Me on the Mountain* (western)

Markoooosie (Inuit). *Harpoon of the Hunter* (novel for teenagers)

Simon Ortiz (Acoma). *Fight Back* (poetry); *Going for the Rain* (poetry); *The Good Journey* (poetry)

Peter Blue Cloud. *Elderberry Flute Song* (poetry and tales)

Joy Harjo. *What Moon Drove Me to This* (poetry); *In Mad Love and War* (poetry)

Linda Hogan (Chickasaw). *Mean Spirit* (historical novel)

Hanay Geiogamah (Kiowa). *New Native American Drama: Three Plays*

Vine Deloria, Jr. (Sioux). *Custer Died for Your Sins* (nonfiction); *We Talk, You Listen* (nonfiction)

A. Grove Day, editor. *The Sky Clears: Poetry of the American Indian* (songs and chants)

136. Native American—American Relations: Westerns

See also List 136, Native American Literature; and List 135, Native American Authors/Characters.

Apache — Will L. Comfort

Between the Worlds — John Byrne Cooke

Big with Vengeance — Cecil Snyder

Blood Brother — Elliott Arnold

Bones of the Buffalo — Lewis B. Patten

The Bronc People — William Eastlake

Forked Tongue — Hunter Ingram

From Where the Sun Now Stands — Will Henry

Go in Beauty — William Eastlake

Gone the Dreams and Dancing — Douglas C. Jones

The Hanging Tree and Other Stories — Dorothy M. Johnson

Hondo — Louis L'Amour

House Made of Dawn — N. Scott Momaday

Indian Country — Dorothy M. Johnson

Indian Hater — Glenn R. Vernam

Jeremiah Thunder — Harold Heifetz

The Last Frontier — Howard Fast

Laughing Boy — Oliver La Farge

Little Big Man — Thomas Berger

Lords of the Plain — Max Crawford

The Magnificent Future — Giles A. Lutz

Nino — Clay Fisher

Nobody Loves a Drunken Indian — Clair Huffaker

The Pipe Carriers — John Byrne Cooke

Portrait of an Artist with Twenty-Six Horses — William Eastlake

The Searchers — Alan LeMay

Season of Yellow Leaf — Douglas C. Jones

Shoot an Arrow to Stop the Wind — Colin Stuart

Two Rode Together — Will Cook

The Unforgiven — Alan LeMay

The Vanishing American — Zane Gray

Whistle in the Wind — John H. Culp

White Apache — Benjamin Capps
The White Man's Road — Benjamin Capps
The Wolf Is My Brother — Chad Oliver
A Woman of the People — Benjamin Capps
Yellow Raft on Blue Water — Michael Dorris

137. POE: COMPLETE STORIES AND POEMS

Edgar Allan Poe, heralded as one of the most gifted American writers of all time, is often studied only for his outstanding tales of horror and a handful of notable poems. To limit oneself to his more familiar works, however, is to miss a great deal of enjoyment. Below are categorized all his known stories and poems. In addition, Poe gave lectures and wrote profound essays, editorials, magazine and newspaper articles, and at least one textbook. A few of these other works are included in a separate section at the end of the list. To use Poe, his works, and life as a theme of study will provide engrossing material.

MYSTERY AND HORROR STORIES

The Assignation
Berenice
The Black Cat
The Cask of Amontillado
The Conversation of Eiros and Charmion
A Descent into the Maelstrom
Facts in the Case of M. Valdemar
The Fall of the House of Usher
The Gold-Bug
Hop-Frog
The Imp of the Perverse
Ligeia
The Man of the Crowd
The Masque of the Red Death
Metzengerstein
Morella
MS. Found in a Bottle
The Murders in the Rue Morgue
The Mystery of Marie Roget
The Oblong Box
The Pit and the Pendulum
The Premature Burial
The Purloined Letter
A Tale of the Ragged Mountains
The Tell-tale Heart
Thou Art the Man
William Wilson

STORIES OF FANTASY

The Balloon-Hoax
The Colloquy of Monos and Una
The Domain of Arnheim
Eleonora
The Island of the Fay
King Pest
Landor's Cottage
Mesmeric Revelation
The Oval Portrait
The Power of Words
Shadow — a Parable
Silence — a Fable
The Unparalleled Adventure of One
    Hans Pfaall
Von Kempelen and His Discovery

POETRY

"Al Aaraaf" (*Note:* Second published work of Poe; highly acclaimed)
"Alone"
"Annabel Lee"
"The Bells"
"Bridal Ballad to ___ ___"
"The City in the Sea"
"The Coliseum"
"The Conqueror Worm"
"A Dream"
"Dream-land"
"A Dream within a Dream"
"Dreams"
"Eldorado"
"Elizabeth"
"An Enigma"
"Eulalie-a Song"
"Evening Star"
"Fairy-land"
"For Annie"
"The Happiest Day, the Happiest Hour"
"The Haunted Palace"
"Hymn"
"Hymn to Aristogeiton and Harmodius"
"Imitation"
"Israfel"
"The Lake: To ____"
"Lenore"
"A Paean"
"The Raven"
"Romance"
"Scenes from "Politian" (unpublished drama)"
"Serenade"
"The Sleeper"
"Sonnet-Silence"
"Sonnet-to Science"
"Sonnet to Zante"
"Spirits of the Dead"
"Stanzas"

"Tamerlane" (*Note:* This was Poe's first published work, under the title *Tamerlane and Other Poems*, with the author's credit "By a "Bostonian.")
"To ____"
"To ____"
"To ____ ____"
"To ____ ____"
"To F ____"
"To F ____ S S. O____D"
"To Helen"
"To Helen"
"To Isadore"
"To M. L. S."
"To My Mother"
"To One in Paradise"
"To the River"
"Ulalume"
"A Valentine"
"The Valley of Unrest"

HUMOROUS STORIES AND SATIRES

The Angel of the Odd
Bon-Bon
The Business Man
The Devil in the Belfry
Diddling
The Duc de l'Omelette
Four Beasts in One
How to Write a Blackwood Article
Lionizing
The Literary Life of Thingum Bob, Esq.
Loss of Breath
The Man that Was Used Up
Mellonta Tauta
Mystification
Never Bet the Devil Your Head
A Predicament
Some Words with a Mummy
The Spectacles
The Sphinx
The System of Doctor Tarr and Professor Fether

A Tale of Jerusalem
The Thousand-and-Second Tale of
    Scheherazade
Three Sundays in a Week
Why the Little Frenchman Wears His
    Hand in a Sling
X-ing a Paragrab

OTHER UNCLASSIFIED WORKS

The Conchologist's First Book (textbook)
Eureka (treatise on theory of the universe)

The Literati (articles on New York
    personalities)
The Narrative of A. Gordon Pym of
    Nantucket (adventure novelette)
Von Jung, the Mystific
The Poetic Principle (lecture)
The Rationale of Verse (important essay
    on meter in lyric poetry)
The Philosophy of Furniture
Landscape Gardening

138. RELIGION: BIBLE

The Bible consists of the Old Testament (the Holy Scriptures of Judaism) and the New
Testament. There have been more copies of the Christian Bible sold than any other book in
history. The King James Version, published in 1611 is the best-known translation of the Christian
Bible in the English language. Most of the familiar biblical quotations come directly from this
translation, so-called because it was commissioned by King James I of England. The Bible is the
sacred book of many Christians, who believe the words were inspired by God. For others, it is
studied as great literature, history, or myth. The following books are contained in the King James
Bible. See also List 140, Religion: Biblical Quotations.

OLD TESTAMENT (39 BOOKS)

Genesis	II Chronicles	Daniel
Exodus	Ezra	Hosea
Leviticus	Nehemiah	Joel
Numbers	Esther	Amos
Deuteronomy	Job	Obadiah
Joshua	Psalms	Jonah
Judges	Proverbs	Micah
Ruth	Ecclesiastes	Nahum
I Samuel	Song of Solomon	Habakkuk
II Samuel	Isaiah	Zephaniah
I Kings	Jeremiah	Haggai
II Kings	Lamentations	Zechariah
I Chronicles	Ezekiel	Malachi

NEW TESTAMENT (27 BOOKS)

Matthew
Mark
Luke
John
Acts
Romans
I Corinthians
II Corinthians
Galatians
Ephesians
Philippians
Colossians
I Thessalonians
II Thessalonians
I Timothy
II Timothy
Titus
Philemon
Hebrews
James
I Peter
II Peter
I John
II John
III John
Jude
Revelation

Note: According to the *Guinness Book of World Records*, 1991 edition, a single volume, incomplete version of the Gutenberg Bible (printed circa 1455) was auctioned off in 1987 by Christie's of New York for $5,390,000 (the highest known price paid for a *printed book*). It contained the Old Testament from Genesis to the Psalms. A two-volume, complete edition of a Gutenberg Bible previously sold in 1978 for $2,200,000. It was printed between 1450 and 1456 in Mainz, Germany.

139. RELIGION: BIBLICAL QUOTATIONS

These oft-quoted words are from the King James Version of the Bible. Many of the quotations are alluded to in other great literature. See also List 7, Allusions: Biblical.

"Am I my brother's keeper?"
> **From story of Cain and Abel (Genesis 4:9)**

"A prophet is not without honor, save in his own country."
> **Jesus (Mark 6:4)**

"Ask, and it shall be given you. Seek, and ye shall find; knock, and it shall be opened unto you."
> **From Sermon on the Mount (Matthew 7:7)**

"Beware of false prophets, which come to you in sheep's clothing, but inwardly they are ravening wolves."
> **Jesus (Matthew 7:15)**

"By their fruits ye shall know them."
> **From Sermon on the Mount (Matthew 7:20)**

"Cast thy bread upon the waters."

   (Ecclesiastes 11:1)

"Do unto others as you would have them do unto you." (or) "All things whatsoever ye would that men should do to you, do ye even so to them."

   From Sermon on the Mount (Matthew 7:12)

"Dust thou art, and unto dust shalt thou return."

   God speaking to Adam when sending Eve and him from the Garden of Eden for eating the forbidden fruit (Genesis 3:19)

"Father, forgive them, for they know not what they do."

   Jesus (Luke 23:34)

"Get thee behind me, Satan."

   Jesus to Peter (Matthew 16:23)

"Give not that which is holy unto the dogs, neither cast ye your pearls before swine, lest they trample them under their feet, and turn again and rend you."

   From Sermon on the Mount (Matthew 7:6)

"He that is not with me is against me."

   Jesus (Matthew 12:30)

"He that is without sin among you, let him cast the first stone at her."

   Jesus (John 8:7)

"I am Alpha and Omega, the first and the last."

   God saying he is the beginning and the end, and will so remain to the end of time. Alpha and Omega are first and last letters in the Greek Alphabet. (Revelation 1:11)

"In the beginning God created the Heaven and the Earth."

   (Genesis 1:1)

"It is easier for a camel to go through the eye of a needle than for a rich man to enter into the Kingdom of God."

   Jesus (Matthew 19:24)

"It is more blessed to give than to receive."

   Apostle Paul (Acts 20:35)

"Judge not, that ye be not judged."
    From Sermon on the Mount (Matthew 7:1)

"Let the dead bury their dead."
    Jesus (Matthew 8:22)

"Let there be light."
    (Genesis 1:3)

"Love thy neighbor as thyself"
    (Leviticus 19:34)

"…love your enemies…"
    From Sermon on the Mount (Matthew 5:44)

"Man shall not live by bread alone."
    Jesus (Matthew 4:4)

"Many are called but few are chosen."
    Jesus (Matthew 22:14)

"My God, my God, why hast thou forsaken me?"
    (Psalms 22:1, recited by Jesus, Matthew 27:46)

"No man can serve two masters: for either he will hate the one, and love the other, or else he will hold to the one, and despise the other."
    Jesus (Matthew 6:24)

"Now abideth faith, hope, charity, these three; but the greatest of these is charity."
    Apostle Paul (I Corinthians 13:13)

"Render unto Caesar the things which are Caesar's, and unto God the things that are God's."
    Jesus (Luke 20:25)

"Take, eat; this is my body… this is my blood… this do in remembrance of me."
    Jesus at the last supper; basis for Holy Communion (I Corinthians 11:24-25)

"…the blind leading the blind"
    Jesus (Matthew 15:14)

"The last shall be first and the first last."
    Jesus (Matthew 19:13)

"The letter killeth, but the spirit giveth life."
   Apostle Paul, referring to the letter of the law (II Corinthians 3:6)

"The Lord is my shepherd, I shall not want..."
   (Psalms 23:1-6)

"The meek shall inherit the earth."
   From Sermon on the Mount (Matthew 5:5)

"The thing that hath been, it is that which shall be; and that which is done is that which shall be done: and there is no new thing under the sun."
   (Ecclesiastes 1:9)

"The voice of one crying in the wilderness: prepare ye the way of the Lord, make his paths straight."
   (Luke 3:4)

"The wolf shall also dwell with the lamb."
   (Isaiah 11:6)

"Thomas, because thou hast seen me, thou hast believed; blessed are they that have not seen, and yet have believed."
   Jesus to Apostle Thomas (John 20:29)

"Thou shalt give life for life, eye for eye, tooth for tooth, hand for hand, foot for foot."
   (Exodus 22:24)

"To every thing there is a season, and a time to every purpose under the heaven: a time to be born, and a time to die;..."
   (Ecclesiastes 3:1-2)

"Upon this rock I will build my church... and I will give unto thee the keys of the kingdom of heaven."
   Peter (Matthew 16:18-29)

"Vanity of vanities... all is vanity."
   Referring to the meaninglessness of life (Ecclesiastes 1:2)

"Whither thou goest, I will go; and where thou lodgest, I will lodge."
   Ruth to Naomi (Ruth 1:16)

"Whosoever shall compel thee to go a mile, go with him twain."

From Sermon on the Mount (Matthew 5:41)

"Why take ye thought to raiment? Consider the lilies of the field, how they grow; they toil not, neither do they spin. And yet I say unto you that even Solomon in all his glory was not arrayed like one of these."

Jesus, speaking of raiment (clothing) and material things (Matthew 6:28-29)

"Ye are the salt of the earth. If the salt have lost his savour, wherewith shall it be salted?"

From Sermon on the Mount (Matthew 5:15)

"Ye cannot serve God and Man."

Jesus (Luke 16:13)

"Ye have heard that it hath been said, 'An eye for an eye, and a tooth for a tooth'; but I say unto you, that ye resist not evil: but whosoever shall smite thee on thy right cheek, turn to him the other also."

(Matthew 5:38-39)

THE TEN COMMANDMENTS

The Ten Commandments are phrased differently in various religions and denominations. These commandments are said to have come directly from God to Moses. Jewish, Lutheran, and Catholic versions vary somewhat in wording and meaning.

   I.   I am the Lord thy God; thou shalt have no other gods before me.
  II.   Thou shalt not take the name of the Lord thy God in vain.
 III.   Remember the Sabbath Day, to keep it holy.
  IV.   Honor thy father and thy mother.
   V.   Thou shalt not kill.
  VI.   Thou shalt not commit adultery.
 VII.   Thou shalt not steal.
VIII.   Thou shalt not bear false witness against thy neighbor.
  IX.   Thou shalt not covet thy neighbor's house.
   X.   Thou shalt not covet thy neighbor's wife, nor his manservant, nor his maidservant, nor his ox, nor his ass, nor anything that is thy neighbor's.

THE TWENTY-THIRD PSALM

A psalm is a song, hymn, or poem. The Book of Psalms contains 150 songs of praise. The Twenty-Third Psalm is probably the most popular. It is often recited at funerals and on other occasions.

The Lord is my shepherd; I shall not want.

He maketh me to lie down in green pastures;

He leadeth me beside the still waters.

He restoreth my soul;

He leadeth me in the paths of righteousness for his name's sake.

Yea, though I walk through the valley of the shadow of death, I will fear no evil;

For thou art with me;

Thy rod and thy staff, they comfort me.

Thou preparest a table for me in the presence of mine enemies;

Thou anointest my head with oil; my cup runneth over.

Surely goodness and mercy shall follow me all the days of my life:

And I will dwell in the house of the Lord for ever.

THE LORD'S PRAYER

This prayer is the most popular Christian prayer in the English language. Two versions are found, first in Matthew 6:9–13 and again in Luke 11:2–4. The first version is the most often quoted.

Matthew 6:9–13

Our Father, which art in heaven,

Hallowed be thy name.

Thy kingdom come.

Thy will be done in earth as it is in heaven.

Give us this day our daily bread.

And forgive us our debts, as we forgive our debtors.

And lead us not into temptation, but deliver us from evil:

For thine is the kingdom, and the power, and the glory, forever.

Amen.

Luke 11:2–4

Our father, which art in heaven,

Hallowed be thy name.

Thy kingdom come.

Thy will be done, as in heaven, so in earth.

Give us day by day our daily bread.

And forgive us our sins, for we also forgive every one that is indebted to us.

And lead us not into temptation, but deliver us from evil.

SEVEN DEADLY SINS

The seven deadly sins, according to St. Thomas Aquinas, are listed below. Definitions have been added.

1. **anger** — outrage, wrath, hostility
2. **covetousness** — strong desire for what belongs to another
3. **envy** — resentment, jealousy, or rivalry between people
4. **gluttony** — excess, greediness, or insatiability, especially with food or drink
5. **lust** — passion and craving, especially for sensual pleasures
6. **pride** — haughtiness, arrogance, conceit
7. **sloth** — idleness, laziness

140. RELIGIONS OF THE WORLD

The following list includes those generally considered the major religions of the world (Buddhism, Christianity, Hinduism, Islam, and Judaism) and others. Their basic beliefs are taught in a few high schools and many colleges. The writings of each religion are often included in comparative religion or world literature courses. Literate people have at least a cursory knowledge of them all. See also List 139, Religion: Bible; List 140, Religion: Biblical Quotations; and List 143, Religious Documents and Holy Literature.

Buddhism — founded by Siddhartha Gautama (the Buddha) in India about the fourth or fifth century B.C. and flourishes today in Asia. It teaches the practice of meditation and the "four noble truths."

Christianity — monotheistic religion includes Roman Catholics, Protestants, Orthodox, Anglicans, and others who believe in Jesus Christ as the saviour.

Confucianism — early Chinese religion with its origins in the sayings of Confucius. It is a system of practical ethical and social precepts.

Hinduism — major religion in India; advocates the caste system and prescribes the roles each class of people should play in society. Four major goals are religious duty, earthly gain, physical pleasure, and spiritual liberation.

Islam — monotheistic religion of Muslims (Moslems). Islam means "surrender" (to the will of Allah) and acceptance of Muhammad as Allah's prophet.

Judaism — oldest monotheistic religion in Western world; practiced by Jews; belief in one God (monotheism) and adherence to the laws handed down through Moses.

Shintoism — ancient native religion of Japan; practiced today with festivals, by revering ancestors, and by pilgrimages to shrines.

Taoism — began about third century B.C. in China, but flourishes mainly in Taiwan today; the system derives from the *Tao-te-ching*, a book attributed to Lao-tze, describing an ideal state of freedom from desire and accenting simplicity.

141. RELIGIOUS DOCUMENTS AND HOLY LITERATURE

See also List 139, Religion: Bible; List 140, Religion: Biblical Quotations; and List 142, Religions of the World.

Bhagavad-Gita (401 B.C.) — Includes dialogues reflecting the fundamental beliefs of Hinduism.

Bible — Old Testament written about 1000 B.C.; New Testament written about 100 A.D.; King James Version prepared at King James's direction and published in 1611. King James version ncludes both Old and New Testaments and is the Protestant version of the Bible; a Roman Catholic version also exists; sacred writings of Christianity.

Book of Mormon (1830) — Word of Jesus Christ through translations of hieroglyphic writings on tablets found by Joseph Smith, founder of Church of Jesus Christ of Latter Day Saints (Mormons), in 1830.

Buddha, Life and Teachings (99 B.C.) — Buddha's enlightenment, experiences, and lessons; principles of Buddhism.

Egyptian Book of the Dead (2401 B.C.) — Oldest known work about religion; tells of life after death.

Koran (550–650 A.D.) — Muslim holy book, written in Arabic, of the word of God and revelations as told to Mohammed by Allah (God).

Torah (Pentateuch), and **Talmud** — The Torah contains some of the sacred writings of Judaism, the first five books of the Old Testament; the Talmud includes the Mishnah (in Hebrew) and the Gemara (in Aramaic), the text of oral law and clarifications of scholars.

Tripitaka — Collection of the teachings of Buddha, who arrived at his conclusions through meditation.

Veda — Any of four sacred books of rituals, myths, epics, philosophical works, and other literature relating to the Hindu religion.

142. SCHOOL

See also List 153, Young Adult Concerns.

Brush Up Your Shakespeare — Michael Macrons

By Jove! Brush Up Your Mythology — Michael Macrons

Closing of the American Mind: Education and the Crisis of Reason in America — Allan Bloom

College Admissions: Cracking the System — Adam Robinson and John Katzman

Cultural Literacy: What Every American Needs to Know — E. D. Hirsch, Jr.

The Elements of Grammar — Margaret Shertzer

The Elements of Style — William Strunk, Jr. and E. B. White

Final Grades — Anita Heyman (school pressures)

First Dictionary of Cultural Literacy — E. D. Hirsch, Jr.

Friends — April Smith (new school adjustment)

Getting It Down: How to Put Your Ideas on Paper — Judi Kesselman-Turkel and Franklynn Peterson

Getting Straight A's — Gordon W. Green

The Giver — Lynn Hall

How to Study — Harry Maddox

I Hate School: How to Hang In and When to Dropout — Claudine G. Wirths and Mary Bowman-Kruhm

Insider's Guide to the Colleges — Yale Daily News Staff

I've Missed a Sunset or Three — Phyllis Anderson Wood

James at Fifteen — April Smith (new school adjustment)

Libby on Wednesday — Zilha Keatley Snyder (new school adjustment)

Lifetime Reading Plan — Clifton Fadiman

The Mentor Guide to Writing Term Papers and Reports — William C. Paxson

The New York Times Guide to Reference Material (rev. ed.) — Mona McCormick

The Princeton Review Word Smart: Building an Educated Vocabulary — Adam Robinson

Read with Me: The Power of Reading — and How It Transforms Our Lives — Walter Anderson

Reading Critically, Writing Well: A Reader and Guide — R. B. Axelrod and C. R. Cooper

Remember Everything You Read: The Evelyn Wood 7-Day Reading Program — Stanley D. Frank

Roget's Thesaurus of English Words and Phrases: The Everyman Edition — D. C. Browning

Scholastic A+ Guides:
  The A+ Guide to Good Grades — Louise and Doug Colligan
  The A+ Guide to Book Reports — Louise Colligan
  The A+ Guide to Research and Term Papers — Louise Colligan
  The A+ Guide to Taking Tests — Louise Colligan
  The A+ Guide to Good Writing — Dianne Teitel Rubins
  The A+ Guide to Better Vocabulary — Vicki Tyler

Shrinklits: Seventy of the World's Towering Classics Cut Down to Size — Maurice Sagoff

Small Victories: The Real World of a Teacher, Her Students, and Their High School — Samuel G. Freedman

Thirty Days to a More Powerful Vocabulary — Wilfred Funk and Norman Lewis

Two Point Zero — Anne Snyder and Louis Pelletier (cheating)

Which Word When? The Indispensable Dictionary of 1,500 Commonly Confused Words — Paul Heacock

143. SPORTS

Any reader who enjoys sports as a fan or participant will find several of these fiction and nonfiction books of interest. Both individual and team sports are included. Type of sport is indicated in parentheses.

Amazing But True Sports Stories — Phyllis Hollander and Zander Hollander (collection)

Anybody's Skateboard Book — Tom Cuthbertson (skateboarding)

Archery for Beginners — John C. Williams (archery)

Arnold: The Education of a Bodybuilder — Arnold Schwarzenegger and Douglas Kent Hall (bodybuilding)

Ball Four — Jim Bouton (baseball)

Baseball Chronicles — David Gallen, editor (baseball)

Baseball in April and Other Stories — Gary Soto (collection of stories about various sports)

Brogg's Brain — Kim Piatt (track)

Cheerleader-Baton Twirler: Try Out and Win — Susan Rogerson Smith (cheerleading)

The Complete Book of Swimming — James E. Counsilman (swimming)

The Contender — Robert Lipsyte (boxing)

A Different Season — David Klass (baseball)

Even Big Guys Cry — Alex Karras (football)

Fire and Ice — Eric Lindros (hockey)

Football Dreams — David Guy (football)

Footfalls — Elizabeth Harlan (track)

Getting Started in Tennis — Paul Metzler (tennis)

Go! Fight! Win! The NCA Guide for Cheerleaders — Betty Lou Phillips (cheerleading)

Grass Roots and Schoolyards: A High School Basketball Anthology — Nelson Campbell, ed. (basketball)

The Great American Balloon Book — Bob Waligunda and Larry Sheehan (hot air ballooning)

Halfback Tough — Thomas J. Dygard (football)

Half Mile Up Without an Engine — Robert Gannon (sailplaning)

Heart of a Lion: The Bobby Layne Story — Bob St. John (football)

Hoops — Walter Dean Myers (basketball)

Hoosiers — Phil M. Hoose (basketball)

Ice Castles — Leonore Fleischer (figure skating)

The Illustrated Sports Record Book — Zander Hollander and David Schulz (most sports)

Inner Game of Skiing — W. Timothy Gallwey (snow skiing)

It's a Mile from Here to Glory — Robert C. Lee (track)

The Joy of Running — Thaddeus Kostrubala (running)

The Joy of Snorkeling: An Illustrated Guide — Steve Blout and Herb Taylor (snorkeling)

Just for Kicks — Paul Baczewski (football)

The Martial Arts — Susan Ribner and Richard Chin (kung fu, judo, karate, and other martial arts)

Mastering Bowling — Dawson Taylor (bowling)

Muhammad Ali, a Life — Thomas Hauser (boxing)

The Official Cheerleader's Handbook — Randy L. Neil (cheerleading)

The Official Soccer Book of the United States Soccer Federation — Walter Chyzowych (soccer)

Oh, Baby, I Love It! — Tim McCarver and Ray Robinson (baseball)

The Olympics: Smitty II — Bill Gutman (basketball)

Once Around the Park — Roger Angell (baseball)

Out of Bounds — Lori Boatright (basketball)

Play Better Golf (Volumes I, II, III) — Jack Nicklaus and Ken Bowden (golf)

Pumping Up! Super Shaping the Feminine Physique — Ben Welder and Robert Kennedy (bodybuilding)

Rabbit Ears: A Sports Novel — Robert Montgomery (baseball)

Racquetball the Easy Way — Charles Garfinkel (racquetball)

Record Breakers: One-Hundred-One Winning Streaks in Sports — Zander Hollander (many sports)

Running Free: A Book for Women Runners and Their Friends — Joan L. Ullyot (running)

Sailing "The Annapolis Way" — Ernie Barta (sailing)

Skills and Tactics of Gymnastics — Peter Aykroyd (gynmastics)

Sports Illustrated Badminton — Sports Illustrated, eds. (badminton)

Sports Illustrated Scuba Diving — Sports Illustrated, eds. (scuba diving)

Sports Lingo — Harvey Frommer (language of most sports)

Stolen Season — David Lamb (baseball)

The Throwing Season — Michael French (shot put)

Total Impact — Ronnie Lott (football)

Tournament Upstart — Thomas Dygard (basketball)

Vision Quest — Terry Davis (wrestling)

Volleyball: The Game and How to Play It — Gary Rosenthal (volleyball)

You Are the Coach (series) — Nate Aaseng
    Baseball: It's Your Team
    You Are the Coach: Football
    You Are the Coach: Basketball
    You Are the Coach: College Football
    You Are the Coach: Hockey
    You Are the Manager: Baseball

Zanballer — R. R. Knudson (football)

Zanbanger — R. R. Knudson (basketball)

Zanboomer — R. R. Knudson (baseball)

Zan Hagen's Marathon — R. R. Knudson (track)

144. SYMBOLISM IN LITERATURE

Writers often use symbols to impart hidden meaning, second — level insights, and levels of understanding beneath the surface of a work. The term symbolism generally refers to the use of specific objects, people, or things to represent ideas, moods, or emotions. The following are examples of literary works that employ symbolism. Brief notations of symbolic meanings are shown in some cases. See also List 10, Famous Characters from Literature; List 13, Famous Places from Literature; List 126, Allegories; and List 147, Symbols.

All Quiet on the Western Front — Erich Remarque
    Earth symbolizes a mother's security and protection; whirlpool represents "the front."

Amerika — Franz Kafka
    Symbolism of sunlight and darkness; going down a rope ladder represents character's descent from higher society to low-life companions; apple given to main character by woman represents his fall.

Animal Farm — George Orwell
Animal behavior symbolizes human characteristics.

Ariel — Sylvia Plath
Christian symbolism.

Beloved — Toni Morrison
Main character, Beloved, is symbolic; milk symbolizes mother-child bond; tree represents strength, characters called Life and Mr. Death; bird symbolism of flight; forest represents blindness; red ribbon symbolizes blood of slave's suffering; water variously represents life, death, and rebirth.

Call of the Wild — Jack London
Red represents blood and savagery; savagery versus civilization symbolized by confrontation between beast and man.

The Castle — Franz Kafka

Catch-22 — Joseph Heller

A Farewell to Arms — Ernest Hemingway
Mountains and snow represent noble aspirations, virtues, and good; plains and rain represent realities of war, death, and evil.

The Flowers of Evil — Charles Baudelaire

Free Fall — William Gelding

Gargantua — François Rabelais

The Golden Bowl — Henry James

Gravity's Rainbow — Thomas Pynchon
Pigs represent alternatively fertility, the unsaved, the saved, anti-dogs and ultimately both the anti-hero and hero; Tarot cards represent a series of characters and life from the fool to the mature fool, a high priestess, an earth mother, a magician, an emperor, and so forth, throughout the book; white and black are used symbolically, but sometimes white is a reverse symbol (death).

Heart of Darkness — Joseph Conrad

Henry IV — William Shakespeare
The lion is used variously throughout the play as a symbol; Falstaff represents human shortcomings.

Invisible Man — Ralph Ellison

King Lear — William Shakespeare
Nakedness of Edgar symbolizes his defenselessness; clothing gives him a fresh start. Images of night and darkness have symbolic meanings.

King Richard II — William Shakespeare
The sun is used throughout as a symbol of the monarch, along with the rain as its opposing element. Plants and flowers present symbolic images.

The Land of Heart's Desire — William Butler Yeats

Lord of the Flies — William Golding

Macbeth — William Shakespeare
Act III soliloquy uses the scorpion or serpent as a symbol of Macbeth's betrayal (as it was of Judas in the Bible). Banquo symbolizes good traits Macbeth wants.

The Masque of the Red Death — Edgar Allan Poe

The Naked and the Dead — Norman Mailer

1984 — George Orwell
Dream sequence uses Freudian symbols.

The Old Man and the Sea — Ernest Hemingway

To One in Paradise — Edgar Allan Poe
Island represents innocence; fountain represents life; shrine represents devotion. These mix together to symbolize love for deceased lady.

Othello — William Shakespeare
Iago a symbol of betrayal; Desdemona's ordering wedding sheets for her bed symbolizes her desire for reconciliation.

Out of Africa — Isak Dinesen

The Plague — Albert Camus

A Portrait of the Artist as a Young Man — James Joyce
Bird, water, and religious symbolism of meals.

Pseudepigrapha; Enoch; Jubilees; Apocalypse of Baruch
Apocalyptic Jewish writings.

The Red Badge of Courage — Stephen Crane
Sunlight represents victory; cloudy sky represents defeat.

The Scarlet Letter — Nathaniel Hawthorne

A Separate Peace — John Knowles
Tree symbolically represents war; leper's attraction to dining room represents search for order; snowball fight represents last of the war games.

The Trial — Franz Kafka
Door is authority symbol; children playing game where they can't touch symbolizes lack of human bonding.

The Waste Land — T. S. Eliot

Which Was the Dream? and Other Symbolic Writings of the Later Years — Mark Twain

The Yearling — Marjorie Rawlings
Yearling symbolizes both vulnerability and wildness; the sinkhole represents the character's resting place.

145. SYMBOLS

A symbol is something that stands for something else. It is often a word, color, object, picture, person, setting, or happening that represents a deeper or broader meaning. This list shows frequently used items and their common symbolic meanings. See also List 10, Famous Characters from Literature; List 13, Famous Places from Literature; List 126, Allegories; and List 146, Symbolism in Literature.

animals

- donkey — Democratic political party; stubbornness
- elephant — Republican political party; forgetfulness
- fox — slyness; cleverness
- lamb — gentleness; purity; sacrifice; innocence
- lion — nobility; ferocity; royalty
- octopus — greed; enveloping evil
- powerful animal — father; dominance
- rat — contemptible person
- serpent — poison; evil; lowness; unworthiness; betrayal

barrenness

(trees, plants, or land) — infertility

birds

- bird on the wing — freedom
- caged bird — imprisonment
- cock crowing — morning; warning
- dove — peace; purity; peaceful person
- eagle — power; vision; clear-sightedness; protection
- falcon — greed; vanity
- hawk — war; warlike person; pugnacity
- owl — wisdom
- robin — spring
- vulture — loathsome evil waiting to devour humans

blood — life; sacrifice

bread — material things; life

chaff — foolish ideas or people

chains — binding together; imprisonment

clock chime — warning

coldness — fear

colors

- black — death; poverty; famine; evil
- green — envy; vegetation; earth; fertility; nature
- grey — sickness; frailty
- rainbow colors — diverse races
- red — passion; sensuality; revolution; violence; war; blood
- white — purity; power; conquest; good; sickliness
- yellow — light; brightness; comprehension

cross — crucifixion; Christianity

darkness — mystery; gloom; confusion

dreams — subconscious thoughts; subconscious desires

eating — self-gratification; pleasure; taking communion

fire/burning — hell; punishment; passion

fisherman — searcher for truth; Jesus

flag — patriotism

flying — sexual intercourse; freedom from restraint

fountain — life source

fruit — fertility

gold — wealth

heart — life force; love

island — innocence; freedom

king — father; authority

midnight — evil hour; mystery

money — labor; evil

monster — evil or supernatural forces

moonlight — romance

nakedness — naturalness; primitive instincts; savagery; innocence

numbers

one — unity; unity with God

seven — sacred; lucky

twelve — sacred

thirteen — unlucky

obesity — greed; materialism; self-indulgence; joviality

petals (dropping from flowers) — life ebbing away

queen — mother; authority

rain — sadness; sorrow

river journey — journey of life

rocking chair — lifelessness; apathy

rose — love; lips; lovely woman; kindness

sackcloth — repentance; mourning

sapphire — chastity; spiritual peace

scaffold — justice

scales (balancing) — justice

sea — danger; evil

sea monster (many sided) — hell

search for gold (gold coins) — worthless pursuit of false goals

seasons

autumn — last few years of life

spring — new beginnings; birth

summer — prime of life

winter — end of life

shadows — ominous foreboding; mystery

shrine — devotion

sun — happiness; cheerfulness; clearness of vision; power

sunset — waning life

thinness — self-sacrifice; grimness; meanness; prudishness; miserliness

thunderstorm — impending danger; violence

volcanic eruption — sexuality

warmth — security

water — birth; cleansing

waterfalls — serenity; calmness; insight

wheat — divine ideas or people; fertility

wine — blood

146. TRANSCENDENTALISTS

In mid-nineteenth-century New England, a group of writers and intellectuals began translating, writing, and publishing a profusion of literary works. Their philosophy centered on protest against the Puritan ethic and materialism; it encompassed individualism, freedom, inquiry, experiment, and intuitive spirituality.

The literary leader of the Transcendentalist movement was Ralph Waldo Emerson. The group, sometimes called the "Concord Group," even had an official organization, the Transcendental Club. (Asterisks* show actual members.) The following men and women of New England, all of whom embraced Transcendentalism, comprised the literary center of America for a half century.

Major works are listed beneath each author's name. See also List 46, Essays: Collections; and List 48, Essay Masters.

*RALPH WALDO EMERSON

"Nature" (essay)
"The American Scholar" (address)
"Literary Ethics" (address)
"The Method of Nature" (address)

Essays, First Series
    "Self Reliance"
    "History"
    "Compensation"
    "Spiritual Laws"
    "Love"
    "Friendship"
    "Prudence"
    "Heroism"
    "The Over-Soul"
    "Circles"
    "Intellect"
    "Art"

Essays, Second Series
    "The Poet"
    "Experience"
    "Character"
    "Manners"
    "Gifts"
    "Nature"
    "Politics"
    "Nominalist and Realist"

Representative Men (essays)
English Traits (travel book)
Parnassus (Emerson's favorite poems)
The Conduct of Life
    "Power"
    "Wealth"
    "Fate"
    "Culture"
Society and Solitude (lecture materials)
Letters and Social Aims
Fortune of the Republic

Poems
May Day and Other Pieces (poems)
"Divinity School Address"
"New England Reformers" (speech)
Journals (posthumously published)
    "The Philosophy of History"
    "Human Culture"
    "Human Life"
    "The Present Age"
Natural History of Intellect
Selected Individual Poems:
    "Each and All"
    "The Rhodora"
    "The Concord Hymn"
    "Hamatreya"
    "The Humble-Bee"
    "Woodnotes"
    "The Apology"
    "The Problem"
    "Politics"
    "Forbearance"
    "Brahma"
    "Terminus"
    "The Problem"
    "Threnody"
    "Days"
    "Uriel"

JOHN GREENLEAF WHITTIER (POET)

"Maud Muller"
"Barbara Frietchie"
"Snowbound"
"The Barefoot Boy"

NATHANIEL HAWTHORNE

The Scarlet Letter (novel)
The House of the Seven Gables (novel)
The Marble Faun (novel)

The Blithedale Romance (based on Brook Farm experience)

Twice-Told Tales (stories)

The Snow Image and Other Twice-Told Tales (collection)

Life of Franklin Pierce (biography)

Our Old Home (last book)

Mosses from an Old Manse (collection of stories and sketches)

"Grandfather's Chair" (historical sketch for children)

The Wonder Book (storybook for children)

Tanglewood Tales (storybook for children)

"Sights from a Steeple" (sketch)

Night Sketches from Under an Umbrella

Selected Individual Titles of Short Works:
- "Roger Malvin's Burial"
- "Rappaccini's Daughter"
- "Young Goodman Brown"
- "The Old Manse"
- "Ethan Brand"
- "The Gentle Boy"
- "The Great Stone Face"
- "The White Old Maid"
- "Endicott and the Red Cross"
- "The May-Pole of Merry Mount"
- "The Birthmark"
- "David Swan"
- "The Grey Champion"
- "Dr. Heidegger's Experiment"
- "Lady Eleanore's Mantle"
- "The Ambitious Guest"
- "The Minister's Black Veil"
- "Feathertop"
- "The Artist of the Beautiful"
- "Drowne's Woodman Image"
- "Wakefield"

HENRY DAVID THOREAU

A Week on the Concord and Merrimac Rivers (collection of poems, essays, and miscellany)

Of Civil Disobedience

Walden; or Life in the Woods (these and others tell of two-year experiment at Walden Pond):

"The Pond"

"Brute Neighbors"

"Winter Visitors"

"The Pond in Winter"

Excursions

"A Winter Walk" (essay)

The Maine Woods

Cape Cod

*AMOS BRONSON ALCOTT

(father of Louisa May Alcott; founded controversial school based on teaching through conversations)

Observations on the Principles and Methods of Infant Instruction

Conversations with Children on the Gospels

Spiritual Culture

Table-Talk

Sonnets and Canzonets

HENRY WADSWORTH LONGFELLOW (POET)

"Evangeline"

"The Song of Hiawatha"

"The Courtship of Miles Standish"

"Paul Revere's Ride"

Ballads and Other Poems
- "The Wreck of the Hesperus"
- "The Village Blacksmith"
- "Excelsior"

OLIVER WENDELL HOLMES

"Autocrat of the Breakfast Table" (essay)

"The Professor's Story" (essay)

"The Guardian Angel" (essay)
"The Poet at the Breakfast Table" (essay)
Pages from an Old Volume of Life
Medical Essays
"Old Ironsides" (poem)
Ralph Waldo Emerson
A Mortal Antipathy
Our Hundred Days in Europe
Before the Curfew (poems)
"The Moral Bully" (poem)
"The Chambered Nautilus" (poem)
"The Deacon's Masterpiece"; or "The Wonderful 'One Hoss Shay'"
"Over the Tea-Cups" (essay)

JAMES RUSSELL LOWELL

A Year's Life (poems)
Poems
The Biglow Papers: First Series (poems in dialect)
The Biglow Papers: Second Series (poems in dialect)
Under the Willows (poems)
Prometheus
Three Memorial Poems
Heartsease and Rue (poems)
The Cathedral (poems)
A Fable for Critics
Conversations on Some of the Old Poets
Fireside Travels (essays)
Among My Books (essays)
My Study Windows (essays)
Political Essays
On a Certain Condescension in Foreigners
Individual Poems:
    "To the Dandelion"
    "The Commemoration Ode"
    "The Present Crisis"
    "The Vision of Sir Launfal"

*SARAH MARGARET FULLER

(founded Transcendentalist magazine *The Dial*, with Emerson and Ripley)

Conversations with Goethe (trans.)
Woman in the Nineteenth Century (women's rights)
Summer on the Lakes
Papers on Literature and Art

*WILLIAM ELLERY CHANNING

(poet; pastor of Boston Church)

On the Character and Writings of Milton
Negro Slavery
The Perfect Life (collection of sermons)

*GEORGE RIPLEY

(critic; pastor; reformer; founded Brook Farm-Utopian community)

Foreign Standard Literature

WALT WHITMAN

Leaves of Grass

*ORESTES A. BROWNSON

(clergyman; part of Brook Farm experiment)

Charles Elwood, or the Infidel Converted
The Spirit-Rapper (novel)
The Convert (autobiography)
The American Republic

*GEORGE BANCROFT

(historian)

A History of the United States

OTHER TRANSCENDENTALISTS

*Theodore Parker

*E. P. Peabody

*C. P. Cranch

*Dr. Follen

*James Freeman Clarke

*W. H. Channing

*Dr. Hedge

*C. A. Bartol

147. UTOPIA/DYSTOPIA

A utopia is an ideal, peaceful state or society. Many older (and a few modern) authors, social reformers, and philosophers have written about the possibility of creating such a society. Conversely, other authors have written antiutopian works about dystopias, or exaggeratedly imperfect and oppressive societies. Authors of dystopias project what might happen if certain ideas (often technological, political, sociological, or scientific) were carried to extremes; in some cases, they simply wish to satirize utopian ideas. Here are several works that might be considered utopian or dystopian.

Always Coming Home — Ursula Le Guin

Animal Farm — George Orwell

Bible ("Garden of Eden" story)

The Birds (Play) — Aristophanes

The Blithedale Romance — Nathaniel Hawthorne

The Book of Being — Ian Watson

The Book of Rivers — Ian Watson

The Book of Stars — Ian Watson

Brave New World — Aldous Huxley

"Brave New World Revisited" — Aldous Huxley (essay)

Candide — Voltaire

Cat's Cradle — Kurt Vonnegut, Jr.

The City of the Sun — Tommaso Campanella

The Dispossessed: An Ambiguous Utopia — Ursula Le Guin

Erewhon — Samuel Butler

Fahrenheit 451 — Ray Bradbury

Foundation Series — Isaac Asimov

Gather, Darkness! — Fritz Leiber

Insatiability — Stanislaw Witkiewicz

The Island — Aldous Huxley

The Joy Makers — James E. Gunn

Limbo — Bernard Wolfe

Looking Backward, From the Year 2000 — Mack Reynolds

Looking Backward, 2000–1887 — Edward Bellamy

Lost Horizon — James Hilton

Major Barbara (Play) — George Bernard Shaw

Make Room! Make Room! — Harry Harrison

A Modern Utopia — H. G. Wells

The New Atlantis — Francis Bacon

News from Nowhere — William Morris

1984 — George Orwell

Nova Express — William S. Burroughs

Oceana — James Harrington

Ossian's Ride — Fred Hoyle

Player Piano — Kurt Vonnegut, Jr.

Republic — Plato

R. U. R. (Play) — Karel Capek

Shockwave Rider — John Brunner

The Space Merchants — Frederik Pohl and Cyril Kornbluth

Starship Troopers — Robert Heinlein

Utopia — Sir Thomas More

Walden — Henry David Thoreau

Walden Two — B. F. Skinner

The Wanting Seed — Anthony Burgess

We — Yevgeny Zamyatin

UTOPIAN EXPERIMENTS

Those listed below planned or carried out experiments in utopian living. Some lasted a while, but all except the Amana Society finally failed. It is intriguing to read about the people, philosophies, and communities involved in these experiments.

Henry Thoreau — Walden

Robert Owen/Robert Dale Owen (son) — New Harmony, Indiana; New Lanark, Scotland; Queenwood, Hampshire, England

Sainte-Simon — France

Etienne Cabet — France

Charles Fourier — France

Samuel Taylor Coleridge/Robert Southe — Susquehanna River in Pennsylvania (planned only)

Amana Society — Iowa River commune (east central Iowa)

Tecumseh — Prophet's Town (Tippecanoe River, near Lafayette, Indiana)

George Ripley — Brook Farm (West Roxbury, Massachusetts)

Bronson Alcott — Fruitlands (Harvard, Massachusetts)

148. WAR

The following fiction and nonfiction works deal with war and its effects. See also List 108, War and Antiwar Poems/Songs.

Across Five Aprils — Irene Hunt (Civil War)

All Quiet on the Western Front — Erich Maria Remarque (World War I)

The American Revolutionaries: A History in Their Own Words, 1750–1800 — Milton Meltzer, editor (Revolutionary War)

Anne Frank's Tales from the Secret Annex — Anne Frank (World War II)

Anne Frank Remembered — Miep Gies (World War II)

Born on the Fourth of July — Ron Kovic (Vietnam War)

The Bridges of Toko-Ri — James Michener (Korean War)

The Cage — Ruth M. Sender (World War II)

The Caine Mutiny — Herman Wouk (World War II)

Catch-22 — Joseph Heller (World War II)

Chickenhawk — Robert Mason (Vietnam War)

Children of the Holocaust: Conversations with Sons and Daughters of Survivors — Helen Epstein (World War II)

Code Name Kris — Carol Matas (World War II)

The Coldest War — James Brady (Korean War)

The Coventry Option — Anthony Burton (World War II)

The Dangerous Game — Milton Dank (World War II)

Daughters of the Law — Sandy Asher (World War II)

Don't Cry, It's Only Thunder — Paul G. Hensler and Jeanne Houston (Vietnam War)

Drawing the Line: The Korean War, 1950–1953 — Richard Whelan (Korean War)

The Emerald Illusion — Ronald Bass (World War II)

Fallen Angels — Walter Dean Myers (Vietnam War)

A Farewell to Arms — Ernest Hemingway (World War I)

Farewell to Manzanar — Jeanne Wakatsuki and James D. Houston (World War II)

Fields of Fire — James Webb (Vietnam War)

Fire in the Lake: The Vietnamese and the Americans in Vietnam — Frances Fitzgerald (Vietnam War)

First Blood — David Morrell (Vietnam War)

The Flying Tigers — John Toland (World War II)

For Whom the Bell Tolls — Ernest Hemingway (Spanish Civil War)

Frontier Wolf — Rosemary Sutcliff (Roman War in 5 A.D.)

The Ghosts of War — Daniel Cohen (general)

The Good Shepherd — C. S. Forester (World War II)

The Great Escape — Paul Brickhill (World War II)

Hiroshima — John Hersey (World War II)

Holocaust Testimonies — Lawrence L. Langer (World War II)

Home Before Morning: The Story of an Army Nurse in Vietnam — Lynda Van Devanter (Vietnam War)

I Am Rosemarie — Marietta D. Moskin (World War II)

If I Die in a Combat Zone — Tim O'Brien (Vietnam War)

I'm Fifteen-And I Don't Want to Die — Christine Amothy (World War II)

In Country — Bobbie Anne Mason (Vietnam War)

The Italians and the Holocaust — Susan Zuccotti (World War II)

Johnny Got His Gun — Dalton Trumbo (World War I)

Khaki Wings — Milton Dank (World War I)

King Rat — James Clavell (World War II)

The Last Mission — Harry Mazer (World War II)

The Last Silk Dress — Ann Rinaldi (Civil War)

Lines of Battle — Annette Taper (World War I I)

The Mad Game — James Forman (antiwar)

Maus — Art Spiegelman (World War II)

Maus II — Art Spiegelman (World War II)

Missing in Action — Bill Linn (Vietnam War)

Mister Roberts — Thomas Heggen (World War II)

The Naked and the Dead — Norman Mailer (World War II)

A Nation Torn: The Story of How the Civil War Began — Delia Ray (Civil War)

Neverlight — Donald Pfarrer (Vietnam War)

Never to Forget: The Jews of the Holocaust — Milton Meltzer (World War II)

No Hero for the Kaiser — Rudolf Frank (World War I)

The Other Victims: First-Person Stories of Non-Jews Persecuted by the Nazis — Ina R. Friedman (World War II)

The Red Badge of Courage — Steven Crane (Civil War)

Rescue: The Story of How Gentiles Saved Jews in the Holocaust — Milton Meltzer (World War II)

A Rumor of War — Philip Caputo (Vietnam War)

Secret Missions of the Civil War — Philip Van Foren Stern (Civil War)

A Separate Peace — John Knowles (World War II)

A Ship Must Die — Douglas Reeman (World War II)

Smoke and Ashes: The Story of the Holocaust — Barbara Rogasky (World War II)

Summer of My German Soldier — Bette Greene (World War II)

The Things They Carried — Tim O'Brien (Vietnam War)

Till the End of Time — Allen Appel (World War II)

The Times of My Life — Brent Ashabranner (life changed by war)

Torpedo Run — Douglas Reeman (World War II)

Travelers — Larry Bograd (Vietnam War)

Under the Apple Tree — Dan Wakefield (World War II)

The Unknown Story of One-Thousand World War II Refugees — Ruth Gruber (World War II)

Walls: Resisting the Third Reich — One Woman's Story — Hiltgunt Zassenhaus (World War II)

Wartime Lies — Louis Begley (World War II)

War Year — Joe Haldeman (Vietnam War)

We Remember the Holocaust — David A. Adler (World War II)

When Heaven and Earth Changed Places: A Vietnamese Woman's Journey from War to Peace — Le Ly Hayslip with Jay Wurts (Vietnam War)

The Winds of War — Herman Wouk (World War II)

The Wooden Horse — Eric Williams (World War II)

Yamamoto — Edwin P. Hoyt (World War II)

150. Women: Books/Stories with Female Emphasis

Westerns

Banis, V. J. — *San Antone*

Bickham, Jack — *The War on Charity Ross; Target; Charity Ross*

Cooke, John Byrne — *The Snowblind Moon*

Frazee, Steve — *A Gun for Bragg's Woman*

Haycock, Ernest — Many of his westerns have strong and interesting female characters.

Locke, Charles O. — *Amelia Rankin*

Olsen, Theodore V. — *Arrow in the Sun*

Overholser, Wayne D. — *The Cattle Queen*

Portis, Charles — *True Grit*

Richter, Conrad — *Tacey Cromwell*

Webster, Jan — *Muckle Annie*

Spies/Adventure/Mystery

Anthony, Evelyn — *Albatross; The Avenue of the Dead; The Company of Saints; The Defector; The Janus Imperative*

Bosse, Malcolm — *The Man Who Loved Zoos*

Cole, G. D. H. and Cole — *The Toys of Death*

Eberhart, Mignon G. — *Murder Goes to Market*

Gilman, Dorothy — *The Unexpected Mrs. Pollifax; Mrs. Pollifax and the Hong Kong Buddha*

Haggard, H. Rider — *She; The Return of She; King Solomon's Mines*

Llewelyn, Morgan — *Grania: She-King of the Irish Seas*

MacInnes, Helen — *Above Suspicion; Ride a Pale Horse*

McCloy, Helen — *Life Is a Brutal Affair*

Muller, Marcia — *The Broken Men; She Won the West: An Anthology of Western and Frontier Stories by Women* (with Bill Pronzini)

O'Donnell, Peter — *Modesty Blaise series*

Rendell, Ruth — *Thornapple*

Rice, Craig — *The Frightened Millionaire*

Robertson, E. A. — *Four Frightened People*

Stevenson, Janet — *Departure*

SCIENCE FICTION

Sargent, Pamela, ed. — *Women of Wonder: Science Fiction Stories by Women about Women*

Sargent, Pamela, ed. — *More Women of Wonder*

Sargent, Pamela, ed. — *New Women of Wonder*

POETRY

Bankier, Joanna, et al, eds. — *The Other Voice: Twentieth-Century Women's Poetry in Translation*

Chester, Laura and Sharon Barba, eds. — *Rising Tides: Twentieth-Century American Women Poets*

Cosman, Carol et al, eds. — *The Penguin Book of Women Poets*

Stetson, Erlene, ed. — *Black Sister: Poetry by Black American Women 1746–1980*

150. WOMEN: IMPORTANT WRITERS

The following women from all parts of the world have been major writers. They refused to take the advice given by poet Robert Southey to Charlotte Bronte: "Literature cannot be the business of a woman's life, and ought not to be . . ." See also List 66, Novelists and Storytellers: Women; List 150, Women: Books/Stories with Female Emphasis; and List 152, Women Writers: Women's Issues.

Anna Akhmatova (Russian poet)

Louisa May Alcott (American novelist)

Sibilla Aleramo (Italian novelist)

Hannah Arendt (German-American philosopher)

Bettina von Arnim (German writer of letters)

Mary Astell (British nonfiction writer)

Jane Austen (British novelist)

Joanna Baillie (British poet and dramatist)

Marie Bashkirtseff (Russian journal writer)

Simone de Beauvoir (French novelist, essayist, nonfiction writer)

Aphra Behn (British playwright)

Elizabeth Bishop (American poet)

Nellie Bly (American journalist)

Enid Blyton (British writer for children)

Anne Bradstreet (British poet)

Anne Bronte (British novelist and poet)

Charlotte Bronte (British novelist and poet)

Emily Bronte (British novelist and poet)

Elizabeth Barrett Browning (British poet)

Frances Hodgson Burnett (British writer for children)

Fanny Burney (British diarist and novelist)

Jane Welsh Carlyle (British writer of letters and history)

Elizabeth Carter (British poet and translator)

Willa Cather (American novelist)

Kate Chopin (American short story writer)

Agatha Christie (British detective novelist)

Chu Shu-chen (Chinese poet)

Colette (French novelist)

Anna Comnena (Byzantine writer of history)

Ivy Compton-Burnett (British novelist)

Emily Dickinson (American poet)

Isak Dinesen (Danish novelist and short story writer)

Marguerite Duras (French writer and film maker)

George Eliot (British novelist)

Marie de France (French poet)

Anne Frank (Dutch diarist)

Hrosvitha von Gandersheim (German poet and chronicler)

Elizabeth Gaskell (British biographist and novelist)

Ellen Glasgow (American novelist)

Nadine Gordimer (South African novelist and short story writer)

Edith Hamilton (American nonfiction writer and novelist)

Lorraine Hansberry (American playwright)

Lillian Hellman (American playwright)

Heloise (French writer of letters)

Julia Ward Howe (American songwriter)

Zora Neale Hurston (American writer)

Marie de la Fayette (French novelist)

Selma Lagerlof (Swedish folklorist and novelist)

Doris Lessing (British novelist and short story writer)

Li Ch'ing-chao (Chinese poet)

Elizabeth Lynn Linton (British journalist)

Amy Lowell (American poet)

Flora Shaw Lugard (Irish journalist)

Mary McCarthy (American novelist, essayist, and nonfiction writer)

Carson McCullers (American writer)

Katherine Mansfield (New Zealand short story writer)

Edna St. Vincent Millay (American poet)

Marianne Moore (American poet)

Lady Murasaki (Japanese novelist)

Iris Murdoch (British novelist)

Walladah al-Mustakfi (Spanish poet)

Anaïs Nin (French/American author)

Flannery O'Connor (American novelist and short story writer)

Pan Chao (Chinese historian and poet)

Dorothy Parker (American drama critic, short story writer, poet)

Christine de Pisan (French poet)

Sylvia Plath (American poet and short story writer),

Katherine Anne Porter (American short story writer, novelist, essayist)

Beatrix Potter (British writer for children)

Anne Radcliffe (British novelist)

Dorothy Richardson (British stream-of-consciousness writer)

Henry Handel Richardson (Australian novelist)

Christina Rossetti (British poet)

George Sand (French novelist)

Sappho (Greek poet)

Lady Sarashina (Japanese nonfiction writer)

Nathalie Sarraute (French novelist)

Olive Schreiner (South African nonfiction writer)

Anne van Schuurman (European dissertation writer)

Madeleine de Scudery (French novelist)

Marie de Sevigne (French writer of letters)

Mary Shelley (British horror story writer and novelist)

Sei Shonagon (Japanese nonfiction writer)

Edith Sitwell (British poet)

Agnes Smedley (American journalist)

Germaine de Staël (Swiss critic and novelist)

Christina Stead (Australian novelist)

Gertrude Stein (American nonfiction writer and playwright)

Harriet Beecher Stowe (American novelist)

Edith Wharton (American novelist)

Virginia Woolf (British novelist, critic, diarist)

Dorothy Wordsworth (British diarist)

Note: For biographical sketches of these women (and others), see *Women of Achievement: Thirty-five Centuries of History* by Susan Raven and Alison Weir. New York: Harmony Books, 1981.

151. WOMEN WRITERS: WOMEN'S ISSUES

From the days when women were denied the vote up to the present day, some women have felt the need to change their lot in life. Here are some representative female writers who have written about issues affecting women. See also List 150, Women: Books/Stories with Female Emphasis; and List 151, Women: Important Writers.

Margaret Atwood — *Surfacing; Bodily Harm*

Simone de Beauvoir — *The Second Sex; Memoirs of a Dutiful Daughter; The Coming of Age*

Susan Brownmiller — *Against Our Will: Men, Women, and Rape; Femininity* (study)

Joan Didion — *Play It As It Lays; The White Album*

Shulamith Firestone — *Dialectic of Sex: The Case for a Feminist Revolution*

Betty Friedan — *The Feminine Mystique; The Second Stage*

Margaret Fuller — *Woman in the Nineteenth Century*

Charlotte Perkins Gilman — *The Yellow Wallpaper; Women and Economics*

Germaine Greer — *The Female Eunuch; Sex and Destiny*

Elizabeth Janeway — *Man's World, Woman's Place: A Study in Social Mythology; Women: Their Changing Roles; Powers of the Weak; Cross Sections: From a Decade of Change*

Diane Jennings — *Self-Made Women: Twelve of America's Leading Entrepreneurs Talk about Success, Self-Image, and the Superwoman*

Erica Jong — *Fanny; Fear of Flying*

Denise Levertov — *Light Up the Cave; A Door in the Hive; Candles in Babylon; Life in the Forest*

Kate Millett — *Sexual Politics; Flying; Sita; The Basement: Meditation on a Human Sacrifice*

Joyce Carol Oates — *Because It Is Bitter, & Because It Is My Heart; I Lock My Door Upon Myself; The Rise of Life on Earth*

Tillie Olsen — *Tell Me a Riddle; Silences; Yonnondio: From the Thirties*

Grace Paley — *The Little Disturbances of Man; Enormous Changes at the Last Minute; Same Day*

Marge Piercy — *Circles on the Water; Woman on the Edge of Time; To Be of Use*

Sylvia Plath — *The Bell Jar; Edge; Daddy; Lesbos; Lady Lazarus; The Colossus; Crossing the Water; Winter Trees; Ariel*

Jean Rhys — *Quartet; After Leaving Mr. MacKenzie; Voyage in the Dark; The Wide Sargasso Sea*

Adrienne Rich — *Adrienne Rich's Poetry; Of Woman Born: Motherhood As Experience and Institution; Diving into the Wreck*

Olive Schreiner — *Women and Labour*

Anne Sexton — *Love Poems of Anne Sexton; No Evil Star: Selected Essays, Interviews, and Prose; Complete Poems; Nineteen Eighty-One*

Mary Wollstonecraft Shelley — *Vindication of the Rights of Women*

Virginia Woolf — *A Room of One's Own; Three Guineas; Orlando*

1532 YOUNG ADULT CONCERNS

See also List 144, School; List 145, Sports; List 149, War.

CHILD ABUSE/RAPE

Sandy Asher — *Things Are Seldom What They Seem* (child abuse)

Maury Blair and Doug Brendel — *Maury, Wednesday's Child* (child abuse)

Janet Bode — *The Voices of Rape*

Patricia Dizenzo — *Why Me? The Story of Jenny* (rape)

Frances Shuker-Haines — *Everything You Need to Know about Date Rape*

Irene Hunt — *The Lottery Rose* (child abuse)

Gloria D. Miklowitz — *Did You Hear What Happened to Andrea?* (rape)

Joanna Lee and T. S. Cook — *Mary Jane Harper Cried Last Night* (child abuse)

Louise Moeri — *The Girl Who Lived on the Ferris Wheel* (child abuse)

Andrea Parro — *Coping with Date Rape and Acquaintance Rape*

Richard Peck — *Are You in the House Alone?* (rape)

COURAGE

Frank Deford — *Alex, the Life of a Child* (girl with cystic fibrosis)

Jack R. Gannon — *The Week the World Heard Gallaudet* (deaf are heard)

Jill Krementz — *How It Feels to Fight for Your Life*

Natalie Kusz — *Road Song*

John Neufeld — *Twink* (cerebral palsy and blindness)

Robert Perske — *Show Me No Mercy: A Compelling Story of Remarkable Courage*

Diana E. H. Russell — *Lives of Courage* (women in South Africa)

Susan Sallis — *Only Love*

Harriet May Savitz — *The Lionhearted*

Julian F. Thompson — *Facing It*

Mala Wojciechowska — *Shadow of a Bull*

DISASTER (NUCLEAR)

Larry Bograd — *Los Alamos Light* (tensions working at Los Alamos)

Gail K. Haines — *The Great Nuclear Power Debate*

Daenis Johnson — *Fiskadoro* (nuclear holocaust)

Arnold Madison — *It Can't Happen to Me* (nuclear threat)

Gloria D. Miklowitz — *After the Bomb* (nuclear war)

Robert Swindells — *Brother in the Land* (nuclear holocaust)

Stephanie Tolan — *Pride of the Peacock* (nuclear fears)

DIVORCE

Judie Angell — *What's Best for You*

Paula Danziger — *The Divorce Express*

Judy Feiffer — *Lovecrazy*

Richard A. Gardner — *The Boys' and Girls' Book About Divorce*

Norma Klein — *Angel Face; Breaking Up; It's Not What You Expect; Taking Sides*

Julie Autumn List — *The Day the Loving Stopped*

Sharon G. Marshall — *When a Friend Gets a Divorce, What Can You Do?*

John Neufeld — *Sunday Father*

Doris Orgel — *Risking Love*

Kit Reed — *The Ballad of T. Rantula*

EATING DISORDERS

Caroline Arnold — *Too Fat, Too Thin? Do You Have a Choice?* (under/overeating)

Adelle Davis and Ann Gildroy — *Let's Stay Healthy* (healthy eating)

Barthe DeClements — *Nothing's Fair in Fifth Grade* (overweight)

Jan Greenberg — *The Pig-Out Blues* (overweight)

Isabelle Holland — *Heads You Win, Tails I Lose* (overweight)

Deborah Hutzig — *Second Star to the Right* (anorexia nervosa)

Rebecca Josephs — *Early Disorder* (anorexia nervosa)

Steven Levendron — *The Best Little Girl in the World* (anorexia nervosa)

Robert Lipsyte — *One Fat Summer* (overweight)

Susan Beth Pfeffer — *Marly the Kid* (overweight)

Ellen Rabinowich — *Underneath I'm Different* (overweight)

Marilyn Sachs — *The Fat Girl* (love; overweight)

Marion Schultz — *The Girl Within* (overweight)

Anne Snyder — *Goodbye, Paper Doll* (anorexia nervosa)

Patti Stern — *I Was a Fifteen-Year-Old Blimp* (overweight)

Margaret Willey — *The Bigger Book of Lydia* (anorexia nervosa)

ECOLOGY

J. Baldwin — *The Whole Earth Catalog*

Michael Caduto and Joseph Bruchac — *Keepers of the Earth: Native American Stories and Environmental Activities for Children*

Earth Works Group — *50 Simple Things Kids Can Do to Save the Earth*

Earth Works Group — *50 Simple Things You Can Do to Save the Earth*

Kathryn Gay — *Greenhouse Effect*

Susan Jeffers — *Brother Eagle, Sister Sky*

Jon Naar — *Design for a Livable Planet*

FAMILY RELATIONSHIPS

Fran Arrick — *Nice Girl from Good Home*

John Bradshaw — *Bradshaw on the Family*

Robin F. Brancato — *Sweet Bells Jangled Out of Tune*

Sue Ellen Bridgers — *Notes for Another Life*

Bruce Brooks — *Midnight Hour Encores; The Moves Make the Man*

Vera and Bill Cleaver — *Where the Lilies Bloom*

Hila Colman — *Sometimes I Don't Love My Mother*

Barbara Corcoran — *Hey, That's My Soul You're Stomping On*

Jean Ferris — *Across the Grain*

Elissa Haden Guest — *Over the Moon*

Lynn Hall — *The Horse Trader*

Hilma Holitzer — *Hearts*

M. E. Kerr — *The Son of Someone Famous*

Caroline Leavitt — *Meeting Rozzy Halfway*

Kevin Major — *Far From Shore*

Norma Fox Mazer — *A Figure of Speech; Three Sisters*

Jane Claypool Miner — *Why Did You Leave Me?*

Philippa Greene Mulford — *If It's Not Funny, Why Am I Laughing?*

Joan Oppenheimer — *Francesca, Baby*

Katherine Paterson — *The Great Gilly Hopkins; Jacob Have I Loved*

Richard Peck — *Don't Look and It Won't Hurt; Father Figure*

Kin Platt — *The Boy Who Could Make Himself Disappear; Chloris and the Weirdos*

Florence Engel Randall — *All the Sky Together*

Gertrude Samuels — *Adam's Daughter*

Ouida Sebestyen — *Far From Home*

Doris Buchanan Smith — *Return to Bitter Creek*

Anne Snyder — *The Best That Money Can Buy; Nobody's Brother*

Stephanie S. Tolan — *No Safe Harbors*

Jean Van Leeuwan — *Seems Like This Road Goes On Forever*

Cynthia Voigt — *Dicey's Song; Homecoming*

Ruth Wolff — *A Crack in the Sidewalk*

PREGNANCY/SEX/TEEN LOVE/UNWED MOTHERS

Gunnel Beckman — *Mia Alone* (teen pregnancy)

Judy Blume — *Forever* (young love)

Leo F. Buscaglia — *Living, Loving, and Learning* (teen relationships)

Leo F. Buscaglia — *Love* (teen relationships)

Leo F. Buscaglia — *Loving Each Other* (teen relationships)

Judith Caseley — *Kisses* (general problems)

Barbara Corcoran — *Making It* (prostitution)

Beverly Donofrio — *Riding in Cars with Boys* (rebellion)

Donny Ewy and Rodger Ewy — *Teen Pregnancy: The Challenges We Faced, the Choices We Made* (teen pregnancy)

Jeannette Eyerly — *He's My Baby, Now* (teen pregnancy)

Ann Head — *Mr. and Mrs. Bojo Jones* (teen pregnancy)

Kayla M. and Connie K. Heckert — *To Keera with Love* (teen pregnancy)

Victor J. Kelly — *MacIntosh Mountain* (teen pregnancy)

Norma Klein — *No More Saturday Nights* (unwed teen parent)

Joanna Lee — *I Want to Keep My Baby* (teen pregnancy)

Mildred Lee — *The Sycamore Year* (teen pregnancy)

Harriet Luger — *Laureen* (teen pregnancy)

Lynda Madaras and Dane Saavedra — *What's Happening to My Body? Book for Girls: A Growing Up Guide for Parents and Daughters* (health)

Lynda Madaras and Dane Saavedra — *What's Happening to My Body? Book for Boys: A Growing Up Guide for Parents and Sons* (health)

Winifred Madison — *Growing Up in a Hurry* (teen pregnancy)

Paula McGuire — *It Won't Happen to Me* (teen pregnancy)

Joe S. McIlhaney, Jr. — *Sexuality and Sexually Transmitted Diseases*

Gloria D. Miklowitz — *Unwed Mother* (teen pregnancy)

Walter Dean Myers — *Sweet Illusions* (teen pregnancy)

John Neufeld — *For All the Wrong Reasons* (teen marriage)

Alison Prince — *Willow Farm* (teen pregnancy)

Bob Stone and Bob Palmer — *The Dating Dilemma* (dating)

Laurel Trivilpiece — *In Love and in Trouble* (teen pregnancy)

Paul Zindel — *The Girl Who Wanted a Boy* (teen relationships)

RUNAWAYS

Fran Arrick — *Steffie Can't Come Out to Play*

Jeffrey Artenstein — *Runaways*

Avi — *Sometimes I Hear My Name*

Hila Colman — *Claudia, Where Are You?*

Marilyn Harris — *The Runaway's Diary*

Fanny Howe — *The Blue Hills*

Kevin Major — *Hold Fast*

Gloria D. Miklowitz — *Runaway*

Scott O'Dell — *Kathleen, Please Come Home*

Richard Peck — *Secrets of the Shopping Mall*

Richard Shaw — *The Hard Way Home*

Susan Shreve — *The Revolution of Mary Leary*

Julia Sorel — *Dawn: Portrait of a Teenage Runaway*

SEARCH FOR SELF/GROWING UP

Patricia Beatty — *Behave Yourself, Bethany Brant*

Sue Ellen Bridgers — *Permanent Connections*

Bruce Clement — *Anywhere Else But Here*

Robert Cormier — *I Am the Cheese; Beyond the Chocolate War*

Andrea B. Eagan — *Why Am I So Miserable if These are the Best Years of My Life?*

Mary Hahn — *Daphne's Book*

Lynn Hall — *The Leaving*

Virginia Hamilton — *Arilla Sun Down*

Robert Hawks — *This Stranger, My Father*

Nat Hentoff — *I'm Really Dragged but Nothing Gets Me Down*

S. E. Hinton — *The Outsiders; Rumblefish*

Mollie Hunter — *Cat Herself*

Anita Jacobos — *Where had Deedie Wooster Been All These Years?*

Paul Janeczko — *Bridges to Cross*

James Joyce — *A Portrait of the Artist as a Young Man*

M. E. Kerr — *If I Love You, Am I Trapped Forever?*

Ronald Kidd — *Dunker*

Lee Kingman — *Break a Leg Betsy Maybe!*

Ron Koertge — *The Boy in the Moon*

Katie Letcher Lyle — *Dark But Full of Diamonds*

Norma Fox Mazer — *Downtown; Dear Bill, Remember Me? and Other Stories*

Jill McCorkle — *Ferris Beach*

Barbara Morgenroth — *Will the Real Renie Lake Please Stand Up?*

Walter Dean Myers — *Fast Sam, Cool Clyde, and Stuff*

Phylis Reynolds Naylor — *A String of Chances*

Jan O'Donnell — *A Funny Girl Like Me*

Zibby Oneal — *In Summer Light*

Joan Oppenheimer — *Working on It*

Barbara Park — *Beanpole*

Katherine Paterson — *Bridge to Terabithia; Come Sing, Jimmy Jo*

Robert Newton Peck — *A Day No Pigs Would Die*

Susan Beth Pfeffer — *A Matter of Principle*

Kin Platt — *Brogg's Brain; The Ape Inside Me*

Padgett Powell — *Edisto*

John R. Powers — *Do Black Patent Leather Shoes Really Reflect Up?*

Ellen Rabinowich — *Underneath I'm Different*

J. D. Salinger — *Catcher in the Rye*

Gertrude Samuels — *Run, Shelly, Run*

Sarah Sargent — *Lure of the Dark*

Sandra Scoppetone — *Long Time Between Kisses*

Bobby Simpson — *Dear Bobby Simpson*

Jan Slepian — *Something Beyond Paradise*

Janice Stevens — *Take Back the Moment*

Jo Stewart — *Andrea*

Judith St. George — *Call Me Margo*

Joyce Carol Thomas — *Marked by Fire*

Marie-Louise Wallin — *Tangles*

Rosemary Wells — *When No One Was Looking*

Jessamyn West — *Cross Delahanty*

Paul Zindel — *Confessions of a Teenage Baboon; To Take a Dare*

SUICIDE AND DEATH

Suicide

Fran Arrick — *Tunnel Vision*

James Bennett — *I Can Hear the Mourning Dove*

Eve Bunting — *If I Asked You, Would You Stay?*

Patricia Calvert — *The Hour of the Wolf*

Jeannette Eyerly — *See Dave Run*

Elizabeth Faucher — *Surviving*

William Faulkner — *The Sound and the Fury*

Corinne Gerson — *Passing Through*

Johann Wolfgang Goethe — *The Sorrows of Young Werther*

Cynthia Grant — *Hard Love*

Judith Guest — *Ordinary People*

R. R. Knudson — *Just Another Love Story*

John Mack and Holly Heckler — *Vivienne*

Gloria D. Miklowitz — *Close to the Edge*

Zibby Oneal — *The Language of Goldfish*

Richard Peck — *Remembering the Good Times*

Stella Pevsner — *How Could You Do It, Diane?*

Luigi Pirandello — *Six Characters in Search of an Author*

Harriet Savitz — *Wait Until Tomorrow*

Brett Singer — *The Petting Zoo*

Paul Zindel — *Harry and Hortense at Hormone High*

Death

Judy Blume — *Tiger Eyes*

Barbara Brenner — *The Killing Season*

Eve Bunting — *A Sudden Silence*

Patricia Calvert — *The Stone Pony*

Julie Reece Deaver — *Say Goodnight, Gracie*

Frances Duncan — *Finding a Home*

James Forman — *The Pumpkin Shell*

Damon Galgut — *A Sinless Season*

Karen Gravelle, et al. — *Teenagers Face to Face with Bereavement*

Virginia Hamilton — *Cousins*

Isabelle Holland — *Of Love and Death and Other Journeys*

June Cerza Kolf — *Teenagers Talk about Grief*

Steven Kroll — *Take It Easy*

Madeleine L'Engle — *A Ring of Endless Light*

Lois Lowry — *A Summer to Die*

Harry Mazer — *When the Phone Rang*

Zibby Oneal — *A Formal Feeling*

Richard Peck — *Close Enough to Touch*

Mary K. Pershall — *You Take the High Road*

Susan Beth Pfeffer — *About David*

Elizabeth Richter — *Losing Someone You Love*

Ann Rinaldi — *Term Paper*

Doris Buchanan Smith — *A Taste of Blackberries*

Todd Strasser — *Friends Till the End*

Marac Talbert — *Dead Birds Singing*

Jill Paton Walsh — *The Unleaving*

Barbara Wersba — *Run Softly*

Patricia Windsor — *The Summer Before*

Literary Periods ...Into One Era and Out the Other

153. CLASSICISM

Early classical writing may not be to everyone's taste today, but certainly literature lovers should be familiar with the names of the classical greats. To read at least one work by an author below will increase your understanding and appreciation of the literature of the period. Classicism in literature refers to writing that has the characteristics of orderliness, reason, clearness, restraint, and altruism. The writings generally present an orderly, harmonious world and are represented by very early Greek and Roman works. These are some of the major authors during classical periods in literature. Each subgroup is arranged in approximate chronological order of major literary works.

GREEK CLASSICAL/HELLENISTIC PERIODS — eighth to second centuries B.C.:

Homer (epic poetry —
  Iliad and *Odyssey*)
Pindar (lyric poetry)
Xenophon (history)
Aeschylus (tragedies)
Euripides (tragedies)
Sophocles (tragedies)
Aristophanes (comedies)
Herodotus (history)
Thucydides (history)
Aeschines (oratorical prose)
Demosthenes (oratorical prose)
Aristotle (philosophy)
Plato (philosophy)
Meander (comedies)
Callimachus (poetry)
Theocritus (idyllic poetry)
Apollonius (epic poetry)

ROMAN CLASSICAL PERIOD "AGE OF AUGUSTUS" — from first century B.C. through the fifth century A.D.:

Romans
Cicero (oratorical prose)
Lucretius (philosophical poetry)
Catullus (lyric poetry)
Horace (lyric poetry and satire)
Virgil (epic poetry — *Aeneid*)
Livy (history)
Seneca (tragedies)
Ovid (lyric poetry — *Metamorphoses*)
Arbiter (novelist)
Lucan (epic poetry)
Juvenal (satirical poetry)
Claudian (last major classical poet)

Greeks
Polybius (history)
Plutarch (biography)
Lucian (satire)
Longus (pastoral romance)
Plotinus (philosophy)

A classic (not to be confused with a classical work, i.e., one created by a Greek or Roman author) is any piece of literature that has stood the test of time, enduring for generations or even centuries. The following authors have all written enduring classics, either for children or adults or both.

Louisa May Alcott
Horatio Alger
Hans Christian Andersen
Jane Austen
James M. Barrie
Lyman Frank Baum
Ludwig Bemelmans
Lucy Boston
Carol Brink
Charlotte Bronte
Emily Bronte
John Bunyan
Frances Hodgson Burnett
Lewis Carroll
Willa Cather
Collodi (Carlo Lorenzini)
Joseph Conrad
James Fenimore Cooper
Stephen Crane
Marguerite de Angeli
Jean de Brunhoff
Daniel Defoe
Antoine de Saint-Exupèry
Charles Dickens
Elsie Dinsmore
Mary Mapes Dodge
George Eliot
F. Scott Fitzgerald
Esther Forbes

Fred Gipson
Kenneth Grahame
Jacob and Wilhelm Grimm
    (collectors)
Thomas Hardy
Joel Chandler Harris
Nathaniel Hawthorne
Ernest Hemingway
Thomas Hughes
Washington Irving
Henry James
Ezra Jack Keats
Rudyard Kipling
Selma Lagerlof
Edward Lear
C. S. Lewis
Sinclair Lewis
Astrid Lindgren
Hugh Lofting
Harriet Mulford Lothrop
    (Margaret Sydney)
W. Somerset Maugham
Robert McCloskey
Herman Melville
A. A. Milne
Lucy Montgomery
Mary Norton
Scott O'Dell
Eugene O'Neill

Charles Perrault
Edgar Allan Poe
Howard Pyle
Marjorie Rawlings
Felix Salten
Sir Walter Scott
Maurice Sendak
Theodore Geisel Seuss
Anna Sewell
William Shakespeare
George Bernard Shaw
Margaret Sidney
Johanna Spyri
Robert Louis Stevenson
Harriet Beecher Stowe
Jonathan Swift
Booth Tarkington
Albert Payson Terhune
J. R. R. Tolkien
P. L. Travers
Mark Twain
Jules Verne
Edith Wharton
E. B. White
Kate Douglas Wiggin
Laura Ingalls Wilder
Thomas Wolfe
Johann Rudolf Wyss

155. Literary, Dramatic, and Other Events: Renaissance

The Renaissance commonly refers to the period of European history from the mid-fourteenth century through the sixteenth century, when learning and the arts (literature, painting, sculpture, architecture, and music) experienced a "rebirth" in Italy, France, Spain, England, Holland, Germany, and parts of eastern Europe. Generally speaking, the Renaissance marks the transition between the medieval era and the modern world. This list provides background information on the events of the Renaissance and is designed to assist readers in understanding the literature of the period. Events relating to literature and drama are emphasized, showing their approximate chronological placement among other events. See also List 157, Literary, Dramatic, and Other Events: 1530–1600; List 158, Literary, Dramatic, and Other Events: 1600–1700; List 159, Literary, Dramatic, and Other Events: 1700–1800; and List 160, Literary, Dramatic, and Other Events: 1800–1900.

c. 1300 — **Marco Polo dictates his memoirs from Italian jail**

1305 — Giotto paints religious frescoes in Italy

— Jews persecuted in France

1307 — **Dante begins to write** *The Divine Comedy*

1308 — One of first indoor tennis courts built in Paris by King Philip IV

1309 — Doge's Palace built (Venice)

— Counterpoint introduced in music

1313 — Gunpowder perfected by Schwarz

1314 — Original St. Paul's Cathedral completed (London)

— Molay burned at stake in Paris (for heresy)

1315 — Italian immigrants to France begin silk industry

1317 — French "Salic Law" excludes women from succession to the throne

1322 — Pope outlaws counterpoint for music in the church

1328 — Sawmill invented

1337 — First scientific weather forecasts made (England)

1341 — **Petrarch emerges as an important poet, laying groundwork for modern Italian**

1347–50 — Black Death (bubonic plague) wipes out one-third of Europe's population

1348 — **Boccaccio achieves prominence as writer of prose, including geographical and mythological dictionaries**

1349 — Jews persecuted in Germany

1350 — Many famous cathedrals built

1351 — **Petrarch writes his autobiography**

— Outdoor tennis developed in England

1354 — Mechanical clock invented

1370 — Steel crossbow used in war

1377 — **Robin Hood makes first appearance in English literature (*Piers Plowman*)**
— Playing cards become popular in Germany
— Rome becomes center of music

1387 — **Chaucer begins *Canterbury Tales***

1400 — Literary tradition develops in Cornwall
— Church drama becomes popular in Italy
— Alchemy falls into disrepute

1403 — Lorenzo Ghiberti works on Florence baptistry

1408 — Donatello achieves fames as a sculptor

1414 — Medici family of Florence become bankers for the Vatican

1415 — Jan Hus is burned at the stake for heresy

1425 — **Chartier writes *La Belle Dame Sans Merci***

1426 — Netherlands becomes Europe's musical center

1428 — Joan of Arc leads French army against England

1430 — Modern English begins to emerge from Middle English

1431 — Joan of Arc is burned at the stake by her English captors

1450 — Florence becomes center of Renaissance and Humanistic movement
— Medici family dominates financial and cultural life of Florence
— **Gutenberg prints *Constance Mass Book***
— **Vatican Library founded**

1452 — **First metal plates used for printing**

1453 — Fall of Constantinople
— End of Hundred Years' War between France and England
— **Gutenberg and Fust print their first Bible**
— **Movable type comes into use, allowing production of books in quantity**

1456 — **Villon writes *The Little Testament***

1461 — Leonardo da Vinci studies under Verrocchio

1466 — **First German Bible printed by Mentel**

1467 — **Ballad of William Tell appears**

1469 — Ferdinand of Aragon marries Isabella of Castille, beginning the rise of Spain as a major power

1470 — Portuguese mariners reach the Gold Coast of West Africa
— **First French printing press established in Paris**

1472 — **Dante's *The Divine Comedy* printed**

1474 — **Caxton prints first book in English language**

1477 — **Caxton prints Chaucer's *Canterbury Tales***

1480 — da Vinci designs a parachute

1484 — Pope issues bull against witchcraft

— Botticelli paints *The Birth of Venus*

1485 — **Caxton prints *Le Morte D'Arthur* (compilation of legends of King Arthur by Sir Thomas Malory)**

1489 — Mathematical symbols + and - are used

1490 — **Spanish drama begins**

— Ballet begins in Italy

1492 — Columbus makes first voyage to the Americas

— da Vinci draws pictures of a flying machine

— Behaim devises first globe of the world

— Jews are expelled from Spain

1493 — **Schedel's *Nuremberg Chronicle* (history of the world) is published**

— Columbus begins second voyage to New World

— Treaty of Tordesillas divides New World between Spain and Portugal

1494 — **Pacioli completes *Algebra***

— da Vinci completes *Madonna of the Rocks* (eleven-year work)

1495 — **Manutius begins printing editions of Greek classics**

— Jews expelled from Portugal

— **First papermill in England established (first European papermill was in Spain about 1150)**

— da Vinci paints *The Last Supper*

1496 — Columbus returns from second voyage to New World

— **Sanudo begins diary of life and politics in Venice**

— Michelangelo begins working in Rome

1497 — Vasco da Gama sails around Cape of Good Hope

— John and Sebastian Cabot reach North America

— Michelangelo sculpts *Bacchus*

— Savonarola excommunicated for opposing pope

— Celtis introduces humanism in Vienna

1498 — **Comedies of Aristophanes's published in Venice**

— Erasmus teaches at Oxford

— Savonarola burned at stake in Florence

— da Vinci produces astounding technical drawings

— Michelangelo sculpts *Pieta*

— Vasco da Gama discovers sea route to India

1499 — Vespucci and Ojeda depart for New World

— **Fernando de Rojas writes *Celestina*, first full-scale drama of modern Europe**

— **First political cartoons emerge during war between France and Italy**

— Signorelli paints frescoes in Orvieto Cathedral

— Dürer paints Krell portrait

— Giorgione completes *Portrait of a Young Man*

1500 — Cabral reaches Brazil

— Vespucci and Ojeda reach mouth of Amazon River

— Petrucci prints music with movable type

— "High Renaissance" begins

— **Italics invented by Aldus of Venice**

— **Erasmus publishes collection of proverbs**

1501 — **Books offensive to the Church are banned and burned**

— Michelangelo sculpts *David*

— **Celtes (Germany) and Gawin Douglas (Scotland) write allegories**

1502 — **Play by Gil Vicente performed in Portugal, marking beginning of modern Portuguese drama**

— **Celtes writes poem "Amores"**

— **Calepino writes *Cornucopiae*, a dictionary in several languages**

— Bellini, Botticelli, and Cranach produce important works of art

— Henlein makes first watch in Germany

1503 — Leonardo da Vinci finishes *Mona Lisa*

1504 — Columbus returns from fourth voyage to the Americas

— Cranach, Dürer, Giorgione, Lippi, and Raphael complete major works

1505 — Martin Luther enters monastery

— Raphael paints *Madonna del Granduca*

1506 — Machiavelli establishes first national army in Italy

— **Johann Reuchlin completes grammar and dictionary**

— Cranach, Mantegna, Raphael, Bellini, Dürer, Lotto, and Giorgione complete major works of art

1507 — **Waldseemüller, a mapmaker, suggests in *Cosmographiae Introductio* that New World be named after Amerigo Vespucci**

1508 — **First book printed in Scotland (*The Maying or Disport of Chaucer*)**
  — Michelangelo begins painting the ceiling of Sistine Chapel in Rome
  — **Ariosto writes Italian comedy, *Cassaria* (Cassaria)**

1509 — Spanish begin taking African slaves to New World
  — Jews persecuted in Germany; **Jewish books banned and burned**
  — **Erasmus writes *In Praise of Folly***

1510 — **Presentation of *Everyman* (English morality play) based on earlier Dutch play**
  — Leonardo da Vinci designs forerunner of water turbine
  — Erasmus, Luther, More, Colet, and von Kaiserberg are active in movement to reform the Church

1512 — Michelangelo finishes work on Sistine Chapel
  — Raphael paints portrait of Pope Julius II

1513 — **Machiavelli writes comedy *La Mandragola***
  — Michelangelo works on tomb of Julius Il
  — Balboa reaches Pacific Ocean
  — Ponce de Leon lands in Florida
  — Copernicus asserts that the planets orbit the sun

1514 — **First book printed in Arabic type (published in Italy)**

1515 — **Printing of books banned except with Catholic Church permission**
  — **First play in blank verse written by Giangiorgio Trissino**

1516 — **Sir Thomas More writes *Utopia, Historie of Edward V,* and *Richard The Third***
  — **Erasmus publishes New Testament in Greek and Latin**
  — Michelangelo completes sculpture of "Moses"
  — Music engraved on plates for first time, in Italy

1517 — **Hans Sachs begins writing songs and poems**
  — Luther mounts powerful challenge to the Church
  — Coffee appears in Europe for first time

1518 — **First book on arithmetic published by Riese**
  — Permission granted to import 4,000 Africans as slaves to American colonies

1519 — Horses reintroduced to North America by Spanish in Mexico
  — Magellan begins historic voyage to circumnavigate globe

1520 — Luther is excommunicated
  — **Royal library of France built at Fontainebleau**
  — Chocolate introduced to Spain from Mexico

1522 — Spaniards reach Peru

— **Luther finishes German translation of New Testament**

— Dürer designs flying machine for military use

1523 — **First English book on agriculture published (written by Anthony Fitzherbert)**

— **Hans Sachs writes poetic allegory honoring Luther**

— **Part I of *Chronicles* of Froissart translated**

1524 — Verrazano reaches Hudson River and New York Bay

— **Ingolstadt writes first geography textbook**

1525 — **Part II of *Chronicles* of Froissart translated**

— Hops introduced to England

— **First geometry book written, by Dürer**

1526 — Jews persecuted in Hungary

— **Italianate School of Literature founded in Portugal**

— **Sir Thomas Wyatt and Henry Howard, Earl of Surrey, write lyrics in England**

1527 — **Book on manners written by Castiglione**

— **Book on poetic theory written by Vida**

— Protestant armies of Charles V sack Rome; pope flees the city; Italian Renaissance comes to an end

156. LITERARY, DRAMATIC, AND OTHER EVENTS 1530–1600

See also List 156, Literary, Dramatic, and Other Events: Renaissance; List 158, Literary, Dramatic, and Other Events: 1600–1700; List 159, Literary, Dramatic, and Other Events: 1700–1800; List 160, Literary, Dramatic, and Other Events: 1800–1900

1531 — **Aristotle's works published by Erasmus**

1532 — **Chaucer's work published**

— **Rabelais's work published**

— French Reformation begins, inspired by John Calvin

1534 — **Allegorical plays performed in France**

— Jacques Cartier voyages to North America

1536 — Danish and Norwegian Reformation

— William Tyndale, reformer, burned at stake

1538 — Calvin expelled from Geneva, Switzerland

1541 — Coronado and de Soto explore United States

1542 — Mary Stuart becomes Queen of Scotland

— Inquisition established by pope in Rome

1543 — Protestants burned at stake in Spain (Spanish Inquisition)

1548 — **Mystery plays forbidden in Paris, France**

— **First English historical drama performed (Kynge Johan)**

1550 — **First English comedy (Ralph Roister Doister)**

— Cellini, Michelangelo, and Titian active in Italy

1555 — Tobacco brought to Spain from America

1556 — Thomas Cranmer burned at stake

1557 — **First censorship of English play, *The Sack-Full of Newes***

— European influenza epidemic

1558 — Elizabeth I becomes Queen of England

— **Torquato Tasso writes epic poem *Rinaldo***

1563 — **First printing presses in Russia**

— Plague sweeps Europe

1569 — Mercator creates map of the world

1574 — **Richard Burbage opens theater in London**

1580 — **Last performance of miracle play in Coventry, England**

1585 — **Cervantes writes pastoral romance *Galatea***

1588 — **Christopher Marlowe writes tragedy *Doctor Faustus***

— **Michel de Montaigne publishes essays**

1590 — **Edmund Spenser completes *The Faerie Queene***

— **William Shakespeare and Christopher Marlowe emerge as important writers**

— **Galileo writes of his experiments**

1592 — **Emergence of Thomas Kyd and John Lyly as important writers**

1597 — **Francis Bacon writes *Essays, Civil and Moral***

1598 — **Lope de Vega writes poem "La Dragontea"**

— **Ben Jonson writes *Every Man in His Humour***

— Bernini, Bruegel, El Greco, and Rubens produce major art works

1599 — **Globe Theater built in London**

157. LITERARY, DRAMATIC, AND OTHER EVENTS 1600–1700

See also List 156, Literary, Dramatic, and Other Events: Renaissance; List 157, Literary, Dramatic, and Other Events: 1530–1600; List 159, Literary, Dramatic, and Other Events: 1700–1800; List 160, Literary, Dramatic, and Other Events: 1800–1900.

1600 — Catholics persecuted in Sweden

— **William Shakespeare active as playwright**

1602 — Johann Kepler leading astronomer/astrologer in Germany

— **Lope de Vega writes epic poem *La hermosura de Angelica***

— Dutch East India Company founded

— Galileo conducts scientific investigations

— **Thomas Campion writes *Observations in the art of English poesie***

1603 — Plague afflicts England

1605 — **Cervantes completes *Don Quixote, Part I***

— **First public library opens in Rome**

— Claudio Monteverdi active as a composer

1607 — Founding of Jamestown, Virginia (first English settlement in North America)

1608 — Champlain creates settlement at Quebec, Canada

1615 — **Cervantes completes *Don Quixote, Part II***

1616 — Catholic Church bars Galileo from further experiments

1617 — **Ben Jonson becomes poet laureate of England**

— **John Calvin's works published posthumously**

1619 — First slaves brought to Virginia from Africa

1620 — Pilgrims land in Massachusetts

— Bernini, Rubens, and Van Dyck create important art works

1623 — **Important collection of Shakespeare's work (*First Folio*) published**

1624 — **John Smith writes a history of Virginia and New England**

1626 — Dutch purchase Manhattan

1629 — **Pierre Corneille, Thomas Heywood, Philip Massinger, and Ben Jonson complete dramas**

— Massachusetts Bay Colony founded

1632 — **Shakespeare's *Second Folio* published**

— **Galileo publishes studies on movement of the Earth**

1633 — **John Donne's poems published posthumously**

— Galileo forced to deny Copernican theories

— **Abraham Cowley, John Ford, Corneille, John Milton, Calderon, and Thomas Heywood publish important works**

1636 — Roger Williams founds Providence, Rhode Island

— Harvard College founded

1639 — **First American printing press (Cambridge, Massachusetts)**

— Rembrandt, Rubens, Poussin, Brueghel the Younger produce important art works

— **Emergence of Milton, Calderon, Corneille, and Massinger in literature**

— Claudio Monteverdi composes operas and madrigals

1642 — **Puritans close theaters in England**

— English Civil War begins

1660 — **Samuel Pepys begins his diary**

— Plague sweeps London

1666 — **John Dryden completes** *Annus Mirabilis*

— **Molière writes** *Le Misanthrope*

— Antonio Stradivari puts name on his first violin

— Great Fire destroys much of London; architect Christopher Wren is appointed to direct the task of rebuilding

1667 — **Milton writes** *Paradise Lost*

1669 — **Pepys completes his diary**

1670 — Hudson's Bay Company chartered for trading in Canada

1675 — Paris emerges as center of European culture

1678 — **John Bunyan completes** *The Pilgrim's Progress, Part I*

— **Jean de la Fontaine's fables published**

1679 — **Fifty plays of Beaumont and Fletcher published**

1682 — **John Dryden completes** *Absalom and Achitophel*

1684 — **Bunyan completes** *The Pilgrim's Progress, Part II*

1687 — Isaac Newton publishes *Principia,* explaining law of gravitation and beginning new era in science

1690 — Henry Purcell and Alessandro Scarlatti complete important musical works

1697 — **Charles Perrault completes collection of fairy tales**

1698 — Manufacture of paper begins in North America

158. Literary, Dramatic, And Other Events 1700-1800

See also List 156, Literary, Dramatic, and Other Events: Renaissance; List 157, Literary, Dramatic, and Other Events: 1530–1600; List 158, Literary, Dramatic, and Other Events: 1600–1700; List 160, Literary, Dramatic, and Other Events: 1800–1900.

1700 — **William Congreve completes** *The Way of the World*

— **Samuel Sewall writes first American work against slavery,** *The Selling of Joseph*

1701 — Yale College founded in New Haven, Connecticut

— **Daniel Defoe completes satire** *The True-Born Englishman*

— Major slave trade begins between Africa and North America

1704 — Bach and Handel produce major musical works

1706 — **London has first evening newspaper**

1707 — **George Farquhar completes** *The Beaux' Stratagem*

1713 — **Joseph Addison writes tragedy** *Cato*

— **Alexander Pope completes his poem "Ode on St. Cecilia's Day"**

— **John Gay writes pastoral** *The Shepherd's Week*

1719 — **Daniel Defoe publishes** *Robinson Crusoe*

1722 — **Defoe completes** *Moll Flanders*

1726 — **Jonathan Swift publishes** *Gulliver's Travels*

— **First lending library opens in Scotland**

1732 — **Benjamin Franklin begins issuing** *Poor Richard's Almanack*

1735 — John Peter Zenger wins "freedom of the press" trial

1741 — Handel completes *The Messiah*

1742 — **Henry Fielding writes** *The History of Tom Jones*

— Sign language for the deaf invented

1750 — **Neoclassical movement spreads through Europe**

— **Thomas Gray writes "Elegy Written in a Country Churchyard"**

— **First New York playhouse opened**

1751 — **Tobias Smollett publishes** *The Adventures of Peregrine Pickle*

— **Denis Diderot and co-editors begin to publish the Encyclopedia in France**

1759 — Franz Josef Haydn dominates European musical world

— **Voltaire publishes** *Candide*

1762 — Wolfgang Amadeus Mozart begins musical career at the age of six

1770 — Industrial Revolution takes hold in England

— Boston Massacre inflames American patriots

1773 — **Oliver Goldsmith completes comedy** *She Stoops to Conquer*

— Waltz craze begins in Vienna, Austria

1774 — **Goethe writes novel** *The Sorrows of Werther*

1775 — **Beaumarchais completes** *The Barber of Seville*

— **Sheridan presents his play** *The Rivals*

— American Revolution begins

1776 — Declaration of Independence severs ties between American colonies and Great Britain

1781 — **Immanuel Kant completes** *Critique of Pure Reason*

1778 — Ludwig van Beethoven begins his musical career at age eight

1779 — **Samuel Johnson completes** *Lives of the Poets*

— **Richard Brinsley Sheridan writes his farce** *The Critic*

1781 — **Publication of French Encyclopedia is completed**

1782 — **Friedrich von Schiller completes his play** *The Robbers*

1783 — Treaty of Paris officially ends American Revolution

1784 — **Beaumarchais completes comedy** *The Marriage of Figaro*

1786 — Francisco de Goya appointed Royal Painter in Spain

— Mozart completes *The Marriage of Figaro*

1787–88 — **Eighty-five essays urging strong central government in the United States are published as** *The Federalist*

1788 — **Jean-Jacques Rousseau's** *Confessions* **are published posthumously**

1789 — **Johann von Goethe writes tragedy,** *Torquato Tasso*

— George Washington becomes first president of U.S.

— French Revolution begins

1790 — **Robert Burns writes** *Tam O'Shanter*

1793 — Alexander MacKenzie explored Canada

— Construction begins on Capitol in Washington, D.C.

1793–94 — Reign of Terror grips France as thousands are put to death

1797 — **Samuel Taylor Coleridge completes "Kubla Khan"**

— Beethoven emerges as a major composer

159. LITERARY, DRAMATIC, AND OTHER EVENTS 1800–1900

See also List 156, Literary, Dramatic, and Other Events: Renaissance; List 157, Literary, Dramatic, and Other Events: 1530–1600; List 158, Literary, Dramatic, and Other Events: 1600–1700; List 159, Literary, Dramatic, and Other Events: 1700–1800.

1800 — Thomas Jefferson elected president of U.S.

1803–15 — Napoleonic Wars dominate European politics

1806 — End of Holy Roman Empire

1807 — **Georg Wilhelm Friedrich Hegel completes** *The Phenomenology of the Spirit,* **which exerts major influence on philosophical thought**

1808 — U.S. bans importation of slaves from Africa

— **Goethe completes** *Faust, Part I*

— **Sir Walter Scott writes** *Marmion*

— End of Spanish and Italian Inquisitions

1809 — **Washington Irving completes** *Rip Van Winkle*

1810 — Napoleon reaches the height of his power in Europe

1811 — **Jane Austen writes** *Sense and Sensibility*

1812 — United States and Great Britain go to war

1813 — **Jane Austen writes** *Pride and Prejudice*

1814 — **Francis Scott Key writes "The Star-Spangled Banner"**

— **Scott publishes** *Waverley*

— **William Wordsworth writes "The Excursion"**

1816 — **Jane Austen writes** *Emma*

1818 — **Major literary works include Byron's** *Don Juan*; **Scott's** *Heart of Midlothian* **and** *Rob Roy*; **Mary Shelley's** *Frankenstein*; **John Keats's** *Endymion.*

1819 — Britain's Queen Victoria begins her reign, which lasts until 1901

1820 — **Washington Irving completes** *The Sketch Book of Geoffrey Crayon, Gent.*

— **Keats writes "Ode To a Nightingale"**

— **Scott publishes** *Ivanhoe*

— **Shelley writes** *Prometheus Unbound*

1821 — **Literary works include James Fenimore Cooper's** *The Spy*; **William Hazlitt's** *Table Talk*; **Thomas de Quincey's** *Confessions of an English Opium Eater;* **Shelley's "Adonais"**

1822 — Franz Liszt begins musical career at age eleven

— **Washington Irving writes** *Bracebridge Hall*

1823 — **Cooper publishes** *The Pioneers*

— Franz Schubert reaches the height of his powers as a composer.

1825 — **William Hazlitt writes** *The Spirit of the Age*

1826 — **Cooper publishes** *The Last of the Mohicans*

1827 — **John James Audubon publishes** *The Birds of America*

1828 — **Alexandre Dumas Père writes** *The Three Musketeers*

— **Noah Webster publishes** *American Dictionary of the English Language*

1829 — **Edgar Allan Poe completes "Al Araaf," "Tamerlane," and other poems**

— Frederic Chopin makes his debut in Austria

1832 — **Tennyson writes "Lady of Shalott"**

1833 — **Literary works include Charles Dickens's** *Sketches by Boz*; **Charles Lamb's** *Last Essays of Elia*; **George Sand's** *Lelia*

1835 — **Literary works include Hans Christian Anderson's fairy tales; William Wordsworth's poems; Robert Browning's** *Paracelsus*

1836 — **Ralph Waldo Emerson writes** *Nature*

1837 — **Nathaniel Hawthorne's** *Twice Told Tales* **enjoy popularity**

1838 — **Elizabeth Barrett Browning writes "The Seraphim" and other poems; Dickens enjoys popular success with** *Oliver Twist* **and** *Nicholas Nickleby*

1839 — **Poe completes "The Fall of the House of Usher"**

1840 — **Cooper publishes** *The Pathfinder*

1841 — **Literary works include Robert Browning's "Pippa Passes"; Cooper's** *Deerslayer*; **Dickens's** *Old Curiosity Shop*; **James Russell Lowell's poems; Emerson's** *Essays, First Series*

— Women granted university degrees for first time in United States

1844 — **Emerson publishes** *Essays, Second Series*

— **Dumas Père writes** *The Count of Monte Cristo*

1845 — **Poe writes "The Raven"**

1847 — **Literary works include Charlotte Bronte's** *Jane Eyre*; **Emily Bronte's** *Wuthering Heights*; **Thackeray's** *Vanity Fair*

1848 — Revolutions erupt in France, Germany, and other nations as republicans try unsuccessfully to overthrow monarchies

1849 — **Dickens completes** *David Copperfield*

— Gold rush begins in California

1850 — **Nathaniel Hawthorne publishes** *The Scarlet Letter*

— **Elizabeth Barrett Browning completes** *Sonnets from the Portuguese*

1851 — **Herman Melville writes** *Moby Dick*

— **Hawthorne writes** *The House of the Seven Gables*

1852 — **Harriet Beecher Stowe publishes** *Uncle Tom's Cabin*

— Liszt, Wagner, Verdi, and Schumann dominate the musical scene

1854–56—Crimean War pits Turkey, France, and Britain against Russia

1855 — **Major poems include Longfellow's "The Song of Hiawatha"; Tennyson's "Maud";**
Walt Whitman's *Leaves of Grass*

1856 — **Gustave Flaubert completes** *Madame Bovary*

1857 — *Atlantic Monthly* **magazine begins publication**

— Jean-François Millet paints *The Gleaners*

— Louis Pasteur conducts important medical experiments

1859 — **Dickens publishes** *A Tale of Two Cities*

— **Tennyson writes** *Idylls of the King*

— **Karl Marx, John Stuart Mill, and Charles Darwin exert major influence on political**
and scientific thought

1860 — **George Eliot completes** *The Mill on the Floss*

— Edgar Degas and Edouard Manet emerge as major figures in the visual arts

1861 — **Literary works include George Eliot's** *Silas Marner;* **Dostoyevsky's** *House of the Dead;*
Dickens's *Great Expectations*

— Abraham Lincoln inaugurated as president of the United States; Civil War begins as
Confederate states secede from Union

1864 — **Leo Tolstoy completes** *War and Peace*

1865 — **Lewis Carroll writes** *Alice's Adventures in Wonderland*

— Civil War ends in the United States; slavery is abolished

1866 — **Dostoyevsky completes** *Crime and Punishment*

1868 — **Louisa May Alcott writes** *Little Women*

— **Dostoyevsky writes** *The Idiot*

1869 — **Twain publishes** *Innocents Abroad*

1870 — Franco-Prussian War leads to the unification of Germany under Prussian leadership

1873 — **Tolstoy completes** *Anna Karenina*

— Tchaikovsky, Rimsky-Korsakov, Bruckner, Brahms, and Mossorgsky compose
important musical works

1875 — **Twain completes** *The Adventures of Tom Sawyer*

1880 — **Dostoyevsky writes** *The Brothers Karamazov*

— Electric lights developed

1882 — **Robert Louis Stevenson writes** *Treasure Island*

— **Henrik Ibsen completes** *An Enemy of the People*

1884 — **Twain publishes** *Huckleberry Finn*

1886 — *Das Kapital* by Karl Marx published in English

1887 — **First Sherlock Holmes Story, "A Study in Scarlet"**

— Vincent Van Gogh produces some of his greatest paintings

1890 — First moving pictures are exhibited

— **Oscar Wilde writes** *The Picture of Dorian Gray*

— **William James publishes** *The Principles of Psychology*

1894 — **Rudyard Kipling writes** *The Jungle Books*

— **George Bernard Shaw writes** *Arms and the Man*

1895 — **H. G. Wells writes** *The Time Machine*

— **William Butler Yeats begins publishing poems**

1897 — **Literary works include Kipling's** *Captains Courageous*; **H. G. Wells's** *Invisible Man*; **George Bernard Shaw's** *Candida*; **Edmund Rostand's** *Cyrano de Bergerac*

1898 — **Literary works include Wells's** *War of the Worlds*; **Shaw's** *Caesar and Cleopatra*; **Henry James's** *Turn of the Screw*; **Thomas Hardy's** *Wessex Poems*

160. NEOCLASSICISM

The term neoclassicism usually refers to periods when writers imitated classical authors. This tendency was most prevalent in English literature from about 1660 to 1780. Neoclassical writers modeled their works on the classicism of the Greeks and Romans, concentrating on literary principles such as balance, harmony, purity of form, reason, and humanism. See also List 154, Classicism.

FRENCH NEOCLASSICAL PERIOD (SEVENTEENTH CENTURY)

Pierre Corneille (tragedies)

Jean Racine (tragedies)

Molière (comedies)

Blaise Pascal (religious philosophy)

François la Rochefoucauld (epigrams)

Jean de la Fontaine (fables)

ENGLISH NEOCLASSICAL PERIOD (SEVENTEENTH AND EIGHTEENTH CENTURIES)

John Dryden (essays; poetry)

Alexander Pope (essays; poetry)

Joseph Addison (poetry; essays; drama)

Sir Richard Steele (essays; drama)

Samuel Johnson (essays; poetry)

Edward Gibbon (history)

Edward Hyde (history)

Oliver Goldsmith (essays; poetry; drama; novels)

Jonathan Swift (satire; poetry)

John Gay (poetry; drama)

GERMAN NEOCLASSICAL PERIOD (EIGHTEENTH AND NINETEENTH CENTURIES)

Gotthold Leasing (drama; criticism)

Johann Herder (history; philosophy)

Friedrich von Schiller (drama; poetry; history)

Friedrich Holderlin (poetry; novels)

Johann Wolfgang von Goethe (poetry; drama; novels; natural science)

161. BRITISH LITERATURE PERIODS

These eras are commonly referred to as the basic periods of British literature. Different authorities may use somewhat different time schemes and terminology; the general literary eras and dates are listed below. Comments on major writings or authors are in parentheses. See also List 129, Authors by Group; List 186, Middle English Period; List 165, England in the Fourteenth Century (Chaucer's *Canterbury Tales*); and List 166, The Romantic Period (1786–1832).

450–1066 OLD ENGLISH/ANGLO SAXON PERIOD (*Beowulf*)

1066–1550 The Middle English Period

1066–1350 Anglo-Norman Period (miracle plays; ballads)

1350–1400 Age of Chaucer (*Canterbury Tales*)

1400–1550 Revival of Learning (More's *Utopia; Everyman;* Malory's *Morte d'Arthur*)

1550–1625 ELIZABETHAN AGE (Shakespeare, Bacon, Marlowe, Spenser)

1550–1603 Elizabethan Age

1603–1625 Jacobean Age

1625–1660 PURITAN PERIOD (Walton, Milton, Bunyan)

1625–1649 Caroline Age

1649–1660 Commonwealth Period (Puritan Interregnum)

1660–1780 THE NEOCLASSICAL PERIOD (Age of Reason)

1660–1700 Restoration Period (Dryden; Pepys)

1700–1740 Classicism (Age of Pope; The Augustan Age)

1740–1780 Age of Johnson (Age of Sensibility)

1780–1840 ROMANTIC PERIOD (Burns, Keats, Shelley, Scott, Byron, Austen)

1840–1900 Victorian Period (Hardy, Stevenson, Browning, Dickens, Tennyson, Bronte sisters)

1848–1860 The Pre-Raphaelites (Christina and Dante Rossetti, Swinburne)

1860–1900 Aestheticism and Decadence (Wilde, Hopkins)

1900–2000 TWENTIETH CENTURY (Hardy, Conrad, Kipling, Wells)

1901–1910 The Edwardian Period

1910–1914 The Georgian Period (Brooke; de la Mare; Hodgson)

1914–1939 The Modern Period (Auden; Sitwell family; MacNeice; Thomas; Joyce)

1939–present Postmodern Period

162. MIDDLE ENGLISH PERIOD

Geoffrey Chaucer, often called the "father of English poetry," wrote in Middle English, the transitional language (used about 1000–1500) between Old English and Modern English. His *Canterbury Tales* are considered by many to be the greatest work written in Middle English. Readers can test their comprehension of Middle English by tackling this passage from the *Prologue* to *The Canterbury Tales*.

> *Bifel that, in that sesoun on a day,*
> *In Southwerk at the Tabard as I lay*
> *Redy to wenden on my pilgrimage*
> *To Caunterbury with ful devout corage,*
> *At night was come in-to that hostelrye*
> *Wel nyne and twenty in a companye,*
> *Of sondry folk, by aventure y-falle*
> *In felawshipe, and pilgrims were they alle,*
> *That toward Caunterbury wolden ryde;*
> *The chambres and the stables weren wyde,*

And wel we weren esed atte beste.

And shortly, whan the sonne was to reste,

So hadde I spoken with hem everichon,

That I was of hir felawshipe anon,

And made forward erly for to ryse,

To take our wey, ther as I yow devyse.

But natheles, whyl I have tyme and space,

Ere that I farther in this tale pace,

Me thinketh it acordaunt to resoun,

To telle yow al the condicioun

Of ech of hem, so as it semed me,

And whiche they weren, and of what degree;

And eek in what array that they were inne:

And at a knight than wol I first biginne.

Hints on Meanings and Pronunciations:

hem: them

hir: their

ech: each

eek: also

Tabard: Tabard Inn in the town of Southwark, England

The vowel *a* is often pronounced as *ah*

The final *e* on many words is pronounced as another syllable (*uh*)
    Example: *space* = SPAH-suh

All consonants are pronounced
    Example: *knee* = *cuh*-NEE

Remember, Chaucer is using iambic pentameter couplets. It might help to think of the rhythm of most lines as tuh-DAH, tud-DAH, tud-DAH, tuh-DAH, tuh-DAH. See List 164, Modern Translation of Middle English Language.

163. Modern Translation of Middle English Language

The following represents a rough translation of part of the *Prologue* from *The Canterbury Tales*. See List 163, for Middle English period.

> It came to pass, in that season on a day,
>
> In Southwark at the Tabard Inn as I lay
>
> Ready to wend my way on my pilgrimage
>
> To Canterbury with a full, devout heart,
>
> At night there came into that inn
>
> At least twenty-nine people in a group,
>
> Of sundry folks, by chance thrown together
>
> In fellowship, and pilgrims were they all,
>
> That would ride toward Canterbury;
>
> The rooms and the stables were large,
>
> And we were set at ease in the best way.
>
> And shortly, when the sun went down,
>
> I had so spoken with everyone,
>
> That I was of their fellowship [friends] right away,
>
> And we agreed to get up early,
>
> To take our way, there as I describe to you.
>
> But nonetheless, while I have time and space,
>
> Before I further in this tale proceed,
>
> I think it according to reason,
>
> To tell you all the condition (social position and occupation)
>
> Of each of them, as it seemed to me,
>
> And who they were, and of what social class;
>
> And also how they were dressed:
>
> And with a knight then will I first begin.

NOTE: At this point in the poem, Chaucer introduces his first character, the Knight, and then continues to tell a bit about each of the people who will be traveling together and telling stories along the way.

The Canterbury Tales consists of prose and poetry about a group of pilgrims who tell stories to pass the time while traveling on horseback from London to the shrine of Saint Thomas à Becket in Canterbury, England. Through this cross-section of characters and the stories they tell, Chaucer gives a realistic view of varied social classes, conduct, and life in the fourteenth century. Each tale is preceded by a prologue, and some have an epilogue.

Chaucer indicates in the general *Prologue* that each person is going to tell four stories (two on the way to Canterbury and two on the way back to London). *The Canterbury Tales*, however, contains only twenty-four tales, and four of them are unfinished. One can only speculate why he did not complete the full complement of tales. Very brief comment is made on each tale below. Chaucer's spelling of characters' names is used, with modern spelling in parentheses.

Knight. Pseudo-historic romance set in Athens about two cousins after the same woman.

Squyer (Squire). Magician gives four gifts to Camuscan, the King of Tartar.

Yeman (Yeoman). Alchemist convinces a priest he can turn metal into gold.

Nonne (Nun, Prioress). Virgin Mary/Christ miracle.

Reve (Reeve, Supervisor). The miller steals from a college, and students try to bring him to justice.

Millere (Miller). John and another man like his wife; she likes another.

Somnour (Summoner). Thomas plans to humiliate the Friar.

Monk. Seventeen tragedies that befall famous men.

Frere (Friar). Friar befriends the bailiff (devil).

Merchant (Merchant). January marries May; when January loses his sight, May tries to help him get it back.

Clerk (Student). Walter tests Griselda's devotion.

Sergeant of the Lawe (Lawyer). Sultan of Syria converts to Christianity.

Frankeleyn (Franklin, country gentleman). Magician tries to help a man steal another man's wife.

Cook. Unfinished bawdy drinking tale.

Shipman (Sailor). A loan of money to a cousin and its unusual repayment by his wife.

Doctour of phisyk (Physician). Virginia must be killed by the judge or shamed by her lover.

Wyf of Bathe (Wife of Bath). Tells of rejecting celibacy, life with her many husbands, and tells an Arthurian fairy tale; trouble comes when women rule in marriage.

Persoun (Parson, priest). Sermon about sin and virtue.

Pardoner (Distributor of pardons). Gives a sermon about three partiers who die because of greed.

Maunicple (Manciple, purchasing agent). About a tattle-tale crow.

Nun's Priest. Mock-heroic "beast fable" of a fox and a cock trying to outsmart each other.

Second Nun. About Valerian and her ever-present angel.

Sir Thopas. Flanders Knight searching for elf-queen's love.

Melibeus (Melibee). Enemies beat his wife and kill his daughter; should he take revenge?

Carpenter

Haberdassher (Haberdasher, hat-seller)

Webbe (Webber, weaver)

Dyere (Dyer of cloth)

Tapicer (Upholsterer)

Plowman (Farmer)

Host

165. THE ROMANTIC PERIOD (1786-1832)

The term *Romantic* has been applied to a number of literary and artistic movements that flourished in Europe and the United States during the eighteenth and nineteenth centuries. Romanticism was essentially a reaction against Neoclassicism. Romantics exalted emotion, imagination, love of nature, and the ideal of liberty, in opposition to balance, reason, and strictly regulated order in art and society. Rejecting the legacy of Greece and Rome, Romantic artists often looked to the medieval era for inspiration, renewing interest in the legends and folklore of their own nations. In the present context, the Romantic Period comprises the years 1786 to 1832 in Britain. The first list includes major poets of the period, along with relatively little-known women poets who brought the era a distinctive point of view. For poetry of the women, see *Women Romantic Poets, 1785–1832* edited by Jennifer Breen (1992). The second list specifies the literary characteristics of the period.

BRITISH ROMANTIC POETS

Joanna Baillie
Anna Barbauld
Elizabeth Bentley
Matilda Bethem
William Blake
Robert Burns
Lord Byron
Thomas Campbell
Samuel T. Coleridge
Anna Dodsworth
Anne Grant
Elizabeth Hands
Felicia Hemans
Thomas Hood
Leigh Hunt

Anne Hunter
John Keats
Charles Lamb
Mary Lamb
Lititia E. Landon
Walter Landor
Helen Leigh
Eliza Mathews
Christian Milne
Elizabeth Moody
Thomas Moore
Hannah More
Carolina O. Nairne
Amelia Opie
Charlotte Richardson
Mary Robinson
Sir Walter Scott

Anna Seward
Percy Bysshe Shelley
Charlotte Smith
Robert Southey
Jane Taylor
Helen M. Williams
Dorothy Wordsworth
William Wordsworth

CHARACTERISTICS OF ROMANTIC LITERATURE

adventurous
aesthetic
antimaterialistic
antimechanistic
chivalrous
confessional

contemplative	interpretive	revelationary
creative	introspective	revolutionary
diverse	lyric	rustic
dreamlike	medieval	sensitive
eccentric	melancholic	sentimental
emotional	moody	sensuous
enthusiastic	mystic	simple
exotic	nationalistic	solitary
expansive	natural	speculative
fanciful	nature-oriented	spiritual
free	observant	supernatural
humanitarian	optimistic	symbolic
idealistic	passionate	transcendental
idiosyncratic	pensive	unconventional
imaginative	precise	Utopian
individualistic	primitive	visionary

166. MAJOR AMERICAN WRITERS BY LITERARY PERIODS

The **Colonial Period** (from about 1630 to 1760) was characterized by religious writings, histories, and diaries.

William Bradford — history

Anne Bradstreet — poetry

William Byrd — history

John Cotton — religious writings

Jonathan Edwards — sermon; autobiography

Benjamin Franklin — autobiography; almanac

Anne Hutchinson — religious writings

Sarah Kemble Knight — diary

Cotton Mather — church history

Thomas Morton — history

Mary Rowlandson — history of captivity by Indians

Samuel Sewall — diaries

Thomas Shepard — autobiography

Captain John Smith — history

Edward Taylor — poetry

Michael Wigglesworth — poetry

Roger Williams — religious writings

John Winthrop — history

The **Revolutionary Period** (from about 1760 to 1787) was characterized by pamphlets, letters, patriotic poetry, histories, journals, diaries, and political writings.

Abigail Adams — letters

John Adams — philosophical pamphlets

William Bertram — journal

Hugh Brackenridge — poetry

John Dickinson — letters

Philip Freneau — poetry

William Godfrey — drama (tragedy)

Alexander Hamilton — essays

John Jay — essays

Thomas Jefferson — Declaration of Independence

James Madison — essays

James Otis — pamphlets

Thomas Paine — political pamphlets

John Trumbull — poetry; satires

Royall Tyler — drama (comedy)

Phillis Wheatley — poetry

John Woolman — journals

The **National Period** (from about 1828 to 1836) produced a variety of novels, poetry, satire, and short stories, and distinctively American literature began. An earlier period, from about 1775 to 1828 when Jacksonian democracy triumphed, is sometimes called the **Early National Period**. These writers are also included here.

Hugh Brackenridge — novels

Charles Brockden Brown — Gothic novels

William Hill Brown — novels

William Cullen Bryant — poetry

James Fenimore Cooper — novels

Ralph Waldo Emerson — essays

Philip Freneau — lyric poetry

Oliver Wendell Holmes — poetry

Washington Irving — satires; tales; essays; stories

Henry Wadsworth Longfellow — poetry

Edgar Allan Poe — short stories; poetry (originated detective story)

John Trumbull — epic poems

Royall Tyler — dramas

Noah Webster — dictionary

John Greenleaf Whittier — poetry

The **American Renaissance Period** (from about 1830 to 1860) includes the Romantic movement and the Transcendentalists, with many writings about nature and self-reliance. Writers from the National Period are included here because they continued to produce major literature during the Renaissance Period. See List 148, Transcendentalists.

William Cullen Bryant — poetry

James Fenimore Cooper — novels

Emily Dickinson — poetry

Ralph Waldo Emerson — essays; poetry

Nathaniel Hawthorne — novels; short stories

Washington Irving — tales

Henry Wadsworth Longfellow — poetry

James Russell Lowell — critical essays

Herman Melville — novels; short stories

Edgar Allan Poe — short stories; poetry;

William Gilmore Simms — critical essays

Harriet Beecher Stowe — novels

Henry David Thoreau — essays

John Greenleaf Whittier — poetry

Walt Whitman — poetry

The **Post–Civil War/Pre–World War I Period** includes the period of the Industrial Revolution, rapid urbanization, and western expansion. It marked the emergence of fiction with a marked regional focus and a literary shift from romanticism to realism and naturalism.

Henry Adams — satiric novel; autobiography

Ambrose Bierce — fiction

William Wells Brown — fiction

Willa Cather — fiction (Midwest and Southwest)

Charles Chesnutt — fiction (South)

Kate Chopin — fiction (Louisiana)

Frederick Douglass — autobiography

W. E. B. Du Bois — history, sociology, and race relations

T. S. Eliot — poetry

Ralph Waldo Emerson — war poetry

Mark Wilkins Freeman — fiction (Massachusetts)

Robert Frost — poetry

Hamlin Garland — fiction (Midwest)

Ulysses S. Grant — autobiography

Joel Chandler Harris — Uncle Remus stories

Bret Harte — fiction (West)

Thomas Wentworth Higginson — autobiography

William Dean Howells — novels; criticism

Henry James — novels; criticism

Sarah Orne Jewett — fiction (Maine)

James Weldon Johnson — autobiography

Vachel Lindsay — poetry

Jack London — adventure novels

James Russell Lowell — war poetry

Edgar Lee Masters — poetry

Herman Melville — novels

Ezra Pound — poetry

Edwin Arlington Robinson — poetry

Carl Sandburg — poetry; biography

Upton Sinclair — social protest

Mark Twain — novels

Booker T. Washington — biography

Edith Wharton — fiction

Walt Whitman — poetry

The **Post–World War I Period** spawned the "Lost Generation" of the 1920s and included literary modernism, with novels and drama the predominant genres.

Maxwell Anderson — dramas

Sherwood Anderson — novels

Philip Barry — dramas

e. e. cummings — poetry

William Faulkner — novels

F. Scott Fitzgerald — novels

Lillian Hellman — dramas

Ernest Hemingway — novels

Ring Lardner — sports novels

D. H. Lawrence — criticism

Sinclair Lewis — novels

H. L. Mencken — essays

Marianne Moore — poetry

Eugene O'Neill — dramas

V. L. Parrington — criticism; history of American literature

Elmer Rice — dramas

Gertrude Stein — criticism; drama; memoir; novels

Thornton Wilder — dramas

Tennessee Williams — dramas

William Carlos Williams — poetry; short stories

Thomas Wolfe — novels

The **Protest/Proletarian Period** (1930s to World War II) included political and social protest writings, detective and other short stories, novels, plays, and the "new criticism."

Richard Blackmur — criticism

Cleanth Brooks — criticism

James M. Cain — detective stories

Raymond T. Chandler — detective stories

John Cheever — short stories

John Dos Passos — novels; proletarian literature

John O'Hara — short stories; novels

James T. Farrell — novels; criticism; poetry

William Faulkner — novels

Dashiell Hammett — detective stories

Zora Neale Hurston — novels

Sidney Kingsley — dramas

Meyer Levin — novels; proletarian literature

Carson McCullers — short stories

Flannery O'Connor — short stories

Clifford Odets — dramas

Katherine Anne Porter — short stories

John Crowe Ransom — criticism

John Steinbeck — novels

Wallace Stevens — poetry

Allen Tate — criticism

Robert Penn Warren — criticism; novels

Eudora Welty — short stories; novels

Yvor Winters — criticism

The **Post–World War II Period** included war novels and memoirs; a resurgence of drama; black literature; antiwar literature; feminist literature; and a variety of experimental forms. See also List 168, 1950s Fiction from Around the World; List 169, 1960s Fiction from Around the World; List 170, 1970s Fiction from Around the World; List 171, 1980s Fiction from Around the World; and List 172, 1990s Fiction from Around the World.

Edward Albee — dramas

John Ashbery — poetry

Louis Auchincloss — novels; short stories

James Baldwin — novels; essays; short stories

Imamu Amiri Baraka — poetry; plays

John Barth — novels; criticism

Donald Barthelme — short stories

Saul Bellow — novels

Elizabeth Bishop — poetry

Robert Bly — poetry

Gwendolyn Brooks — poetry

Truman Capote — nonfiction; novels

Eldridge Cleaver — essays; letters

Joan Didion — novels; essays

Ralph Ellison — novel; essays

Frances Fitzgerald — journalistic prose

Betty Friedan — feminist nonfiction

Allen Ginsberg — poetry

Nikki Giovanni — poetry; autobiography

Herbert Gold — novels

Lorraine Hansberry — drama

John Hawkes — novel

Joseph Heller — novel

Michael Herr — memoirs

Elizabeth Janeway — novels; feminist essays

Randall Jarrell — poetry

James Jones — war novels

Denise Levertov — feminist poetry

Robert Lowell — poetry

Norman Mailer — nonfiction; novels

Bernard Malamud — novels

Mary McCarthy — journalistic prose

James Merrill — poetry

W. S. Merwin — poetry

Arthur Miller — dramas

Kate Millett — memoir; novels; feminist
  nonfiction

Wright Morris — fiction

Toni Morrison — novels

Vladimir Nabokov — novels

Joyce Carol Oates — novels; short stories; plays

Tim O'Brien — novels

Tillie Olsen — novel; short stories

Charles Olson — poetry

Grace Paley — short stories

Walker Percy — novels

Sylvia Plath — poetry

Thomas Pynchon — novels

Ishmael Reed — novels; poetry

Adrienne Rich — feminist poetry

Theodore Roethke — poetry

Philip Roth — novels; short stories

J. D. Salinger — novels; short stories

Delmore Schwartz — poetry

Anne Sexton — feminist poetry

Karl Shapiro — poetry

Gary Snyder — poetry

Susan Sontag — journalistic prose; novel

Robert Stone — novels

Peter Taylor — fiction

John Updike — novels; essays

Gore Vidal — historical novels

Kurt Vonnegut, Jr. — novels

Alice Walker — novels

Robert Penn Warren — poetry; novels; criticism

Eudora Welty — short stories

Richard Wilbur — poetry

Thornton Wilder — dramas

Tennessee Williams — dramas

Tom Wolfe — journalistic prose; novels

James Wright — poetry

Richard Wright — novels; nonfiction;
  short stories

167. 1950s FICTION FROM AROUND THE WORLD

See also List 169, 1960s Fiction from Around the World; List 170, 1970s Fiction from Around the World; List 171, 1980s Fiction from Around the World; and List 172, 1990s Fiction from Around the World.

Anatomy of a Murder — Robert Traver

Atlas Shrugged — Ayn Rand

Bonjour Tristesse — Francoise Sagan

The Catcher in the Rye — J. D. Salinger

The Collected Stories — Isaac Babel

The Cypresses Believe in God — Jose Gironella

A Death in the Family — James Agee

Doctor Zhivago — Boris Pasternak

The Dwarf — Pär Lagerkvist

From Here to Eternity — James Jones

From the Terrace — John O'Hara

Goodbye, Columbus — Philip Roth

The Grass — Claude Simon

Hurry on Down — John Wain

Justine — Lawrence Durrell

The Last Hurrah — Edwin O'Conner

Lie Down in Darkness — William Styron

Lolita — Vladimir Nabokov

Lord of the Flies — William Gelding

The Lord of the Rings — J. R. R. Tolkien

Love Among the Cannibals — Wright Morris

Lucky Jim — Kingsley Amis

Malcolm — James Purdy

Memoirs of Hadrian — Marguerite Yourcenar

Morte d'Urban — J. F. Powers

The Once and Future King — T. H. White

On the Road — Jack Kerouac

Pedro Paramo — Juan Rulfo

Saturday Night and Sunday Morning — Alan Sillitoe

A Separate Peace — John Knowles

South American Jungle Tales — Horacio Quiroga

Things Fall Apart — Chinua Achebe

Thousand Cranes — Yasunari Kawabata

The Tin Drum — Gunter Grass

The Ugly American — William J. Lederer and Eugene Burdick

Under the Net — Iris Murdoch

The Villagers — Jorge Icaza

See List 168, 1950s Fiction from Around the World; List 170, 1970s Fiction from Around the World; List 171, 1980s Fiction from Around the World; and List 172, 1990s Fiction from Around the World.

The Agony and the Ecstasy — Irving Stone

The Andromeda Strain — Michael Crichton

Another Country — James Baldwin

A Beggar in Jerusalem — Elie Wiesel

The Bell Jar — Sylvia Plath

Billiards at Half-Past Nine — Heinrich Böll

Caravans — James Michener

Catch-22 — Joseph Heller

The Chosen — Chaim Potok

A Clockwork Orange — Anthony Burgess

Collected Short Stories — John Cheever

Collected Short Stories — Katherine Anne Porter

The Death of Artemio Cruz — Carlos Fuentes

Enormous Changes at the Last Minute — Grace Paley

Ficciones — Jorge Luis Borges

The Fixer — Bernard Malamud

The French Lieutenant's Woman — John Fowles

The Gabriel Hounds — Mary Stewart

The Garrick Year — Margaret Drabble

The Golden Notebook — Doris Lessing

The Green House — Mario Vargas Llosa

Hopscotch — Julio Cortazar

Hue and Cry — James McPherson

In Cold Blood — Truman Capote

The Interpreters — Wole Soyinka

The Keepers of the House — Shirley Ann Grau

The Left Hand of Darkness — Ursula Le Guin

The Leopard — Giuseppe di Lampedusa

The Loneliness of the Long Distance Runner — Allan Sillitoe

Manchild in the Promised Land — Claude Brown

The Man Who Cried I Am — John A. Williams

The Martyred — Richard E. Kim

The Moviegoer — Walker Percy

Myra Breckinridge — Gore Vidal

One Day in the Life of Ivan Denisovich — Alexander Solzhenitsyn

One Flew Over the Cuckoo's Nest — Ken Kesey

One Hundred Years of Solitude — Gabriel García Márquez

The Pawnbroker — Edward Wallant

Pinktoes — Chester Himes

Rabbit, Run — John Updike

Ship of Fools — Katherine Anne Porter

Slaughterhouse-Five — Kurt Vonnegut

Some Prefer Nettles — Junichiro Tanizaki

The Sot-Weed Factor — John Barth

The Spire — William Golding

Stern — Bruce Friedman

Them — Joyce Carol Oates

To Kill a Mockingbird — Harper Lee

Wide Sargasso Sea — Jean Rhys

The Winter of Our Discontent — John Steinbeck

The Woman in the Dunes — Kobo Abe

169. 1970s FICTION FROM AROUND THE WORLD

See List 168, 1950s Fiction from Around the World; List 169, 1960s Fiction from Around the World; List 171, 1980s Fiction from Around the World; and List 172, 1990s Fiction from Around the World.

August 1914 — Alexander Solzhenitsyn

Beyond the Bedroom Wall — Larry Woiwode

Breakfast of Champions — Kurt Vonnegut, Jr.

Burger's Daughter — Nadine Gordimer

Car — Harry Crews

Chesapeake — James Michener

Corregidora — Gayle Jones

A Crown of Feathers and Other Stories — Isaac Bashevis Singer

Curtain — Agatha Christie

Deliverance — James Dickey

Even Cowgirls Get the Blues — Tom Robbins

Eye of the Needle — Ken Follett

Final Payments — Mary Gordon

Fools Die — Mario Puzo

Gravity's Rainbow — Thomas Pynchon

Grendl — John Gardner

How to Save Your Own Life — Erica Jong

Humboldt's Gift — Saul Bellow

I, Etcetera — Susan Sontag

Jaws — Peter Benchley

The Killer Angels — Michael Shaara

The Last Catholic in America — John R. Powers

The Lonely Passion of Judith Hearne — Brian Moore

Love Story — Erich Segal

Mr. Sammler's Planet — Saul Bellow

My Name Is Asher Lev — Chaim Potok

People Will Always be Kind — Wilfred Sheed

Play it as it Lays — Joan Didion

The Public Burning — Robert Coover

Rabbit Redux — John Updike

Ragtime — E. L. Doctorow

Son of the Morning — Joyce Carol Oates

Strange Things Happen Here — Luisa Valenzuela

Sula — Toni Morrison

Tell me a Riddle and Other Stories — Tillie Olsen

The Tenants — Bernard Malamud

The Thorn Birds — Colleen McCullough

Tinker, Tailor, Soldier, Spy — John Le Carre

Trinity — Leon Uris

War and Remembrance — Herman Wouk

Watership Down — Richard Adams

170. 1980s Fiction from Around the World

See List 168, 1950s Fiction from around the World; List 169, 1960s Fiction from around the World; List 170, 1970s Fiction from around the World; and List 172, 1990s Fiction from around the World.

The Care of Time — Eric Ambler

Collected Stories — Isaac Bashevis Singer

Collected Stories — Eudora Welty

The Color Purple — Alice Walker

A Confederacy of Dunces — John Kennedy Toole

Dinner at the Homesick Restaurant — Anne Tyler

The Dirty Duck — Martha Grimes

Devices and Desires — P. D. James

Famous Last Words — Timothy Findley

A Flag for Sunrise — Robert Stone

The Fourth Protocol — Frederick Forsyth

Gone to Soldiers — Marge Piercy

Gorky Park — Martin Cruz Smith

A House of Stairs — Barbara Vine

Housekeeping — Marilynne Robinson

The Icarus Agenda — Robert Ludlum

If on a Winter's Night a Traveler — Italo Calvino

Jealousy — Alain Robbe-Grillet

Levitation: Five Fictions — Cynthia Ozick

Lie Down with Lions — Kenneth Follett

The Little Drummer Girl — John Le Carre

Love in the Time of Cholera — Gabriel García Márquez

The Lover — Marguerite Duras

Mantissa — John Fowles

A Married Man — Piers Paul Read

A Matter of Honor — Jeffrey Archer

Midnight's Children — Salman Rushdie

A Mother and Two Daughters — Gail Godwin

Mr. Polomar — Italo Calvino

Mrs. Pollifax and the Hong Kong Buddha — Dorothy Gilman

Night of the Fox — Jack Higgins

A Pale Horse — Helen Clark MacInnes

Pinball — Jerzy Kosinski

Prizzi's Honor — Richard Condon

Quartet in Autumn — Horacio Quiroga

The Radiant Way — Margaret Drabble

Rainsong — Phyllis Whitney

Riddley Walker — Russell Hoban

Rights of Passage — William Golding

Sabah Al-Ward — Naguib Mahfouz

Shoeless Joe — W. P. Kinsella

Something Out There — Nadine Gordimer

Souls and Bodies — David Lodge

Spartina — John Casey

Straight — Dick Francis

A Trap for Fools — Amanda Cross

The White Hotel — D. M. Thomas

A Winter's Tale — Mark Helprin

The Women of Brewster Place — Gloria Naylor

World's End — T. Coraghessan Boyle

See List 168, 1950s Fiction from Around the World; List 169, 1960s Fiction from Around the World; List 170, 1970s Fiction from Around the World; and List 171, 1980s Fiction from Around the World. Also check newspaper best-seller lists such as those of the *New York Times* and *Los Angeles Times*.

All the Pretty Horses — Cormac McCarthy

Antoinetta — John Hersey

At Weddings and Wakes — Alice McDermott

Blue Calhoun — Reynolds Price

The Campaign — Carlos Fuentes

Dark Force Rising — Timothy Zahn

The English Patient — Michael Ondaatje

The Evening Star — Larry McMurtry

Eye of the World — Robert Jordan

Guardian Angel — Sara Paretsky

A Hand Full of Stars — Rafik Schami

Haroun and the Sea of Stories — Salman Rushdie

In the Fire of Spring — Thomas Tryon

Jazz — Toni Morrison

Joe — Larry Brown

The Kitchen God's Wife — Amy Tan

Lazarus — Morris West

The Living — Annie Dillard

The Lost Father — Mona Simpson

Mao II — Don DeLillo

Maus II, A Survivor's Tale: And Here My Troubles Began — Art Spiegelman

My Sister the Moon — Sue Harrison

On Fortune's Wheel — Cynthia Voigt

The Pelican Brief — John Grisham

Possessing the Secret of Joy — Alice Walker

Queen of the Summer Stars — Persia Woolley

Rice Without Rain — Minfong Ho

Rise of Life on Earth — Joyce Carol Oates

Saint Maybe — Anne Tyler

Shadows — John Saul

A Soldier of the Great War — Mark Helprin

The Stories of John Edgar Wideman — John Edgar Wideman

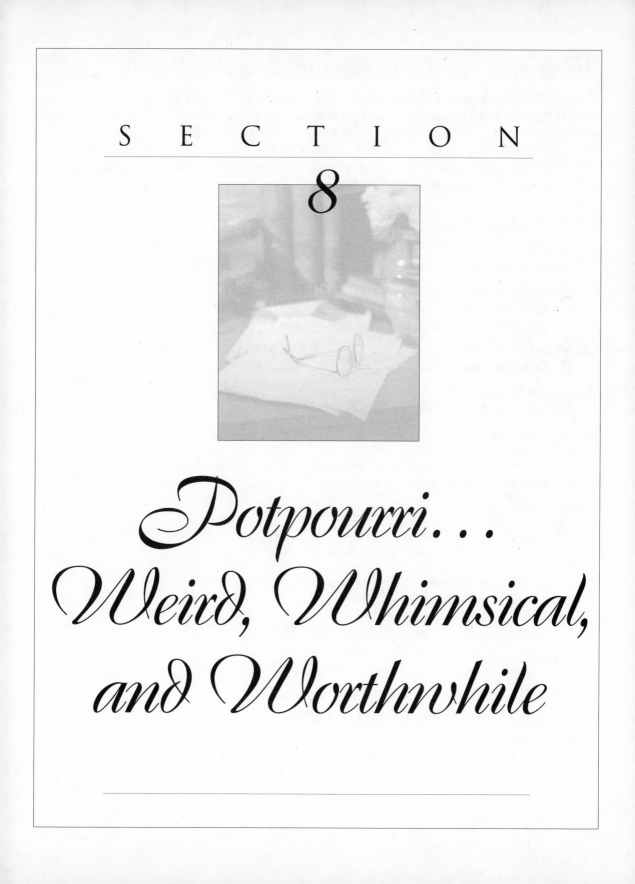

Potpourri...
Weird, Whimsical,
and Worthwhile

172. ANONYMOUSLY WRITTEN BOOKS AND CURRENT VALUES

Many older books, some of which are classics now, were first published without the author's name on the title page. Readers who find any of these in an attic, garage sale, secondhand store, or flea market have found a valuable treasure — if the books are in good condition. The reward may come in the form of money or simply in the form of reading pleasure, but it will be worthwhile either way. This list shows the author, title, and date of publication. The four lists are arranged in order of the general estimated value of the books.

LOWER VALUE

Jane Austen
(2 volumes) *Elizabeth Bennett; or, Pride and Prejudice: Novel* (1832)

James Fenimore Cooper
(3 volumes) *The Bee-Hunter; or, The Oak Openings* (1848)
(3 volumes) *The Chainbearer; or, The Littlepage Manuscripts* (1845)

Leigh Hunt
The Feast of the Poets. By the Editor of the *Examiner* (1814)

Washington Irving
Biography of James Lawrence, Esq. (1813)

Walter Savage Landor
Count Julian: A Tragedy (1812)
(2 volumes) *Imaginary Conversations of Literary Men and Statesmen* (1824)
Legends of the Conquest of Spain (1835)

James Russell Lowell
Class Poem (1838)
A Fable for Critics (1848)

Sir Walter Scott
(3 volumes) *Anne of Geierstein; or, The Maiden of the Mist* (1829)
(3 volumes) *The Antiquary* (1816)
(3 volumes) *The Fortunes of Nigel* (1822)
(3 volumes) *Guy Mannering; or, The Astrologer* (1872)

Alfred Lord Tennyson
In Memoriam (1850)

Edward John Trelawny
(3 volumes) *The Adventures of a Younger Son* (1831)

John Greenleaf Whittier
Leaves from Margaret Smith's Journal (1848)

Oscar Wilde

The Importance of Being Earnest. By the Author of *Lady Windermere's Fan* (1899)
An Ideal Husband. By the Author of *Lady Windermere's Fan* (1899)

MIDDLE VALUE

Elizabeth Barrett Browning

An Essay on Mind, with Other Poems (1826)

Samuel Langhorne Clemens (Mark Twain)

Date 1601. Conversation as it was by the Social Fireside, in the Times of the Tudors (1882)

James Fenimore Cooper

(3 volumes) *The Borderers: A Tale by the Author of 'The Spy'* (1829)
(3 volumes) *The Bravo: A Venetian Story* (1831)
(3 volumes) *The Headsman* (1833)
(3 volumes) *The Heidenmauer; or, The Benedictines* (1832)
(2 volumes) *Home as Found.* By the Author of *Homeward Bound* (1838)
(2 volumes) *The Oak Openings; or, The Bee-Hunter.* By the Author of *The Pioneers* (1848)

T. S. Eliot

Ezra Pound: His Metric and Poetry (1917)

Oliver Wendell Holmes

The Autocrat of the Breakfast Table (1858)

Charles Lamb

The Adventures of Ulysses (1808)
Beauty and the Beast (c. 1810)
A Brief History of Christ's Hospital (1820)
Elia: Essays which have Appeared under that Signature in the London Magazine (1823)
An Eyewitness. Satan in Search of a Wife (1831)
John Woodvil: A Tragedy (1802)

Henry Wadsworth Longfellow

(2 volumes) *Hyperion: A Romance.* By the Author of *Outre-Mer* (1839)

Herman Melville

John Marr and Other Sailors (1888)

George Gordon Noel (Lord Byron)

Beppo, A Venetian Story (1818)

Sir Walter Scott

(3 volumes) *Kenilworth* (1821)

Mary Wollstonecraft Shelley

(3 volumes) *Falkner: A Novel* (1837)
(3 volumes) *The Fortunes of Perkin Warbeck* (1830)

Walt Whitman
   Memoranda: Democratic Vistas (1871)

John Greenleaf Whittier
   Justice and Expediency; or, Slavery Considered with a View to Its Rightful and Effectual Remedy, Abolition (1833)

William Butler Yeats
   Ganconagh, John Sherman and Dhoya (1891)

HIGHER VALUE

Jane Austen
   (3 volumes) *Emma.* By the Author of *Pride and Prejudice* (1816)

William Cullen Bryant
   The Embargo, or Sketches of the Times; A Satire by a Youth of Thirteen (1808)

James Fenimore Cooper
   (2 volumes) *The Deerslayer; or, The First War-Path.* By the Author of *The Last of the Mohicans* (1882)
   (2 volumes) *The Last of the Mohicans.* By the Author of *The Pioneers* (1826)
   (2 volumes) *The Redskins* (1846)
   (2 volumes) *Satanstoe; or, The Littlepage Manuscripts* (1845)

Ralph Waldo Emerson
   Nature (1836)

Thomas Hardy
   (3 volumes) *Desperate Remedies: A Novel* (1871)

Aldous Huxley
   Jonah: Christmas (1917)

Walter Savage Landor
   The Dun Cow: An Hyper-Satyrical Dialogue in Verse (1808)

Edward Lear
   Derry Down Derry: A Book of Nonsense (1846)

Archibald MacLeish
   Class Poem (1915)

George Gordon Noel (Lord Byron)
   The Curse of Minerva (1812)
   English Bards and Scotch Reviewers (1809)
   Ode to Napoleon Buonoparte (1814)

Edgar Allan Poe
   The Narrative of Arthur Gordon Pym (1838)

Sir Walter Scott

    (3 volumes) *Ivanhoe: A Romance* (1820)

    (3 volumes) *Quentin Durward* (1823)

Mary Wollstonecraft Shelley

    Frankenstein; or, The Modern Prometheus (1818)

    (3 volumes) *The Last Man* (1826)

Percy Bysshe Shelley

    Epipsychidion: Verses, Etc. (1821)

    History of a Six Weeks' Tour Through a Part of France, Switzerland, Germany, and Holland (1817)

John Smith

    Capt. Smith and Princess Pocahontas: An Indian Tale (Undated)

Robert Louis Stevenson

    An Appeal to the Clergy of the Church of Scotland (1875)

Johann David Wyss

    (2 volumes) *The Family Robinson Crusoe* (1814)

HIGHEST VALUE

Robert Browning

    Pauline: A Fragment of a Confession (1833)

Nathaniel Hawthorne

    Fanshawe: A Tale (1828)

173. BOOK TERMINOLOGY

Americana — any published matter about North America

anonymous — writing that does not show the author's name

backstrip (spine) — narrow end of book visible when it is on a shelf

belles-lettres — aesthetically valuable literature

bibliography — list of titles in alphabetical order by subject or author

bibliophile — book-lover

bibliophobe — book-hater

bibliopole — book dealer in rare or unique books

binding (covers) — outside parts of book that protect pages from wear

blind stamping — blank letters or designs impressed on book's surface with no coloring, gold filling, etc.

bookplate — ownership label pasted in book

Books in Print — annual multivolume directory containing all currently available books

case (binding) — book cover (not to be confused with dust jacket)

colophon — notice of publisher, typographical details, or other information found either at back of book (older books) or on copyright page (newer books)

copyright page — usually carried on back of title page, providing copyright date, publisher, and other information

dust jacket — printed paper cover that protects the book case

elephant folio — refers to a huge book (size of newspaper)

endpapers — paper pasted onto inside covers of the book

errata slip — printed slip of paper pasted or inserted freely into book to show and correct errors discovered after printing

folio — refers to oversize book, about twelve inches tall or more

foxed (foxing) — "rusting" of pages in older books caused by decomposition of iron oxide in the paper

genre — category of literature (Ex: detective story; novel; western)

half-title (bastard title) — extra book title page with nothing else but the title

hinge — area where covers of book attach to the backstrip or spine

in print — books currently available from a publisher

limited edition — work of which only a specific number of copies were printed

literary — pertaining to writers or books

mainstream — current trend

mint condition — like-new condition

octavo (8vo) — refers to typical hardbound novel size, about eight inches tall

out-of-print — not currently available from a publisher

pirated edition — work reprinted illegally

points — identifying traits that identify edition, issue, or condition of book (Ex: errors, typefaces, errata slips)

rebound (recased) — referring to a book binding that has been replaced

recto — right-hand page of book

rubbed — frayed, worn, or scuffed book binding

scout — person who finds, buys, and sells rare books

shaken — describes a book with pages that are coming loose

verso — left-hand page of book

woodcut — picture made from inked wood blocks (usually in older books)

wraps (wrappers) — paper or flexible material used as book cover

174. DEWEY DECIMAL CLASSIFICATION

The most widely used book classification system in the world is the Dewey Decimal Classification, invented by Melvil Dewey in 1873. The system is used by 95 percent of the public and school libraries in the United States, and in hundreds of other countries. (Most college and university libraries use the Library of Congress system. See List 185, Library of Congress Classification System.) The basic tenet of Dewey's system, which divides the entire world of knowledge into categories so that books can be readily retrieved, is that categories are arranged by discipline (not by subject). This means that information on a particular *subject* will be found in many parts of the library according to the *discipline* involved. Books on *dogs*, for example, might be found under *folklore, literature, music, sculpture, photography, recreation,* and other disciplines. The following list defines the main divisions of the Dewey Decimal system. See also List 176, Dewey Decimal Literature Subdivisions and List 177, Dewey Decimal Breakdowns of Special Interest.

000–099 GENERAL WORKS
010 Bibliography
020 Library Science
030 General Encyclopedias
040 General Collected Essays
050 General Periodicals
060 General Societies
070 Newspaper Journalism
080 Collected Works
090 Manuscripts and Rare Books

100–199 PHILOSOPHY
110 Metaphysics
120 Metaphysical Theories
130 Branches of Psychology
140 Philosophical Topics
150 General Psychology
160 Logic
170 Ethics
180 Ancient and Medieval
190 Modern Philosophy

200–299 RELIGION
210 Natural Theology
220 Bible
230 Doctrinal Theology
240 Devotional and Practical
250 Pastoral Theology
260 Christian Church
270 Christian Church History
280 Christian Churches and Sects
290 Other Religions

300–399 SOCIAL SCIENCES
310 Statistics
320 Political Science
330 Economics
340 Law
350 Public Administration
360 Social Welfare
370 Education
380 Public Services and Utilities
390 Customs and Folklore

400–499 LANGUAGE

410 Comparative Linguistics
420 English and Anglo-Saxon
430 Germanic Languages
440 French, Provençal, Catalan
450 Italian, Rumanian
460 Spanish, Portuguese
470 Latin and other Italic
480 Classical and Modern Greek
490 Other Languages

500–599 PURE SCIENCE

510 Mathematics
520 Astronomy
530 Physics
540 Chemistry and Allied Sciences
550 Earth Sciences
560 Paleontology
570 Anthropology and Biology
580 Botanical Sciences
590 Zoological Sciences

600–699 TECHNOLOGY

610 Medical Sciences
620 Engineering
630 Agriculture
640 Home Economics
650 Business
660 Chemical Technology
670 Manufactures
680 Other Manufactures
690 Building Construction

700–799 THE ARTS

710 Landscape and Civic Art
720 Architecture
730 Sculpture
740 Drawing and Decorative Arts
750 Painting
760 Prints and Print Making
770 Photography
780 Music
790 Recreation/Sports

800–899 LITERATURE

810 American Literature in English
820 English and Old English
830 Germanic Literatures
840 French, Provençal, Catalan
850 Italian, Rumanian
860 Spanish, Portuguese
870 Latin and other Italic Literatures
880 Classical and Modern Greek
890 Other Literatures

900–999 HISTORY

910 Geography, Travels, Description
920 Biography
930 Ancient History
940 Europe
950 Asia
960 Africa
970 North America
980 South America
990 Other Parts of the World

175. DEWEY DECIMAL LITERATURE SUBDIVISIONS

The literature category of the Dewey Decimal System (800s) is subdivided further into the categories below. See List 175, Dewey Decimal Classification.

800 LITERATURE

801 Philosophy and Theory
802 Handbooks and Outlines
803 Dictionaries and Encyclopedias
804 Essays and Lectures
805 Periodicals
806 Organizations and Societies
807 Study and Teaching
808 Literary Composition
809 History and Criticism

810 AMERICAN LITERATURE

811 American Poetry
812 American Drama
813 American Fiction
814 American Essays
815 American Oratory
816 American Letters
817 American Satire and Humor
818 American Miscellany
819 (Unused category)

820 ENGLISH LITERATURE

821 English Poetry
822 English Drama
823 English Fiction
824 English Essays
825 English Oratory
826 English Letters
827 English Satire and Humor
828 English Miscellany
829 Old English Literature

830 GERMAN LITERATURE

831 German Poetry
832 German Drama
833 German Fiction

834 German Essays
835 German Oratory
836 German Letters
837 German Satire and Humor
838 German Miscellany
839 Other Germanic Literature

840 FRENCH LITERATURE

841 French Poetry
842 French Drama
843 French Fiction
844 French Essays
845 French Oratory
846 French Letters
847 French Satire and Humor
848 French Miscellany
849 Provencal and Catalan

850 ITALIAN LITERATURE

851 Italian Poetry
852 Italian Drama
853 Italian Fiction
854 Italian Essays
855 Italian Oratory
856 Italian Letters
857 Italian Satire and Humor
858 Italian Miscellany
859 Rumanian

860 SPANISH LITERATURE

861 Spanish Poetry
862 Spanish Drama
863 Spanish Fiction
864 Spanish Essays
865 Spanish Oratory
866 Spanish Letters
867 Spanish Satire and Humor

868 Spanish Miscellany
869 Portuguese and Galician

870 LATIN LITERATURE
871 Latin Poetry
872 Dramatic Poetry
873 Epic Poetry
874 Lyric Poetry
875 Latin Oratory
876 Latin Letters
877 Latin Satire and Humor
878 Latin Miscellany
879 Other Italic Literature

880 GREEK LITERATURE
881 Greek Poetry
882 Greek Dramatic Poetry
883 Greek Epic Poetry

884 Greek Lyric Poetry
885 Greek Oratory
886 Greek Letters
887 Greek Satire and Humor
888 Greek Miscellany
889 Byzantine and Hellenic

890 OTHER LITERATURES
891 Other Indo-European
892 Semitic and Hamito/Semitic
893 Hamitic Literatures
894 Finno-Ugric And Other
895 Far Eastern Literatures
896 African Literatures
897 North American Indian
898 South American Indian
899 Austronesian and Other

176. DEWEY DECIMAL BREAKDOWNS OF SPECIAL INTEREST

These subcategories of the Dewey Decimal System may be of special interest to the literature student. See also List 175, Dewey Decimal Classification.

000 GENERAL WORKS

010   Bibliography
011   Bibliographies
012   Of Individuals
013   Of Works by Specific Classes of Authors
014   Of Anonymous and Pseudonymous Works
015   Of Works from Specific Places
016   Of Works on Specific Subjects
017   General Subject Catalogs
018   Catalogs, arranged by Author and Date

090 MANUSCRIPTS AND RARE BOOKS

091   Manuscripts
094   Printed Books
096   Books Notable for Illustrations
097   Books Notable for Ownership or Origin

098 Prohibited Works, Forgeries, Hoaxes
099 Books Notable for Format

200 RELIGION

220 Bible
221 Old Testament
222 Historical Books of Old Testament
223 Poetic Books of Old Testament
224 Prophetic Books of Old Testament
225 New Testament
226 Gospels and Acts
227 Epistles
228 Revelation (Apocalypse)
229 Apocrypha and Pseudepigrapha

290 Other and Comparative Religions
291 Comparative Religion
291.13 Religious Mythology
292 Classical Greek and Roman Religion
293 Germanic Religion
294 Religions of Indic Origin
296 Judaism
297 Islam and Religions Originating in It

300 SOCIAL SCIENCES

398 Folklore
398.2   Folk Literature
398.21 Fairy Tales
398.22 Tales and Lore of Historical and Quasi-Historical Persons and Events
398.23 Tales and Lore of Places and Times
398.24 Tales and Lore of Plants and Animals
398.25 Ghost Stories
398.3   Natural and Physical Phenomena as Subjects of Folklore
398.4   Paranatural and Legendary Phenomena as Subjects of Folklore
398.5   Chapbooks
398.8   Rhymes and Rhyming Games
398.9   Proverbs

800 LITERATURE (See also List 176, Dewey Decimal Literature Subdivisions)

808   Literary Composition
808.067   Adult Easy Literature
808.068   Children's Literature

809 **History and Criticism**
809.8 Literature for and by Specific Kinds of Persons
809.801 Literature for and by Specific Racial, Ethnic, National Groups
809.9 Literature Displaying Specific Features

822 **English Drama**
822.3 Elizabethan Period
822.33 William Shakespeare

900 HISTORY

904 **Essays and Lectures**

920 **Biography**
921 Philosophers and Psychologists
922 Religious Leaders, Thinkers, Workers
923 Persons in Social Sciences
923.1 Heads of State
923.2 Persons in Political Science and Politics
923.3 Persons in Economics
923.4 Criminals and Persons in Law
923.5 Public Administrators and Military Persons
923.6 Philanthropists, Humanitarians, Social Reformers
923.7 Educators
923.8 Persons in Commerce, Communication, Transportation
923.9 Explorers, Geographers, Pioneers, Frontiersmen
924 Philologists and Lexicographers
925 Scientists
926 Persons in Technology
927 Persons in the Arts and Recreation
928 Persons in Literature, History, Biography, Genealogy
928.1 Americans
928.2 Others

177. EPITAPHS OF AUTHORS

An epitaph is an inscription on a tomb. Someone once said that a tombstone is the only thing that has a good word for a person when he's down. Ambrose Bierce, in *The Devil's Dictionary*, provided another humorous definition: "Epitaph — An inscription on a tomb, showing that virtues acquired by death have a retroactive effect." The following epitaphs have become memorable for their wit, poignancy, and literary quality.

Epitaph written by Shakespeare for himself:

> *Good Friend for Jesus sake forbeare*
> *To digg the dust encloased heare;*
> *Bleste be the man that spares these stones,*
> *And curst be he that moves my bones.*

Epitaph written by Benjamin Franklin at the age of twenty for himself:

> *The Body of*
> *B. Franklin, Printer (Like the Cover of an old Book*
> *Its Contents torn out*
> *And stript of its Lettering and Gilding)*
> *Lies here, Food for Worms.*
> *But the Work shall not be lost;*
> *For it will (as he believed) appear once more,*
> *In a new and more elegant Edition*
> *Revised and corrected*
> *By the Author*

Note: His real stone says "Benjamin and Deborah Franklin."

Epitaph written for himself by Robert L. Stevenson (from "Requiem"):

> *Under the wide and starry sky,*
> *Dig the grave and let me lie.*
> *Glad did I live and gladly die,*
> *And I laid me down with a will.*
>
> *This be the verse you grave for me:*
> *Here he lies where he longed to be;*
> *Home is the sailor, home from sea,*
> *And the hunter home from the hill.*

Epitaph written by Samuel Taylor Coleridge for himself:

A poet lies, or that which once seemed he —
Oh, life a thought in prayer for S. T. C.!
That he, who many a year, with toil of breath,
Found death in life, may here find life in death.

Epitaph written by John Keats for himself:

Here lies one whose name was writ in water.

Two epitaphs written by Dorothy Parker for herself:

(1) *Excuse my dust.*

(2) *If you can read this, you've come too close.*

Epitaph written by Jonathan Swift (in Latin) for himself:

Here lies the body of Jonathan Swift... where, at last savage indignation can no longer lacerate his heart.

Epitaph written by Will Rogers for himself:

I joked about every prominent man in my lifetime, but I never met one I didn't like.

Epitaph of Joseph Conrad:

Sleep after toyle, port after stormie seas,
Ease after warre, death after life, does greatly please.

Epitaph of Sir Arthur Conan Doyle:

Steel True, Blade Straight.

Epitaph of Jack London:

The Stone the Builders Rejected.

Epitaph of Edgar Allan Poe, from "The Raven":

Quoth the Raven, Nevermore.

Last part of epitaph of Oscar Wilde:

And alien tears will fill for him
Pity's long, unbroken urn.
For his mourners will be outcast men,
And outcasts always mourn.

Epitaph of Richard Mather (father of Increase Mather; grandfather of Cotton Mather):

Under this stone lies Richard Mather,
who had a son greater than his father,
And eke a grandson greater than either.

Epitaph of John Gay, attributed to him:

Life is a jest, and all things show it;
I thought so once and now I know it.

Epitaph of Thomas Jefferson, written by himself:

Here was buried
Thomas Jefferson
Author
of the Declaration of
American Independence
of
the Statute of Virginia
for Religious Freedom, and
Father of the University
of Virginia

Epitaph of Martin Luther King, Jr. (from "I Have a Dream" speech):

Free at last, free at last
Thank God almighty
We are free at last.

Proposed epitaph written by Hilaire Belloc:

When I am dead, I hope it may be said:
'His sins were scarlet, but his books were read.'

Proposed epitaph written by William Faulkner:

It is my aim, and every effort bent, that the sum and history of my life,
which in the same sentence is my obit and epitaph too, shall be them both:
He made the books and he died.

Proposed epitaph written by Robert Frost:

I would have written of me on my stone: I had a lover's quarrel with the world.

Said in eulogy of Jacqueline Susann by Gene Shalit:

Her books were put down by most critics, but readers would not put down her books.

Said of DeWitt Wallace, founder of the *Reader's Digest*.

The final condensation.

Epitaph for Charles II by the Earl of Rochester:

Here lies our Sovereign Lord the King,
  Whose word no man relies on,
Who never said a foolish thing,
  Nor ever did a wise one.

Erica Jong said she thought the following could be her epitaph from the poem "The Buddha in the Womb":

Flesh is merely a lesson
We learn it and pass on.

Ray Bradbury, when asked what he would like on his epitaph:

*Here lies a teller of tales. If he had lived ten centuries ago, you would have walked down a street in old Baghdad or in some Middle Eastern city and there among the menders of copper and the shapers of clay turned into a Street of the Story Tellers and found him seated there among the tellers of tales who have existed since men came out of the caves. This is a proud heritage. This was his.** *

*From *On Being a Writer*, Bill Strickland (editor), Writers Digest Books, F&W Publications, Cincinnati, Ohio, 1989.

178. EPONYMS

Many words originate from the names of people. The people whose names are transformed into new words are called eponyms and are commonly referred to as "the eponymous ___." Here are some common words, along with the person they are named after. Readers who investigate the stories behind these words will find them quite interesting. A good place to begin is *Melba Toast, Bowie's Knife & Caesar's Wife: A Dictionary of Eponyms* by Martin Manser.

America — Amerigo Vespucci

ampere — Andre Ampere

baud — Jean M. E. Baudot

begonia — Michel Begon

bloomer — Amelia Bloomer

bougainvillea — Louis Bougainville

bowdlerize — Thomas Bowdler

bowie knife — James Bowie

boycott — Charles Boycott

braille — Louis Braille

busby — Richard Busby

camellia — Josef Kamel

cardigan — Earl of Cardigan

celsius — Anders Celsius

chateaubriand — Francoise Chateaubriand

chauvinism — Nicolas Chauvin

dahlia — Anders Dahl

decibel — Alexander G. Bell

derby — Earl of Derby

derringer — Henry Deringer

diesel — Rudolf Diesel

Doberman pinscher — Ludwig Dobermann

dunce — John Duns Scotus

epicure — Epicurus

fahrenheit — D. G. Fahrenheit

Fallopian tube — Gabriel Fallopius

gardenia — Alexander Garden

Geiger counter — Hans Geiger

georgette — Georgette de la Plante

gerrymander — Elbridge Gerry

graham cracker — Sylvester Graham

guillotine — Joseph Guillotin

guppy — Robert Guppy

guy — Guy Fawkes

hooligan — Patrick Hooligan

jacuzzi — Candido Jacuzzi

leotard — Jules Lèotard

lynch — William Lynch

macadam — John McAdam

mackintosh — Charles Macintosh

magnolia — Pierre Magnol

martinet — Jean Martinet

masochism — Leopold von Sacher-Masoch

mausoleum — King Mausolus

maverick — Samuel Maverick

Melba toast — Nellie Melba

mesmerize — Franz Mesmer

moonie — Sun Myung Moon

Morse code — Samuel Morse

nicotine — Jean Nicot

ohm — George S. Ohm

pasteurize — Louis Pasteur

peach Melba — Nellie Melba

platonic — Plato

poinsettia — Joel R. Poinsett

pompadour — Marquise de Pompadour

praline — Count Plessis-Praslin

pullman — George Pullman

quisling — Vidkun Quisling
raglan sleeves — Baron Raglan
ritzy — Cesar Ritz
sadism — Marquis de Sade
salmonella — Daniel Salmon
sandwich — Earl of Sandwich
saxophone — Antoine J. Sax
shrapnel — Henry Shrapnel
sideburns — Ambrose Burnside
silhouette — Etienne de Silhouette
sousaphone — John P. Sousa

spinet — Giovanni Spinetti
spoonerism — William Spooner
stetson — John B. Stetson
stonewall — Thomas "Stonewall" Jackson
teddy bear — Teddy Roosevelt
volt — Alessandro Volta
watt — James Watt
wisteria — Caspar Wistar
zeppelin — Count Ferdinand von Zeppelin
zinnia — Johann Zinn

179. "EST" LIST

This list contains the oldest, youngest, largest, smallest, longest, shortest, fastest, and slowest of literary curiosities, gathered from a variety of sources.

Oldest complete novel in world — *The Tale of Genji* (Japan, eleventh century)

Oldest poet laureate — William Wordsworth, age seventy-three (when appointed)

Oldest book printed with movable type — *Gutenberg Bible* (about 1454)

Oldest theater — Teatro Olimico (in Italy — 1508)

Youngest author — Dorothy Straight, age four (*How the World Began*)

Youngest author-illustrator — Dennis Vollmer, age six (*Joshua Disobeys*)

Youngest Oscar winner — Anna Paquin (for *The Piano*)

Youngest special Oscar winner — Shirley Temple, age five (1934)

Youngest poet laureate — Laurence Eusden, age thirty (when appointed)

Largest bookstore — Barnes & Noble (in New York City — 154,250 sq. ft.)

Largest English language dictionary — *Oxford English Dictionary* (twenty volumes)

Largest library — Library of Congress (in Washington, D.C. — 532 miles of shelves containing over eighty-eight million items)

Largest printing company — R.R. Donnelley & Co. (Chicago)

Largest theater — National People's Congress Building in China (seats 10,000 people)

Smallest book — *Old King Cole* (1/25" x 1/25" pages have to be turned with a needle)

Smallest theater — Piccolo (in Germany, seats thirty people)

Longest biography — Winston S. Churchill (unfinished work of five volumes by Randolph S. Churchill and Martin Gilbert)

Longest-lived poet laureate — John Masefield (nearly eighty-nine years old)

Longest movie — eighty-five hours (*The Cure for Insomnia*)

Longest novel — *Les hommes de bonne Volontè* by Louis Farigoule (twenty-seven volumes)

Longest on N.Y. Times best-seller list — *The Road Less Traveled* by M. Scott Peck (more than 300 weeks)

Longest overdue book in U.S. — 145 years (in Ohio)

Longest overdue book in world — 288 years (in Germany)

Longest running comic strip — *Katzenjammer Kids* (since 1897)

Longest Shakespeare play — *Hamlet*

Longest-tenured poet laureate — Alfred Lord Tennyson (nearly forty-two years)

Shortest drama review — "Ouch" (of play called *Wham!*)

Slowest publishing of a book — a German dictionary entitled *Deutsches Wörterbuch* (117 years)

180. EUPHEMISMS AND OXYMORA

Euphemisms are words or phrases that put the best possible, most respectful, and least demeaning slant on a subject. Many have to do with occupations or personality traits. An oxymoron is the result of juxtaposing two or more incongruous or opposite words. Literature is filled with oxymora and euphemisms used for effect. While paradoxical combinations can be expressive, they are often awkward and undesirable.

EUPHEMISMS

(The honest term is on the left; the euphemism is on the right.)

bullying — assertive

cheap — frugal; thrifty

dead — deceased; gathered unto God

die — pass on; pass away

don't agree — two ways to look at it

don't like it — it's interesting

don't want to go — have other plans

garbage collector — sanitation engineer

guilty of crime — boys will be boys

hate it — it's different

impractical; illogical — right-brained; creative

janitor — custodian

lazy — conserves energy

obnoxiously aggressive — assertive

overeats — has a healthy appetite

prostitute — lady of the evening; working girl

short — vertically challenged
two-faced — diplomatic
unattractive — has nice personality
unemployed — between jobs
very angry — offended
wild — hyperactive

OXYMORA

backward progress
bittersweet
black light
bottomless pit
cruel kindness
exact estimate
expecting the unexpected
flat curve
free with purchase
freezer burn
genuine imitation
hopeless optimist
ice water
idle labor
intense apathy
liberal conservative

light heavyweight
liquid gas
metal woods
negative cash flow
nervous calm
new review
original reproduction
passive resistance
peaceful warrior
proud humility
randomly organized
selfish love
silent scream
strong weakness
sweet sorrow
thunderous silence
tragic comedy
unbiased opinion
urban cowboy
wavering steadfastness
working vacation
worthless treasure
zero growth

LATIN

ad absurdum: (carried out) to absurdity

ad hoc: created for a special occasion

ad hominem: to the man

ad nauseam: (to continue on and on) to a sickening extreme

alma mater: the school from which one graduated

annus mirabilis: miraculous year

ante bellum: before the war

ante meridiem (abbreviation: *A.M.*): before noon

a priori: from cause to effect

ars poetics: art of poetry

bona fide: in good faith

causa belli: just cause of war

corpus delicti: facts of the crime; body of the crime

de facto: agreed upon informally

de jure: by law

Deo gratias: thanks to God

de profundis: out of the depths

ergo: therefore

et alii/et aliae/et alibi (abbreviation: *et al.*): and others; and elsewhere

ex cathedra: pronouncement from pope or other authority

exempli gratia (abbreviation: *e.g.*): for example

exeunt: they leave; they go off stage

ex officio: by virtue of office

ex post facto: (rule made up) after the event (after the deed)

ex tempore: without preparation

finis: end

furor poeticus: poetic enthusiasm (fire)

gratia placendi: in order to please

homo sapiens: the human species; a wise man

ibidem (abbreviation: *ibid.*): in the same place in book cited

idem (abbreviation: *id.*): same as ibidem, above

id est (abbreviation: *i.e.*): that is

Iesus: Jesus

in camera: in secret

incipit: here begins (the literary piece)

in loco parentis: in place of the parent

in memorium: in memory (of)

in pace: in peace

in puris naturalibus: naked

in situ: in the original place (in position)

in toto: in total

in vino veritas: There is truth in wine

lapsus calami: a slip of the pen

liber (abbreviation: *L.* or *lib.*): book

lis pendens: pending law suit

literati: literate people

locus criminis: scene of the crime

magna cum laude: with great praise

magnum opus: greatest work of one's career

mea culpa: my fault

modus operandi (abbreviation: *m.o.*): method of operation

momento mori: an object kept to remind one of mortality

non compos mentis: out of one's mind

non sequitur: something that does not logically follow

nota bene (abbreviation: *n.b.*): note well

pater familias: father of the family

pax vobiscum: may peace be with you

per annum: annually

per diem: daily

per se: for itself

persona non grata: unacceptable person

post meridiem (abbreviation: *P.M.*): noon until midnight

post mortem (abbreviation: *P.M.*): lengthy analysis after an event; autopsy

pro forma: doing something by just going through the motions (by form)

pro tempore (pro tem): for the time being

quid pro quo: a fair trade (something for something)

quod erat demonstrandum (abbreviation: *Q.E.D.*): proof completed

requiescat in pace (abbreviation: *R.I.P.*): rest in peace

semper fidelis: always faithful

[sic]: a doubtful or wrong word is quoted accurately

sine qua non: the condition without which something else would be impossible (without which nothing)

status quo/status in quo: the present state

stet: let it stand

sub rosa: in secret (under the rose)

summa cum laude: with highest praise

tempus fugit: time flies

terra firma: solid ground

terra incognita: unknown land (used on older maps)

veni, vidi, vici: I came; I saw, I conquered

veritas: truth

vox Dei: voice of God

vox populi: voice of the people

FRENCH

adieu: good-bye

à la bonne heure: at the right time

amour: love

amour propre: vanity

à propos: directly to the point

artiste: highly skilled performer

au contraire: on the contrary

au jus: served with its natural juice

au naturel: naked

au revoir: good-bye

avant propos: preface

à votre sante: to your health

bon voyage: good and pleasant journey

bourgeois: commoner; middle-class person

carte blanche: power to do as the person wishes (blank card)

cause célèbre: cause arousing public sentiment (celebrated cause)

c'est la vie: that's life

chanson: song

château: castle

cher ami: dear friend

cinq: five

comme il faut: as it should be

coup: uprising

coup de grace: the final blow

crème de la crème: the best of the best

defense de fumer: no smoking

déjà vu: the feeling that something has happened before

de rigueur: necessary because of custom

deux: two

dix: ten

dix-huit: eighteen

dix-neuf: nineteen

dix-sept: seventeen

double entente (also double entendre): double meaning

douze: twelve

eminence grise: gray eminence; person who has behind-the-scenes power

enfant terrible: someone who stirs up trouble irresponsibly (terrible child)

en masse: all together in a huge group

esprit de corps: camaraderie (group spirit)

fait accompli: something already accomplished (an accomplished fact)

farceur: writer of farces; jokester

faux: false

faux pas: mistake; indiscretion (false step)

femme fatale: alluring woman, especially one leading a man to his downfall

fete: holiday or feast

fille: daughter

fils: son

fin: end

fleur de lis: flower of the lily; French national emblem

franc: French monetary unit

garçon: waiter; boy; youth

gens de lettres: literary men (men of letters)

grandmère: grandmother

grandpère: grandfather

hors d'oeuvre: appetizer served before a meal

huit: eight

je ne sais quoi: indescribable something (I do not know what)

joie de vivre: joy of life

Joyeux Noël: Merry Christmas

laissez faire: to leave alone; to do nothing

le monde: the world; society

le mot juste: just the right word

lycée: high school

ma chère (mon cher): my dear

madame: Mrs. or mistress

mademoiselle: Miss; unmarried woman

maître d'hôtel (maitre D.): headwaiter; hotel keeper

merci: thank you

merci beaucoup: thank you very much

metro: subway system

mon cheri: my darling

mon Dieu: my God

monsieur (abbreviation: *M.*): Mr.

née: name born with; maiden name

n'est-ce pas?: isn't that so?

neuf: nine

noblesse oblige: the duty of the rich to help the poor

Noël: Christmas

nom de plume: pen name

non: no

nouveau riche: newly rich

nouvellette: short story or novel

objet d'art: art object

onze: eleven

opèra bouffe: farcical opera

oui: yes

par avion: airmail (by air)

père: father

petit: little

pièce de résistance: main dish; crowning touch

quatorze: fourteen

quatre: four

quinze: fifteen

raison d'etre: reason for existence (reason for being)

repondez s'il vous plait (abbreviation: *R.S.V.P.*): respond if you please *rue:* street

sacré bleu: confound it! (expletive)

sans: without

sans souci: carefree (without care)

savoir-faire: social ease; tact (to know how to act)

seize: sixteen

sept: seven

six: six

soirée: night party

table d'hôte: specialty of the restaurant

tête-à-tête: intimate meeting (head to head)

touché: term used to acknowledge good point made against you in argument (fencing term)

tour de force: outstanding strength or skill

tout de suite: immediately

treize: thirteen

très bien: very well

trois: three

un (une): one

une belle dame: a beautiful lady

vin: wine

vingt: twenty

vis-à-vis: in comparison to (face to face)

voilà: there you have it; there it is

SPANISH

a caballo: on horseback

adios: good-bye

a Dios gracias: thanks be to God

afectisimo/afectisima: most affectionately; very truly (used in letter closing)

aficionado/aficionada: fan, usually sports fan

alcazar: castle; palace

Americano: American

apellido: family name; surname

A su salud!/A vuestra salud!/Salud!: To your health

bambino: baby; child; image of Jesus

bandido: bandit

bandolereo: robber

buenas dias: good morning

buenas noches: good evening

buenas tardes: good afternoon

catorce: fourteen

chicano: North American of Mexican descent

chico: small; small boy

cinco: five

comandante: commanding officer

comida: meal

compadre: companion

conquistador: conqueror

cuatro: four

cuidado: look out!

diecinueve: nineteen

dieciocho: eighteen

dieciseis: sixteen

diecisiete: seventeen

diez: ten

doce: twelve

dos: two

en paz descanse: may he rest in peace (abbreviation: *E.P.D.*)

Felices Pascuas: Happy Easter

Feliz Navidad: Merry Christmas

gaucho: cowboy

gracias: thank you

gringo: foreigner held in disdain

hacienda: large country estate and house

hija: daughter

hijo: son

hola: hello; hi

hombre: man

los Estados Unidos (abbreviation: *EE.UU* or *E.U*): the United States

luna (also Italian): moon

macho: male

madre (also Italian): mother

mañana: tomorrow; morning

muchacha: girl

muchacho: boy

mucho: much; many

niño: child

nueve: nine

ocho: eight

once: eleven

padre: father; priest

paisano: fellow countryman; pal (slang)

por avion: airmail; by air

por favor: please

pronto: soon

quince: fifteen

se prohibe escupir: no smoking

seis: six

señor (abbreviations: *Sr./Sor.*): Mr.

señora (abbreviations: *S.a/Sra.*): lady; Mrs.

señorita (abbreviations: *Srta./Sta.*): young lady; Miss

si: yes

siesta: afternoon rest

siete: seven

sol: sun

sombrero: hat

trece: thirteen

tres: three

uno: one

vaquero: cowboy

veinte: twenty

viva (also Italian): hurrah

vivo: alive

GREEK

alpha: beginning (first letter of alphabet)

efharisto: thank you

hoi polloi: common people

omega: end (last letter of alphabet)

Eureka: I have found it

speude bradeos: make haste slowly

HAWAIIAN

aloha: hello; good-bye; love

lei: garland of flowers

malahini: newcomer to Hawaii

poi: food made of mashed taro root, bananas, or pineapple

ITALIAN

adagio: slowly

afetto: passion

Aiuto!: Help!

Alla salute!/A vostra salute!: To your health!

amore: love

andiamo: let's go

arrivederci/arriverderla: good-bye; til we meet again

autore (abbreviation: *aut.*): author

avanti Cristo (abbreviation: *av. C.*): before Christ

avvocato del diavolo: Devil's advocate

bambino: child

Basta!: Stop!; Enough!

benvenuto: welcome

casa: house; mansion (also Spanish and Portuguese)

che bel Tempo!: What fine weather!

ciao!: Hello!; So long!

con amore: with love

coraggio!: courage!

diavolo: devil

Dio vi benedica: God bless you

duomo: cathedral

evviva!: hurrah!

fine: end

grazie!: thanks!

Mafia: crime organization

mafioso: member of the Mafia

prima donna: leading female opera singer; also anyone who likes to be center of attention

signor/sinore: gentleman; mister

signora: lady; Mrs.

signorina: young lady; Miss

terra cotta: baked clay of an earthy orange-tan color

GERMAN

Achtung!: Attention!

Aufklärung: enlightenment (especially eighteenth century)

Auflage (abbreviation: *Aulf.*): edition of a book

auf Wiedersehen: good-bye

bitte: please; don't mention it (you're welcome)

Blaustrumpf: literary woman (blue stocking)

danke schon: thank you

der Führer: the Nazi German leader

Deutsches Reich: German Empire

Deutschland: Germany

Dichter: poet

Donner!: Nuts!; Darn it!

Druck and Verlag (abbreviation: *Dr.u.Vrl.*): printed and published by

Dummkopf: blockhead; stupid fellow

Eisen und Blut: iron and blood

Ersatz: compensation; amends

Frau: female honorific

Fräulein: Miss

Gasthaus: restaurant; inn

Gasthof: hotel; inn

geboren (abbreviation: *geb.*): born

Gesundheit: Bless you! (usually after a sneeze)

gluckliche Reise!: Have a good journey!

gute Nacht: good night

guten Morgen: good morning

guten Tag: good day

Gymnasium: school preparing students for university

Herr: Sir or Mister

im Jahre (abbreviation: *i.J.*): in the year

lieblich: charming

Reich: realm

Schmalz: excessive sentimentality (rendered fat)

wie heissen Sie?: What is your name?

Zeitgeist: spirit of the times

HEBREW

ahava: love

bar mitzvah: ceremony at coming of age of a male

bas/bat mitzvah: ceremony at coming of age of a female

boker tov: good morning

chutzpah (also *hutzpah*): nerve; gall; "guts"

erev tov: good evening

l'chaim: to your health; to your life

shalom: hello, good-bye, and peace

RUSSIAN

babushka: scarf that ties around head; grandmother

Blagodar'yoo vas!: Thank you!

kharosho: good

da: yes

dobre din: good afternoon

dobre utra: good morning

intelligentsia: the intellectual elite

nyet: no

yah vahs loobloo: I love you

CHINESE

chow: food

ding hao: very good

gung ho: work hard together

182. GET IT STRAIGHT!

There are a number of literary or linguistic faux pas that true scholars of literature are able to avoid. Some common mistakes are cleared up below.

1. Frankenstein was a doctor, not a monster. Dr. Frankenstein *created* the monster.

2. Joyce Kilmer, poet famous for "Trees," was a *man*, not a woman.

3. George Sand, French novelist, was a *woman*, not a man.

4. Dr. Jekyll and Mr. Hyde are two sides of *one* fictional person.

5. Sherlock Holmes was a *fictional* detective, not a real one.

6. Sherlock Holmes never said, "Elementary, my dear Watson." This was said by an actor portraying Holmes in the movies. See also List 8, Quotations from Literature.

7. A *ballad* and a *ballade* are not the same. The former is a folk poem; the latter, a sophisticated verse form.

8. Little John (of Robin Hood's band of men) was big and brawny.

9. Voltaire never said, "I disapprove of what you say, but I will defend to the death your right to say it." This quotation was used to describe Voltaire's sentiments, but the words were not his.

10. Neither Mark Twain nor Will Rogers uttered the famous line, "Everybody talks about the weather, but nobody does anything about it," though it has been attributed to one or both.

11. Disraeli, not Twain, said, "There are three kinds of lies: lies, damn lies, and statistics."

12. "All Americans are deaf, blind, and dumb," traditionally attributed to George Bernard Shaw, was not said by him.

13. Richard Armour, not Ogden Nash, wrote: "Shake and shake the catsup bottle. None will come, and then a lot'll."

14. "That government is best which governs least" is often attributed to Thomas Jefferson or Henry David Thoreau, but even Thoreau put quotations around it when he wrote it.

15. Horace Greeley did not say, "Go west, young man."

16. "Fools rush in where angels fear to tread," is not from the Bible, but from an essay by Alexander Pope.

17. "Cleanliness is next to Godliness" is not from the Bible but from a sermon by John Wesley.

18. "God helps those who help themselves" is not from the Bible but from Benjamin Franklin's *Poor Richard's Almanack*.

19. "Then spare the rod and spoil the child" is not from the Bible, but Samuel Butler, English poet. The Bible does refer to the "rod," in Proverbs, however.

20. "Pride goeth before a fall" is a misquotation from the Bible. The correct quotation is, "Pride goeth before destruction, and an haughty spirit before a fall."

21. "He who hesitates is lost," should be, "The woman that deliberates is lost," from an eighteenth-century play by Addison.

22. People refer to "the patience of Job" because he never lost faith, but he did complain bitterly about his afflictions!

23. Don't confuse Henry *Wadsworth* Longfellow, nineteenth-century American poet, with William *Wordsworth*, nineteenth-century English poet laureate.

24. Evelyn and Alec Waugh are brothers, not husband and wife.

25. Oliver Wendell Holmes was an American author; his son, Oliver Wendell Holmes, Jr. was a longtime justice of the U.S. Supreme Court.

26. There were at least five famous Lowells: Amy Lowell and Robert Lowell (not related) were both Pulitzer Prize-winning poets; Amy's brother, Percival Lowell, was a world-famous astronomer; another brother, Abbott Lowell, was president of Harvard University; James Russell Lowell (not related) was also a renowned American poet. This profusion of Lowells may account for the famous, though anonymous, poem:

> *I come from the city of Boston,*
> *The home of the bean and the cod,*
> *Where the Cabots speak only to Lowells,*
> *And the Lowells speak only to God.*

27. There are *two* authors named Alexandre Dumas. The father (referred to as "Alexandre Dumas, père") wrote almost 300 books, including *The Count of Monte Cristo* and *The Three Musketeers*. Alexandre Dumas, fils (the son) was a dramatist who wrote *Lady of the Camellias*, the basis for Verdi's opera *La Traviata*.

28. Heinrich Mann and his brother, Thomas Mann, were both German novelists. Thomas Mann was the Nobel Prize winner in Literature in 1929. Though Heinrich's novel *Professor Unrat* was made into a movie, he never won high literary honors.

29. Stephen Vincent Benet and his brother, William Rose Benet, were both notable American poets. Stephen won *two* Pulitzers for poetry, William *one*.

30. The American poet *e .e. cummings* signed his work in lowercase letters as a sign of individuality. It is not a misprint.

31. Thornton Wilder (*Our Town* dramatist) and Laura Ingalls Wilder (*Little House* books) are not related. Thornton won the Pulitzer; Laura's books were the basis for famous TV series.

32. Elizabeth Barrett Browning and Robert Browning, both famous English poets, were husband and wife.

33. Charlotte, Emily, and Anne Bronte were sisters who lived in the north of England. They all wrote famous novels: Charlotte Bronte wrote *Jane Eyre*; Emily Bronte wrote *Wuthering Heights*; Anne Bronte wrote *Agnes Gray*.

34. Don't confuse *e.g.* and *i.e.* The former means *exempli gratia* (for the sake of example) and should precede a series of examples. The latter means *id est* (that is) and should precede explanatory, clarifying material.

35. Don't confuse *et al.* and *et cetera*. The former means *and other things or people;* the latter means *and so forth* or *and the rest* and should never refer to people.

36. *Homographs* are spelled the same, but have different meanings or pronunciations; *homophones* are pronounced the same, but have different spellings and meanings.

37. "Oh, what a tangled web we weave when first we practice to deceive" was written by Sir Walter Scott, not Shakespeare.

38. Don't confuse *pathos* and *bathos.* The former brings about sympathy; the latter brings about laughter because it is an attempt at pathos, but is trite, mushy, and overdone.

39. *Playwright* is the correct spelling of a person who writes plays; not playwrite, or playright.

40. Becky Thatcher was Tom's sweetheart in Mark Twain's *Tom Sawyer*, and Becky Sharp was a character in William Makepeace Thackeray's *Vanity Fair*.

Elizabeth Barrett Browning, English poet: "Knowledge by suffering entereth, And life is perfected by death."

Robert Browning, English poet: "How gratifying!"

Lord Byron, English poet: "The damned doctors have drenched me so that I can scarcely stand. I want to sleep now."

Hart Crane, American author (as he jumped overboard): "Good-bye, everybody!"

Benjamin Franklin, American statesman and writer: "A dying man can do nothing easy."

Johann Wolfgang von Goethe, German poet: "More light!"

Joel Chandler Harris, American author of Uncle Remus stories: "I am about the extent of a tenth of a gnat's eyebrow better."

Alfred Houseman, English poet: "Yes, that's a good one, and tomorrow I shall be telling it again on the Golden Floor." (after hearing an off-color story)

Washington Irving, American author: "Well, I must arrange my pillows for another weary night! When will this end?"

John Keats, English poet: "Lift me up for I am dying. I shall die easy. Don't be frightened. Thank God it has come."

Cotton Mather, American clergyman and author: "Is this dying? Is this all? Is this what I feared when I prayed against a hard death? Oh, I can bear this! I can bear it!"

Sir Thomas More, English statesman and author: "Pluck up thy spirits, man, and be not afraid to do thine office: My neck is very short; take heed, therefore, thou strike not awry, for saving of thine honesty." (said to executioner)

Edgar Allan Poe, American writer: "Lord, help my poor soul."

George Bernard Shaw, English playwright: "Sister, you're trying to keep me alive as an old curiosity, but I'm done, I'm finished, I'm going to die."

Robert Louis Stevenson, Scottish writer: "My head, my head!"

Henry David Thoreau, American author: "Moose, Indian."

Walt Whitman, American poet: "Garrulous to the very last."

Oscar Wilde, Irish writer: "I am dying as I've lived: beyond my means; this wallpaper is killing me; one of us has got to go."

184. Library Of Congress Classification System

Herbert Putnam, head of the U.S. Library of Congress in Washington, D.C. for forty years, originated the Library of Congress Classification for library books. (The Library of Congress now contains more than 80 million items in 470 languages.) Most colleges and universities in the U.S. use this system. The Library of Congress system consists of three lines — a letter (top); a number (middle); and a letter/number combination (bottom). Untold combinations accommodate large numbers of books. Basic divisions, with the language/literature section (P) expanded, are as follows:

A: General Works (including Newspapers, Yearbooks)

B: Philosophy and Religion (and Metaphysics, Psychology, Ethics)

C: Auxiliary Sciences of History (like Archaeology, Genealogy)

D: History and Topography (except America)

E–F: History: America (Western Hemisphere)

G: Geography (including Anthropology, Folklore, Manners and Customs, Recreation, Sports, Games, and Dance)

H: Social Sciences (including Statistics, Economics, Sociology)

J: Political Science (including International Law)

K: Law

L: Education (including History of Education, Teaching)

M: Music (Musical Scores, Music Literature, Music Instruction)

N: Fine Arts (including Architecture, Graphic Arts, Engraving)

P: Philology and Linguistics (General)

    PA Classical Languages and Literatures

    PB Modern European Languages

    PC Romance Languages

    PD Germanic Languages

    PE English Languages

    PF West Germanic Languages

    PG Slavic, Baltic, Albanian Languages and Literature

    PH Finnish, Ugrian, Basque Languages and Literature

    PJ Oriental Languages and Literature

PK Indo-Iranian

PL Eastern Asia, Africa, Oceania

PM Indian and Artificial Languages

PN General Literature (Literary History and Collections)

PQ Romance Literature (French, Italian, Spanish, Portuguese)

PR English Literature

PS American Literature

PT Germanic Literatures (German, Dutch, Flemish, Afrikaans, Scandinavian)

PZ Fiction and Juvenile Literature

Q: Science

R: Medicine

S: Agriculture

T: Technology

U: Military Science

V: Naval Science

Z: Bibliography and Library Science

185. LITERARY CHARACTERS BASED ON REAL PEOPLE

Hundreds of famous literary characters were based on real people; some were self-portraits. Usually authors kept their prototypes secret to protect themselves from unhappy consequences, but the following have come to light. The character is listed first with the name of the real-life model in parentheses; the work and author follow. A bit of research will reveal fascinating stories behind each entry.

Captain Ahab (Owen Chase, seaman). *Moby Dick* — Herman Melville

Don Armado (Sir Walter Raleigh, soldier-poet). *Love's Labour's Lost* — William Shakespeare

Barabas (David Passi, ambitious merchant). *The Jew of Malta* — Christopher Marlowe

Norman Bates (Ed Gein, convicted Wisconsin killer). *Psycho* — Robert Bloch

Peggy Nash Belmont (Jacqueline Kennedy, wife of President John Kennedy). *The Greek* — Pierre Rey

Juliana Bordereau (Claire Clairmont, Lord Byron's lover). *The Aspern Papers* — Henry James

Madame Bovary (Louise Colet, author's lover, and Delphine Delamare). *Madame Bovary* — Gustave Flaubert

Gareth Brendan (Hugh Hefner, magazine publisher). *Dreams Die First* — Harold Robbins

Natty Bumppo (Daniel Boone). *Leatherstocking Tales* — James Fenimore Cooper

Tony Camonte (Al Capone, notorious Chicago gangster). *Scarface* (movie) — Ben Hecht

Hunt Conroy (F. Scott Fitzgerald). *You Can't Go Home Again* — Thomas Wolfe

Jonas Cord (Howard Hughes, eccentric movie mogul and businessman). *The Carpetbaggers* — Harold Robbins

Robinson Crusoe (Alexander Selkirk, Scottish seaman). *Adventures of Robinson Crusoe* — Daniel Defoe

Mr. Cypress (Lord Byron, poet). *Nightmare Abbey* — Thomas Love Peacock

Cyrano de Bergerac (Cyrano de Bergerac, French dramatist). *Cyrano de Bergerac* — Edmond Rostand

Dracula (Prince Vlad Dracula, sadistic ruler of Wallachia). *Dracula* — Bram Stoker

Martin Eden (Jack London). *Martin Eden* — Jack London

Richard Fiddes (author John LeCarre). *Some Gorgeous Accident* — James Kennaway

Marguerite Gautier (Marie Duplessis, lover). *The Lady of the Camellias* — Alexandre Dumas, fils

Scythrop Glowry (Percy Bysshe Shelley, poet). *Nightmare Abbey* — Thomas Love Peacock

Clyde Griffiths (Chester Gillette, who murdered Grace Brown). *An American Tragedy* — Theodore Dreiser

Captain Harville (Frank Austen). *Persuasion* — Jane Austen

Prince Hohenstiel-Schwangau (Napoleon Bonaparte III). *Prince Hohenstiel-Schwangau, Saviour of Society* — Robert Browning

Sherlock Holmes (Dr. Joseph Bell, Edinburgh surgeon). Numerous detective stories — Sir Arthur Conan Doyle

Jekyll and Hyde (William Brodie, businessman by day, criminal by night). *The Strange Case of Dr. Jekyll and Mr. Hyde* — R. L. Stevenson

Lucky Jim Dixon (Philip Larkin, poet). *Lucky Jim* — Kingsley Amis

Don Juan (Lord Byron). *Don Juan* — Lord Byron

Claude Lantier (Paul Cèzanne and Eduard Manet, the artists). *L'Oeuvre* — Emile Zola

Annabel Lee (Virginia Poe, the poet's wife). *Annabel Lee* — Edgar Allan Poe

Maggie (Marilyn Monroe, actress, and the author's ex-wife). *After the Fall* — Arthur Miller

Camille Maupin (George Sand, writer and Frederic Chopin's lover). *Beatrix* — Honorè de Balzac

Lloyd Mcharg (Sinclair Lewis). *You Can't Go Home Again* — Thomas Wolfe

Richard Monckton (Richard Nixon, president forced to resign). *The Company* — John Ehrlichman

Clay Overbury (John Kennedy, thirty-fifth president of United States). *Washington D.C.* — Gore Vidal

Peter Pan (Peter Llewelyn Davies, son of friends of author). *Peter Pan* — J. M. Barrie

Uncle Remus (Remus, former slave from Georgia). Uncle Remus stories, songs and sayings — Joel Chandler Harris

Christopher Robin (Christopher Milne, the author's son). Winnie-the-Pooh series — A. A. Milne

Marie Roget (Mary Cecilia Rogers, murder victim). "The Mystery of Marie Roget" — Edgar Allan Poe

Romeo and Juliet (Giuletto Cappelletto and Romeo Montecchi). *Romeo and Juliet* — William Shakespeare

Samson (John Milton). *Samson Agonistes* — John Milton

Harold Skimpole (Henry Leigh Hunt, writer). *Bleak House* — Charles Dickens

George Smiley (Rev. Dr. Vivian H. H. Green, Oxford historian). Numerous spy stories — John Le Carre

Nigel Strangeways (W. H. Auden, the poet). Numerous novels — Nicholas Blake (Cecil Day-Lewis)

Charles Strickland (Paul Gauguin, French impressionist painter). *The Moon and Sixpence* — W. Somerset Maugham

Una (Queen Elizabeth I, Queen of England). *The Faerie Queene* — Edmund Spenser

Jean Valjean ("Gaillard," flamboyant French assassin and thief). *Les Misérables* — Victor Hugo

William Wilson (Edgar Allan Poe). *William Wilson* — Edgar Allan Poe

186. LITERARY LAPSES

Even good writers sometimes make mistakes, and their literary lapses can be amusing. Printers are to blame for a fair share of blunders, too. The errors catalogued in this list demonstrate the need for careful proofreading.

Daniel Defoe — Robinson Crusoe comes out of the water naked to board a ship, then fills his *pockets* with biscuits.

Sir Arthur Conan Doyle — According to the author, Dr. Watson suffered a war injury. In *A Study in Scarlet* the injury was to Watson's shoulder, but in *The Sign of Four*, it has moved to his leg.

George Eliot — Maggie Tulliver and her brother in *The Mill on the Floss* are supposedly drowned when heavy debris overtakes their light boat. The laws of physics make such an event impossible.

Rider Haggard — In *King Solomon's Mines* an eclipse occurs at the time of a new moon, instead of a full moon.

Eugene O'Neill — A character in *Where the Cross Is Made* has his right arm amputated at the shoulder. He is subsequently described as resting on his elbows with his head in his hands.

Carl Sandburg — In *Abraham Lincoln –The Prairie Years*, Sandburg has Lincoln's mother singing a song that was not written until twenty-two years after her son's death.

Sir Walter Scott — In *Ivanhoe*, Scott has a horse, laden with armor, run an impossible distance in intense heat.

William Shakespeare — Wrote of cannon in the reign of King John (cannon were unknown until about 150 years later); clocks striking the hour in the days of Julius Caesar; and printing in the days of King Henry II.

Several older editions of the Bible contain amusing errors:

The "BUG" Bible — Translates Psalms 91:5 saying you should not be afraid of *bugs* by night. Other Bibles say *terror*.

The "FOOL" Bible — Misquotes Psalms 14:1 indicating the fool says there *is* a God.

The "LIONS" Bible — Misquotes I Kings 8:19 indicating that a son will come forth out of the *lions*, instead of *loins*.

The "WICKED" Bible — Misquotes Exodus 20:14 saying a person *should* commit adultery.

187. "MOST" AND "FIRST" LISTS

These literary records were gathered from a variety of sources.

Most Academy Awards — Walt Disney (20); Katharine Hepburn (4)

Most autobiographies — Georges Simenon (22)

Most commercially successful poem — "If" (by Rudyard Kipling)

Most comprehensive encyclopedia — *New Encyclopaidia Britannica* (32 volumes)

Most lingual man in world — Powell Alexander Janulus (41 languages)

Most often portrayed characters — Sherlock Holmes; Dracula

Most rejections of an eventual best-seller — *Zen and the Art of Motorcycle Maintenance*, by Robert Pirsig (121 rejections)

Most sales of one author — Barbara Cartland (500,000,000 copies)

Most titles and shelving of bookstore — W. & G. Foyle, Ltd. (in London, 30 miles of shelving)

Most Tony Awards — Julie Harris (5)

Most widely distributed book — *Bible* (over 2,500,000,000 copies)

Most widely distributed comic strip — *Peanuts* (over 2000 newspapers)

First American novel — *The Power of Sympathy* (attributed to William Hill Brown and Sarah Wentworth Morton, 1789)

First American Nobel Prize in Literature — Sinclair Lewis (1930)

First best-selling author — Harold Bell Wright (*The Shepherd of the Hills*, 1907)

First best-selling novel — *Charlotte: A Tale of Truth* (Susanna Haswell Rowson, 1794)

First book-binder in America — John Ratliffe (1663)

First book by African-American author — *Poems on Various Subjects, Religious and Moral* (Phillis Wheatley, 1773)

First book fair — New York City (1802)

First book in Braille — Louis Braille, publisher (1829)

First book-store in the U.S. — Boston, Massachusetts (1830)

First book-of-the-month club — United States (1926)

First comic strip — *The Yellow Kid* (1896)

First copyrighted book — *The Philadelphia Spelling Book* (John Barry, 1790)

First detective story — *Murders in the Rue Morgue* (Edgar Allan Poe, 1841)

First English Nobel Prize in Literature — Rudyard Kipling (1907)

First known autobiography in English — Thomas Whythorne (1576)

First modern novel — *Don Quixote* (Cervantes, 1576)

First novel by an African American — *Clotel, or the President's Daughter: A Narrative of Slave Life in the United States* (William Wells Brown, 1853)

First poet laureate of England — John Dryden (1670)

First publisher in English-speaking world — Cambridge University Press (1534)

First use of flashback in Western literature — *Odyssey* (Homer)

First woman to win Pulitzer Prize for Fiction — Edith Wharton (*The Age of Innocence*, 1921)

Many writers publish works under assumed names. In the days when it was not "proper" for women to write about certain topics, female authors sometimes used male names. In other cases, writers may conceal their identities to avoid the wrath (or lawsuits) of those who appear in the book. Some writers may conceal their identity when producing commercial books below their usual standard, while others do it simply for their own amusement. Pen names (pseudonyms) are alphabetical; real names follow.

Sholom Aleichem (Solomon Rabinovitch)

Acton Bell (Anne Bronte)

Currer Bell (Charlotte Bronte)

Ellis Bell (Emily Bronte)

Nicholas Blake (Cecil Day-Lewis)

Nellie Bly (Elizabeth Cochrane Seaman)

Boz (Charles Dickens)

Max Brand (Frederick Faust)

Ned Buntline (Edward Zane Carroll Judson)

Lewis Carroll (Charles Lutwidge Dodgson)

Manning Coles (Cyril Henry Coles)

A. B. Cox; Francis Iles (Anthony Berkeley)

Edmund Crispin (Robert Bruce Montgomery)

Amanda Cross (Carolyn Heilbrun)

E. V. Cunningham (Howard Fast)

Carter Dickson; Carr Dickson (John Dickson Carr)

Isak Dinesen (Baroness Karen Blixen)

Elia (Charles Lamb)

**George Eliot (Mary Ann (Marian) Evans)

Paul Eluard (Eugene Grindel)

A. A. Fair; Carleton Kendrake (Erle Stanley Gardner)

Maxim Gorky (Aleksey Maximovich Peshkov)

Kafiz (Shams-ud-din Muhammad)

Knut Hamsun (Knut Pedersen)

O. Henry (William Sidney Porter)

Victoria Holt (Eleanor Burford Hibbert)

Horace (Quintus Horatius Flaccus)

Michael Innes (John Innes MacKintosh Stewart)

Cyril Judd (Cyril M. Kornbluth)

**Carolyn Keene; Ralph Bonehill; Franklin W. Dixon; Arthur M. Winfield (Edward Stratemeyer)

Diedrich Knickerbocker (Washington Irving)

*Emma Lathen (Mary J. Latis and Martha Hennissart)

John le Carré (David John Moore Cornwell)

Richard Llewellyn (Richard Lloyd)

Hugh MacDiarmid (Christopher Murray Grieve)

Ross MacDonald; John MacDonald (Kenneth Millar)

Naguib Mahfouz (Abdel Aziz Al-Sabilgi)

Katherine Mansfield (Kathleen Mansfield Beauchamp)

J. J. Marric; Gordon Ashe; Robert Caine; Kyle Hunt; Anthony Morton; Jeremy York; and over twenty others (John Creasey)

André Maurois (Emile Herzog)

Ed McBain (Evan Hunter)

*Judith Michael (Judith Bernard and Michael Fain)

Yukio Mishima (Kimitake Hiraoka)

Molière (Jean Baptiste Poquelin)

Pablo Neruda (Neftali Ricardo Reyes Basoalto)

Frank O'Conner (Michael O'Donovan)

George Orwell (Eric Arthur Blair)

Lewis Padgett (Henry Kuttner)

Harry Patterson (Jack Higgins)

Jean Paul (Johann Richter)

Petrarch (Francesco Petrarca)

Poor Richard (Benjamin Franklin)

*Ellery Queen (Manford B. Lee —
 born Manford Lepofsky; and Frederick
 Dannay — born Daniel Nathan)

Sax Rohmer (Arthur Sarsfield Ward; also
 Arthur Sarsfield Wade)

Jonathan Ryder (Robert Ludlum)

Francoise Sagan (Francoise Quoirez)

Saki (Hector Hugh Munro)

**George Sand (Amandine Aurore Dupin
 Lucie, Baronne Dudevant)

Sapper (Herman Cyril McNeile)

Giorgos Seferis (Giorgos Sefirades)

Margaret Sidney (Harriet Lothrop)

Cordwainer Smith (Paul Myron Anthony
 Linebarger)

Burt L. Standish (Gilbert Patten)

Richard Start; Tucker Cole (Donald Westlake)

Stendahl (Marie-Henri Beyle)

Theodore Sturgeon (Edward Hamilton Waldo)

Abram Terts (Andrei Sinyavsky)

**Josephine Tey; Gordon Daviot (Elizabeth
 MacKintosh)

Ironi Mazel Tof (Shmuel Yosef Agnon or
 Samuel Czaczkes)

Mark Twain (Samuel Langhorne Clemens)

Tristan Tzara (Samuel Rosenfeld)

S. S. Van Dine (William Huntington Wright)

Barbara Vine (Ruth Rendell)

Voltaire (Francois-Marie Arouet)

Mary Westmacott (Dame Agatha Christie)

Émile Zola (Edouard Charles Antoine)

*Examples of two people assuming a pseudonym and writing as if they were one person. In the first instance, two women; in the second instance, a husband and wife; in the last instance, two men.

**Examples of authors sometimes assuming opposite sex names.

189. READING THE QUEEN'S ENGLISH

Even though people who live in Great Britain and the United States speak and write the same language, there are many words, phrases, colloquialisms, and slang terms American readers need to know in order to appreciate contemporary British literature. This list will make the "Queen's English" a bit more accessible. See also List 192, Understanding the Queen's Spelling.

aerodrome: airport

A-level: test for students going to university
 (advanced)

angling: fishing

baths: pools

bed and breakfast: inn

best book: paper assignment booklet (like
 college "bluebook")

bird: young woman

biro: ball-point pen

biscuit: cookie or cracker

bloody: swear word like g-damn; used as adjective

bob: shilling

bobby: policeman

bonnet: hood of car

boot: trunk of car

bowler: derby hat

braces: suspenders

brolly: umbrella

caravan: trailer

cats' eyes: reflectors on roads (for use during fog)

cheerio: good-bye

chemist shop: drugstore

Chunnel: tunnel under the English Channel, connecting England and France

cooker: stove or oven

cot: baby crib

court shoes: dress shoes

crown: five shillings

cubby: compartment

cupboard: closet

dampers: car shock absorbers

digs: apartment or house

draughts: checkers

electric fire: electric heater

flat: apartment

football: soccer

form: grade in school

fringe: bangs (hair on forehead)

games: gym classes

garden: yard

grammar school: secondary school

greengrocer: grocer carrying fruits and vegetables

gum boots: overshoes

ha'penny (half penny): one-half penny coin

handle: crank for cranking car engine

high tea: late-afternoon or early-evening meal

holiday: vacation

jumper: pullover sweater

kirby grips: bobby pins

knickers: girls' underpants

knock up: visit someone

lay-by: roadside turnoff

lift: elevator

loo: bathroom; water closet

lorry: truck

luv: equivalent to honey, as in "good morning, luv."

maize: corn

maths: mathematics class

motorway: expressway

naked lights: headlights lit

nappy: diaper

netball: like girls' basketball

nick: police station

O-level: test before A levels

paper store: retail shop for paper/wood products (Ex: paper napkins)

pence: penny

petrol: gasoline

plimsoles: tennis shoes

pound: unit of currency

prefect: honor student; helps teacher in various ways

pub: tavern

public school: private school

pulling the micket: poking fun

queue: line (of people)

rates: taxes

ring up: call someone on the telephone

roundabout: traffic circle

rounders: game like baseball

Royals: the Royal Family

rubber: eraser

running lights: small, exterior car lights left on while driving at night

school-leavers: students who will leave school at age fifteen

scone: tea cake; biscuit

Scotland Yard: detective bureau

serviette: napkin

shilling: five pence

sponge: cake

stream: academic track

suspenders: garter belt

sweets: candy

ta: thank you

tea: break for a snack; evening meal

Teddy boys: teenage punks

telly: television

the green: large lawn area

the commons: common land; field

tube: subway

tuck: snack

tuck shop: snack shop

turf accountant: bookmaker

twit: scatterbrained person

vest: undershirt

waistcoat: vest

wellingtons: boots

white horses: whitecaps

wireless: radio

190. TITLES TAKEN FROM PREVIOUS WORKS

Many times, authors (or editors) choose their book titles from memorable phrases found in the Bible, poems, classical literature, and other influential works. Here are a few examples.

Absalom! Absalom! — William Faulkner (from the story of Absalom, King David's rebellious son, in the Old Testament: 2 Samuel)

Brave New World — Aldous Huxley (from *The Tempest*, Act III, Scene 2 — Shakespeare)

For Whom the Bell Tolls — Ernest Hemingway (from *Devotions upon Emergent Occasions* — John Donne)

The Four Horsemen of the Apocalypse — Vincente Blasco Ibanez (from the New Testament: Revelation, Chapter 6)

Gone with the Wind — Margaret Mitchell (from "Non sum qualis eram bonae sub regno cynarae" — Ernest Dowson)

Grapes of Wrath — John Steinbeck (from *The Battle Hymn of the Republic* — Julia Ward Howe)

Horseman, Pass By — Larry McMurtry (from "Under Ben Bulben" — William Butler Yeats)

A House Divided — John Barth (from the New Testament: Matthew, Chapter 12)

Metamorphosis — Franz Kafka (from *Metamorphosis* — Ovid)

Notes of a Native Son — James Baldwin (from *Native Son* — Richard Wright)

The Sound and the Fury — William Faulkner (from *Macbeth*, Act 5, Scene 3 — Shakespeare)

The Sun Also Rises — Ernest Hemingway (from the Old Testament: Ecclesiastes, Chapter 1)

Where Angels Fear to Tread — E. M. Forster (from "Essay on Criticism" — Alexander Pope)

The Winter of Our Discontent — John Steinbeck (from *King Richard III* — Shakespeare)

191. UNDERSTANDING THE QUEEN'S SPELLING

The Queen's spelling (British spelling) takes a bit of getting used to. Britons spell many words differently than Americans. Readers who think they have found a misprint in a British book or story can consult this list. See also List 190, Reading the Queen's English.

British Spelling	American Spelling	British Spelling	American Spelling
aeroplane	airplane	kerb	curb
aluminium	aluminum	labour	labor
centre	center	organisation	organization
cheque	check	parlour	parlor
colour	color	pedlar	peddler
connexion	connection	programme	program
diplomatist	diplomat	pyjamas	pajamas
enquire	inquire	realise	realize
flavour	flavor	recognise	recognize
gaol	jail	theatre	theater
grey	gray	tumour	tumor
harbour	harbor	vice	vise
honour	honor	vigour	vigor
jewellery	jewelry	waistcoat	weskit

Note: British use of quotation marks also differs from American. The Britons use single quotes ('…') around actual words of a speaker; Americans use double quotes ("…"). In addition, the placement of periods and commas in relationship to the quotation marks is exactly opposite, with the British putting them outside the quotation marks and Americans putting them inside the quotation marks. All this is background so you don't think you have misunderstood certain principles when you are reading British literature.

192. Weird and Wonderful Tidbits

The following is a collection of unique, unusual, weird, or wonderful tidbits about authors or their works. See also related List 194, Weird Words.

Authors who Wrote When Old or Young

Winston Churchill, 82, wrote *A History of the English-Speaking Peoples*.

Johann von Goethe, 81, completed *Faust*.

Aleksandr Kerensky, 83, wrote *Russia and History's Turning Point*.

W. Somerset Maugham, 84, wrote *Points of View*.

Alice Pollock, 102, wrote *Portrait of My Victorian Youth*.

George Bernard Shaw, 93, wrote *Farfetched Fables*.

Leo Tolstoy, 82, wrote *I Cannot Be Silent*.

Griffith R. Williams, 102, published autobiography, *Cofio Canril* (A Century Remembered), on birthday (June 5, 1990).

Stephen Crane wrote all books before age 28 (died of tuberculosis).

F. Scott Fitzgerald, 24, wrote famous novel, *This Side of Paradise*.

John Keats, English poet, wrote all works before age 25 (died of tuberculosis).

Georges Simenon, when 7, published first novel, *Au Pont des Arches*.

Dorothy Straight, 4, wrote *How the World Began* (Pantheon Books).

Dennis Vollmer, 6, wrote *Joshua Disobeys* (Landmark Editions, Inc.).

Phillis Wheatley, African-American poet, was published at age 20.

Dissident Authors

Many writers had to write secretly; some were even exiled or banished from their native countries for writing literature that offended political leaders. Here are a few of the most prominent.

Vasily Pavlovich Akesenov — Russian writer and novelist

Joseph Brodsky — Russian poet

Yuli Daniel (pseudonym: Nicolay Arzhak) — Russian author/translator

Francesco de Sanctis — Italian writer

Esteban Echeverria — Argentine poet

Boris Pasternak — Russian novelist

Anatoly Ryabkov — Russian novelist

Lucius Annaeus Seneca — Roman philosopher and writer

Andrei Sinyavsky (pseudonym: Abram Tertz) — Russian novelist

Aleksandr Solzhenitsyn — Russian writer and novelist

Vladimir Voinovich — Russian short story writer and novelist

Yevgeny Zamyatin — Russian novelist

Weird Behavior of Authors

Louisa May Alcott — Did not like little children; only wrote her best-sellers to please her publisher.

Hans Christian Andersen — Was afraid of being pronounced dead before he really died; left notes saying he only "seemed dead."

Joseph Conrad — Hated the works of D. H. Lawrence.

Thomas Gray and Sir Walter Scott — Refused position of Poet Laureate of England.

Ernest Hemingway — Liked to write first drafts with a #2 pencil.

Samuel Pepys — Thought Shakespeare's *Midsummer Night's Dream* was terrible.

George Bernard Shaw — Hated Shakespeare and his works.

Walt Whitman — Wrote in free verse, but did not like to read free verse by others.

William Wordsworth — Thought Shakespeare's sonnets were terrible.

Ernest Vincent Wright — Wrote entire novel, *Gadsby*, without using the vowel e.

Imprisoned Authors

Several authors wrote while imprisoned; some, in fact, wrote their most impassioned works in captivity. Most were imprisoned for political/social crimes or financial offenses such as fraud, embezzlement, and debt, but some committed more serious crimes. Below are some of the most famous:

Roger Bacon	Leigh Hunt	Marquis de Sade
John Bunyan	Yasanari Kawabata	Torquato Tasso
Miguel de Cervantes	Richard Lovelace	Cesar Vallejo
John Cleland	Sir Thomas Mallory	Paul Verlaine
Daniel Defoe	Karl May	François Villon
Fyodor Dostoyevsky	Yukio Mishima	Voltaire
Galileo Galilei	Jawaharlal Nehru	Oscar Wilde
Jean Genet	Marco Polo	
O. Henry	Sir Walter Raleigh	

AUTHORS WITH DISABILITIES

Jorge Luis Borges (*blind*)
Miguel de Cervantes (*lost left arm*)
Homer (*blind*)
Helen Keller (*blind and deaf*)

John Milton (*one eye, then blind*)
Joseph Pulitzer (*blind*)
Charles Steinmetz (*hunchback*)
James Thurber (*blind*)

WRITERS WHO DID NOT ATTEND COLLEGE

Joseph Conrad
Noel Coward
Hart Crane
Charles Dickens
Kahlil Gibran
Maxim Gorky

Ernest Hemingway
Rudyard Kipling
H. L. Mencken
Jack London
Rod McKuen
Sean O'Casey

Will Rogers
William Saroyan
George Bernard Shaw
Dylan Thomas
Mark Twain
Virginia Woolf

INSOMNIACS

Winston Churchill
Charles Dickens
Alexandre Dumas
Benjamin Franklin

Franz Kafka
Rudyard Kipling
Marcel Proust
Jacqueline Susann

James Thurber
Evelyn Waugh

FORMER OR CONCURRENT OCCUPATIONS OF AUTHORS

Louisa May Alcott — teacher
Aristotle — librarian
Robert Burns — farmer
Edmund Crispin — musical composer
William Faulkner — house painter
Dick Francis — jockey
Benjamin Franklin — librarian
O. Henry — cowboy
James Herriot — veterinarian

Gerard Manley Hopkins — priest
Thomas Jefferson — librarian
D. H. Lawrence — teacher
Jonathan Miller — physician
Thomas Paine — corset-maker
Henry David Thoreau — pencil-maker
Mark Twain — river pilot
Joseph Wambaugh — police detective

AUTHOR SUICIDES

Petronius Arbiter, *Roman writer*

John Berryman, *American poet*

Tadeusz (Thomas) Borowski, *Polish writer*

Thomas Chatterton, *British poet*

Hart Crane, *American poet*

Sergei Esenin, *Russian poet*

Alexander Fadeyev, *Russian novelist*

Romain Gary (Emile Ajar), *French poet*

Ernest Hemingway, *American author*

Arthur Koestler, *Hungarian writer*

Jack London, *American author*

F. O. Matthiessen, *American critic and writer*

Vladimir Mayakovski, *Russian poet and playwright*

Yukio Mishima, *Japanese writer*

Gerard de Nerval, *French author*

Cesare Pavese, *Italian poet and novelist*

Sylvia Plath, *American poet and short story writer*

Aleksandr Radishchev, *Russian writer*

Anne Sexton, *American poet*

Alfonsina Storni, *Argentine poet and novelist*

John Kennedy Toole, *American novelist*

Heinrich von Kleist, *German poet*

Gustav Wied, *Danish writer*

Bernd Heinrich Wilhelm, *German poet, novelist, dramatist*

Virginia Woolf, *British novelist*

Stefan Zweig, *Austrian writer, biographer*

SELECTED MONEY-MAKING AUTHORS

There are many writers, but only a few actually make a substantial living solely from writing. Here are some who had lucrative careers as authors.

Peter Benchley — novels

Lord Byron — poetry

Barbara Cartland — romances

Agatha Christie — crime novels

Catherine Cookson — novels

Ian Fleming — James Bond books

Frederick Forsyth — novels

Erle Stanley Gardner — crime novels

Zane Grey — westerns

Rudyard Kipling — poetry; novels; stories

Ann Landers (Eppie Lederer) — newspaper columns

Thomas Macaulay — histories; essays

Alistair MacLean — novels

Peggy Marsh — television writer (*Upstairs, Downstairs*)

Margaret Mitchell — novel (*Gone with the Wind*)

Harold Robbins — novels

Sir Walter Scott — novels; poems

Dr. Seuss (Theodor Seuss Geisel) — children's books

Mickey Spillane — detective novels; comics

Benjamin Spock — classic child-care book

Danielle Steel — novels

Jacqueline Susann — novels

Alfred, Lord Tennyson — poetry

Sue Townsend — humorous books

193. WEIRD WORDS

The following list may be useful for solving crossword puzzles, playing super Scrabble™, or simply impressing friends. The following unusual words are all legitimately contained in an average-sized dictionary. Most are not long — just weird combinations of letters that look strange to the eye. See also List 193, Weird and Wonderful Tidbits.

aalii: tree; wood

acta: deeds

adit: mine entrance

agee: awry; askew

ait: islet; island in river

alar: winged

ana: collection

ankh: Egyptian symbol

ansa: loop; handle

apod: footless

bleb: blister

cos: lettuce

crambo: rhyming game

dado: groove

dop: diamond holder

dopp: dip

dyad: pair

emu: ostrichlike bird

epée: fencing blade

esse: existence; being

fils: son
fyke: restlessness
gnu: antelope; wildebeest
gowl: monster
grigri: witch doctor's charm
hadj: pilgrimage
hoicks: call to the hounds
iamb: verse foot (in poetry)
ibex: goat
ibis: wading bird
inee: poison on arrow
jako: parrot
jo: sweetheart
junu: charm
ka: ancient Egyptian religion
kerf: notch
kibe: opening in the skin
kudu: type of antelope
leet: petty court
lehr: complexion
limn: portray
limu: edible seaweed
liss: fleur-de-lis
moho: bird
mohr: gazelle
mumm: disguise

neb: nose; beak
née: born; maiden name
nu: Greek alphabet letter
obi: oriental sash
olla: dish; jar
oy: exclamation of emotion
phat: profitable
pi: mixture; 3.1416
ria: inlet; estuary
rotche: type of auk
rotl: oriental unit of weight
rynd: iron fitting
ryot: Indian peasant
skua: type of sea bird
snee: knife
titi: South American monkey
tutu: ballet skirt
ungula: hoof
uvic: grapelike
wadi: dry river bed
xema: gull
xyster: surgical instrument
yak: Tibetan ox
yoicks: same as hoicks
zebu: oxlike animal
zori: Japanese sandal

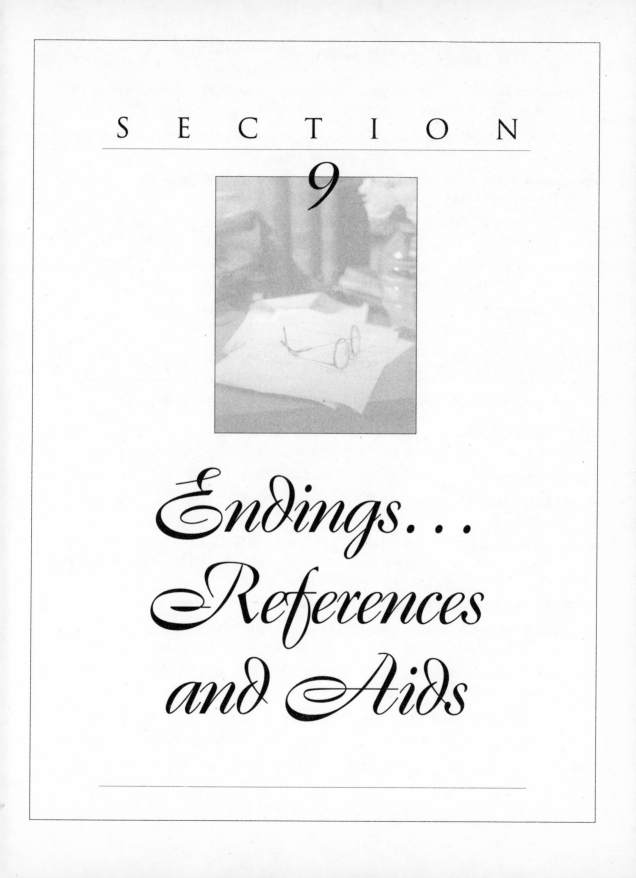

SECTION

9

*Endings...
References
and Aids*

194. CASSETTES: GREEK CLASSICS

Audio cassettes can add interest and sparkle to literature. These Greek myths and legends are available on cassettes, translated into conversational English.

The Odyssey — Homer's heroic tale of adventures of Odysseus, the Greek warrior, as he journeys back to Ithaca and his wife, Penelope, after the Trojan War.

Agamemnon — This Greek legend of crime and retribution after the Trojan War influenced art and literature in future years.

Oedipus the King — The first play in Sophocles's trilogy tells the tragic tale of Oedipus and his family.

Antigone — The last play in Sophocles's trilogy tells of Oedipus's daughter and her defiance of the king. Issues of the state versus individual freedoms are paramount.

The Execution of Socrates — Dramatization of Socrates's final hours.

195. CASSETTES AND CDS: POETRY

The following list contains only a few examples of poetry available on audio.

Wallace Stevens Reading His Poems — "The Poem that Took the Place of a Mountain," "Final Soliloquy of the Interior Paramour," and fourteen others.

Dylan Thomas Reads — "A Winter's Tale," "And Death Shall Have No Dominion," and others.

Robert Lowell Reads His Poetry — "The Exile's Return," "Skunk Hour," "Epilogue," and other material.

Modern Poets Reading Their Own Poetry — One and one-half hours of Aiken, Auden, Cummings, Eliot, Prost, Graves, MacLeish, MacNeice, Moore, Pound, Sitwell, Spender, Stein, Stevens, Thomas, Wilbur, Williams, and Yeats.

William Carlos Williams Reading His Own Poetry — forty-two-minute cassette.

T. S. Eliot Reading His Poems — One and one-half hours of "The Wasteland," "The Hollow Men," "Whispers of Immortality," "Macavity: The Mystery Cat," and others.

T. S. Eliot — "The Lovesong of J. Alfred Prufrock," "Ash Wednesday," "A Song for Simeon," "O Light Invisible," and others.

e. e. cummings — e. e. cummings reading his own poetry.

Langston Hughes Reading His Poems — "One Way Ticket," "Negro Speaks of Rivers," and others.

Sylvia Plath — One cassette of Sylvia Plath reading her own poems.

Robert Frost Reading His Poems — "The Road Not Taken," "Death of a Hired Man," "Fire and Ice," and others.

Anne Sexton Reading Her Poems — "Music Swims Back to Me," "The Touch," and twenty-two others.

81 Famous Poems — Two and one-half hours of works of thirty-nine major poets read by Alexander Scourby, Nancy Wickwire, and Bramwell Fletcher.

196. CASSETTES: POPULAR BOOKS

An extensive variety of fiction, inspirational, business, and spy books are available on audio cassettes, read by famous actors and readers. They are available in major bookstore chains, by mail order, via the World Wide Web, or directly from the publisher.

Alaska — James Michener

All I Really Need to Know I Learned in Kindergarten — Robert Fulghum

The Best of Benchley — Robert Benchley

The Bonfire of the Vanities — Tom Wolfe

Caribbean — James Michener

Dazzle — Judith Krantz

Dorothy Parker Stories — Dorothy Parker

Eudora Welty Reads (five short stories) — Eudora Welty

The Fledgling Spy — John le Carré

Gift from the Sea — Anne Morrow Lindberg

The Glass Menagerie — Tennessee Williams

Hawaii — James Michener

The Holcraft Covenant — Robert Ludlum

The Icarus Agenda — Robert Ludlum

In Harry's Bar in Venice (excerpts) — Ernest Hemingway*

Interview with the Vampire — Anne Rice

It Was on Fire When I Lay Down on It — Robert Fulghum

The Matlock Paper — Robert Ludlum

Murder at the National Cathedral — Margaret Truman

The Old Man and the Sea (excerpts) — William Faulkner

The Osterman Weekend — Robert Ludlum

Patriot Games — Tom Clancy

The Pit and the Pendulum — Edgar Allan Poe

A Prairie Home Companion — Garrison Keillor

The Prophet — Kahlil Gibran

The Queen of the Damned — Anne Rice

Red Storm Rising — Tom Clancy

The Russia House — John le Carré

Slaughterhouse Five — Kurt Vonnegut, Jr.

The Source — James Michener

Space — James Michener

Tales of Mystery and Horror — Edgar Allan Poe

Texas — James Michener

Trump: The Art of the Deal — Donald Trump with Tony Schwartz

Trump: Surviving the Top — Donald Trump with Charles Leerhsen

The Vampire Lestat — Anne Rice

The Witching Hour — Anne Rice

Often periodicals are preferred to lengthy books. This list suggests popular, good-quality magazines. After each magazine is the address for ordering, a brief comment, the number of issues per year (in parentheses), and the targeted audience (last line).

Baseball Digest
Century Publication Co.
990 Grove Street
Evanston, Illinois 60201
(847) 491-6440

Major league baseball players
and races (12)
Junior High through Adult

Boy's Life
Boy Scouts of America
1325 Walnut Hill Lane
Irving, Texas 75038
(972) 580-2366

Sports/hobbies/jokes/fiction (12)
Junior/Senior High School

Classical Calliope
Cobblestone Publishing, Inc.
30 Grove Street
Peterborough, New Hampshire 03458
(603) 924-7209

Ancient history/language arts
/puzzles (4)
Junior/Senior High School

Cobblestone
Cobblestone Publishing, Inc.
30 Grove Street
Peterborough, New Hampshire 03458

American historical people
and events (12)
Junior High

**Cricket: The Literary Magazine
for Children**
Open Court Publishing Co.
315 Fifth Street
Peru, Illinois 61354
(800) 827-0227

Children's literature (12)
Junior High

They also publush :
Babybug 6 mo. – 2 yrs.
Ladybug 2 – 6 yrs.
Spider 6 – 9 yrs.
Muse 6 – 14 yrs.
Click 3 – 7 yrs.

Dolphin Log
Greenbrier Circle; Suite 402
Chesapeake, Virginia 23320
(757) 523-9335

Sea life (4)
Junior High

Faces
Cobblestone Publishing, Inc.
30 Grove Street
Peterborough, New Hampshire 03458

Natural history and culture (10)
Junior High

National Geographic World
National Geographic Society
P.O. Box 63001
Tampa, Florida 33663-3001
(202) 857-7000

History/science/travel (12)
Junior High

Odyssey
Cobblestone Publishing, Inc.
30 Grove Street
Peterborough, New Hampshire 03458

Astronomy and outer space (12)
Junior High

Plays
120 Boylston Street
Boston, Massachusetts 02116
(617) 423-3157

Lighthearted original drama (7)
Junior/Senior High

Ranger Rick's Nature Magazine
National Wildlife Federation
8925 Leesburg Pike
Zienna, Virginia. 22184
(703) 790-4274

Nature activities (12)
Junior High

Stone Soup
Children's Art Foundation
P.O. Box 83
Santa Cruz, California 95063
(408) 426-5557

Poems/stories/artwork
Junior High

3–2–1 Contact
Children's Television Workshop
1 Lincoln Plaza
New York, New York 10023
(212) 595-3456

Science (10)
Junior High

198. POPULAR AMERICAN MAGAZINES

Magazines can be an interesting source of both fiction and nonfiction reading. This list includes widely circulated, popular magazines of general interest.

American Health	*Jet*	*Prevention*
Business Week	*Travel and Leisure*	*Psychology Today*
Car and Driver	*Life*	*Reader's Digest*
Consumers Digest	*Money*	*Scouting*
Discover	*National Geographic*	*Seventeen*
Discovery	*Nation's Business*	*Smithsonian*
Ebony	*Natural History*	*Sports Illustrated*
Field and Stream	*Newsweek*	*'Teen*
Golf	*The New Yorker*	*Time*
Golf Digest	*Outdoor Life*	*U.S. News and World Report*
Health	*Popular Mechanics*	*Weight Watchers*
Home Mechanix	*Popular Photography*	*Workbench*
Hot Rod	*Popular Science*	*Yankee*

E

L

S

Saberhagen, Fred, 128
Sachar, Louise, 54
Sachs, Hans, 313
Sachs, Marilyn, 299
Sachs, Nelly, 219
Sackler, Howard, 221, 222
Sagan, Carl, 64, 65, 133
Sagan, Francoise, 68, 142, 246, 334
Sagoff, Maurice, 278
Sainte-Beuve, Charles Augustin, 108
Saint-Exupery, Antoine de, 55, 58, 67, 241
Sakharov, Andrei, 79
Saki, 128, 155, 157, 245
Salerno-Sonnenberg, Nadja, 79
Salinger, J. D., 73, 80, 138, 154, 303, 333
Sallis, Susan, 298
Salny, Abbie F., 73, 74
Salten, Felix, 246
Sampson, Fay, 62
Samuels, Ernest, 84
Samuels, Gertrude, 300, 303
Sanchez, Sonia, 253
Sand, George, 142, 295, 320, 365
Sandburg, Carl, 56, 57, 79, 131, 169, 177, 187, 206, 212, 331, 373
Sanders, Dori, 254
Sanders, Lawrence, 98
Sandoz, Mari, 80, 260
Santayana, George, 28
Santee, Ross, 164
Sappho, 295
Sarashina, Lady, 295
Sardar, J'afre, Ali, 213
Sargent, Sarah, 303
Saroyan, William, 131, 138, 154, 157, 219, 221, 222
Sarraute, Nathalie, 295
Sarton, May, 245

Sartre, Jean-Paul, 31, 108, 218
Sassoon, Siegfried, 212
Saul, John, 338
Savitz, Harriet May, 298, 304
Sawyer, Ruth, 58
Saxe, John Godfrey, 51, 206
Sayers, Dorothy L., 67, 98, 245
Scarron, Paul, 145
Schaefer, Jack, 55, 58, 164, 247
Schami, Rafik, 338
Scharf, Lois, 80
Schenker, Dona, 248
Schenkkan, Robert, 222
Schiller, Friedrich von, 318, 323
Schiller, Johann, 187
Schlesinger, Arthur M. Jr., 84
Schmitt, Lois and Joyce Price, 258
Schnitzler, Arthur, 142
Schopenhauer, 75
Schorske, Carl E., 133
Schreiner, Olive, 295, 297
Schulberg, Budd, 138
Schuller, Robert, 258
Schultz, Marion, 299
Schuurman, Anne van, 295
Schuyler, James, 169
Schuyler, Montgomery, 207
Schwartz, Alvin, 66
Schwartz, Delmore, 154, 169, 333
Schwartz-Bart, Andrè, 69
Schwarzenegger, Arnold, and Douglas Kent Hall, 278
Scoppetone, Sandra, 303
Scott, Sir Walter, 16, 73, 126, 142, 156, 171, 172, 178, 207, 319, 340, 341, 343, 373, 381, 384
Scudery, Madeleine de, 295
Seami, Motokiyo, 216
Sebestyen, Ouida, 300
Sedgwick, Henry Dwight, 249
Seeger, Alan, 181, 212

Segal, Erich, 138, 336
Selden, George, 245, 248
Seldon, Frank H., 249
Sender, Ruth M., 79, 289
Seredy, Kate, 56
Serraillier, Ian, 58
Seton, Ernest Thompson, 58
Seuss, Dr. (Theodore Seuss Geisel), 34, 51, 244, 384
Sevigne, Marie de, 295
Sewall, Samuel, 317, 329
Sewell, Anna, 32, 56, 247
Sexton, Anne, 170, 297, 333, 383
Seymour, William, 226
Shaara, Michael, 121, 336
Shadwell, Thomas, 171
Shaffer, Peter, 218
Shakespeare, William, 6, 12, 31, 32, 33, 34, 35, 36, 37, 45, 67, 75, 172, 179, 181, 192, 193, 202, 216, 226-233, 244, 282, 314, 315, 351, 370, 372, 373
Shange, Ntozake, 253, 255
Shannon, Monica, 56
Shapiro, Karl, 131, 170, 213, 333
Shaw, George Bernard, 4, 75, 108, 218, 236, 288, 322, 365, 368, 380, 381
Shaw, Irwin, 71, 139
Shaw, Richard, 301
Shea, Michael, 118
Sheed, Wilfred, 336
Sheehan, Neil, 133
Sheehan, Susan, 133
Sheldon, C. M., 50
Sheldon, Sidney, 139, 219
Shelley, Bruce, 258
Shelley, David, 164
Shelley, John, 164
Shelley, Mary Wollstonecraft, 33, 81, 98, 118, 126, 128, 142, 144, 295, 297, 319, 341, 343